A ROBERT PENN WARREN READER

BOOKS BY ROBERT PENN WARREN

John Brown: The Making of a Martyr (1929)
Thirty-six Poems (1935)
Night Rider (1939)
Eleven Poems on the Same Theme (1942)
At Heaven's Gate (1943)
Selected Poems, 1923–1943 (1943)
All the King's Men (1946)
Blackberry Winter (1946)
The Circus in the Attic (1947)
World Enough and Time (1950)
Brother to Dragons (1953)
Band of Angels (1955)
Segregation: The Inner Conflict in the South (1956)
Promises: Poems 1954–1956 (1957)
Selected Essays (1958)
The Cave (1959)
All the King's Men (play) (1960)
You, Emperors, and Others: Poems 1957–1960 (1960)
The Legacy of the Civil War (1961)
Wilderness (1961)
Flood (1964)
Who Speaks for the Negro? (1965)
Selected Poems: New and Old 1923–1966 (1966)
Incarnations: Poems 1966–1968 (1968)
Audubon: A Vision (1969)
Homage to Theodore Dreiser (1971)
Meet Me in the Green Glen (1971)
Or Else—Poem/Poems 1968–1974 (1974)
Democracy and Poetry (1975)
Selected Poems: 1923–1975 (1976)
A Place to Come To (1977)
Now and Then: Poems 1976–1978 (1978)
Brother to Dragons: A New Version (1979)
Being Here: Poetry 1977–1980 (1980)
Jefferson Davis Gets His Citizenship Back (1980)
Rumor Verified: Poems 1979–1980 (1981)
Chief Joseph of the Nez Perce (1983)
New and Selected Poems: 1923–1985 (1985)
A Robert Penn Warren Reader (1987)

A ROBERT PENN WARREN READER

VINTAGE BOOKS
A DIVISION OF RANDOM HOUSE
NEW YORK

FIRST VINTAGE BOOKS EDITION, August 1988

All rights reserved under International and Pan-American
Copyright Conventions. Published in the United States of America by
Random House, Inc., New York, and simultaneously in
Canada by Random House of Canada Limited, Toronto.
Originally published, in hardcover, by
Random House, Inc., in 1987.

Library of Congress Cataloging-in-Publication Data
Warren, Robert Penn, 1905–
A Robert Penn Warren reader.
I. Title.
PS3545.A748A6   1988   813'.52   87-45945
ISBN 0-394-75762-9 (pbk.)

Portions of this work were originally published in
the following periodicals: *American Caravan, Antaeus,*
The Atlantic Monthly, Encounter, The Georgia Review,
Harper's Magazine, The Kenyon Review, Life, The London Times,
The New Leader, The New Republic, The New Yorker,
The Ohio Review, Partisan Review, Saturday Review,
The Southern Review, The Yale Review.

Grateful acknowledgment is made to Harcourt,
Brace Jovanovich, Inc., for permission to reprint the
following works by Robert Penn Warren. "Prime Leaf" and
"Blackberry Winter" from *The Circus in the Attic and Other*
Stories. Copyright 1947 by Robert Penn Warren. Copyright
renewed 1975 by Robert Penn Warren. "Cass Mastern's
Wedding Ring" from *All the King's Men.* Copyright 1946
by Robert Penn Warren. Copyright renewed 1974 by
Robert Penn Warren. Rights in the United Kingdom
(excluding Canada) for *All the King's Men* are
administered by Martin Secker & Warburg Ltd.

Manufactured in the United States of America
10 9 8 7 6 5 4 3 2 1

CONTENTS

POETRY

EDITOR'S NOTE

In the fall of 1930, at the beginning of my junior year at Southwestern College at Memphis (now Rhodes College), I passed several times in the corridors a student, obviously not a freshman, whom I did not know. This was slightly unusual because by this time I had become a campus politician with an interest in knowing everybody, but at the start of a new year, new faces were to be expected. The stranger was not long unknown, however, for one day he stopped me to say he had seen me playing chess in one of the common rooms and suggested that we have a game. Thus began a chess combat that was to last for years and of which each of us fondly recalls having won the most games.

I learned that my new opponent, Robert Penn Warren, who looked younger than his twenty-five years, was not a student. He had just returned from earning, as a Rhodes Scholar, his B.Litt. from Oxford and now had a one-year appointment to our English faculty—his first teaching job. I should have known, but did not, that in 1929 he had published a biography, *John Brown: The Making of a Martyr;* that he was one of the twelve contributors to *I'll Take My Stand* (1930); or that for almost a decade his poems had been appearing in well-known literary magazines I had never heard of. What more was one to expect from a nineteen-year-old student, literate but not literary, more interested in social activities than in his classes?

Gradually I found out who Red Warren was and what he did, but more importantly, that he was different from anyone I'd previously encountered—wittier, more erudite, more interesting to listen to. Our chess contest expanded, and soon he and his wife invited me to bring a student friend to their apartment to make a foursome for bridge, at which we were enthusiastic amateurs, and this broadened the relationship.

At the end of that year the Warrens departed for Nashville, where Red would teach English at Vanderbilt, leaving behind a different kind of student, a senior who dropped economics and took three English courses. I was determined to qualify for a Vanderbilt graduate fellowship that Red suggested I apply for, and which I obtained. When he moved to Louisiana State University in 1934, he and Cleanth Brooks found a fellowship that enabled me to continue graduate work by teaching freshman English. This made three places where during the thirties I was a student and Red was teaching, yet I never took one of his courses, though I knew many others were profiting from them, but I know I learned more from his conversation than I ever did from formal instruction.

We had been in Baton Rouge only a few months when he and Cleanth and I began to share an office and to put out a new literary quarterly, *The Southern Review*. During the forties this trio left Louisiana for various parts of the country—Brooks and Warren to other universities, I to publishing—but our friendship continued, and we soon found ourselves living not too far apart in Connecticut. In 1947, I became an editor at Random House, which in 1950 began (with *World Enough and Time*) its long history of publishing Robert Penn Warren.

When the opportunity came to decide on the contents for this reader, it was most welcome, and at first seemed a relatively easy assignment because there is so much good work to choose from. But since a reader must be limited in size—it must at least be portable—after the initial enthusiasm of selecting, one faces the problem of what has to be left out from such a multiplicity. For example, there are the ten novels, the inclusion of any one of which, complete, would preempt space needed to properly represent other forms.

The fiction selections presented here begin with "Prime Leaf," the author's first published story, which appeared in *American Caravan IV* (1931) and was called a short novel by the editors. The last selection is the ending of Warren's most recent novel, *A Place to Come To* (1977), and in between these earliest and latest examples of his fiction—a space of forty-six years—are the story "Blackberry Winter" (1946); three excerpts from novels that editors of literary quarterlies chose to present as stories, which in fact they are—self-contained, but thematically related to the larger wholes; and two selections from *At Heaven's Gate* (1943) that are connected with an event in literary history.

In the summer of 1952, Warren and William Faulkner were both in New York, and I had known for some time that, strangely, they had never met, a situation I hoped to remedy. Both accepted my invitation to come to my apartment for drinks and then to a nearby restaurant for dinner. So Bill and I left Random House together and walked the few blocks to my place, and when shortly thereafter Red arrived, I made the toddies.

For a while I feared I had set up a real disaster: Red in high spirits, talkative; Bill grunting his dour and seemingly reluctant responses. But things soon began to thaw a bit, and at dinner Bill was doing most of the talking. In fact, he took over the management of the evening, which turned out to be delightful, with a ferry ride in the balmy summer air across the Hudson and back, and then to his hotel for champagne to crown it off.

But the dinner-table talk was what is most memorable about the occasion. At one point Bill was expounding one of his favorite precepts: in fiction, truth is more important than fact. I had heard him on this subject before and had at least partially understood, but on this night he began to give examples, summarizing scenes from other people's work that met his criterion for truth. Soon Red became aware that some of his own writing was thus being praised, and this, along with the good Bordeaux, contributed a further sense of warmth to the event. I believe that an episode in "Prime Leaf" concerning a touching relationship between a boy and his grandfather was one of the things singled out, as was also a complex father-son relationship in *At Heaven's Gate*—themes that are frequent in Warren's work. Both are in this book, and both justify the praise.

Though a vast number of readers around the world are familiar with Warren's distinguished career as poet and novelist—and his numerous awards, including three Pulitzer Prizes, the Bollingen Prize in Poetry, the Presidential Medal of Freedom, and the designation in 1986 as this country's first Poet Laureate—it is likely that many of them are less aware of his eminence in other fields: as respected literary critic, as shrewd observer of and commentator on American history and social issues, and as creator (with Cleanth Brooks) of influential textbooks for the teaching of literature, of which, among others, *Understanding Poetry* and *Understanding Fiction* have benefited many thousands of students.

The middle section of this reader presents six characteristic examples of Warren's nonfiction writing: three literary essays; his introduction to The Modern Library edition (1953) of *All the King's Men,* which was needed to educate certain critics who persisted in misinterpreting the novel; and, in their entirety, two short books, *Segregation: The Inner Conflict in the South* (1956) and *The Legacy of the Civil War: Meditations on the Centennial* (1961).

In the last fifty years—including the narrative poems *Brother to Dragons* (1953, new version 1979) and *Chief Joseph of the Nez Perce* (1983)—Warren has published sixteen volumes of poetry. That ten of these have appeared in the last two decades is indicative of the surge of creativity that took place when he reached his sixties and seventies with no diminution of his imaginative power. In fact, a number of well-known critics and scholars are of the opinion, by no means universal, that his "later" poems are markedly superior to the "earlier." The author has seemed in some measure to agree, favoring the new at the expense of the old when choosing the contents for his "selected" volumes, and for the most recent of these—*New and Selected Poems: 1923–1985*—he contemplated eliminating all but one of the poems published before the 1950s, but fortunately reconsidered. Except for the addition of four earlier poems, two excerpts from *Brother to Dragons: A New Version,* and a section of *Chief Joseph,* all of the poems here are from the 1985 selected volume, where, as has been his practice in the past, the poems begin with the new and end with the old. Here they are in chronological order.

When I was assigned to compile this reader, the author and I agreed that he should not advise, and that I should do the choosing on my own and then seek his consent, which has been granted. What I have tried to do is to make selections which will fairly represent the rich variety of his work of over half a century and which, I hope, other readers besides me will admire and enjoy and profit from.

ALBERT ERSKINE

FICTION

PRIME LEAF

"Lord, make us thankful for these blessings. Make our salvation commensurate to Thy mercy. Bless this food to the purposes of our bodies and us to Thy service. Amen." Little Thomas looked up promptly, just as the last word of the grace was uttered, and then seemed abashed when he met the incurious glance of his grandfather. His mother, at the foot of the big table, had not seen. Now she was turning with an appearance of hospitable interest to their guest.

"Did you have a good trip this time, Mr. Wiedenmeyer?"

"Vell, no," answered Mr. Wiedenmeyer. "I come on the steamboat up the river. Paducah to Clarksville, I come. I vill tell you, Mrs. Hardin, not one vink of sleep did I get."

Little Thomas took the wide bowl of soup, which made his fingers quiver slightly with its weight, and passed it into his father's large hand.

"It was mighty hot here Thursday night," Mrs. Hardin was saying. "That was the night three nights ago—wasn't it?"

"Ja, Thursday night vas the night all right I guess, but that vas not the trouble." Mr. Wiedenmeyer's moist thumb with its broad, glisten-

First published in 1931 in *American Caravan IV*. In 1947 it was included in *The Circus in the Attic and Other Stories*, from which this text was taken.

ing nail closed over the edge of the second bowl. He settled it in front of him, very near to him. "But that vas not the trouble all right." He picked up the spoon and waggled it gently in Mrs. Hardin's direction. "Three drunks get on at Paducah and have the room next to my room. All night they sing, they yell, they stomp. One drunk, he has a harmonicer and he plays it all night. It vas terrible, Mrs. Hardin, I vill tell you. A man not so young any more like me not to get his sleep. Terrible. That so, Mr. Hardin?" he asked, turning to old Mr. Hardin and shaking his head with a vague air of self-commiseration.

"I reckon so. I'm sixty-nine—about twenty years older than you— but two years ago this coming fall I went coon hunting with Big Thomas here and the niggers, and we didn't come back till half past four. We got two coons," he added like an afterthought.

"Yes, and kept me up all night waiting for you men to come in," Mrs. Hardin said sharply, but with a smile. "And you, Papa, almost had a chill the next night and I had to sit up with that."

"Humph!" The old man half snorted, and then, catching himself, laughed.

"Edith." There was a note of rebuke in the young Mr. Hardin's voice. His father appeared to pay no notice and gravely tilted his bowl to get the last spoonful of soup and the bright disk of carrot submerged in its midst.

Mrs. Hardin tapped the brass bell in front of her. A large Negro woman padded in from the pantry passage and began clumsily to transfer the dirty china to the sideboard, where a scrawny and very black boy stacked it with more than necessary clatter. He started toward the door.

"Careful, Alec," admonished Mrs. Hardin.

"Yas'm, Miss Edith," the black boy said, and disappeared with the precarious load.

"I done tole him," the large Negro woman remarked to no one in particular, and she followed her son into the pantry passage.

"Shiftless, these neggers, shiftless," said Mr. Wiedenmeyer, and again shook his head with that vague air of commiseration. Mrs. Hardin looked up quickly at him and then fixed her eyes on the brass bell, as if she had been about to speak and then, in the nick of time, had recollected herself. There was silence, except for the faint, pleasant sounds from the kitchen, until the Negro woman reappeared with a platter. Her boy was behind her with two covered dishes.

"I hope your business has been good, Mr. Wiedenmeyer," Mrs. Hardin said. The tone seemed to imply that she had put away completely whatever other remark she had been considering a few minutes before.

"Ja, ja, but business is nefer too gud in this business."

"It ain't ever too good in any business," the young Mr. Hardin interrupted. "But how is the crop looking over in Tennessee? I haven't heard anybody say recently."

"Gud, gud enough if tings they go gud now."

"Do you reckon you'll get much buying done down there when buying time comes?"

"Vell, to tell the truth among friends, I don't know. It looks like a gud crop all right, all right. But it's a leetle early to be talking about the tobacco-buying business so soon in the season."

"If it turns out a good crop," said young Mr. Hardin, "I hope you all will be paying a price to match it. Do you think it'll fetch a good price this year, Mr. Wiedenmeyer?"

"Vell, it's a leetle early like I say to be talking about the tobacco-buying business yet a time. But it vill be a gud price, I bet."

The young Mr. Hardin laid down his knife and fork with deliberation and looked steadily across at his guest. "It wasn't too early to talk about the tobacco-buying business August last year when you were down here. You talked a right smart about it. And just like now you said, 'Oh, it will bring a good price all right, all right.'" There was the slightest hint of mimicry in his tone. "I recollect well what you said. You said eleven cents, maybe twelve cents, for good prime leaf. All I wonder is if 1907 is going to be just like 1906. Eleven, maybe twelve cents, you said, and when you came around after and we did business with you it was prime leaf, eight cents, lugs, three cents. And we had a lot of good prime leaf. It was a fine crop. I reckon you were well pleased with that lot, weren't you, Mr. Wiedenmeyer?"

"Sure, it vas a fine crop you had. But the profit, there vas not much profit." Again he shook his head, but this time did not look up from the plate. "Eleven cents, I said. Maybe I said eleven cents, ven I vas here last year August. If you say I said eleven cents, eleven cents is vot I said. You alvays vas a careful man, Mr. Hardin. You got a long memory, Mr. Hardin."

"I reckon it pays to be careful, sometimes."

Old Mr. Hardin glanced at his son in the same incurious fashion, not quite a reproof, which had met Little Thomas after the blessing. Big Thomas ignored it completely. He continued with studied innocence.

"I'm mighty sorry to hear you don't expect to get your proper amount of buying done towards Clarksville."

"I vasn't saying I didn't expect to get no buying done towards Clarksville, Mr. Hardin. It is early a time yet to talk."

"Maybe. But then I sorter understand there ain't going to be much tobacco buying done down there, or anywhere much else. That is, there ain't going to be—yet."

"Ja? Ven the time come, they vill sell all right, all right. The fellers I talked to down there ain't got a crop so far along like you. They didn't get a gud season in setting-out time like you got."

"Yes, sir, we had a good early season this last spring and there was mighty little resetting of plants to do. But I reckon folks won't be so quick to do business this year."

"Vell, I don't know. Ve all gotta do business. Some gotta sell, some gotta buy. Ve all gotta live, ain't ve? Ain't that true, Mrs. Hardin?" And he turned to her flatteringly and waited for the agreement which, as his posture seemed to imply, would settle the matter for good and all.

"You are right, of course, Mr. Wiedenmeyer. We all have to live."

The Negro woman removed the plates, and again Alec stacked them on the deep walnut sideboard. This time there was no rebuke from Mrs. Hardin, despite the careless clatter, and Alec went out, pressing the pile against the faded blue front of his Sunday overalls with one hand while with the other he opened the door. After he passed, it creaked shut with a slight musical whine from its heavy hinges.

"Lemon custard," old Mr. Hardin observed to his grandson. "Don't you like lemon custard, Tommy?"

"Sure I do," Little Thomas answered. And then, almost pertly, "Don't you?"

"Sure," said Mr. Hardin, nodding with a fine show of gravity. The old man, his son, and his grandson ate in silence. Only Mrs. Hardin was still trying to keep up some sort of conversation with the guest. Then Alec burst open the pantry door, perspiring from the heat of the kitchen and very excited.

" 'Scuse me, Mr. Hardin, but, Mr. Hardin, dere one er dem hawks atter de chickens agin."

"I'm coming," said old Mr. Hardin. "Tommy, get me my gun, won't you?"

Thomas pushed back his chair with a rasp and ran into the next room. He found the gun in its corner, jerked off the oil-spotted paper envelope over the muzzle, and dropped it on the floor. He glanced over at another corner where a second shotgun and two rifles stood.

"Can't I use your gun just for one shot, Daddy?" he shouted.

"No," his father called back, "and how about hurrying a little?"

Thomas went to the writing desk under the window, opened one of the lower drawers, and fumbled in a box of shells. He dropped two shells into his pocket. Then he slipped one into each barrel of the gun and looked quickly at the safety-catch.

"Here it is, loaded," he said as he ran back into the dining room. His grandfather was already standing.

"Mr. Wiedenmeyer, why don't you come out back and talk to me while I wait for that God-damned hawk? Big Thomas hasn't finished his pie yet. But I still do most of the shooting around the house." He spoke between puffs while he lighted his pipe.

"All right." Mr. Wiedenmeyer got up very laboriously and leaned slightly over the back of his chair, with his large stomach pressing against it. "You vill excuse me please, Mrs. Hardin."

"Yes, of course."

"Come on, Mr. Wiedenmeyer." Mr. Hardin was already at the side door which opened on a porch. "Come on, Thomas."

They went out to the broad porch and down the stone steps. A dirt path led back to the left, past the painted rain barrel which stood under the gutter, and through a wooden gate into the chicken yard. Alec came running out from the kitchen after them.

"Dat hawk done gone long ago. He done flew ten miles away by now."

"That's all right. He'll come back if he wants his dinner."

"If'n he wants our dinner," Alec replied, and grinned at his own joke.

"Well, we'll wait for him then. We can sit over here, Mr. Wiedenmeyer, and talk till that hawk gets back." With his pipe he pointed to a wooden bench under the enormous maple which shaded a corner of the chicken run. They walked toward the tree, Alec and Thomas a little way in front. Alec paddled up the soft yellow dust with his bare feet, so that it rose in little clouds as high as his knees.

"For God's sake, Alec," Mr. Hardin mildly rebuked him.

"Yassuh."

Thomas looked at him slyly. "I told you so." This was spoken very low.

"Naw, you did'n." And Alec devoted his attention to making elaborate and perfect footprints in which the dust outlined the creases of the skin and stood up beautifully in the spaces between his toes.

There was no sign of the hawk. Already the full-grown white leghorns were picking about in the few patches of grass in the large yard.

One hen with her brood still squatted anxiously just inside the door of the whitewashed chicken house, and another had sought safety close against the base of the big iron wash kettle. In a minute or so she came out and the awkward chicks began to stray over the yard. She looked very harassed and the soot from the kettle still clung to the white feathers of her back.

It was hot, even under the shade of the maple. Mr. Wiedenmeyer's ruddy forehead had tiny beads of perspiration, and he seemed to lack the energy to wipe it again. His damp handkerchief lay spread out over one knee, with streaks of yellow where the dust had settled. Obviously he was very uncomfortable. Mr. Hardin was not inclined to renew conversation, but held his pipe between his teeth and idly fingered the point of his trimmed gray beard. Now and then he looked at the expanse of bright blue sky above the cedar grove which began at the very edge of the woodlot to the north.

"Me, I guess that bird vill not come back maybe." Mr. Wiedenmeyer looked hopefully down the slope of lawn toward the deep cool porch, where the young Mr. Hardin and his wife could be seen through the vines.

"Let's wait."

Now Mr. Wiedenmeyer studied the sky, as if his added attention might bring the hawk a little sooner and end the unpleasant affair. After a time he spoke again.

"Didn't you, Mr. Hardin, think I'm right? Ain't ve all gotta live?"

"Sure," said Mr. Hardin. He did not take his pipe from his teeth.

"I hear about this pool, this tobacco fellers' association, a long time back—last spring, I guess. But I say to myself, It is all the same, some gotta sell, some gotta buy." He paused, waiting for an answer. There was no sign from Mr. Hardin.

"Me, I think this tobacco association is all foolishness. If a feller, he knows the honest man to buy his crop, he don't need this association business. Sometimes the price fall low, like last year, but nobody, he can help that. This association vill not help ven the end come. It vill ask a high price and nobody vill buy, and then somebody vill sell his tobacco, a little higher than most year maybe, and then somebody else and somebody else. Somebody in this association business, maybe, somebody out, maybe. Then everybody want to sell quick and get the price before it drop. People need money bad that time year. And the price vill drop—quick. You vill see. It vill end like that—cost everybody money and do nobody gud. You vill see."

"Some of us don't think exactly like that, Mr. Wiedenmeyer."

"You vill see, I guess." He picked up the damp handkerchief, pressed it into a dull-colored pad, and slowly wiped his forehead. With great care he spread it back on his knee and again looked at Mr. Hardin, waiting for his words to take effect. Then he continued less vehemently. "Besides, I don't see vy a feller like you want to be in this association for. You alvays got a gud crop if there is any gud crop in the country. You got gud land and you know how to verk it. And this year you got a extra fine crop, and it vill be early."

Mr. Wiedenmeyer turned around on his bottom and gestured vaguely off to the left, beyond the house. A half mile away, beyond the lawn, beyond the driveway and the irregularly spaced forest trees which bordered it, the fields began. They dropped away gradually to the south and east, ending in a point where the creek joined the river. On the other side of the brush and sycamores which followed the curve of the creek bottom was a pasture land. Some red cattle, very small and far away, were grouped at a gap in the line of sycamores where the ford of the creek was. The heat waves shimmered up from the broad ripe green of the tobacco, from the sycamores, and from the browning pasture land beyond.

Mr. Hardin had turned to follow the gesture, as if some new sight had been pointed out to him. For a moment he contemplated the fields, and then took the pipe from his mouth. Deliberately he knocked it out and laid it on the bench near the propped shotgun.

"It is pretty good, even if it ain't extra fine. And we got it in early. That's usually something."

"It is almost extra fine, but you alvays did have a gud crop. Sometime people say they don't see how you do it." He suddenly seemed to think of something else. "But if you are mixed up with this association business, getting a crop in early von't help much, vill it?"

"Getting it in early won't help one way, I reckon, but a man likes to have things over and done with. It's satisfying that way."

"That is all right, but you lost some money."

"Maybe."

"Maybe, but all the same I don't see vy a feller fixed like you get mixed up for."

"Well, it's about like this. I'm not generally a man to join up with societies and associations and things. I think most of the time you have to stand on your own, and I like to pick and choose my friends some other way, too. I didn't take to the idea in the beginning. And Big Thomas was all dead set against it. He said pretty much what you've been saying, so I've heard all those arguments before."

"But Big Thomas don't talk that vay now, Mr. Hardin. You just seen him."

"But he did talk that way. And I thought about it a right smart. I had some long talks with Old Man Hopkins, over there across the river. He was strong for the association idea. Said all of us growers wasn't getting our due, even if one or two of us made good money now and then off a crop, and we couldn't do anything about it unless we stuck together. Old Hopkins is a mighty clever feller, and maybe he talked me into it. All the same I believe he's right now. And I talked Big Thomas into it. All the association is after is our due." He looked amiably at Mr. Wiedenmeyer, and then almost smiled as he added, "But I reckon some of us could be content with just a little bit more than our due. We're all human."

"You alvays got your due from me, Mr. Hardin. Alvays the top price for the season. Ja?"

"Sure, nobody's blaming you if the price is dirt sometimes."

"It vud not be dirt a year like this with a crop like that." And again he turned heavily about on his bottom and gestured toward the fields and the river.

"We ain't intending for it to be dirt this year. The price won't be dirt for this or any other crop. You see, we expect to fix that matter up ourselves."

Mr. Wiedenmeyer spread his hands out in the air before him, the soft fingers standing apart, and then brought them down with deliberate emphasis on his knees. "Ven the end come, don't say I didn't tell you. It vill be bad for everybody. And it vill be mighty bad fer fellers like you vot didn't need to have nothing to do with the business."

"I reckon we'll all take our chances together on that."

"Together. You don't have to take chances together. I tell you it is nefer too late. Anyvay, it ain't too late a time yet."

"Yes?"

"Ve have done a lot of business with each other, Mr. Hardin. Ve is like old friends, and it is like an old friend I talk to you. Understand me, Mr. Hardin?"

"I don't exactly know whether I do or not."

"De hawk, Mr. Hardin! Here come de ole debbil!" Alec was pointing off to the north.

The hawk floated very high over the hill crest and the cedar trees. It passed over, still very high, and then tilted into a long bank, slipping down like a leaf across the air.

"He shore is comin' back," Alec exulted.

"Alec, you and Thomas get back here under the tree or he won't come back. Come here, Thomas."

The boys stood behind the bench, very quiet, as if the least sound might carry far up into the air and frighten the hawk away at the last. Then Thomas whispered, "Can't I take a shot?"

"No."

"Just one. I'll hit him. Please." It was not quite a whisper now.

"No."

Thomas was quiet again. The chickens had not yet taken alarm. The old leghorn hen, the soot from the kettle still on her feathers, crouched in the yellow dust, ruffling it luxuriously with her wings. The chicks and a few young pullets wandered aimlessly. The hawk had drifted to the north again, over the cedars, sinking in a broad unhurried circuit.

"Thomas, you can have one shot," Mr. Hardin said. "Come around here on this side the bench."

Thomas made no answer. He came around in front of the bench, looking very grave under the new responsibility. His grandfather handed him the gun.

"The safety's off. Be damned careful. Don't shoot while he's circling around over the trees, even if he gets low. He's too far for the gun. Wait till he stops that foolishness and starts straight down at the yard. He'll come whizzing down, so shoot plenty in front. And don't try to follow him down with the sight. You'll sure miss him. Sorter let him and the sight almost meet. See?"

Thomas nodded. His knuckles were white from gripping the gun. The hawk still drifted lazily around the big spiral. The boy's gray eyes squinted at the sky, following its course. Now and then the tip of the hawk's wing caught the sun and glittered like metal.

"Funny the fool chickens ain't worried yet," Mr. Hardin remarked.

The hawk dropped suddenly, checked, tilted sidewise, and came swooping down across the tree tops. Thomas' gun rose to meet it. For a second it wavered, and then jerked back with the explosion. The lowest maple leaves shivered with the gust.

"Missed," said Mr. Hardin and seized the gun. The hawk, within ten feet of the ground and the terrified chickens, did not strike, but veered off and bounded upward with a deep beat of its wings. Mr. Hardin ran out from under the tree and fired at the high hawk. The wings beat again. The hawk seemed to rest on the air for a moment and glide hesitantly. Then one wing crumpled. The hawk tumbled on the hurt wing, downward, fluttering and turning, making no resistance. It struck on the other side of the wire fence in the wood lot.

Alec and Thomas ran toward the place like dogs.

"Shut that gate, or the chickens will get out," Mr. Hardin called, but the boys paid no attention.

He came slowly back to the bench and sat down beside his guest again. Very carefully he broke the gun and flicked the empty shells away.

"Fine," said Mr. Wiedenmeyer, "you got him all right. A feller might know a boy like Thomas vud not get him. I knew he vud not get him."

"I knew it too."

"Vell," Mr. Wiedenmeyer began, and then thought better of it when he realized that Mr. Hardin was paying no apparent attention to his impending remark.

The boys came back, quieter now. Thomas was holding the hawk by its legs. The head swung listlessly in time with Thomas' quick step. The broken wing drooped forward and down, occasionally brushing the dust, while the other fluttered out stiffly and awkwardly.

"Here he is. He's a big one," Thomas said to his grandfather.

Mr. Hardin took the hawk and stretched out the broad wings to their full span. "More'n three feet. He is a mighty big one. A red shoulder. They get bigger than this, though, sometimes."

The hawk's small head had fallen forward. The beak, slightly parted, was pressing against the downy feathers of the breast where a few beads of blood stood.

"Dat hawk, he done had his las' dinner," said Alec, grinning at Mr. Hardin. "He wuz deader'n a door-nail when we fotched him."

Mr. Hardin handed the hawk to Alec. "Thomas, take the gun back to the house, and if you've got any more shells, don't forget to put them back in the box. And when Sam comes up after milking tonight, you might tell him to clean the gun if he's got time."

Thomas picked up the gun and followed Alec down the path toward the kitchen porch. He was furtively rubbing his right shoulder. Alec, turning, caught him at it.

"Dat gun done kick like a mule, I bet. You ain't helt it right."

"It didn't kick. I just itch. I reckon I held that gun all right."

Alec sniggered. "But yore gran-pappy, he got de hawk."

"Darn," said Thomas. "Can't I scratch myself where I itch without you going and giggling like Susie?"

"I bet you itch." And Alec began whistling.

Mr. Hardin was still sitting on the bench. He made no sign of going back to the house. "Where were we when the hawk came?"

"I vas saying ven it come that it might not be too late yet. It vill not be too late some time yet, for a feller like you to get vot is coming to him."

"I'm expecting to get what's coming to me."

"Maybe, you might not get it some vays. You got a gud crop, a gud early crop. Some vays you vill not get your right money out of it. It is like the old friend I vant to talk to you, Mr. Hardin."

"I reckon you're making me an offer, Mr. Wiedenmeyer?"

"I vas not making any offer yet. It is early some to be making offers. Soon maybe, ven the time come, I vill make you the offer. A extra gud offer, Mr. Hardin. Then ve vill talk business."

"We might talk a little business right now."

"Ja!"

"I just want to ask you one question. You knew when you came out here today that I was in the association. You knew that, didn't you?"

"Ja, I knew it. I knew it a long time before I come down here. It vas in the paper you vas a director."

"That's true, too. I'm one of the directors."

"Fine, fine. I give you my congratulations. It is a honor sure."

"That don't matter much. What I want to say is something like this. If you knew I was in the association, why, for the love of God, did you reckon I'd be open to any offers you might have to make? Why now, Wiedenmeyer?"

"I just thought maybe you vas not sure how ve stood. I just vanted you to know ve could still do business yet. I vanted you to know I do vot is right with you."

"If you've got any more right offers to make, it might be a pretty good idea, I guess, for you to make them a little later when the association starts fixing prices. And then you might just make them direct to the association. Don't you think it might be a good idea, Mr. Wiedenmeyer?"

"Plenty of fellers is not in the association."

"That's true too. Some of them will come in though. But it might be a good idea all the same to make any private offers just to those people. Some people in the association might not take it right. It's funny the way people take things sometimes, ain't it?"

"Ja." Mr. Wiedenmeyer paused for a minute. "You vud not be mad, vud you?"

"No, I'm not mad. It's only that I want us to understand each other."

Mr. Wiedenmeyer did not speak. He was studying his companion with a puzzled expression.

"And I reckon we understand each other well enough now. Let's go down to the house."

They got up and left the bench in silence. Mr. Wiedenmeyer walked a little bit behind, regarding the unstooped shoulders before him with the same bewildered look. When they were halfway down the path, near the rain barrel, Mr. Hardin turned pleasantly.

"You might sit around a time and have supper with us. We always have early supper on Sunday. It'll be cold though."

"Thank you all the same, I vud have to be going. I'm crossing the river this afternoon."

"Dropping by to see Old Man Hopkins?"

"No."

Young Mr. Hardin and his wife were still on the side porch when the two men came up. She looked at them questioningly.

"Mr. Wiedenmeyer says he can't stay for supper, Edith. He's got to be crossing the river this afternoon."

"I'm sorry you're not staying."

"Thanks all the same. I got to go now. Good-bye. Good-bye, Mr. Hardin."

"Good-bye."

Mr. Hardin leaned against the trellis post and watched the stocky man walking down the long path to the front gate. Mr. Wiedenmeyer went out, untied his horse from the hitching rack, and got in his buggy. He did not wave back, or even turn around, as he drove off under the trees by the edge of the nearest field.

"You didn't make him mad, did you, Papa?" asked Mrs. Hardin. "He acted a little funny."

"No," said Mr. Hardin cheerfully. "I didn't. He ain't exactly mad. He's just worried."

His son looked up suddenly. "I hope you gave him hell. I wish to God you had made him good and mad. What does he want coming around here for? The old Jew," he added.

"I didn't give him hell, I just gave him some advice. And you can't make a man like that mad anyway. And besides, he ain't a Jew. He's just a German. A German who feels sorter sorry for himself."

"What did you tell him?"

"I just advised him if he had any more offers to make, to make them to the association direct or make them to people not in the association."

"Well, you wasted your breath."

"No doubt about it," Mr. Hardin complacently agreed. "But he's got something to figure about while he rides over to Hopkins' place."

"He better not. Hopkins'll just take one good look at him and then dump him in the river before he opens his damned mouth. Did he say he was going over there?"

"I asked him, and he said, as I recollect, that he wasn't. But he will." Mr. Hardin looked very cheerful about the whole matter. "It'll be good for both of them, too. Old Man Hopkins can get some steam worked off, and maybe Wiedenmeyer will learn something."

"Well, we should worry," and Thomas gave an elaborate late afternoon yawn and settled back in the swing.

"We've got considerable to worry about. The reason Hopkins will probably dump Wiedenmeyer in the river is because he's worried. If he weren't worried, he'd listen to all Wiedenmeyer had to say, not saying anything, just sitting with that crab-apple grin of his on his face. That's the way with Hopkins. He's a clever fellow, a mighty clever fellow, but when he gets worried he's just got to do something all of a sudden. He's similar to you that way, Thomas. And Hopkins is worried pretty much right now. You know people ain't coming in the association like they ought. But do you know that if things don't pick up, we'll be short about a hundred-fifty or two hundred names when the fun starts."

"I didn't think it was quite that bad, Papa," said Mrs. Hardin. "What are you all going to do?"

"We can't do anything in the world right now but wait. There's a meeting of the board of directors in about a month. We can tell better then. But if we don't get a bigger membership, we can't make a real fight this year. And the only thing that'll get a bigger membership for next year is a real fight now. It looks to me the association is about the only chance of getting our rights, but some people can't see any farther than their noses. They think the dues are too high or, if they're real skunks, they figure that they'll get the good out of the association without it costing them anything. But in general it's just that people here don't like to join up with things much. That is, except the Baptist Church or a possum hunt."

He came up on the porch and stood, with legs apart, in front of the swing where his son and daughter-in-law sat.

"Lord knows we need money," he said, speaking directly to Mrs. Hardin, "but I reckon we can hang on another year. But don't fret yourself, Edith. It'll all come out right."

He turned and opened the big screen door of the dining room. Holding it back with his body, he stood there fumbling about in his pocket for his watch. He seemed to study its thick face as if he expected to find something there of more importance than the time of day.

"It's just about five o'clock," he said. "I'm going upstairs and take me a nap before supper. If you see Sam, tell him to clean my gun, will you. I asked Thomas to tell him, but he'll sure forget."

"Close the door, Papa," said Mrs. Hardin. "You're letting all the flies in the county get in."

Without a word he stepped inside and the door slammed with a crash. Then from the dining room came his voice, half singing, half humming.

> *The old gray mare come trottin' through the wilderness,*
> *trottin' through the wilderness . . .*

A minute later there was the sound of his step in the bedroom just over the dining room, and then, in the late afternoon quiet, the faint creak of the bed springs as he lay heavily down.

II

The meeting had just adjourned. Near the unlit grate at the side of the room, the directors were standing in a silent group. "It's about time for dinner," one man remarked tentatively, then turned to pick his hat from among those scattered on the threadbare sofa. "It's time," said Mr. Hopkins, who still sat in the chairman's place at the head of the long table. He did not even glance up when he spoke. He sat very erect in his chair, filling it. One heavy sunburned hand lay flat out on the table before him, palm down, while the other plucked at a rip in the old green-baize table-cover. The rest of the men, all except Mr. Hardin, moved toward the door. The last one hesitated a moment with his hand on the knob.

"You all will lock the door and leave the key downstairs, won't you? I'm not coming back this afternoon. I've got a case on."

"Listen, Sullivan," said Mr. Hopkins, "why don't you hang around a spell? Maybe you can have dinner with Mr. Hardin and me. We are going over to the Ellis House."

"I'll stay a few minutes, but I can't eat with you, I've got to hurry." He came over and leaned against the table, facing Mr. Hopkins. Mr. Hardin stood across the room looking out of the window. There were not many people in the street, even on Saturday, at noontime. A few buggies and a surrey stood on the far side; the horses were tied to iron rings set in the stone curb of the pavement, and their heads drooped down over their hoofs. Sunlight filled the narrow street, and glittered on the few puddles left by the rain of the night before. It was all very familiar to him. He was paying no attention to the low voices from the table.

"Hey, Joe, wake up," Mr. Hopkins called to him. "Sullivan can't eat dinner with us, but he's got time for a drink."

Mr. Hardin turned slowly. "All right, let's go to the Utopia."

While sitting, Mr. Hopkins looked like a very big man. A certain impression of size and endurance came from the heavy shoulders, the large bald head and deep-set eyes, the muscular wrists. But now, when he stood, his head came only a little above Mr. Hardin's shoulder. His thick legs were ridiculously short, and the boots which he wore almost gave the look of a deformity.

He led the way out. Sullivan pulled the door shut and locked it.

"A. M. Sullivan, Lawyer," Mr. Hardin read aloud the lettering on the frosted glass. "If I was you, Mike, I'd sell my farm and stick to the law."

"I sorter like my place, though, even if it don't pay some years," answered Sullivan as he followed his friends down the dark stairs.

"Well, I just like my place the years when it pays," interrupted Mr. Hopkins sardonically.

"You sure muster hated it last year," Mr. Hardin said with mild good humor. "I like my farm well enough to keep it as long as tobacco buyers and banks will let me. All the same, it might be good to be a lawyer in these days and times, if I was as young as you are, Mike. My father was a lawyer, but he had a place in the country, too, like you. It was all right then. In South Carolina—that's where I was born—they raised cotton and weren't bothered with this God-damned tobacco crop. I started out to be a lawyer myself."

"I didn't know that," said Sullivan.

"That was long before your time. It was before the war. Somehow I never got settled back to it after the war."

They came out on the street and turned to the left. Without speaking again, they walked the hundred yards to the saloon. The lawyer paused in front of the swinging doors of the Utopia, and tapped the uneven crumbling brick of the sidewalk with his stick.

"They're going to put in a concrete sidewalk for seven blocks along here sometime next year. The contracts haven't been let out yet though."

"More damned foolishness," said Mr. Hopkins. "Better put that money in the schoolhouse or some place where it'll do some good."

"Or in the jail house maybe," Mr. Hardin suggested.

It was crowded inside the saloon. Dozens of farmers were about the bar, and others sat at the little marble-topped tables across the room. Some were wearing their good clothes—dark suits and collars very white against the red of their necks and faces. There were others whose trousers were tucked into mud-splattered boots and whose loose coat pockets bagged with small packages and freshly folded newspapers. These had ridden in on horseback. All of them leaned over their glasses, looked at each other or into the broad bar mirror which reflected the whole scene, and talked. When one of them picked up a glass or pipe, the ends of his fingernails showed white where they had been scraped carefully and deep with the point of a heavy knifeblade. The blue tobacco smoke rose slowly through the thick air and puddled against the painted ceiling.

The three men found a small space at the bar. "Hello, Jerry," Mr. Hopkins said to the sad-faced fellow who was fishing glasses from a basin and wiping them bright. "I see you've got a good run today."

"Good for cutting time. What'll you have?"

Mr. Hopkins turned to his friends. "How about three Jack Daniel's?"

"No, I reckon not," said Sullivan. "I'll have a beer. I never drink whisky, not even a little whisky, before I have a case on. Some people don't like it for you to do their business when you've got whisky on your breath."

"The hell you say," answered Mr. Hopkins. "But you'll have your whisky, won't you, Joe? You haven't got any case on."

Mr. Hardin only nodded. Mr. Hopkins turned back to Sullivan. "Well, you can have my cases whether you're drunk or sober, Mike."

"Thanks, but I lost the only case I ever had for you."

"It wasn't exactly your fault. I ought never fought that case. I knew that son-of-a-bitch Mitchell had a lot of law on his side, but I was so mad at him that if I hadn't sued him, I would have thought about the whole business till I cut his heart out. I saved his life maybe."

"All the same I'm sorry I didn't win for you." Then Sullivan grinned. "But I'm glad you didn't cut his heart out."

"Mitchell just had more law than I did. I reckon the rights were about even, but the rights and the law of things ain't exactly the same thing sometimes."

"We lawyers do the best we can. God-a-mighty Himself frequently don't make things and the rights of things match up. We just do the best we can and try to make a living out of it at the same time."

"God-a-mighty ain't even got that excuse." Mr. Hopkins picked up his full whisky glass and laughed. "Let's drink. Let's drink to the rights of things." He held up the glass and, still smiling, looked at the clear gold liquor. They drank quickly. He and Mr. Hardin set the empty tots back on the bar.

"Two more, Jerry," said Mr. Hardin, "and one for yourself."

Jerry brought the drinks and Mr. Hardin paid him. "Let's go get that table before somebody else wants it. It looks quieter over there."

They went over to the corner and settled themselves.

"I'm glad you made it up with Mitchell," said Mr. Hardin.

"I am too. I like to be at peace with my neighbors like the Bible says," Mr. Hopkins remarked and again laughed. "And Mitch is a good neighbor, but he's a son-of-a-bitch. I like lots of sons-of-bitches though. If I went to law with all the sons-of-bitches I know, you'd have your hands full, Mike, fighting my cases. I've noticed that the sons-of-bitches have the law on their side right frequent."

"Mitchell ain't exactly a son-of-a-bitch," said Mr. Hardin reflectively, "but I know he's a pretty hard man to deal with sometimes. Thank the Lord he ain't on the board."

"I don't mind a man being hard and grasping, because you generally know what to do about that. What I mind is a man being hard and grasping and still telling you he wants to do what's right by you and that it hurts him more than it hurts you. I wouldn't be surprised if some day Mitch don't sit on my front porch and look down the road to that patch of woods that caused all the trouble and say, Well, Bill, I reckon it was God's will and mercy you lost that suit to me. . . . And just let him."

"All the same," said Sullivan blandly, "I hear you two spent a right smart time sitting on each other's porches this summer. I'll bet you didn't talk about lawsuits or politics. Or religion. You old infidel."

"Well, I don't know," Mr. Hardin suggested. "Being a good Episcopalian, I can see how an old infidel, like Bill here, and an old Baptist, like Mitchell, might get together on a good many points of common interest."

"Damn," Mr. Hopkins said. Then he winked at Sullivan.

Sullivan grinned and got up. "I've stayed too long now. Good-bye, gentlemen." He picked up his stick from the table and started for the doorway. He turned, fumbling in his inside coat pocket, and stepped back to the table. "I was about to forget something, Mr. Hopkins. Here's this little item I promised you for today. Good-bye." He laid an envelope on the table in front of Mr. Hopkins.

"Thanks, Mike."

"Good luck, with your case," Mr. Hardin called after him. Sullivan, already at the entrance, waved back and was gone. Mr. Hopkins half turned in his chair and stared at the doors as if to assure himself that his friend had really left the bar room. The doors swung lightly back and forth from Sullivan's passage, weakened in their irresolute arcs, and settled into place. Only then did Mr. Hopkins pick up the long manila envelope from the table. Mr. Hardin looked casually at it; it was unsealed and tied with a red band, and on neither side was there a word of writing.

Mr. Hopkins caught the look, and his strong forefinger slipped under the red tape as if he intended to snap its fold and satisfy whatever idle curiosity prompted that glance. Searchingly, but for only the fraction of a second, he hunched forward against the edge of the table and looked into his companion's eyes. Mr. Hardin deliberately met his gaze and then looked slowly down at the envelope. The strong forefinger relaxed and carefully withdrew from under the tape. Once or twice Mr. Hopkins turned the packet over in his hands and then, with the slightest air of regret, slipped it into his pocket.

"A little legal work Mike did for me. Sorter a last will and testament." He saturninely tapped the right breast of his coat, which bulged slightly from the envelope. "I might fall off a horse some night in the dark of the moon and break my neck."

"Not much chance. A man that rides like you and holds his likker like you ain't going to fall off any horses," said Mr. Hardin. "But let's go get our dinner."

"Can I have one more drink? Besides, we'll miss the first rush at the Ellis House if you can hold out a little longer. This is Saturday and the town is stinking full."

"All right. I'm not specially hungry. But no drink."

Mr. Hopkins held up one finger in the air; Jerry caught the sign and came across the room with another whisky. Mr. Hopkins did not pick it up, but sat back in his chair with one hand flat out on the table before him, palm down, just as he had sat in the chairman's seat in Sullivan's law office. His large head hung a little forward, crinkling into deep furrows the strong red flesh of his jowls. The least breath of air from the saloon's half-doors disturbed the red fine hair which fringed his head, and fluttered the leaves of the calendar on the wall above. Mr. Hardin watched him calmly, waiting for him to speak. Finally he looked up.

"It's pretty bad, ain't it, Joe?" Though the voice was still harsh, it was somehow different, with a deeper and more resonant tone.

"It's bad, and there ain't a doubt. The worst is we can't do much about it. We didn't start organizing soon enough, and in a thing like this you haven't got anything really but the time between one crop and the next. If we lose out this year, we'll lose members instead of gaining them for next year. If people could only see what we're up against. I reckon people usually see things clear enough in the end, but it sure takes a devil of a long time."

"We ain't going to lose this year," said Mr. Hopkins with the old voice. "I'll be damned to hell if we lose."

"Yes."

"People always see too late. A hell of a lot of good it'll do next year when prime leaf is six cents and dropping for people to say that maybe, maybe, the association was a good thing. See for them, and cram it down their throats. I know the association is a good thing, and you know it's a good thing, and there's dozens of men that know it's a good thing. See for the rest and cram it down their throats." He picked up his glass to drink. "And they'll like it in the end," he said.

"Things don't work that way, Bill. I sometimes wish they did," Mr. Hardin answered. "You can work them that way a little while maybe, but you lose something else. Too much."

"I know all about that, Joe. Hell, Joe, I've heard you talk like that before."

"And I reckon you're right apt to hear me talk like that again before I die."

"Sure. About once a month for the next twenty-five years. And I don't go so far as to say that you ain't right in a majority of cases. It wouldn't surprise me a bit if you are right. But you can't play that way when you're playing against time, and we're sure playing against time right now. If people won't see, we've got to make them see. Cram it down their throats. Do you know, Joe, that if we could get twenty-odd more names, the right names, in this county, and about the same number in a few other sections, we might stand a chance of getting our figure when selling time comes?"

"I know it. The devil of it's going to be getting them."

"We're going to get them."

"I hope to the Lord we do, but I don't quite see how."

"I see one way. I grant you, Joe, it's a way I don't cotton to much, but it's a way. There's two things about people; one of them is that they won't see what's good for them till it's too late, and the other is they're always wanting to play safe. They're afraid, they're afraid of their shadow. They're downright timid, Joe." Again he hunched forward a little against the table and looked into Mr. Hardin's eyes, and again Mr.

Hardin deliberately met his gaze. He shook his head before he spoke.

"It ain't that people are so much afraid. It's just that they're fuddled. Fuddled as hell right frequent. When they see straight they ain't generally afraid."

Mr. Hopkins said nothing. Motionlessly he still leaned forward and watched his friend's face.

"And, Bill, I sorter suspect," Mr. Hardin continued, "that you've already shown your hand."

"And you're dead right."

"I suspected it. I suspected it pretty strong just this minute."

"It was just a little private experiment I made. I wrote some friendly little letters to some people I ain't so fond of. That is, I signed them 'A friend.' You know this fellow Jerdan over in Trigg County, and you remember how he was almost stumping against the association. Writing damn-fool letters to the papers and going on. Well, he stopped it pretty sudden, you remember, and it wasn't long before he signed up. I've tried it three or four times on the quiet, and, by God, it's worked. It's worked sweet. There ain't even a whimper, for if a man's afraid enough to mind a dirty scrap of paper, he's afraid to do much complaining. And nine out of ten are afraid."

"Well, Bill, number ten is going to take his letter out of his postbox some morning, and he's going to look at that little tin American flag on the box, and there's going to be hell breaking loose in Georgia."

"Look here, Joe. Damn your tin flags, Joe. A lot of good we get out of it. A farmer pays his taxes and gets a vote—and he's lucky if some fellow in shirt sleeves don't throw it in the paper basket instead of counting it. But does he ever get time on his loans, or roads, or a decent price for his crop? Give us a chance and we'll fix those things ourselves."

"I still think we'll get them fixed, but I don't believe your way can do the job. I don't claim all the tin flags either. I used to see that particular flag behind some guns pointing in my general direction, and Lord knows it wasn't my flag then. But I managed to keep a certain amount of respect for it." He surveyed Mr. Hopkins humorously. "A little more respect, I reckon, when it was on the other side of those dog-gone guns than now when it ain't."

"Well, just let number ten look at his little tin flag all he wants. But that's all."

"Um-huh." Mr. Hardin was leaning back and filling his pipe with an excess of care. No longer was he looking at Mr. Hopkins, and Mr. Hopkins seemed just a little disturbed by the fact.

"You know that when I write a letter, any letter," Mr. Hopkins went on, "I mean what I say. Of course now," and he seemed pleased with his whimsicality, "I'm pretty long-suffering."

"Um-huh."

"The only people we wouldn't be long-suffering with would be those that bolted the association. After they bolted, there won't be any tobacco for them to sell. Of course, they might collect a little insurance. No objection to that."

"I guess this project you propose couldn't be called exactly private?"

"No. I've talked it over with plenty—or rather I fixed it so they talked it over with me—and there's plenty people that hold my views. I didn't mention what made Jerdan change his mind though. That was just a little private experiment."

"Funny I didn't get wind of all these goings-on."

"You see, it wasn't like something official for the board. Some of the others sorter felt it might be better if you didn't get spoken to yet a while. They sorter felt—" Mr. Hopkins hesitated vaguely.

"I get your point, Bill. They sorter felt I was getting old and set in my notions. They felt that if I happened to agree, I was too old to be much good to them, and that if I didn't agree, I'd better not be told. I'd better read it in a newspaper—after it was over."

"Well, Joe, that's putting it a little hard."

"Do you think so?"

"I do," Mr. Hopkins said. He seemed not to notice whatever sarcasm lay in the question. "And I'm telling you all this now on my own responsibility. Mike and me thought you ought to know."

"So Mike's in it too?"

"Sure, Mike's in it. In it up to the neck. Hell, Mike's a farmer before he's a lawyer."

"Thanks for telling me."

"We thought you had a right to know where you stood. Mike thought you might see like we do, but I never thought so. I hoped so a little maybe, but I knew you too well, and when I saw you sitting there in Mike's office today, I was dead sure of it. I ain't even asking you, Joe."

"You needn't. I'm against it on every point and every way you look at it. And the next board meeting I'm putting the matter on the table and we'll have it out in the open. If the board don't see sense and decency, they can have my resignation. I reckon from what you've just said that they don't need my efforts much anyway."

"You're crazy. You carry influence around here, and if you resign, there'll be trouble."

"That don't matter. If it happens, I'm resigning, and on the morning when our friend number ten starts to collect insurance because somebody's decided that a tobacco crop had better be smoked up in one pile, I'm getting out of the association altogether."

"The hell you say, Joe! You can't get out."

"I can. I reckon you figure you're doing right according to your lights, but they ain't my lights."

"It's a question of getting our rights. Isn't that so?"

"It depends on how you get them. I've set a lot of store by the association, but if things go that way, I'm getting out. You see, I have to get out if things go that way."

"You're a fool, Joe. A perfect damn fool."

"Maybe. But I get out if things go that way."

"Well, Joe, I tell you this much. They go that way if they have to go that way to win. I'd see every leaf in two states burned up in a bonfire before I'd see one hand of tobacco sold half a cent under the association price. We'll fix a fair price and we'll have it. It ain't just the money—it's our rights in that and everything else."

"You'll need that sorter last will and testament Mike so kindly fixed up for you. You'll need it bad, maybe. But you won't fall off any horse in the dark of the moon. Some fool farmer that wants his rights will shoot you off in the light of the moon, Bill."

"The hell he will. There won't be any shooting done."

"There'll be a little shooting, one way and another. I reckon you know that you're proposing a sort of revolution. You say you usually mean what you say, and I guess you do. Well, in revolutions I've noticed that right frequent there's a little shooting."

Mr. Hopkins stood up with a violence that sent his chair spinning to the floor. The clatter of its light metal back against the tiles suddenly hushed all of the talk of the saloon as if it had been the crash of a gavel in the courtroom. Every man lounging along the bar or sitting at the other tables was now staring at Mr. Hopkins. Only Jerry, who had seen a good deal in his job, gave a glance and kept on polishing his glass. One fellow heard the clatter just as he passed the doors, turned and saw its cause, and then, with the easiest air in the world, sauntered back into the saloon. He leaned against the near end of the bar, watching. Mr. Hopkins neither stooped to pick up the chair nor paid the least attention to the score of farmers who were regarding him with covert curiosity. He stood very straight, with his legs wide apart, and he was white to the lips.

"I won't be threatened. I'll be damned if I'll be threatened." He spoke very low, almost in a harsh whisper. "Let them shoot and shoot their bellyful. We're going to beat them."

"I wasn't threatening you, Bill. I was just remarking."

"We're going to beat them. And you, you haven't got any right to get out. You won't get out!"

"I've had my say."

"You have?" He stepped back and took his hat from the hook on the wall. "Well, so long, Hardin." He smiled heavily, sarcastically down at him. "I'll see you in the board meeting."

He strode toward the door. His direct stare met the group about the bar, but gave them not a sign of recognition. They all might have been strangers to him.

"Good-bye, Bill," called Mr. Hardin. "Don't fall off any horses."

Mr. Hopkins did not turn to the joke, or to the farewell. The curious eyes watched his broad back and red creased neck under the brim of his black hat disappear through the swinging doors and out into the street.

"Well, I'll be damned," someone remarked in a reflective monotone. In the silence the words carried distinctly across the room.

For a little while Mr. Hardin kept his seat in the corner. He got up finally and, hat in hand, walked across to the bar.

"I'll pay for Mr. Hopkins' last drink, Jerry." He laid a silver dollar carefully on the bar. While Jerry got the change he turned to a man at the nearest table.

"Hopkins certainly gets heated up about his politics on one or two points. You know, Mr. Jackson, I have times when I almost believe Bill is just a black Republican." He spoke carefully, putting his words out as he had put the silver dollar on the onyx top of the bar. Then he shook his head and, smiling, repeated, "Just a black Republican."

"Hopkins gets heated up pretty easy," agreed the man at the table.

"Good-bye, Mr. Jackson. Give my respects to Mrs. Jackson. You all ride over to see us sometime when the season slacks a little. Edith gets right lonesome, I guess, with just us men around. Good-bye."

He picked up his change and moved toward the door. To one or two familiar faces he lifted his hand gravely in a sort of salute, but he did not pause to speak again.

He stood for a moment irresolutely in front of the Utopia, and then looked at his watch. A little after one o'clock. He put it back in his pocket and turned to the right in the direction of Sullivan's law office. He passed the door to the dark stairs which led up to it without a glance. Farther down across the street stood the Ellis House. Along its front ran a two-story gallery, which sagged with decrepitude between the supporting posts and sloped perilously out toward the pavement. Men who had finished their dinner now lounged there on both levels and smoked and talked in the sunshine with their feet propped up on the green iron grillwork of the railing. Without quickening his pace, Mr. Hardin walked past it, giving it no more attention than he had given to the dark stairs. A few blocks farther on he turned into a side street and entered a small restaurant.

"Hello, Mr. Hardin," said the fat little man who came over to his table. "I ain't seen you in town for a coon's age."

"I ain't been in much lately. We've been pretty busy getting the cutting done and the firing started."

"I reckon you're in over Sunday, ain't you?"

"No. Just for today. I'm going back tonight on the eight-fifty train."

"Just in for the 'sociation meeting, I reckon. I seen about it in the paper, and there's been right smart talk about it, too."

"Yes, we had a meeting this morning."

"Well, I shore hope you git yore price. If tobacco gits right in this section, everything gits right, and when it gits wrong, they ain't nobody got any money."

"That's true," agreed Mr. Hardin. "But what's good to eat today, Jake?"

"We've got first-class ham. A first-class ham, Mr. Hardin."

"Give me some ham and vegetables then. You needn't hurry. I'm not in a hurry this afternoon. And a cup of coffee, Jake."

He climbed into a coach and found himself a seat near the end. Across from him sat an old woman dressed in a black silk dress. She did not notice Mr. Hardin, for she was already dozing, with her head resting on the back of the seat and her respectable black hat just the least bit crooked. Looking at her, Mr. Hardin smiled, then he began to survey the station platform. Just by his window some people stood while they took their good-bye. Another old woman, very much like the one who slept so peacefully opposite him, kept leaning down to kiss a little boy who held the hand of a young woman. The young woman paid no attention, but talked busily to another young woman. Once the old woman blew the little boy's nose on her own small white handkerchief, wiping it gently as a sort of token of service and affection at parting.

Beyond them, almost in the shadow, two men conversed. Their backs were to the train, but one of them was a powerful man whose thick, booted legs almost gave the look of deformity. The other man, who waved his hands now and then as in argument, was tall and stooped. At last they walked over to the other side of the platform where the east-bound local waited. The powerful man fumbled in his coat pocket and produced a packet which he passed into the emphatic hands of the friend. The packet was a long envelope bound in two folds of red tape; in the light from the vestibule of the local it showed plainly. The friend mounted the steps of a coach, leaned to shake hands with the powerful man, and disappeared. Mr. Hopkins turned away and walked the length of the platform and into the door of the waiting room. Then the local drew out of the station, bearing Blake Mitchell and the long envelope away to the east.

"Well, I'm damned," said Mr. Hardin aloud, and then glanced across at the old woman. "Well, I'm damned. Old Man Hopkins giving his last will and testament to Blake Mitchell." He chuckled to himself. "His last will and testament."

The train pulled out with a jerk and left the station. Slowly it passed a grade crossing on a street which led up into the town where people walked about under the lights. Then came the flour mill by the river, the warehouses, and then the scattered Negro cabins where black faces pressed against the windowpanes as the train went by. After that there was the open country with the occasional gleam of a light in the distance.

The conductor put his head in the door of the dim coach. "Thomasville," he called, "Thomasville." Mr. Hardin stood up as the train swayed to a stop, and collected the packages beside him on the seat. Only the stationmaster and a few Negroes were on the platform when he got off. The brakeman on the rear of the last coach leaned out to wave his red lantern and the train drew quickly away down the valley cut. Once or twice the trail of smoke above the engine glowed with a soft cumulous rose in the reflected light from the firebox door, showing that the fireman was stoking for the grade ahead. Just after Mr. Hardin had turned away from the station toward the town the full moan of the engine whistle blowing for Johnson's Crossing came drifting back on the still night air.

"OO—oo, OO—oo," one of the Negroes behind on the platform mocked the echo. It was a deep and melancholy voice, full like the distant whistle. "OO—oo, OO—oo." Then there was the sound of laughter.

The door of the livery stable was locked when he got there, but he could see the light of a lantern through the broad cracks. He kicked the boards, and when that brought no one to open, he shouted. At last there was the rattle of the bolt and the big door grated outward, showing a stooped old fellow, who blinked in the lantern light.

"I'm sure sorry I didn't hear right off, Mr. Hardin. You been here long?"

"No, I just got here," Mr. Hardin said as he followed back to the box stall where his mare was. The keeper disappeared into it and his voice came vacantly from its gloom.

"Mr. Hopkins didn't come by like he said for his hoss after the early train, so I says to myself, both you and him was staying over till tomorrow about that 'sociation business. So I shuts up and goes to bed."

"Mr. Hopkins didn't come on the last train either, so you can shut up for good this time. I reckon he's staying in on association business."

"Funny he didn't git back. He generally gits back soon's he can." He emerged from the stall leading the saddled mare, and stood there with the bridle ends dangling idly from his hand. He made no sign of turning Jenny over to her owner and saying good night. "Yeh, he generally gits back right prompt. He won't be away from that farm of his'n half a minute, if he can help. He sticks to his business, sure, and he always has. If I'd stuck to my business when I was young, I might a-had a fine place like him now. I just gallivanted when I'se young and look at me now. That's what I says to these shiftless boys around here. I says, Just look at me now." He spat into the dung and straw of the stable floor, and then put his broken shoe over the spot. A streak of tobacco juice clung on his long mustache, glistening like dew in the lantern light. His head hung forward and he looked up in an anxious doglike way at Mr. Hardin, seeming to expect some answer that would set straight the shiftless years.

"Lord knows, John, you haven't got much to worry about." Mr. Hardin leaned down and took the bridle rein from the old man's loose hand as if he were lifting it from a peg. "You're pretty well fixed here for the rest of your life. Mr. Alexander's a good man to work for. You haven't got a thing in the world to worry about."

Mr. Hardin swung easily up to the saddle and Jenny walked toward the door. He lifted the bridle and turned. "John, I'm leaving some bundles over there on the bench. I'll get them tomorrow when we drive in for church. Good night."

"Good night," answered John, "good night, Mr. Hardin." The voice sounded impersonal and thin, like the voice of a man coming from a trance. He stood in the middle of the wide doorway while Mr. Hardin trotted off down the street. Even after Mr. Hardin turned out of sight beyond the station, he still stood in the door, against the lantern light from the cavernous stable hall.

Beyond the station the road ran steeply up a hill, and there Jenny dropped into a walk. After the crest of the hill it was an easy ride of two and a half miles to the farm gate. By the time Mr. Hardin reached it, the last bit of cloud had drifted away to the horizon on the north and the moon was clear. He took the long lane between the fields and grove, and Jenny, knowing that she was nearly home, went into a brisk canter. The shadow of the tall trees which bordered the fields lay blackly across the moonlit lane. The fields were bare now, with only the regular stubs where the tobacco had been cut. Jenny's hoofs clattered hollowly over the wooden bridge where the lane crossed the creek, then, far away in the direction of the house, came the answering bay of a hound. Just beyond the bridge the house could be seen, and farther down the sweep of land toward the river, the bulk of the firing barn. The smoke stood up from its roof in thin unperturbed plumes and lay over the fields like the faintest strata of mist. In the middle of the nearest field stood a wagon, deserted after the day's work. Not a breath of wind stirred, and everywhere hung the scent of burning.

The house showed no light. Mr. Hardin took the branch of the lane which led toward the barn, and rode straight to it without going to the stable. He hitched Jenny to the prong of a peeled sapling near the barn and entered by a small side door. In the middle of the dirt floor two logs smoldered. Their smoke lifted heavily and spread out in the upper obscurity of the barn where the ripe tobacco hung in tier after tier. A Negro man lay on an old quilt near the stack of fresh logs on the other side of the fire, lying on his stomach with his head on his arm and his legs sprawled straight out. In the firelight the upturned soles of his feet showed a creased and ashen gray. His shoes were set carefully side by side at the end of the pallet.

Mr. Hardin stepped noiselessly across the powdery floor to the Negro. For a long time he looked down at him. There was no sound in the barn except the steady draw and whisper of the sleeper's breath and the occasional crackling of the logs as they dropped apart and settled into ash. Finally Mr. Hardin bent over and shook the Negro firmly by the shoulder.

"Wake up, Sam. Wake up."

The Negro rolled over and rose to a sitting posture and leaned back on both stiff arms like a clumsy child. Then he recognized Mr. Hardin. "I jes' gone to sleep," he said. "I jes' done napped off this minute."

"Well, you better not nap off any more. For God's sake, Sam, what do you think you're down here for?"

"Yassuh. I jes' napped off this very minute though."

"Get up and put Jenny in the stable. I'll stay here till you get back."

He sat down on the pile of logs and watched Sam as he laboriously pulled on his shoes. Sam stood up, stretched himself, and moved toward the door.

"Sam," Mr. Hardin said, "I'm not much sleepy, I reckon I ain't sleepy a bit. If you hurry and put that mare up, I'll be down here a time yet, and you can do some more of your damn-fool napping."

"Yassuh," Sam answered, and closed the door behind him.

III

Mrs. Hardin laid her book down on the sofa beside her and looked up at the big clock above on the mantelshelf. As she looked, the minute hand twitched over a space and somewhere in the bowels of the clock began the whirr and catch which presaged the half-hour stroke. The two strokes came, muffled and deliberate, in the afternoon silence. The setter bitch on the hearth drowsily raised her head, blinked at the fire, and again settled the black nose between crumpled forelegs. It was half past three.

Mrs. Hardin had no sooner begun to read once more than the dog scrambled up and stood with ears cocked. There was the sound of steps from the rear of the house and stamping as if a man were knocking the mud off his feet before entering. The dog ran to the dining room and whined to be let out.

"Thomas," called Mrs. Hardin.

"Coming!"

Big Thomas entered from the dining room, with clothes wet and his black hair a tangle of damp curls. He came over and kissed his wife, who ran her hands through his hair and then brought them down on his shoulders.

"You're mighty wet, Thomas," she said. "Maybe you better change."

"I guess not. I'll just dry off by the fire. I'm a little cold."

"Is it cold out now?"

"It's cold, but it doesn't get cold enough to stop this infernal raining. It's been raining all winter. It didn't really let up today till fifteen minutes ago. We may get an early spring out of it though. Where's Papa?"

"Papa went out when the rain let up. He said he was going down to the road and get the afternoon mail."

"I guess he wanted his paper. He gets mighty restless for his paper in the afternoon. But I could tell him what's going to be in it this time. Jones just told me when I went over to his place about that heifer."

He leaned from his stool, by the hearth, spreading his big hands to the fire and gazing into its depth. He appeared to be disturbed, almost truculent. The vapor from the drying clothes ascended in thin clouds about his head, caught the drift of air to the chimney, and vanished. Once or twice he flexed his hands; a few drops of water still clung to the black hairs on the back of his hands and wrists. Mrs. Hardin waited for him to go on, but he gave no sign.

"What was it?" she asked at length.

"What's been going on for some time maybe, but there can't be a doubt about it now. Nightriders."

"They're sure, Thomas?"

"My Lord, honey, they burned up two barns full of tobacco, and then when old Mr. Salem's barn didn't burn proper, they used dynamite. People saw them, too, plain as day, riding down the pike this side of Hubertsville. There wasn't much secret about it.

"I hoped those burnings last fall were accidents, but I bet, by God, most of them weren't accidents. But those fellows were clever about it. Some people who bucked the association got letters, but the people who got the letters didn't get their barns burned; it was people who didn't get letters that had their barns burned. But almost every time, the man who lost his barn wasn't in the association either, and the fellow who had the letter got the point right quick. But when the fire marshal came around about a burnt barn and asked if there'd been any threats, they had to tell him no. And there weren't any tracks. Last night's job was different; there were plenty of tracks and they burned the barns belonging to men who've had letters and been standing out against them since last fall. The fire marshal will sure find plenty of tracks this time, but he'll have a devil of a time finding the men who made them. And then he might not be so anxious to find the men that made them." He did not look at his wife as he talked; his eyes were still fixed on the depths of the burning coals. "If I happened to be the fire marshal or the sheriff and knew who made the tracks, I wouldn't be anxious to have the job of serving any warrants."

"I guess you would serve your warrants all right, Thomas, if you had them." She spoke sharply, in a voice that demanded reply. He did not answer or look up, but stretched his hands again before the fire. He seemed very cold and his eyes stared into the depth of the embers like those of a man who sees something he desires but may not have. Then his wife laughed. "But of course you aren't the sheriff."

"That's just one piece of luck and not enough. There's going to be a lot of trouble around here soon. I wish Papa would come on back to the house. I hope to God he doesn't get any more of his notions."

"He's already got them, Thomas. You know how he is."

"I can see how he felt about getting off the board. I reckon they sorter crowded him off maybe. The only thing I'm sorry about is his breaking up with Hopkins. I like Hopkins pretty well, and he's got lots of influence in this section."

"Papa's always been thick as thieves with Mr. Hopkins, and he still likes him. They just didn't think alike."

"I wish I knew just exactly what they had to row about. Papa just shuts up when I ask him and nobody else knows much about it. People just say that Hopkins jumped up and kicked his chair over and walked out the door. Then Papa went over and paid for Hopkins' drink. Did you know that, Edith? He just walked over in front of all those people and paid for his drink. He muster been crazy. I'd go to jail before I'd do a thing like that."

"I know, Thomas. You and Papa are mighty different. I don't know which one of you I like the best."

"I know which one. It's him."

"Maybe so, maybe you're right." And then she caught sight of her husband's face. "Why, Thomas! You crazy old goose. I do believe you're jealous of your own father. You ought to be spanked like Tommy."

He turned and stared directly at her with the same look in his eyes as when he had been staring into the center of the fire. Startled, she met his eyes.

"Papa and I ain't a damned bit alike," he said in a quiet voice. "I take more after Mother's people. Papa and I don't think the same thing about anything in the world. Just wait about ten minutes till he comes up to the house and comes in here with his newspaper stuffed in his pocket and that set look on his face. Talking won't help any, for he just listens and then acts like he'd never heard a single word."

"Why, Thomas! You know that's not true. Thomas, I don't know what's the matter with you."

"Nothing is the matter. I'm just not going to be ruined now by any of Papa's damned foolishness. He never knows on which side his bread's buttered. I didn't want to get in this association mess in the first place. We don't make much out of our crop some years, but we manage better than most. We always manage to pull through with a little to show for it. Papa talked me into this, and look what a hell of a mess it's turned out to be. What a hell of a mess. The only thing we can do now is to stick it out and get what we can from the association. I'm just not going to let any of Papa's damned highfalutin notions ruin us all. That's what's the matter."

His wife got up quickly from the sofa and went over to him. She put her hands on his forehead and then leaned down and kissed his hair. "Thomas, I do believe you've got fever. You don't feel like a chill coming on, do you?"

"No. I don't. Didn't I tell you, Edith, that I'm all right? I haven't got any fever."

She drew his head back against her breast, her fingers still on his forehead. He sat erect on the low stool with his arms straight and his hands on his knees. His body was perfectly rigid, resisting, but his eyes were closed.

"Oh, Thomas," she whispered. Her mouth was almost against the damp black hair.

Again the dog stirred by the hearth. There was a sound of voices from the outside, and the dog went to the door that opened on the front porch.

"It's Papa. Get away, Edith, get away."

She moved to the sofa again without speaking.

"Tommy is with him," he said. "Back from school early today."

Mr. Hardin came in with Thomas at his heels.

"Hello," Mr. Hardin said, but before either of the others could answer, the boy ran across and stood in front of his father.

"The nightriders were out last night, Father. They were out for sure this time. They burned up three barns. They burned up old Mr. Grey's barn and Jack Grey said at school today that Mr. Grey said he thought Mr. Mitchell helped do it. He said he thought he saw Mr. Mitchell's horse and if he ever found out for sure, he'd shoot Mr. Mitchell if it's the last thing he ever does. I'll bet he does, too. I'll bet Mr. Mitchell did it. I'll bet—"

"I know all about it," said his father. "I've heard the whole story already."

"Listen, Tommy," rebuked Mrs. Hardin, "you don't know whether Mr. Mitchell had anything to do with it or not. Don't you say one word about all this at school or anywhere else. Not a word. Do you hear?"

"But, Mother, everybody knows about it. Jack said his father said he bet Grandpa was kicked off the board just so they could put Mr.

Mitchell on and the association could nightride all it wanted and he said he'd shoot every man on the whole board 'fore he'd ever join up with a bunch of skunks like that. And Mrs. Grey's mighty sick today. She's caught a breakdown."

"Tommy, I've told you. Don't say a single word to anybody. And your grandfather wasn't kicked off the board either. He resigned because he wanted to. Now go upstairs and change your clothes. You're wet as can be. Then go back and get yourself something to eat. It's a long time till supper."

"They say Grandpa had to resign and that he got kicked off. It's the same thing, Grandpa, ain't it?"

Old Mr. Hardin looked down at his grandson with puzzled eyes. "Do what your mother says, Thomas, before you catch cold."

"I'm not cold."

"Do what your mother says, son," Big Thomas threatened, "or you'll get your hide frailed off in about a minute."

The boy looked at his father with a sort of impudent amusement at the terror of the threat; then he turned and left the room. The noise of his feet, as he took each stair with a solid deliberate stamp, carried his protest back to the hearthside.

"He ought to be spanked," said Big Thomas. "I've got half a mind to spank him right now."

"I expect you've about forgotten how to spank him," smiled his wife, "it's been so long since you've spanked him." She paused a moment and studied him. "And besides, Thomas, it's you who need a spanking."

"He's a mighty bright little boy," old Mr. Hardin remarked, just as the feet reached the last stair with especial violence. "He's mighty clever. He understands everything as clear as can be."

"You didn't talk to him about the nightriding, did you, Papa?" asked Mrs. Hardin with a trace of anxiety in her tone. "You ought not to, you know."

"I didn't say a word about it to him. I just let him talk about it to me coming up to the house. I met him down at the big gate."

Big Thomas looked directly at his father for the first time since the old man had come in. "You mean he came while you were sitting on the gate reading your paper," he said. "I wish you wouldn't sit on the gate. It's ruining the gate."

"I sit up pretty near the post, son. It don't hurt the gate any more anyway. The gate's already solid down on the ground."

"Your sitting on it put it solid on the ground."

"I reckon so, even if I always do sit up pretty near the post, but the gate's the only place to sit down there. When the weather warms up, maybe I'll put me a bench down there. There's a right pleasant place for a bench under that big white oak. Don't you think so, Edith? It'll be nice to sit down there some when summer comes. It's nice and close to the road."

"Yes, Papa," she answered, "it's nice and close to the road for you."

The old man came around by the fire opposite his son and took the big chair reserved for him. He propped his stick against the stonework of the fireplace, and began filling his pipe. When that was lighted and the first blue puff or two had been dissipated into the upper air of the room, he took the folded paper from his pocket. Slowly, he spread it on his knees.

"You seen this, Thomas?"

"No, I haven't seen it, but Jones told me all about it when I went over about that heifer. Jones sorter thinks it's a good thing, even if he is a friend of Mr. Salem's. He says he feels sorry for Mr. Salem because of Mr. Salem not having any insurance to speak of, but he says it's a time when you can't think too much about friends. You've got to think about the future for everybody. Let's see the paper."

Without a word his father passed him the newspaper. He began to read, holding the sheets firmly with both of his large hands and leaning forward over them. His father watched him; he still held the pipe fixed between his teeth while he watched, but no more puffs of smoke came from it. Mrs. Hardin's book lay open in her lap with her hand on it to hold the place, but she, too, was watching her husband. When he turned the sheet, hunting the rest of the story, the paper crackled sharply in the silence, like a new-lit log at night. He finished, folded the paper, and passed it back to his father.

"I suppose you've made up your mind," he said.

"That ain't exactly the point," the old man answered. "The point is, What do you think about it?"

"You won't see it the way I do. I don't see much use in talking about it." The voice was sullen, constrained. For a moment his wife seemed about to speak, and then, with an effort, turned her eyes from him.

"Son, that ain't the point either. What do you think about it?"

"I feel about like Jones, I reckon."

"You feel that the association's got to win, no matter how?"

"I reckon so."

"Not feeling that way made me get off the board. I can't feel that way now since it's come to this. Nothing in the world's worth winning or doing, no matter how. You always cut your own throat that way."

"I'd take a chance right now on cutting my own throat. We've got a crop on our hands and we've got to sell it. And next year we'll have a crop and we'll want to sell that for enough money to pay hands and pay taxes and pay this and pay that. And everybody's in the same boat. I'd take a chance all right."

"Well, I told Hopkins something when we had our little disagreement."

"I can guess what you told him."

"Maybe you can guess. You ought to be able to guess. I told him that the first time I was certain the association burned a barn, I was getting out and was going to stay out. I can't stop them being damned fools, but I can get out myself. I might've stayed on the board if I thought I had a chance of stopping it, but I didn't see a single chance. Now they've got that fellow Mitchell in my place, most likely they'll be singing a hymn before and after setting a fire to a barn. Well, I just don't see that singing one of Mitchell's hymns changes things. I'm getting out right away."

Big Thomas got up from the stool and stepped to the center of the hearth. His father, sitting in the chair with the newspaper on his lap, looked very small before him.

"You are going to ruin us, Papa. Just as certain as you get out, you are going to ruin us. But I'll not have it. I'm not going to be ruined now by any notion of yours. God knows I've worked hard enough on this place, but always what you say runs it. But it's not going to run it this time. You helped start this association. You got us in it and you got a lot of other people in it. You've started something and you can't stop it, so you're getting out. You made your mistake when you got off the board. Papa, you're on horseback now, you're on horseback, and it's a wild piece of horseflesh. By God, Papa, it's you or the horse. A bad horse don't let you step down at the block just because you've decided you can't ride him. He throws you. You just try easing out now and see what happens. It'll be ruin. And I'll not be ruined by you."

"It won't be ruin, son, but even if it is, I'm going to try to keep my hands clean as I can."

"Clean? Clean? Why, if you keep on this sort of thing, your hands'll be dirty from grubbing in somebody else's tobacco patch. It's ruin, I tell you."

"You're crazy, Thomas."

"It's not me that's crazy. It's you. I've got other people to think about. I've got Edith here and Tommy. You're crazy, and you don't think about anybody in the world except yourself when it come to do something like this. Keep your hands clean? Why don't you think about the rest of us a little? Keep Edith's hands clean. Keep them out of somebody's dishwater."

"Thomas, Thomas," implored his wife, "don't be such a fool. Come over and sit down. Sit down over here with me."

He swung around toward her, his head drooping a little, but without shame, and his arms straight at his sides.

"Come here, Thomas."

He followed the direction of her extended hand and came to sit beside her on the sofa. Mr. Hardin regarded the proceeding with no apparent interest; he looked like one finally detached from it, a spectator who had no concern with its outcome. There was silence in the room. Each of the three seemed to be completely unaware of the others, and lost in thought.

"Why don't you say something?" Thomas demanded at last.

"I don't know if there's anything for me to say now."

"Are you getting out?"

"I might say this, Thomas, after all. I've broken horses since I was fifteen years old and I've been thrown by them, but I always rode them in the end. I guess I understand them all right. I thought I understood something about men, too. But I guess I don't understand a thing in the world about them."

"Are you getting out?"

"Yes. I'm getting out. No, don't say anything, Thomas." He lifted his hand, palm outward, toward his son. "That don't mean you're getting out at all. I can't see any reason why we ought to stay together on this business. I think one way and you think another. We've both got our reasons, but there's mighty little use in talking about them. We'll divide the crop up right now, and we can divide the land up for this year's crop before it's set out. We'll let people know right away, too."

"But, Papa," Mrs. Hardin begged, "you can all fix it up. You don't have to do that."

"Hush, Edith," he said gently. "There's nothing to fix up. Thomas, are you satisfied?"

"I'm satisfied."

"We might even build a new barn. We need another barn pretty bad. That'll make things easier."

"Yes, I reckon we need another barn."

"Well, I'll write a letter to the board tonight and tell them I'm out. And I'll write to Wiedenmeyer tonight, too."

"To Wiedenmeyer?"

"Yes. I ain't going to try to ride in on the tail of the association price. The buyers are getting a good deal of tobacco round the country but maybe they'd be glad for a little more good prime leaf. We've got a right smart good leaf down there. I'll ask Wiedenmeyer for an offer right away tonight. He won't pay the association price, but his figure ought to do me."

"Do it quick. I'll feel better with your tobacco sold. The nightriders won't be wanting to see a good lot like that just put in the buyers' hands. I wish it was off the place right now."

"It'll be off soon enough. I'll get shet of it just as quick as I can, son."

"Well, hurry. I wouldn't write to the board just yet. I'd wait a day or two maybe, till I heard from Wiedenmeyer."

"No, I'm writing both the letters tonight."

Thomas got up and moved toward the door. "Suit yourself," he said. There was an air of victory, of business, about him. "Just suit yourself," he repeated, "but it's playing with dynamite to wait around."

"Where are you going?" his wife asked.

"To hunt Sam," he answered, with the air of achievement still about him.

"Just a minute," his father said. "I'd like to ask you a question. Don't you think the association'll think you're acting a little funny in just helping me to turn over a good crop to the buyers? You, a strong association man. Me, a man that's been kicked off the board and bolted the association?"

"You're my father." The answer was again sullen.

"Sure. I'd just forgotten that for a minute," the old man said reflectively. "I'd just about forgotten about that, thinking of this other."

"Why, Papa," Mrs. Hardin protested with genuine alarm. "You hadn't forgotten anything of the sort."

"Oh, yes, I had. But I just forgot for a minute. And, Thomas, I'd like to ask something else if you don't mind."

"Ask it."

"You're a strong association man. What are you going to do if they ask you to do a little nightriding? Being a strong association man, why don't you do a little nightriding? Most likely they're going to need a few more men that can ride and can shoot pretty well. That is, shoot if they have to shoot. What about Simmons over here? He ain't in the association. He's got a good crop over at his place. More'n likely he'll be ready to sell soon, and they won't want to see that much tobacco put on the market right off. Simmons is a friend of yours. What are you going to do if they ask you to ride with them? Are you going to ride? Or are you going to tell Simmons to get ready, Simmons being a good friend of yours?"

"I'm not telling anybody anything."

"Just going to wash your hands. Just going to call for the bowl and pitcher and wash your hands? Going to keep your hands clean?" The old man's voice was innocent of sarcasm. His question was almost gentle.

"I'm not telling anybody anything," Thomas repeated slowly, his hand on the knob of the door. "I'd be a fool to tell anybody."

"Why don't you ride? Maybe you ought to ride, son, feeling like you do."

Thomas hesitated a moment and then pointed at his wife. "I've got other things to think about. There's Edith, and there's Tommy for me to think about."

His wife looked at the hand outstretched toward her, the stubborn index finger and the black hairs on the back of the hand. "You needn't bother about me," she said.

"God damn it to hell!" said Thomas in a voice that filled the room. "Maybe I will ride."

He went out, slamming the door behind him; the heavy pictures, indistinct now in the late afternoon light, rattled on the walls.

Mrs. Hardin walked over to one of the deep windows and stood with her back to the room. It had begun to rain again. It was a slow, nerveless rain, dropping to earth like an embodiment of the winter twilight. Already the path to the gate was filled with a small riffled flood, and to the left, in the low part of the lawn, water stood almost over the grass. The water reflected nothing in such a light and at such a distance, but a gray splatter which the drops made in the east corner told that it stood there, like a miniature marsh, among the roots and unclipped stems of the grass. The nearer trunks of the leafless trees between the drive and the stagnant fields were visible, but the farther ones of the row gradually dissolved into the opacity of rain. To the left, toward the river, the firing barn was a scarcely distinguishable hulk; to the right, the cedar grove seemed a dim but solid body which pressed, nearer than ever, against the white palings of the lawn fence. The water dripped from the eaves of the veranda and rustled in the overflowing gutter, and immediately in front of the window where Mrs. Hardin stood it plunged in steady, swollen drops from a leak in the veranda roof. Their more regular beat, among the other noises of the weather, was audible in the still room.

"Papa," said Mrs. Hardin, "there's that leak again."

"Yes, honey, it needs fixing soon. Maybe I better write it down so I'll remember it. I'll write it down when I start my letters."

"Why don't you do them now before supper? There won't be anybody in here to bother you now. I'm going back and start Sallie with supper."

"All right. I'll fix them now."

He got up from his chair and knocked his pipe out against the blackened stone of the inner chimney. Mrs. Hardin walked across the room to the sofa where her book lay face down. She picked it up and then closed it with a faint snap. The place was lost. Just as she turned to the door, Mr. Hardin spoke.

"Honey, I'm sorry I said that last to Thomas. I reckon I oughtn't. After all, it's his business."

"Nothing turns out to be just anybody's business all to himself, Papa. That's the trouble."

He made no answer, even though she stood there for a moment or two as if she expected one. She was a tall woman with loose dark hair which looked heavy above her white face. She stood, as her husband had stood, with one hand on the knob of the door, while with the other she held the red-backed book which she had been reading. "But it doesn't matter in the least," she finally said.

Not until after the sound of her steps on the uncarpeted dining-room floor had died away did he go to the desk under the second window. The top rolled back with difficulty, for the wet weather had swollen it in the grooves and age had loosened the joints so that it no longer ran true. He sat in front of the desk, staring at the loose papers which cluttered its interior, the two tarnished silver inkpots, and the silver tray where the pens lay on a matrix of paper clips, pins, and faded stamps. It was a long time before he began to write. Then his pen moved slowly, almost painfully, to form the meticulous, small letters, whose outline wavered a little even though the fingers which held the penstaff seemed firm. Once he laid the pen back in the silver tray and looked out of the window before him. It was still raining and the light was dim.

Just as he finished the first letter and laid it aside, unblotted, to dry, the door of the dining room opened and Alec entered with an armful of wood for the fire.

"Better put some on the fire," Mr. Hardin said. "It's pretty chilly now. And don't put the rest in the box, Alec. Just put it out on the hearth to dry a little. It gets right wet in the shed."

The Negro boy stooped before the fire and lowered his arms slowly so that the sticks slipped off heavily to the stones of the hearth. Then he put two on the fire, dropping them quickly on the andirons to snatch his thin curled fingers back from the heat like a hurt animal. As he leaned forward the new flame lighted up his small, intent face.

"Alec, won't you bring me a lamp right away?"

"Yassuh, Mr. Hardin."

Mr. Hardin got another sheet of paper from one of the pigeonholes before him and laid it on the desk. Across the top of the sheet ran the business caption: *Cedardale—J. C. Hardin & Son—Tobacco Growers and Stock Breeders.* Carefully he drew a single line through the "& Son" of the caption, but he did not begin to write again.

Alec did not bring him the lamp. It was Mrs. Hardin herself who came with it, holding it almost at arm's length before her in steady hands. The clear light fell on her arms and breast, but across her face was the shadow of the opaque roses which garlanded the lamp's frosted shade. With the burden of the lamp she moved slowly; there was a certain gravity, like that of a ritual, in her step and bearing as she crossed the room to Mr. Hardin. She set it on the upper part of the desk in front of the window. Immediately the world outside vanished, and the panes, which separated it from the room, went flat and black to reflect the glowing shade with its wreath of roses, her tall figure, and Mr. Hardin's bearded head.

"I've got something to tell you, Papa."

"Yes, Edith," he said.

"It's Thomas. Thomas just came up to the kitchen a minute ago and said to tell you that he thought he might sell his crop with you. And he wants to resign from the association. He said tell you that, too. Have you written the letter yet?"

"I'll write another one."

"Are you glad, Papa?"

"I can't tell, honey, whether I'm glad or not, it's all so mixed up. But I'll write the letters."

IV

Mrs. Hardin rose on her elbow and then sat bolt upright in the bed. Somewhere, very faintly, a dog was barking. She got out quietly and went across the room to the dim square of the south window. For a minute or two she leaned over the sill while the slight wind ruffled her nightgown.

"Thomas," she called softly.

There was no answer from the dark side of the room where the bed stood. Very quickly she crossed to it and bent above her husband.

"Thomas," she said, but he only stirred in his sleep. She took him by the arm and shook him. "Thomas, wake up. Wake up. I think there's somebody down by the barn."

Suddenly he was awake and rising from the bed as if his deep slumber had only been a joke played on her.

"What is it?"

"Down at the barn. I heard the dogs. And I think the gate to the drive is open. I couldn't see plain."

Without a word he strode to the window and peered out. "I can't see either. I'm going down. Don't light the lamp."

She stood at the window, while he fumbled with his clothes in the dark.

"Can you see anything?" he asked in a low voice.

"Nothing. You can't see the barn from here for the trees." And then, just as she spoke, the faintest glow, like early dawn, spread above the tree tops. "They are, Thomas! They are there!"

He was at the window beside her in a single awkward bound. "Oh, the dogs! The dirty dogs! The dirty sons-of-bitches!" His voice was almost a sob. "Wake Papa," he called back from the door. And then there was the noise of his feet pounding down the stairs, in the living room, and across the hollow floor of the veranda.

She ran out of the room and down the pitch-dark hall to the last door. She beat on the panels with the flat of both hands, calling over and over again. Then his voice came from within.

"Hurry! Hurry!" she called. "Thomas has gone."

He found her in the hall, standing at the head of the stairs. She was quiet now, but she gripped him by the arm when he reached her side. "Take care of Thomas" was all she said.

"I'll take care of him."

He hurried down, stumbling once in the dark. At the bottom he turned and looked up at the almost indistinguishable white figure at the head of the stairs. "Dress, Edith," he ordered. "You'll catch cold."

A flickering light fell through the windows of the living room, more a reflection than a light, and the grass between the trees to the east of the lawn was faintly luminous with what seemed to be a light of its own. Just as Mr. Hardin reached the front gate, there came the protracted empty staccato of hoofs from the wooden bridge down the lane. By the time he reached the gate off the drive, the barn was in full blaze, and, as he turned there, an enormous flame spun up from the roof and plunged through the high drift of smoke above. The bulk of the cedars behind the barn leaped from black to green, and the wide expanse of the field shimmered like water as the innumerable small shadows cast by inequalities of its surface flickered with the flickering of the tall flame. Near the barn three or four men rushed about. Then the roof of the barn collapsed with the cracking of a broken bough. The single flame plunged again, a little higher, held for a moment, and dropped into the tangled blaze below. The barn and the tobacco in it had burned like tinder.

Mr. Hardin slowed his pace to a walk. His lips were open, and between his teeth the breath came in quick gasps. When he got to the barn the men were standing close together in silence. They were all Negroes.

"Where's Mr. Thomas?" he asked.

"I ain't seen him," said one.

"He ain't bin here a-tall," Sam interrupted. "I wuz here at de fust. I heared dem dogs an' I say ter myself, Dey's at de barn. An' dar dey wuz. I come up de back way an' dey wuz ridin' off down tow'd de gate, jes' lopin' along, an'—"

"You haven't seen him, Sam?"

"Naw, suh. Jes' as dey rode off—"

Mr. Hardin turned abruptly away. "Thomas! Thomas!" he shouted, and then hurried out across the rough earth of the field. He stumbled a little, caught himself, and ran on. He stopped, shaking as with a chill, and put his hands, trumpetwise, to his mouth. "Thomas! Thomas!" There was no answer. He ran again, but more slowly. Again he stopped and lifted his hands to his mouth and called. "Thomas! Thomas! O Thomas!" There was no answer, not even an echo of his own voice in the broad field. For several minutes he stood there in the middle of the field. "God-a-mighty," he said aloud, "what a fool I am." Then he began to walk slowly back to the barn.

The four Negro men stared curiously at him when he came up. Their eyeballs were white and wide, and their cheeks, on the side toward the fire, glistened dully in its light. None of them spoke. They seemed embarrassed, almost guilty.

"How many men were there, Sam?" Mr. Hardin spoke very deliberately as if he were making an effort to control his heavy breathing.

"I doan know egzackly, Mr. Hardin. I reckin maybe fifteen. Maybe more'n fifteen. I jes' seen them hawses lopin' down tow'd de gate an' den dem nightriders muster seen me. Dey turn de gate an' den dey go jes' as fas' as dey can down tow'd de big-road. Den I go roun' ter de udder side de barn whar they lit de fire fust, but it wuz a big fire den. Dar wuzn' trompin' er nuthin' could put dat fire out den. Dar jes' wuzn' nuthin' I could do den, Mr. Hardin."

"I know it, Sam."

"I'd er done sumthin' ef'n I could, Mr. Hardin."

"Sure, Sam."

Again the Negroes relapsed into the vague embarrassment with which they had met Mr. Hardin when he came back from the field. He left them and walked as near as he could for the heat to the spot where the barn had stood. It was a glowing, oblong heap from which a perfunctory blaze now and then spurted. Some of the heavy beams still burned steadily with thin, clinging flames. It had been an old barn, and the frame timbers of the lower part had been cut with ax and adze, not sawed, from solid tree trunks. They would burn all night like backlogs in a fireplace. As he watched, the length of one which protruded from the mass broke off and dropped flatly to the glowing bed. The sparks spattered under the impact like molten iron and for a second the flame leaped again, higher than a man's stature, to light up the space around. But it sank quickly, and again the darkness began its gradual encroachment from the field and from the cedars on the other side of the place.

"Look, Mr. Hardin, look yonder."

He swung about and peered in the direction of the Negro's pointing arm. A lank hound was sniffing at something over by the fence. Mr. Hardin ran to the spot, shouting at the hound as he ran. He dropped on his knees by the fence, while the hound stood behind him with lowered head.

"Come here," he called back to the Negroes.

They came, walking almost timidly in a close group, and gathered about him. The hound moved back behind them.

"It's old Bess," Mr. Hardin said slowly. "It ain't anything in the world but old Bess," he repeated half to himself, and rubbed the coat of the setter's back with a hand that trembled.

"She daid?" one of the Negroes asked.

Mr. Hardin did not answer. Sam stooped to feel with his hand over the bitch's head and throat.

"Yeh," he said. "She's daid. Daider'n a doornail."

One of the other Negroes had picked up a heavy stick of firewood from the ground at his feet. It was a short, gnarled stick, and at one end the bark was matted with blood and hair.

"Dey done it wid dis." He turned the stick over in his hands, looking at it stupidly, and then hefted it. "Yeh, dey done it wid dis. Dis stick enuff ter kill enybody." He hefted it again, and then struck a wide, sweeping blow in vicious pantomime.

"Dem houn' dawgs jes' barked," said Sam. "Dey didn't try ter bite dem nightriders. Dey ain't nuthin' but ole coon-dawgs. But ole Bess, I bet she try an' bite. Den dey kilt her."

Mr. Hardin rose from his knees and reached out for the stick. The Negro passed it to him. Without a word he laid it on the ground by the fence away from sight. He leaned against the top rail of the fence for a moment looking at the Negroes.

"I reckon you boys better go home to bed," he said. "Just take old Bess down to the stable first. We'll bury her tomorrow."

Two of the men picked up the dog, one with the fore and one with the hind legs, and started off with their burden toward the clump of cedars. Another walked beside them, talking in a low voice. Sam loitered behind. He stood a few feet away from Mr. Hardin as if waiting to speak.

"Better go to bed, Sam."

"I'se goin' ter bed."

"Good night, Sam," said Mr. Hardin, and turned away.

"Mr. Hardin." He hesitated a moment. "Mr. Hardin, I bet Mr. Thomas'll sure be all right. He's a pow'ful good man, Mr. Thomas. He kin take care uv hisself."

"Yes, Sam," agreed Mr. Hardin, and turned away, this time quickly, in the direction of the house.

A light was burning in the living room when he turned into the lawn. Halfway up the veranda he paused, put his hands to his mouth, and then withdrew them. He crossed the veranda in three long steps, flung the door open, and stood at the sill. A small lamp burned on the mantelshelf, near the clock, but in the big room its light was feeble. Some expiring coals had been raked together against the backlog in the depth of the fireplace and blown to life in the midst of the bed of cold ashes. Very close, almost in the mouth of the fireplace, Mrs. Hardin sat on the low stool. She had not dressed herself but wore a blue flannel robe which dropped loosely from her shoulders to the stone of the hearth and crumpled there to give a strange impression of arrangement in the cold disorder of the room. The wide sleeves of the robe dropped from her bare arms, stretched out toward the fire, and her hands, which shifted above the flame with a tentative, weaving motion, showed a sudden whiteness against the sooty stone of the fireplace. They seemed almost too thin for the hands of a young woman. Her son crouched opposite her.

"Where's Thomas?" she asked.

Mr. Hardin did not answer.

"Come in, Papa. Close the door and tell me where Thomas is."

"Thomas is all right, honey," he said, and he pulled the door gently into its place. "Thomas said tell you he'd be back before morning and for you to get to bed. He said he'd be mad if he found you up when he got back. He looked at the light up here and he said to me, I bet Edith's up catching her death of cold and her not strong this season. That's exactly what he said. Now, Edith honey, you get to bed."

Mrs. Hardin's hands continued to weave their deliberate, invisible thread above the flame.

"Where is Thomas?" she said.

"Honey, he's ridden over to Simmons' place to tell Simmons the nightriders are out and to watch for them. He took my mare and went by the short cut so he'd beat them there if they aim to get Simmons' barn tonight. He had to go because of Simmons not having a telephone yet. He oughter almost be there now. He'll be back long before morning. Simmons has got three big boys and all of them can go out and lie behind that stone wall and when the nightriders come up they can call to them and say, We got you now. Then the nightriders'll go off. They don't want any stand-up fight and they'll know they're beat. But Thomas won't stay. He promised me not to stay. He knows he's got you to think about, honey, and he won't stay a minute after he tells Simmons." His voice went on impersonally, as if he were recounting a story that had happened long before. "Now, Edith, you just get along to bed and get some sleep."

She neither moved nor answered.

"Get up, Edith, and go to bed. Thomas'll be mighty mad if he comes back and finds you here. There ain't even any fire in the fireplace to speak of." He went to her and took her hands and drew her up beside him. "You're cold already, your hands are as cold as ice. Go to bed. Thomas just rode over to do something neighbor-like, being a good friend of Simmons. He'll be back long before morning."

He led her to the hall door and then in the darkness to the foot of the stairs.

"Good night, Edith," he said.

She climbed the stairs silently, faced about for a moment at the landing, and vanished. Mr. Hardin went back into the living room. Little Thomas was still crouching beside the fire.

"Get up, boy, and go to bed."

Little Thomas rose, but made no sign of going off. "I hope Mr.

Simmons shoots a dozen nightriders. Red Simmons is a good shot, too, and I'll bet he shoots a nightrider. The dirty skunks. I'd like to shoot all those nightriders."

"There won't be any shooting, Tommy, because the nightriders will just go off when Mr. Simmons calls to them. People that ride around like that at night and burn other people's barns don't want to fight. They're just cowards, Tommy."

"I'll bet Mr. Mitchell's a coward. But Mr. Hopkins, Grandpa, if he's there, I'll bet he ain't a coward even if he is a dirty nightrider."

"No, I wouldn't call Bill Hopkins a coward. I guess I can't tell who's a coward. But you don't know whether he's a nightrider or not."

"He's on the board."

"Yes, he's on the board all right. But you, Tommy, you get to bed right now. You've got to go to school tomorrow, and if you don't get to bed, you'll be sleepy all day like last Monday. I mean what I say, Tommy."

The boy walked toward the door and then turned. "Can't I just run down and look at the barn once? Mother wouldn't let me go. I'll be right back. Please?"

"No."

When his grandson had gone, Mr. Hardin went to the hall door and listened for a moment. He pulled it shut and then moved hurriedly to the far corner of the room where the rays of the lamp did not penetrate. There were the two shotguns propped in the corner with the white oil-stained envelopes pulled over their muzzles. His foot touched something on the floor, and he stooped to pick it up. It was a rifle. He went to the other corner and looked. The second rifle was gone. The lower drawer of the desk beside him was half open. He pulled it out and peered inside. There were two solid square boxes with the picture of a shotgun shell on their tops, and beside them lay a smaller oblong box overflowing with brass cartridges. His hand plunged in the drawer and withdrew, clenched full of them. He let the cartridges slip between his fingers into the palm of the other hand like heavy, swollen grains of corn. He inspected them as they lay in the cupped palm, stirring them gently with a forefinger as a farmer inspects seed corn, and then let them trickle through his fingers again and thump into the obscurity of the drawer.

He wandered aimlessly out to the porch and down the low stone steps to the grass. To the left a light still glowed from the barn. The front windows of the living room did not reflect it now, but shone with the faint light from within, and the grass under the trees was dark. He walked to the gate and stood there, leaning over its top, while he regarded the lighter strip of the drive, which wound off between the cedar grove and the fields. A hound came cautiously out from the shadow of the trees on the east side of the lawn and approached him with tail wagging and head lowered. When the hound nuzzled at his knees he dropped his hand to fumble with its head and soft loose ears, but he did not look down. At length he turned from the gate and began to walk back up the path; the hound gave the dangling hand a clumsy final lick and was gone, sniffing the grass, into the shadows.

Back in the house Mr. Hardin took the lamp from the mantelpiece and went into the dining room. The unwashed dishes from the Sunday night supper were still on the table, waiting for Sallie in the morning, and about the table stood four chairs pushed irregularly back as they had been left the evening before. Mr. Hardin went to the sideboard and opened one of the panels. From the interior gloom he took a large square decanter and a tumbler. He slipped the tumbler into the pocket of his coat and, with the decanter in one hand, and the lamp in the other, returned to the living room. The whisky, sloshing about inside the cut glass, gave off thin prismatic gleams from the light of the lamp. When he had set the lamp carefully on the mantel and the decanter and glass on the stool he got down to his knees and began to blow Edith's remnant of coals back to flame; he fed it with shags of cedar gently, and at last trusted two heavier sticks to its heat. Only then he poured out a drink for himself, three fingers in the tumbler, and sat down in his chair. Once he got up to put more wood on the fire, which now leaped cleanly toward the chimney, and once to pour himself another drink, three fingers in the bottom of the tumbler.

Shortly after three o'clock there was a noise from the dining room. Mr. Hardin stood up from his chair and stepped forward, but before he could reach the door, the knob turned in the socket and it swung gently inward. Half concealed by the shadow stood his son, filling the space of the doorway.

"Put out the light," he ordered. The voice was scarcely more than a whisper.

Mr. Hardin turned about casually, took down the lamp, and moved to the other side of the hearth. Then, cupping his hand behind the glass chimney, he blew sharply, and the room went dark except for the firelight. Thomas came in. He was wringing wet and shivering with cold, but he did not approach the lighted hearth.

"God-a-mighty, son, what is it?"

"I got one of them, maybe two. I saw one fall off his horse. I ran down across the field and cut them off at the pike and when they rode by I got them. If my rifle hadn't stuck, I'd a gotten some more. The God-damned rifle stuck and I had to run. They chased me down toward the river, but they didn't have anything but pistols. I lost them in the cane down there and swam the creek where it's deep near the river. God, if my rifle hadn't stuck, I'd gotten some more of the sons-of-bitches when they came across the field toward the cane, running and shooting off their pistols, and me in the cane. But I got one, I know. I saw him fall off his horse in the road. I hope I killed the son-of-a-bitch."

"Son, you fool, you fool."

"Maybe I am a fool, but I hope he's dead. Oh, the dirty sons-of-bitches."

"You're cold, son." Mr. Hardin picked up the decanter and poured a drink and took it across to him. "Drink it, son," he said gently.

Thomas swallowed the whisky in two choking gulps. "We've got to hurry," he said, and coughed. "I reckon they'll be here any time now if they ain't here now."

"Get some clothes, Thomas. You'll find some in the closet in the hall. Hurry. And, Thomas, in God's name don't wake Edith up."

Thomas went out into the hall, leaving a trail of water drops behind him; on the wood floor the water looked dark. His father got the rifle from the corner and a handful of cartridges from the desk. When Thomas came back he was standing in the middle of the room loading the magazine of the weapon. Thomas pulled off the wet shirt, dropping it with a soft smack to the floor, and began to wipe his muscular chest and belly. He put on an old sweater and a coat and twisted a scarf about his throat. He watched his father slip the last cartridge in.

"God, I'm cold," he said, picking up the decanter. He drank directly from it, thirstily, without troubling to use the tumbler.

"Get some pants," advised Mr. Hardin.

"I couldn't find any pants, and I haven't got time."

Mr. Hardin passed him the rifle. "I don't reckon this one will stick. I used it just the other day and oiled it."

"You using the shotgun?"

"I won't need anything. Now you get along, son. Better get down to the woods by the river."

"The hell I will. I'm staying. This is my house."

"Tommy, you better get along."

"I'm staying. I'm not leaving you here."

Mr. Hardin regarded him for a moment with that incurious gaze. "All right," he said.

"I better go out back."

"Yes, you go out back. Get up by the chicken house and you can see all the backyard. I'm going down in the edge of the cedars by the drive. Go on. I'll get me another coat first. Go on, son."

As soon as Thomas left the room, Mr. Hardin went into the hall to return with a coat. From the corner he took a shotgun, dropped a shell into each barrel, and slipped out, closing the front door softly behind him. He did not go directly to the gate, but skirted the front of the house, close to the shrubbery, and crossed the lawn to the fence. He climbed it quickly, and in two or three paces more, was wrapped in the dense shadow of the cedars. He picked his way among them, his feet making no sound on the bed of needles which cloaked the wood earth. Some ten feet from the drive, beyond the gate which opened off toward the barn, he found a gap and settled himself with his back against a tree trunk.

The branches spread out flat and fanwise above him, drooping at the tips, but they were still high enough to give a view of the drive, the field beyond it, and the open space outside the lawn fence. The broad strip of whitewashed paling made an excellent background for any object which might move between it and the cedars, but nothing, not even a prowling hound, came again into that obscure area which intervened. Once or twice some animal stirred in the grove, and once an owl called from the hill back of the house. Before dawn the slight wind, which had shifted the cedars to a pervasive whisper, died altogether, and there was perfect stillness. The glow from the barn declined with the first light, was lost in it, and then, long before the sun, the casual smoke took substance above the spot. Finally the sun lifted across the higher land beyond the river, the last rooster crowed and drummed his wings, and the whole scene, the river bottom, the fields, the house, and even cedar grove, appeared again as a place of use and familiar habitation.

In the broad daylight Mr. Hardin walked up the little rise, through the gate, up the path to his house, and opened the door. He broke the gun, put the shells back in the drawer, and set the gun in its corner with the envelope again over the muzzle. Then he passed the length of the house, through the dining room where the unwashed dishes still cluttered the table, through the kitchen, and across the back porch. He was halfway to the chicken run when Thomas rose from hiding and walked down to meet him. The rifle dangled like an ineffectual toy, almost dragging the ground, at the end of his long arm. Mr. Hardin stopped and waited until his son approached.

"God, I'm cold," Thomas said. His face was very pale, and a black stubble of beard stood out against the white skin like the beard on a sick man's face.

"Hurry, son, and get dressed. Maybe a drink would help first."

"I don't want a drink."

Just inside the privacy of the kitchen they stopped.

"Thomas, you better hurry and get dressed. You want to be dressed like usual when Sallie comes to get breakfast and Sam comes up after milking. I've got to get dressed, too."

Thomas made no move. "I don't know what I'm going to do," he said.

"Go on, son. We'll talk about that later. Maybe it ain't so bad."

"I don't much care how bad it is. God, the dirty bastards."

"Hush, son, hush. You go and get dressed proper."

In the living room he stopped and Thomas obediently went upstairs. Mr. Hardin rang the telephone, turning the little crank with a cautious hand while with the other he muffled the bells. For almost a minute he waited and then there came an answer.

"Central," he said with his mouth close to the transmitter, "this is Hardin speaking. I understand there was a little shooting down on the west pike last night. Can you tell me if anybody got hurt? . . . No, we didn't hear any shots. One of my niggers that lives on the river down closer to the pike says he heard a right smart shooting. . . . No, don't ring me up, I'll ring you up in a few minutes again. I'm much obliged, Miss Turner." And he, too, left the room.

It was Thomas who first reappeared, to kneel on the hearth and begin rebuilding the fire. When the door closed behind his father he did not even glance up from his task.

"I've told Edith," he said into the black hollow of the chimney.

Mr. Hardin stood behind him, staring down at his son's broad back. He did not answer.

"I've already told her," Thomas repeated.

"How did she take it, Thomas?"

"She's taking it bad," he said, with his face still averted. "I told her quick, and she didn't say anything to me. She just began to walk around the room, walking around in her nightgown, crying and brushing her hair. God, I couldn't stay up there and stand in the middle of the floor and watch her crying like that."

"Maybe you better go back up, son."

"I can't go back up there," he said, rising to face his father. "She didn't even say anything to me. She's just walking around, brushing her hair, and crying and crying. I don't know what to do."

"There ain't but one thing to do, that I can see. Call up the sheriff and tell him you shot somebody when they burned your barn and you're coming in to him. I'll call him. I know Jack Burton. He'll take my word and he won't come get you, son. It'll be all right, son."

Thomas looked at him steadily for a moment, and then spoke very slowly. "Papa, I'll be damned to hell if I'll go in. They know where to find me if they want me. This is my house. They can find me here."

Mr. Hardin reached out to touch him lightly on the arm. "Thomas, you can't do that, you just can't. You can't let them ride up here and let Edith see them take you. It would about break her heart, son."

For a long time Thomas stood there looking stupidly down at the fingers which touched his sleeve. "I reckon I'll go," he said.

Mr. Hardin moved to the telephone. "We better find out who got hurt. Miss Turner is going to tell me." Again he muffled the bells and rang. While he waited for an answer with his bearded lips close to the instrument, Thomas stood on the hearth, rigidly erect, and never shifted his eyes from his father's face. The face was inscrutable and tired.

"That you, Miss Turner? . . . Yes, this is Hardin." There was a pause, and then, "My God, you don't say! My God." Thomas started as if a bull whip had cracked about his ears. Mr. Hardin hung up the receiver and turned.

"It's Bill Hopkins, Thomas. But he'll live, Thomas. The doctor says he'll live. But, Thomas, it's old Bill Hopkins that you saw fall off his horse down on the pike."

"He'll live?"

"Yes, he's going to live. Dr. Jacob told Miss Turner that he's hurt bad, but he'll live. He'll live all right. But, Thomas, it's Bill Hopkins."

"It don't matter who it is. He rode, didn't he?"

"But, Thomas, you don't understand."

"It don't matter." The voice was stubborn. "He rode."

"All right, son. You go up and tell Edith quick. Tell her he'll live and she'll be glad and she won't take it so hard then."

Thomas stepped off the hearth toward the hall door and then paused at its edge. "It don't matter," he said, "but I reckon I'm glad he's going to live." He hesitated again. "Call the sheriff," he ordered and was gone.

"Central, give me Mr. Jack Burton's place, please." The only sound in the house while he waited was Sallie's voice singing in the kitchen as she got the breakfast. "That you, Jack?" he finally said. "This is Hardin, Joe Hardin. . . . The nightriders burned our barn last night, and, Jack, my boy shot one of them, down on the pike. . . . He muster been a little crazy and mad when they burned our barn. Yes, it was Old Man Hopkins he shot, but Hopkins'll live the doctor says. . . . Listen, Jack, I'm sending my boy in to you. I'll go his bail, I reckon I'll be good for his bail all right. Get him back quick as you can, because my daughter-in-law, Edith, she's in a bad shape about it. . . . Much obliged, Jack. . . . And listen, he belongs to you now, and if anybody tries to stop him on the road, he's coming on in anyway. Understand? . . . Take care of him. . . . And, Jack, listen to me, Jack, for God's sake don't go bothering Old Man Hopkins. He's hurt pretty bad the doctor says. And you know him, he wouldn't get away if he could. Much obliged." He hung the receiver up with awkward fingers.

They ate breakfast in silence, each in the usual place. Big Thomas was dressed in his good clothes, a blue serge suit and white stiff collar. His face was shaven now. Mrs. Hardin, at the foot of the table, poured the coffee and passed the large cups without a tremor, but she ate little. At length Mr. Hardin rose from the table and pushed his chair into place.

"I'll go see about saddling up," he said. "You, Tommy, you better get ready for school. Get along."

Almost with an air of relief the boy slipped down and left the room. Mrs. Hardin rose to go around behind her husband's chair. She put her hands on his shoulders and stood there.

"I'll go," said Mr. Hardin, and left them so, her hands on his shoulders and his reaching up to cover them.

On the back porch he found Alec sitting propped against the post with a nearly empty plate of bread and molasses on his lap. A cup of coffee was on the floor beside him. He looked up and grinned.

"Mawnin', Mr. Hardin."

"Hello, Alec. Alec, do you know where your pappy is?"

"He down at de cawn crib. He done et his brekfus'."

"Alec, I want you to go and tell him to saddle up for me and Mr. Thomas. I ain't feeling very well this morning."

"Yassuh, Mr. Hardin." Alec took one more mouthful and wiped his sticky hands on the trousers of his overalls. Whistling, he strolled off toward the side gate of the yard. Mr. Hardin sat on the floor of the porch, his back to the post against which Alec had been leaning, and watched him go. He was still sitting there when his son came to tell him that the horses were ready.

Mrs. Hardin stood at the gate while they mounted. "Come back, honey, as soon as you can," she said to her husband. "I'll be worried till you get back."

"I'll hurry. I'll telephone from town, too, before I start."

"Good-bye," she said. Her eyes were dry but her lips trembled a little when she spoke.

"Good-bye, Edith."

"Good-bye," said Mr. Hardin, and lifted the rein.

The two men rode easily down the slight dip of the drive. At the last bend before the bridge Thomas looked back to wave, but his wife had turned and was walking up the path to the house. The soft earth and gravel of the drive was scored with the deep hoof marks of galloping horses. Studying the surface, Mr. Hardin remarked, "Looks like there might have been nigh onto a score of them."

"No," said Thomas. "Just about a dozen. I watched them coming down the pike."

They rode slowly for another mile, and spoke no more; they were absorbed in their own meditation as if they were strangers riding the same road by the chance of travel who had talked out the commonplaces of greeting and crops and weather. At the branch of the road Mr. Hardin drew rein.

"I reckon I turn off here," he said.

"You ain't going in with me?"

"No, I reckon I better not. It might be better for you to go riding up to Jack Burton's office by yourself."

"Yes," said Thomas in a voice of some trifling bitterness, "it might look like you brought me in."

"It never crossed my head once that way. You know it never did."

"You going to Hopkins' place?"

"Yes, I'm going over and see how he's making out. There ain't anything else I can do."

Thomas hesitated a moment, seeming to suppress something. "I guess I better be getting on," he said finally, and touched his heel to the horse's flank.

"I'll meet you in town before long," Mr. Hardin said. "Good-bye, Tommy, and take care of yourself."

"Good-bye," Thomas called. Again he gave his mount the heel and took the road toward town.

Mr. Hardin picked up the rein, and Jenny wheeled to the left branch. He rode off down the gentle grade to the river, sitting the trot like a cavalryman, and disappeared beyond a clump of sycamores which guarded the first bend of the road.

The schoolroom was warm even though the fire in the big iron belly of the stove had run low. The children bent above their books with a hint of restlessness of the impending season or stared with rebellious frankness out of the windows. The teacher, a young woman, was writing figures on the strip of blackboard which ran across the front of the room. There came a knocking at the door and she laid the bit of chalk on her desk and went to open it. A tall Negro man stood there, hat in hand. He spoke to the young woman in a voice which did not carry distinctly back to the curious children. The young woman turned and walked to her desk.

"Thomas," she said, "Thomas Hardin, you can get your books and go. Somebody has come for you."

She herself brought his cap and coat from the hook on the wall and handed them to him as he stood just inside the open door. He stepped out and Sam reached clumsily down to take the cloth satchel from his shoulder.

"What's the matter?" the boy asked.

"Nuthin'," answered Sam, "yore mammy jes' wants you home."

The Negro led the way to the buggy and unhitched the horse from the top bar of the fence. He got up to the seat, unlooped the reins from the splatterboard, and clucked to the horse.

"Sam, what's the matter? I know something's the matter."

The Negro did not look around but continued to stare toward the front, over the horse's jogging back, down the gray road between the fields and trees.

"Dey done shot yore pappy, son. Dey done kilt him down on de pike tow'd town."

The boy hid his face against the Negro's rough coat, which smelt of sweat and tobacco, and wept, weeping silently, as they rode along through the clear, premonitory sunlight of early spring.

HOW
WILLIE PROUDFIT
CAME HOME

High up, on the bluffside of the hill, a spring poured out of an archway of stone. In its basin there, the perfectly clear water eddied ceaselessly, braiding and swelling, swaying the young fronds of fern and the grass which trailed lushly down to the surface, spilling over the lip of stone and plunging down the slope to join the creek below. "Soon's I laid eyes on hit," Willie Proudfit would say, "come-en slide-en down that rock that a-way, I says, thar my house will set. Sometimes a-nights I lays in bed and I kin hear hit. I lays in bed and I kin recollect the times out in the dry country I laid out a-nights and studied on water. In this country the Lord's done give a man water which ever way he turns, fer drinken and washen, hit looks lak, and a man don't know how hit is in the dry country, and the thirsten. But even here ain't ever man got him a spring come-en nigh outer the top of a hill, lak me, and fall-en so he kin lay and hear hit. Nor ever man got him a cold-air cave to keep his milk sweet to his mouth."

He had built his house right at the creek bank, with the little branch from the falls running into the creek just behind it. And the cave, where the moisture dripped from the pelt-thick green moss, was at the foot

Text taken from *The Southern Review*, Vol. 4, Autumn 1938; became part of *Night Rider* (1939).

of the bluff, just beside the house. Inside the cave, in the chill shadow, the crock jars of milk stood in rows. Willie Proudfit's wife would set her candle on a shelf of stone, for even at noon a candle was needed, and dip up the milk with a tin dipper and pour it into her big blue pitcher. Then, from another crock, she would take a pat of butter. Holding the heavy pitcher in one hand, but out from her body strongly and easily, she would move across the patch of grass toward the house. She would set the pitcher on the table, by her husband's plate, and smile. "Willie, now he's the beatenest," she would say, "fer milk."

"Now I thank you," he might say, and pick up the pitcher; or he might only look up at her, not quite smiling, and say nothing, for he was not a man to talk much except on those rare occasions, in the evenings usually, when, lying stretched out like a cat on the boards of the little porch, he would reach back into his mind for some incident out of those years he had spent on the plains. He would tell it, not exactly for us, it seemed, but for the telling, speaking slowly and tentatively. Reaching back into those past times, he was like a man who, in a dark closet, runs his fingers over some once-familiar object and tries, uncertainly, to identify it. "They's a passel of things," he would say, "on God's earth fer a man to study about, and ain't no man e'er seen 'em all. But I seen some. I seen gullies so deep and wide, you could throw that-air hill in hit, lock, stock, and barr'l, and ne'er no difference to a man's sight. And the gully with colors spread out in the light, far as air eye could see, lak a flag. Colors lak the colors in the sky at sun, and layen thar on the ground, lak the sky had come a-fall-en down." Then he might pause. His wife, Adelle, and her niece and nephew and I would be sitting in chairs propped back against the wall, with Willie Proudfit lying there on the floor, scarcely visible in the darkness. We would wait for him, not saying anything. If the season was right, the frogs would be piping down the creek, in the place where the ground gets marshy.

"The Indians taken them colors outer the earth," he would say, "and paint theirselves." And he would pause again, and there would only be the night sounds. Then he would say: "When they dance."

"Heathen," the nephew, Sylvestus, said in the darkness, for he was a pious man.

"Heathen," Willie Proudfit said in his soft, slow voice, "heathen, in a way of speaken." Then he fell silent, brooding backward into those times. Then he said: "But them dance-en, hit ain't just frolic and jollification." Then, later: "They's a passel of things, and the Lord God, He made ever one. In His mighty plan, and ain't a sparrow falleth."

But some evenings he didn't speak a word.

He was a medium-sized man. His face was thinnish, and it had lines in it, tiny lines that meshed multitudinously in the leathery-looking skin, but it was neither an old nor a young face. The skin was brown like an oak leaf, so brown that against it the bluish-green eyes looked pale, and the very blond hair silvery like the hair of an old man. He wore his hair longer than any man I had ever seen, down to his neck behind and cut off square. Sometimes on Sunday mornings, just after breakfast, he would sit out on the chunk of limestone that formed the back step, and his wife would cut his hair. She had a pair of big clumsy-looking shears she used for that, and when the blades engaged on his thick hair, they made a sound like a heel on sand. He was a quiet and smooth-tempered man, even when times got bad and it looked like he was going to lose his place, and even when he knew he would lose it. He did lose it, and moved away. Before he lost it, he talked once or twice about going back west, like he had when he was a boy. One night, lying there on the porch boards, he suddenly said, quietly and offhand, "Oklahoma," like the answer to a question somebody had asked him. But nobody had said anything for quite a while.

"Oklahoma," the nephew said, and added, "they say a man kin git a start out thar."

"A long time since I seen hit," Willie Proudfit said. He shifted a little, and the boards of the porch floor creaked in the dark. Then he said: "Folks was goen in, then. To git a start. And fer one reason or 'nuther. Some just a move-en kind of folks, just move-en on. Lak I was, them days. The buffalo petered out, and they wasn't no more, whar I'd seen 'em black the ground off yander when a man looked. So I moved on, west. But I come back here. But a lot of folks, they ne'er come back, no-whar."

He waited a while, then he said: "I come back, and left the dry country. But a man ne'er knows. Maybe I'll be goen back. To Oklahoma, maybe."

"Sweat fer nuthen," the nephew said, "in this country."

"Maybe I'll be goen agin," Willie Proudfit said, "and the time comes. If they's a place for a man to go nowadays. My pappy up and left here, and he ne'er aimed to, till the time come. Hit was in 'sixty-one and the war a-starten. My pappy wasn't easy in his mind. He never was no Bible-man exactly, but he studied on the shooten and the killen, and he prayed the Lord to show him which side to take. Which was the Lord's side. One mornen he said, 'I ain't a-stayen in this country, on-easy in my mind and with my neighbors.' He said, 'I'm a-leave-en.'"

"So he got shet of what he had, land and gear, what he couldn't git on a wagon. And he put two span oxen to the wagon, and we all hit out towards north Arkansas. Pappy had a cousin in north Arkansas who wrote him a letter sayen north Arkansas was air man's country, free fer the gitten, a fair land and flowen. We went down west Tennessee, whar hit was cotton, everwhar a man looked. And to Memphis. We got on a steamboat at Memphis and went down the Mississippi and up the Arkansas, the country flat lak a man's hand, and the ground black and greasy-looken, and dead tree trunks standen in some fields, black with fire whar folks had been ringen and burnen to clear, and the cotton come-en on a-tween. But the good ground was all took. Been took a long time. Then we come to Little Rock. We stayed in Little Rock nigh onto three weeks waiten fer pappy's cousin. And me, I got so I knowed my way all over the hull town, you know how a kid is, a-pryen and a-prowlen. We was campen down on a little crick, and pappy was a-fretten and a-fume-en to be gitten on, and the season wearen. He wanted to be gitten some ground broke, even if hit was late, and a house up fore winter. And the drinken water in Little Rock, hit wasn't so good and pappy one to be cantankerous about drinken water. They's water in that country, but hit ain't good water lak the water here. Lots of folks them days had the flux in Little Rock, they said, and hit was the drinken water. I ain't ne'er been back in Little Rock, not since I went on outer Arkansas west, but I seen a man not more'n five years back, come from Arkansas, and I says to him, how's the drinken water in Little Rock now? They git right good water now, he said. But not them days. And pappy was a-fume-en to git on.

"But me, I was ten-'leven year old, and ever day Sunday. I'd go up and see the men drillen and gitten ready, some of them drillen with sticks, not have-en no guns yit. One day I says, 'Pappy, ain't you gonna be a sojer?' 'Sojer, sojer,' he said, 'you stay away from them sojers, or I'll whale the tar.' But I'd slip off and go watch them sojers, lak a kid will. I had ne'er seen sich.

"Then pappy's cousin come. 'Amon,' he said to my pappy, fer Amon was his name, 'I been slow a-gitten here, but sumthen crost my path.' He taken a piece of paper outer his pocket, and he had drawed a map on hit, with everthing marked good. My pappy studied on the map, then he said, 'Ain't you goen back?' 'Naw, Amon, I ain't,' pappy's cousin said, 'I'm a sojer now.'

" 'Sojer,' my pappy said, and looked at him.

" 'Sojer,' pappy's cousin said, 'but I ain't a family man, lak you.'

"Pappy shook his head, slow. 'Naw,' he said, 'hit ain't that. I had me a good place in Kentucky. And my wife, she's a clever woman and fore-minded. I'll lay her agin air woman I e'er seen. She and my boys, they could run my place, and I could been a sojer. If I had hit in my mind and heart. But I ain't. I ain't clear and easy in my mind, this rise-en and slayen and a man not knowen.'

"So pappy taken the map, and we loaded up the wagon, and put the oxen in, and crost over the river. That same, blessed day. Fer north Arkansas.

"Hit was air man's country, and the Lord's truth. Fair and flowen, lak pappy's cousin done said. Pappy found him a place in a fork of two cricks, bottom ground and high ground layen to a man's use-en, and a spring outer the ground, and timber standen, scalybark and white oak and cedar and yaller poplar and beech. And squirrels so thick they barked to wake you up of a mornen. 'Lord God, Lord God,' pappy said real soft, just standen there looken, after he'd done settled his mind on a spot to set his house. Then he said to ma, right sharp and sudden, 'Henrietta, gimme that axe!' And ma done hit.

"Some of the folks round there went off and went to the war, like pappy's cousin, but pappy never the hull duration. Folks would be a-talken, and a man mought name the war, and pappy, he'd just git up and walk off. Then word come the war was over. I was a big feller then, goen on sixteen, and handy if I do say so. Us boys worked with pappy round the place, and we done right well. Hit was a good country, fer fair. Ever fall we'd go down to Little Rock and do our big trade-en. Down at Mr. Wolff's wagon yard. When the time come on, pappy would cast round, and load up what hides layen round, and what tallow they was we didn't need, and sich truck, and honey—Lord God, the honey, you'd go out and knock over a bee tree, and honey to spare— and we'd start down to Little Rock. They wasn't nuthen Mr. Wolff wouldn't buy off'n a man, and give him cash money or swap outer his wholesale store. We done swappen fer the majority, fer you taken cash money and give it right back to Mr. Wolff fer what you was gitten. So pappy'd swap, and load up the wagon with plunder, and we'd start on back home.

"Time come I was goen on nineteen, and I said to pappy, 'Pappy, I been studyen about goen up to Kansas.'

"And pappy said, 'Boy, I been notice-en you sorter raise-en yore sap.'

"So I taken out fer Kansas. Pappy gimme a horse and saddle and fifty dollars and hit gold. I figgered I'd go to Kansas and be a buffalo hunter, lak I'd heared tell. I figgered I was handy with a rifle as the next man. Many's the time, shooten fer a steer, I'd took hind quarter, hide, and tallow, that being top man. Fellers would put up fifty cents a-piece and buy a steer and shoot fer choice, high man, hind quarter, hide, and tallow, next man, hind quarter, and next man, fore quarter and head, and next man, fore quarter. Shoot at a shingle and a little heart drawed on hit in white clay, forty paces free style or sixty paces layen to a chunk.

"Hit was in Hays City I taken up with a feller named Mingo Smith. He was a Yankee and he fit the war. He got mustered out and he come to Kansas. He'd been a muleskinner down to Santa Fe, and a bull-whacker out Colorado way, and a boss layen the Kansas Pacific railroad, and he'd hunted buffalo fer the railroad, too, to feed the men, they wasn't nuthen he hadn't took a turn to, hit looked lak. He was a long skinny feller, didn't have no meat on his bones to speak of, and his face was all yaller and he didn't have no hair to his head, and hit yaller, too. And him not more'n thirty. 'Some day I'll shore be a disappointment to a Cheyenne,' he'd say, and rub his hand over whar his hair oughter be. He figgered he'd take one more turn, the price on hides goen up lak hit was. Men come-en out to Hays City to buy hides, and all. Mingo, he had some money he'd got fer freighten up from Fort Sill, and a old wagon, and he bought and paid fer what all we needed, and said I could pay him my part outer what we took. So I thanked him kindly, and we hit out, him and me.

"Seven-eight year, and durn, we was all over that-air country, one time and ernuther. North of Hays City to the Saline, and up Pawnee Crick and the Arkansas, and down in the Panhandle on the Canadian, and down to Fort Sill. They had been a time a man couldn't git nuthen fer a hide not seasonable, with the fur good, and summer hunten didn't pay a man powder and git. But we come in to Hays City our first trip, loaded down, and figgeren on what to do till the cold come, and a feller what bought hides for Durfee, over to Leavenworth—give us two dollars and a dime fer prime bull, I recollect—he says, 'Boys, just belly up quick, and quench yore thirst, and hit out agin, I'm buyen now, summer or winter, rain or shine!' 'Is that a fact,' Mingo says, 'summer hide?' 'Hit's a fact,' that feller says.

"Mingo up and buys ernuther wagon, and hires two fellers to skin—Irish, they was, the country was plumb full of Irish—and a feller to cook and stretch, and I says to him, 'Lord God, Mingo, you act lak we was rich.' And he says, 'We ain't, but Lord God, we gonna be. And I durn tired of skinnen, durned if I ain't. I don't mind shooten, but I hate to skin. One thing hit was, shooten rebels, a man ne'er had to skin 'em. Hit's gonna be shooten now, like a gentleman, till the barr'l hots.'

"And durn if he didn't say the God's truth. The barr'l hot to a man's hand. The day a still day, and the smoke round a man's head like a fog, and yore ears ringen. If'n you got a stand—the buffalo standen and graze-en—and drapped the lead one, the others mought just sniff and bawl, and not stampede. If you was lucky. Nuthen to hit then, keep on shooten fer the outside ones that looked lak they mought git restless, take hit easy and not git yore gun barr'l too hot. That next year, I mind me we got two good stand, Mingo one and me one. I was come-en up a little rise south of a crick runnen in the Pawnee, and I raised up my head, keerful, and thar they was, a passel of 'em. Bout a hundred and fifty paces off yander, and me downwind. I propped my Sharp's to my prongstick, and cracked down. I started to git up—a man would git up and run to git him his next shot—and got on one knee, and I see they wasn't no buffalo down. I figgered I'd missed, and a easy shot, and I laid back down fer a try. Then I seen a buffalo just lay down, and the rest standen thar, not move-en. I shot agin, and a buffalo come down, and the rest a-standen. And agin. I said, 'Lord God,' I said, 'I do believe hit's a stand!'

"A stand hit was. I laid thar, looken down the barr'l of my Sharp's and the buffalo standen. I laid thar, counten out loud betwixt shots not to go too fast and hot the gun. A long time, and I could see 'em come down, slow, to the knees, when the ball found. Then keel over and lay. And the rest standen round, sniffen and bawlen. A man lays thar, the sun a-bearen down, and keeps on a-pullen on the trigger. He ain't lak his-self. Naw, he ain't. Lak he wasn't no man, nor nuthen. Lak hit ain't him has a-holt of the gun, but the gun had a-holt of him. Lak he mought git up and walk off and leave them buffalo down the rise, a-standen, and leave the gun lay, and the gun would be shooten and a-shooten, by hitself, and ne'er no end. And the buffalo, down the rise, standen and bawlen. Hit comes to a man that a-way.

"Seventy-two buffalo I shot that afternoon, layen thar, a-fore they broke and run. Gitten on to sun, they broke. I laid thar, and seen 'em go, what was left, not nigh a score, and the dust a-rise-en behind 'em. They run north. I seen 'em past sight, but I kept on a-layen thar, lak I couldn't uncrook my hand-holt off'n my Sharp's, and the barr'l hot to a man's flesh. I laid thar, lak a man past his short rows.

" 'Durn,' Mingo said, 'them buffalo down thar, and you a-layen here lak hit wasn't nuthen!' I ne'er heared him come-en. 'Boy, go git them Irish,' he said, 'hit's gonna be night work, a-skinnen.' I didn't say nuthen, I taken out fer the wagons to git them skinners when they done got done with the ones they was skinnen. We got back hit was night, and Mingo down thar, skinnen and cussen. But the moon come up, red and swole layen thar to the east, bigger'n a barn,. Ain't no moons in this country lak them moons in west Kansas. We skinned by the moon. Didn't nobody say nuthen. Nary a sound but a man grunten, or a knife whetten on a stell, maybe, soft and whickeren lak when hit's a good temper to the blade, and the sound hit makes when the hide gives off'n the meat to a good long pull. Then, off a-ways, the coyotes singen, and come-en closter.

"We skinned 'em all, all seventy-two, and taken the tongues. And the mops off'n the bulls. We loaded the wagon, and started up the rise, not have-en et, and plumb tuckered. Nigh halfway up the rise, I recollect, I looked back. The moon was ride-en high, and the ground down thar looked white lak water, I recollect, and them carcasses sticken up lak black rocks outer water.

"But a man didn't make him a stand ever day. Not by a sight, I kin tell you. He'd try the wind and git downwind, and start move-en in, slow and keerful, crawlen a good piece maybe. They started move-en, and hit was time. Two hundred paces and you was lucky. But a Sharp's will shoot lak a cannon. Hit's a fact. Three-quarter mile ain't nuthen fer a Sharp's, not even on a bull buffalo, if'n you kin hit him. Which you caint. But two-fifty, three hundred paces, a man kin. And under the hump. You shoot, and the herd breaks and runs, and stops, and you run to ketch up, and lay and shoot. And they run agin. That a-way, till they done left you. Or you kin ride with 'em, shooten alongside with a carbeen. A Spencer, I had me. But we ne'er done that but to be a-doen. Hit was a sporten man's way, you might say. And the way with the Indians. Only they used a bow and arrow, ride-en alongside, and one arrow doen hit sometimes. Or two.

"But one way and ernuther, by and large we taken our share, Mingo and me. Winter and summer. And not us only. In Charlie Rath's sheds in Dodge City, many's the time with my own eyes I seen fifty-sixty thousand hides baled up and waiten, and his loaden yard so thick with wagons a man could nigh cross hit and ne'er set foot to ground. Wagons standen nigh hub to hub, and loaded, and fellers just in and likkered up and rare-en and cussen, waiten to git shet of their take. A time hit was, with money free lak sweat on a nigger, and men outer the war and from fer countries, and the likker runnen lak water. A power of meanness, and no denyen. But a man could git a-long, and not have him no trouble to speak on. If'n he tended to his business, and was God-fearen, and ne'er taken no back-sass off'n no man.

"We got our'n and didn't reckon on no end, hit looked lak. But a man's that a-way. He sees sumthen, and don't reckon on no end, no way, and don't see hit a-come-en. They's a hoggishness in man, and a hog-blindness. Down off'n Medicine Lodge Crick, one time, I was a-standen on a little rise, in the spring, and the buffalo was a-move-en. North, lak they done. All the buffalo trails run north-south, and hit was spring. They was move-en north, and fer as a man could see, hit was buffalo. They was that thick. No pore human man could name their number, only the Lord on high. That a-way, and no man to say the end. But I seen 'em lay, skinned and stinken, black-en the ground fer what a man could ride half a day. A man couldn't breathe fresh fer the stinken. And before you knowed hit, they wasn't no buffalo in Kansas. You could go a hull day and see nary a one. 'Hit's me fer Oklahoma,' Mingo said, 'whar thar's buffalo yit. Down Cimarron way, or Beaver Crick.'

" 'Hit's Indian country,' I said, 'I ain't a-relishen no Indians.'

" 'They's fellers been down thar and done right good,' Mingo said. 'I heared tell of a feller come out with nigh onto a thousand hides, and not down thar no time.'

" 'And fellers been down thar and ain't come back,' I said.

" 'Indians,' Mingo said, 'I fit Indians down in Oklahoma, when I was freighten. Hit ain't nuthen to brag on. They ain't got nuthen lak this-here.' And he give his Sharp's a little h'ist. 'The guns they got, ain't no white man would have 'em.'

" 'I ain't skeered,' I said, 'but hit ain't the law. Hit's Indian country down thar, by law.'

" 'Indian country,' and Mingo give a spit, 'hit ain't Indian country fer long. A feller from Dodge City said they's a gang gitten ready to go down fer buffalo, all together. Said Myers was gonna go down and buy hides and set up to do business right thar, down in Oklahoma, or maybe Texas toward the Canadian. Hit's big doens.'

" 'You figgeren on goen down with 'em?' I ast him.

" 'Naw,' Mingo said, 'folks gits under my feet.'

"We went down to Oklahoma, just us and our skinners. New skinners, they was, our old skinners quitten, nor wanten to go to Indian country. We got two new ones, a French feller and a nigger. We had to give 'em eighty dollars a month and found, because hit was Indian country. We went down thar. 'Seventy-four, hit was, and a drout year with the cricks dryen. And they was grasshoppers come that year, I recollect. But we made out, and they was buffalo thar. Hit was lak a-fore, the buffalo move-en and fillen the land. Hit was lak new coun-try. Fer a spell. And we worked fast and fer. But a man had to keep his eyes skinned, looken fer Indians. And somebody watchen all night, turn a-bout. We ne'er seen none till we got our first take out, up to Dodge City, and come back. Then we seen some, one time. The nigger was down a little draw, skinnen some buffalo Mingo shot, and French was at the wagon, stretchen hides, and Mingo and me was move-en out in the open. They come over a rise, between the draw and the wagons, and we seen 'em. We high-tailed fer home, and beat 'em to the wagons, and started shooten. 'Whar's the nigger?' Mingo said.

" 'He ain't here,' French said.

" 'God dammit,' Mingo said, layen thar shooten, 'that black bastud lets 'em slip up and git him, and me with a dislak fer skinnen lak I got. Hit's the thanks a man gits fer fighten rebels four years to set a nigger free.'

"We laid thar a-shooten at 'em all afternoon. French loaden, and Mingo and me shooten. When they was a-way off, we used our Sharp's, and when they come ride-en in clost, we used our carbeen and Colt guns. A Spencer carbeen shoots twelve times without stoppen, and heavy lead. Hit was that a-way all afternoon, and hit was a clear night and they couldn't git in clost and us not see. They tried hit, but we seen 'em ever time. They left a-fore day.

"Hit come day, and they was gone. They was some ponies layen off here and yander, and clost in, not more'n fifteen paces, a Indian. I ne'er knowed one got that nigh, but nighttime'll fool you. If'n we got airy other, they carried him off. But this one was too clost. We walked out to whar he was a-layen. 'Tryen to make a *coup*,' Mingo said, 'come-en in clost, that a-way. Wanted to git to be a chief.' He was a young Indian, and he was shot in the guts. 'The durn fool,' Mingo said. He poked him with his foot. 'Kiowa,' he said. Then he squatted down and taken out his knife.

" 'What you aim to do?' I ast him.

" 'Git me a scalp,' Mingo said.

" 'Hit ain't Christian,' I said.

" 'Hell,' he said, 'I knowed Christians as skinned Indians. I knowed a feller made him a baccy sack outer squaw-hide. But hit didn't do so good,' he said, and started cutten, 'hit wore out right off. But a scalp now, hit's diff'rent, hit's a keepsake.'

"He scalped him, then we looked down the draw fer the nigger. Thar he was, but they'd done taken his scalp. 'They made a pore trade,' Mingo said, 'a nigger's scalp ain't no good, hit ain't worth beans. Hit ain't much better'n mine.'

"Them was the only Indians we had trouble with that year, but them fellers went down from Dodge City all together, they had plenty trouble over in Texas. They had a big fight down at a place called 'Dobe Walls, and some got killed, and a passel of Indians. But the Indians was still bad on south a-ways. They was fighten at Anadarko with the sojers, and killen and scalpen here and yander. And raiden down to Texas. And the Kiowas caught a supply train—hit was Captain Lyman's wagons, I recollect—and give 'em a big tussle. We was down to Fort Sill the next spring, and we heared tell from the sojers. How they laid out four days in holes they dug, a-thirsten and no water, and the Indians all round, a-ride-en and a-whoopen and a-shooten. They was one Indian tied a white sheet round him and come ride-en through the sojers four times, and back agin, and lead cut that-air sheet off'n him, but ne'er a slug teched him. Doen hit made him a big chief, and they give him a new name fer hit, lak they done. But hit's done left me now, and I cain't name hit to you. All them days them sojers laid thar, thirsten. Then the rain come, heavy lak when the drout breaks in that-air country, and hit durn nigh drowned 'em layen thar in them holes they dug. But a scout got through to Camp Supply, and more sojers come.

"Hit was a bad year, and no denyen, and the Gin'al over to Fort Sill —hit was Gin'al Sheridan as fit in the war—a-gitten ready and sot to stomp 'em out. And he done hit. They was run here and yander, lak a coyote and the dogs on him. They run 'em and ne'er give no breathen. Some of 'em come in and give up, but some of 'em kept on a-runnen and a-fighten, the wildest what went with the war chiefs Lone Wolf and Maman-ti and sich. But they come in, too, a-fore hit was done. I seen 'em. Hit was at Fort Sill I seen 'em. They was another chief, named Kicken Bird, what got 'em in. He seen how hit would be, and he said hit to his people, and he made 'em come in. I seen 'em at Fort Sill. They put them Indians in the corrals—they was stone corrals— and the bad chiefs locked up in the jail, and chained, and in the stone ice-house they was a-builden. Ever day the wagons with meat come, and they throwed the meat over the wall—raw meat and in chunks lak you was feeden a passel of painters. They taken what stock the Indians had and drove 'em outside and shot 'em and let 'em lay, stinken. Hit was lak the stink when they'd been shooten buffalo and skinned 'em. Git a west wind, and couldn't no man in Fort Sill git the stink of them ponies outer his nose, wake-en nor sleepen. And hit ne'er helped no man eat his vittles.

"They was gonna send the bad chiefs off and git shet of 'em. A fer piece, to Florida. Kicken Bird, they was gonna let him pick out the ones to go, the ones he knowed was dead-set agin the white folks. And he done hit. He named Lone Wolf and Maman-ti, and a passel more, and said they would ne'er have hit in their hearts not to scalp a white man. The time come to git shet of 'em, and I seen hit. Them army wagons was standen thar by the ice-house, and sojers drawed up with guns, and they taken out the Indians from the ice-house. They had chains on 'em. And thar Kicken Bird come ride-en on his big gray stallion—a man he was to look on, tall and limber, and he could evermore set a hoss, a sight to see. He got off, and come up close to Maman-ti and Lone Wolf and them was standen thar. 'Hit's time,' he said, 'and my heart is full of a big sadness. But it will be. I love you, but you would not take the right road. But I love my people. I send you away because I love my people, and you would make them kill theirselves a-beaten their head agin the stone. Fighten the white man is lak beaten yore head on a stone. When yore hearts is changed, you kin come back to yore people, and you will find love in my heart for you.' That's what they said he said, fer I didn't know no Kiowa talk to speak of.

"The chiefs standen thar, the chains a-hangen off'n 'em, didn't say nuthen. They just looked at Kicken Bird. Then Maman-ti, he said: 'You think you are a big chief, Kicken Bird. You think you have done a good thing. The white men talk to you and puff you up, Kicken Bird. But you are lak a buffalo cow, dead and layen in the sun and swole with rot-wind. Indians ought to be a-dyen together, but you would not die with us, Kicken Bird. Now you will die by yoreself, Kicken Bird. You are dyen now, Kicken Bird, and the rot-wind is in you.' The wagons started rollen, the black-snakes a-cracken, off toward Caddo crossen. Kicken Bird stood thar, and watched 'em go. The sojers marched off, but Kicken Bird kept on a-standen thar, looken whar the wagons done gone.

"They's things in the world fer a man to study on, and hit's one of 'em. What come to Kicken Bird. He stood thar, a-looken, and then he went to his lodge, down on Cache Crick, nigh Sill. They say he just set thar, not give-en nuthen to notice, to speak of. He et a little sumthen, but he didn't relish nuthen. He ne'er taken his eyes off'n the ground. Five days that a-way, and come the fifth mornen and he keeled over and died. 'I done what come to me,' he said, layen thar, 'and I taken the white man's hand.' Then he was dead. Nary a mark on him, and him in the prime.

"But they ain't no tellen. Some said as how Maman-ti, when the wagons camped outer Sill, prayed and put a strong medicine on Kicken Bird to die. Then he died his-self fer putten medicine on ernuther Kiowa. But agin, maybe his heart was broke in two. Maybe Kicken

Bird's heart broke in two lak a flint rock when you put hit in the hot fire. They ain't no tellen. But hit's sumthen fer a man to study on.

"Hit was in May they taken them Indians away from Sill, and me and Mingo hit out agin. Buffalo hunten agin. But we didn't do so good that year. They was peteren out. That's what made them Indians so durn bad, some folks said, them buffalo goen. They didn't git no vittles then, but what the gov'mint give 'em, and hit spiled more'n lak. We taken what we could find, but the time was goen in Oklahoma. We heared tell they was buffalo down Brazos, and Charlie Hart's boys a-gitten 'em, so hit was down Brazos and up Pease River. We done what we could, but the time was a-goen. Mingo got lak I'd ne'er seen him git a-fore. We'd sight buffalo, and he'd go nigh loco. 'Durn, God durn,' he'd say, his voice lak a man prayen, 'God durn the bastuds.' And his eyes with a shine in 'em lak a man got the fever. 'Durn,' he'd say, 'what you a-waiten fer, you Kentuck bastud,' and we'd move out on 'em. Light or dark, he'd be at hit. Past sun, I seen him, and not light fer a man to aim by. Him a-waste-en lead, and them Sharp's evermore et lead lak a hog slop. Two ounce the slug, and powder to back hit. 'Mingo,' I says to him, 'hit's a willful waste.' 'I'll cut yore scaggly thote,' he said, and ne'er said one more word all night.

"We come outer Brazos and up Kansas way. 'They's buffalo north,' Mingo'd say. Days, and we'd see a old bull, maybe, and a couple of cows. And bones layen white on the ground, fer as a man's sight, white lak a salt flat. The wagon wheel went over 'em, cracken. We come to Dodge City. They was bones piled and ricked up thar, a sight of bones. Them nesters and 'steaders done picked up and brung 'em in to sell 'em. They was buyen 'em back east to make fert'lizer to put on the wore-out ground. Bones ricked up thar along the Santa Fe, a-waiten, you ne'er seen sich. They was fellers in Dodge City, but not lak a-fore. Fellers was setten round didn't have a dime, what had been throwen round the green lak a senator. Bones and broke buffalo hunters thar, them days. We was in Dodge City, and Mingo ne'er outer spitten-range of a bottle. 'Buffalo gone,' he said, 'durn, and hit'll be whisky next, and no country fer a white man.' But they shore-God wasn't no drout in sight yit. Not with Mingo.

"We was in Dodge City, and word come the Santa Fe was payen out good money fer men to fight the Denver and Rio Grande fer putten the track through where the Arkansas comes outer the mountains, out in Colorado. Mingo come and said to git ready, we was goen. But I said, naw, I wasn't gonna be a-shooten and killen no human man, not fer no railroad, no way. 'Me,' Mingo said, 'I kilt plenty fer the gov'mint goen on four years, and kill a man fer the gov'mint, I shore-God oughter be willen to kill me one fer anybody else. Even a railroad.' But naw, I said. But Mingo went on and done hit, and me waiten in Dodge City. Then he come on back, and money he had. 'Hit'll be Santa Fe line,' he said, 'and Irish fer cross-ties.'

"Then Mingo said: 'Yellowstone, up Yellowstone and they's buffalo lak a-fore. Hit's the word. Git ready.' But I ne'er said nuthen. 'What you setten thar fer?' he said. 'Git ready.' Then I said I wasn't aimen to go. 'What you aimen to do?' Mingo said. I said I couldn't rightly name hit, but hit would come to me. I said I might take me out some ground, have-en a little money left to git me gear and a start. Mingo looked at me lak he ne'er laid eyes on me a-fore, and he give a spit on the ground. 'A fool hoe-man,' he said, 'you be a durn fool hoe-man.' 'Maybe,' I said, 'if'n hit comes to me.' 'A bone-picker,' he said. He give me a look, and that's the last word I e'er heared him say. 'Bone-picker,' he said, and give me a look, and walked off. He was gone, a-fore sun next mornen. Yellowstone way, they said.

"I taken me a claim, lak I said. Up in Kansas. And I done well as the next one, I reckin. I ne'er minded putten my back to hit, and layen a-holt. And I had me money to git a start, gear and stock and sich. Two year, goen on three, I stayed. I was a-make-en out, that wasn't hit. Hit was sumthen come over me. I couldn't name hit. But thar hit was, sleepen and wake-en. I sold my stock and gear. I said to a man, 'What'll you gimme fer my stock and gear?' And he named hit. Hit wasn't nuthen, not to what a man could a-got. But I taken hit, and hit was ample. To git me a outfit. And I started a-move-en. Down through Oklahoma, and west. West, lak a man done them days when hit come over him to be a-move-en.

"I went down the way I'd been a-fore, and hit was diff'rent a-ready. But not diff'rent lak when I come back in 'ninety-one on my way back here. The Indians was dance-en then, when I come back through, tryen to dance the buffalo back. They'd been gone a long time then, and the bones. Them Indians was a-tryen to dance 'em back. And Indians everwhar, I heared tell, up in Dakota and west. The ghost-dance, they named hit. They was make-en medicine and tryen to dance back the good times, and them long gone. Hit would be a new world, and fer Indians, they claimed. A new earth was a-come-en, all white and clean past a man's thinken, and the buffalo on hit a-move-en and no end. Lak that time I stood on a rise near Medicine Lodge Crick and seen 'em a-move-en, and ne'er reckined on the end, how hit would be. That-air new earth was a-come-en, they figgered, a-slide-en over the old earth whar the buffalo was done gone now and the Indians was dirt, a-blotten hit out clean, lak a kid spits on his slate and rubs hit clean. And thar all the Indians would be, all the nations a-standen and callen, all them what had died, on that-air new white earth. The live ones was dance-en to bring hit.

"They was them as had seen hit. They was them as fell down in the dance and had died, lak they named hit, when they was a-dance-en, and laid on the ground stark and stiff lak dead. They was the ones as had seen hit, the new land. They'd come to, lak a man wake-en, and tell as how they had seen hit. They seen the new earth, all white and shine-en, and the dead ones thar, happy, and beckonen with the hand, and they talked to 'em. Squaws what had chil'en what was dead, they'd see 'em. And they'd git busy a-make-en moccasins and toys, lak hummers and bull-roarers and sich, and bring 'em to the dance next time to have 'em ready to give to the chil'en when they seen 'em. They'd see 'em, and give 'em the toys and sich. Then they'd come round, layen thar, and thar'd be that-air truck they'd done fixed fer the chil'en. Layen thar on the ground. They didn't know what to make on hit. See-en hit thar.

"They was some folks as was laughen and scornen. Said them Indians was gone plumb crazy. But not me. One time, long a-fore, when I was young and sallet-green, I mighter scorned. But not then, in 'ninety-one, when I was a-come-en back, after what hit was I'd seen. I'd laid dead lak them Indians, and seen hit come to me. Hit was how I was a-come-en back. In 'ninety-one.

"But them Indians. They come together in a big ring, a-dance-en. Round and round, and a-singen. Them songs they made up, how they'd been dead and what they seen in that-air new land a-come-en. And the medicine man, he was in the middle, a-shake-en his eagle feather, and them Indians move-en round, and a-singen. Then somebody starts to feel hit a-come-en, and starts a-shake-en and shudderen, lak the chill. And the medicine man, he waves that-air eagle feather a-fore his face what's a-shake-en, and he blows out his breath at him and says, 'Hunh, hunh, hunh, hunh!' And that feller comes outer the ring in the middle, lak the blind-staggers, and the medicine man waves the feather a-fore him, and ne'er stops, and says, 'Hunh, hunh, hunh!' Till that-air feller gits the jerks, lak a man when the gospel hits him. Then the jerks is gone, and him a-standen, stiffer'n a man on the coolen board, and eyes a-stare-en lak a-fore the pennies is put. He stand thar, how long hit ain't no tellen, and them dance-en and singen, and hit come-en on more Indians, too, and them a-fall-en. They lays on the ground thar, lak dead, and broad daylight, maybe. And the singen and dance-en not stoppen.

"But that was in 'ninety-one, when I was a-come-en back, not when I was a-goen. A-goen, I was headed west, lak I said, lak a man them days when hit come on him to be move-en. I was down in Santa Fe and seen hit. I went to the middle of town, and seen the folks a-move-en and doen, and I figgered I'd lay over and rest up, maybe. Then hit come on me. Naw, I said, I ain't a-stoppen, hit's on me not to be a-stoppen. I didn't tarry none, only to git me grub and sich. A feller said to me, 'Whar you goen?' I said I didn't know, and he said, 'God-a-mighty, stranger, goen and don't know whar!' And I said, 'Naw, I don't know, but hit'll come to me when I git thar.' And he said, 'God-a-mighty!' And I went on.

"I come into the mountains. Them mountains wasn't lak no moun-tains you e'er seen. Nor me. Not lak them hills in Arkansas or in this-here country in Kentucky. That-air country was open and high, and the mountains rise-en outer hit. Hit was June when I come in the high country, and they was flowers everwhar. I ne'er seen sich. Grease-wood with blooms plumb gold, and little flowers on the ground. And the cactus, flowers a-bloomen fer as a man's sight. But no smell. Put yore nose to hit, but they ain't no smell, fer all the brightness.

"I went on to the high mountains. Cedar and juniper I come to, but scrub and not fitten fer nuthen. Then up higher, piñons, then oak but hit scrub. Then high up in them mountains, the big pines standen, and no man e'er laid axe. Look down and the land was all tore up down below, ever which way, tore up and a-layen on end. And the ground with colors lak the sky at sun. Look up, and snow was still layen when I come, and the sun white on hit, lak on cloud-tops in summer. The wind come down off'n the snow, cold to yore face and the sun shine-en.

"I come in that-air country, and ne'er ast no man the way. Outer Santa Fe I seen folks a-goen and a-come-en, then they wasn't none to speak on. In the high country I seen Indians sometimes, ride-en along, or standen, and I made 'em signs and them me, but I ne'er ast 'em the way. A man could be in a place in that-air country and they'd be Indians live-en thar, not a pistol-shot, and him ne'er knowen. Not the way they fixed them houses, dirt piled up round looken lak a hump outer the ground. Hogans, they named them houses. The cold come or hit git dry and the grass give out, and they'd up and move and build 'em a new house. One day, sun to sun, and hit was built.

"Summer I was in the mountains, high up. The cold come, and I moved down and built me a house, lak them Indian houses, only mine set south, backed up under a hunk of rock. Them Indian houses sets east, ne'er no other way. Hit's agin their religion. And I fixed me a shed fer my ponies. That winter I laid up thar. I lived off'n the land. A man kin do hit, put to hit, what with a rifle and snare-en. But I traded the Indians fer some corn, now and agin. But two-three months, and I ne'er seen nobody, hair nor hide. I didn't miss hit, somehow. I'd a-come thar, and thar I was. Hit's past name-en, how the Lord God leads a man some time, and sets his foot. Thar I was, and I knowed they was a world of folks off yander, down in the flat country. A-gitten and a-begetten, and not knowen the morrow. I knowed how they'd been war and killen in the country, and folks rise-en in slaughter, brother agin brother. And men was dead and under the earth, as had walked on hit, standen up lak me or airy breathen man. And no man to name the reason. Only the Lord God. I minded me on the power of meanness I'd seen in my time. And done, to speak truth. A man does hit, some more, some less, but he's got hit to think on.

"Hit looked lak my head was full, one thing and ernuther. Sometimes hit was lak I could see, plain as day, everthing and everbody I'd e'er knowed layen out a-fore me, all at one time. They ain't no tellen how hit was, but hit was that a-way. All together, lak a man lived his life, and the time not a-passen while he lived hit. Hit's past sayen, and they ain't no word fer me to say hit, but hit was that a-way. A-fore God. Hit's sumthen to study on. Then a man feels clean, hit's ne'er the same.

"Summer come, and the snow gone, and I started up to the high mountains. I seen Indians a-move-en, too. They made me signs, and I taken up with 'em. They had 'em sheep and ponies, and was goen whar the grass was good. They was two or three of 'em knowed our talk, not good but some. All summer I was with them Indians, off and on. The grass gone and time to be a-move-en, and they ast me to move too, and I done hit. A man could git along with them Indians if'n he had a mind to. I done hit. They ne'er had nuthen agin me, nor me agin them. Hit come cold, and they was a-move-en down low, and I went with 'em. They helped build me a winter hogan, lak their'n, and they rubbed corn meal on the posts, the way they done fer luck, and sprinkled hit on the floor, and said the words they says to make the live-en in the house be good live-en. They throwed a handful on the fire they'd built under the smoke hole, and said the words. They fixed vittles, and we set on the floor, on sheep skins, and taken sup, side by side. They made cigarettes, lak they do, outer corn shucks and terbaccer, and set thar smoke-en and talken. Hit was lak a log-raise-en in this-here country, and folks jolli-fyen.

"Five year, and hit was that a-way. Hit was a way of live-en, if'n hit's in a man's heart. And I ne'er had no complaint. I was easy in my heart and mind, lak ne'er a-fore in my time of doen and strive-en. I'd a-been thar yit, I reckin, if'n I had'n a-took sick, and hit bad. Hit was in the summer of 'ninety, and we was in the high country, but hit looked lak sumthen went outer me. I wasn't good fer nuthen. Looked lak I couldn't raise my hand, the pith gone out of me. I'd jist set on the ground, and look up at the sky, how thin and blue hit was over them mountains. Then the fever come. Hit taken me, and I said, 'Willie Proudfit, you gonna die.' That's what I said, and the words was in my head lak a bell. Then hit come to me, how other men was dead, and they taken hit the best they could and the bitterness, and I said, 'Willie Proudfit, what air man kin do, you kin do.' But the fever come agin, and I said, 'You gonna die, and in a fer country.'

"The Indians done what they could. They give me stuff to drink, black and bitter hit was, outer yerbs and sich, but hit ne'er done no good. I'd burn up with fever, then I'd lay and look and everthing in the world was diff'rent to me. Wouldn't nuthen stay on my stomach, looked lak. And then the fever agin. The Indians treated me good. A man couldn't a-ast more. They give me them yerbs and sich, and hit ain't all foolishness. They knows what grows outer the earth in their country, hit's use the Lord give hit. I seen some mighty sick Indians them years I was thar, and seen 'em get well and walken. But the Lord had laid a powerful sickness on me, and I said, 'Willie Proudfit, you gonna die.'

"But no, ain't no man knows what the Lord's done marked out fer him. And many's the pore, weakid man done looked on the face of blessedness, bare-eyed, and ne'er knowed hit by name. Lak a blind man a-liften his face to the sun, and not knowen. Hit was a blessen the Lord laid on me, and I praise hit.

"Them Indians seen I was witheren up, lak a tree in the sun done had the axe at hits root. Because they done called me brother and give me a name, they done everthing they could. They built the medicine house, made a fire thar, and set me in the medicine house, and tried to take out the evil. Not jist one day, they was tryen to git the evil out. They set in thar and some of 'em had their faces all covered up with masks made outer leather and painted, and they waved eagle feathers on me to bring out the evil, and sometimes they put stuff on my head and my feet and my knees and my chist, stuff they done mixed up, and sometimes corn meal. Sometimes hit was sand on my head. And some-times they washed me with suds, just lak soap suds, they done made outer yerbs, and done dried me with corn meal. And agin they done put pine branches on me, and put stuff on the fire fer me to breathe and one thing and ernuther, and me too nigh gone to keer. And sometimes they done made pictures outer colored sand on the floor, and feathers and beads and sich, and they was singen and hooten, sometimes. To git out the evil. And they put me in them sweat houses, little houses not much bigger'n fer a man to lay in, and covered with dirt and sand, and pictures in colored sand, and a curtain outer deerskin fer a door. But hit had to be skin off'n a deer they done run down and smother with a man's hand, not shot or cut fer the killen. They put me in hit, and rocks they done got red hot, and sweated me. And one night they was dance-en all night hit looked lak, and singen, naked and painted white, I recollect, and the fires was burnen big.

"But the fever done had me sometimes, and hit was lak a dream. I was a-goen, and nuthen to lay holt on. And I didn't keer. The time comes and a man don't keer. They taken me out and laid me on the ground. Hit was night. I knowed that then I was a-goen. I might been gone, fer all I know. They ain't no sayen.

"I might been gone, when hit come to me, what I seen. I seen a long road come-en down a hill, and green everwhar. Green grass layen fresh, and trees, maple and elm and sich. And my feet was in the road, and me a-move-en down hit. They was a fire in me, thirsten. Hit was a green country, and the shade cool, but the fire was in me. I come down the hill, and seen houses setten off down the valley, and roofs, and the green trees standen. I taken a bend in the road, and thar was a little church, a white church with a bell hangen, and the grass green a-fore hit. Thar was a spring thar, by the church, and I seen hit and run to hit. I put my head down to the water, fer the fire in me, lak a dog gitten ready to lap. I didn't take no water in my hand and sup. Naw, I put my face down to the water, and hit was cool on me. The coolness was in me, and I taken my fill.

"No tellen how long, and I lifted up my head. Thar a girl was sitten, over thar nigh the spring, and she was a-looken at me. I opened my mouth but nary a word come out. Hit looked lak the words was big in me to busten, and none come.

"Then hit was finished and done, and I'd ne'er spoke. The dream, if'n hit was a dream. No tellen how long I laid thar, but I come to, hit was mornen light, gray, fer the rain was fall-en. I didn't have no fever. I laid thar, and my head was full of what all I'd been a-dreamen. They taken me in, and a-fore night I et a little sumthen, and hit stayed on my stomach. My strength come back, not fast, but hit come. All the time I was a-thinken what I'd seen, the church and the green trees standen, and the spring. Everday. I'd seen hit, I knowed I'd seen hit, but I couldn't give hit the name. Then I knowed. Hit was the road come-en down to Thebes, in Kentucky, when I was a kid thar, and the church setten thar whar hit takes a bend. I ne'er seen hit since pappy done up and taken outer Kentucky fer Arkansas when the war come and he was on-easy in his mind, but hit come to me plain as day, and I said, 'I'm a-goen thar.'

"My strength come, and I done hit. I told them Indians goodbye, and they taken my hand. I come to Santa Fe, and up Oklahoma, lak I said, and on to Arkansas. I was gonna see my pappy, and my mammy, if'n the Lord had done spared 'em. I come in Arkansas at Fort Smith, and on east, whar my folks had been. My mammy was dead. Been dead a long time, folks said. And my pappy, he was dead too, but not more'n goen on a year. He was kilt, with a knife. A feller from up Missouri kilt him. He was setten down at a store one night, at the settlement, and everbody was talken and goen on. They was a-talken about the war, and how hit come. The feller from up Missouri, he was cussen the rebels, and my pappy said, naw, not to be a-cussen 'em that a-way, they didn't do hit, no more'n no other man. They had a argument, and the feller from up Missouri, he cut my pappy, and him a old man. The feller from up Missouri taken out, and was gone, no man knowed whar. And my pappy died, layen thar on the floor. I seen the place he was buried, and my mammy. Nobody knowed whar my brothers was gone, been gone a long time. Strange folks was a-live-en in the house my pappy'd done built long back, the house I'd seen him start builden that day he'd stood thar and looked whar hit was gonna set, sayen, 'Lord God, Lord God,' right soft, and then, sudden-lak, to ma, 'Henrietta, gimme that-air axe!' I seen hit, the logs notched clean and set tight, and the chimney true, ne'er sunk nor slipped yit.

"I sold the place fer what I could git. I ne'er hemmed and hawed. Then I come on, on here to Kentucky, acrost Tennessee. I come on to Thebes. Hit was a hot day, when I come, but summer not on good yit. I come over the hill, down the road, and thar was the grass and the trees standen green. Lak hit is, and lak hit come to me that time. I taken the turn in the road, and thar was the church. New Bethany church, hit is. And the spring, and I run to hit, on-steady and nigh blind, with what come on me when I seen hit. I put my face down to the water. I taken my fill.

"I lifted up my head, slow. And thar she set."

His voice stopped. In the silence, in the marshy ground down the creek the frogs were piping. Then he said: "Hit was Adelle."

"Yes," his wife's voice said, quietly, from the shadow where her chair was, "I was setten thar, in the shade of a sugar-tree, and I seen him come down the hill."

FROM
AT HEAVEN'S GATE
(1943)

*The first of these two excerpts is near the beginning
of the story, when Gerald (Jerry) Calhoun, on first
meeting Sue, the daughter of his employer Bogan
Murdock, clumsily overturns an ashtray, and the
accident triggers a flashback to episodes of his childhood. In the second selection, at the end of the novel,
Jerry and others have been arrested on suspicion of
fraud after the collapse of the Murdock financial
empire. Jerry is waiting in the jail for his friend
Duckfoot Blake (a former employee and critic of
Murdock) to arrange his release.*

—A. E.

Crouched on the floor before Sue Murdock, feeling his cheeks flush
at his own clumsiness, watching his hands fumble to collect the scattered butts, Jerry Calhoun suddenly saw, in his mind's eye, his own
father; a big man, his blue shirt soaked with sweat, stooped to some
small occupation—to buckle a harness or set a staple over a strand of
wire—while his breath came in quick gasps, or while he held his breath
and his face grew purple, while the thick, scarred fingers crooked
ineptly and the sweat rolled down his cheeks into the neatly trimmed
black beard. At that moment, Jerry Calhoun, tangled in his own clumsiness, aware of the sweat starting at his own temples, had that vision of
his father, or rather, felt himself somehow as merged into, and identified
with, that image.

His father was a strong man, and his shoulders seemed to be stooped
from the knotted pads of muscle. He was a man who would sweat
easily, and his shirt would stick to the flesh, showing the twin humps
of muscle knitted into the crevice where the backbone was. Jerry had
seen him crouch and grapple his hands under the hub of a wagon wheel
stuck in the mud, and heave it out while the mules strained forward.
"You always put your feet together, son, this-away, and lift straight,
just rise up, son," he would say. "You don't want to be spilling your
bowels in the road." But when he had some small thing to do, he was

no good. The stiff fingers could not hold the buckle, the wrench, the staple right, the face would work with the agony of its intenseness, and the sweat would start. He did not break into fury on these occasions, as big, clumsy men often do, but, when the effort became too much for him, he would lay down his tool, or the object with which he had been struggling, laying it down very gently, solicitously, and would stare at it and shake his head almost imperceptibly, while the sweat streaked his face and his breathing subsided to a normal rate.

That was the image of his father which had dominated his childhood, not the image of his father performing his casual and unprideful feats of strength, or holding him on his lap to read to him, to make him spell out the words, on Sunday afternoons, on the front porch of the big old brick house, or, in winter, before the fire in the draughty living room; and that was the image which now struck him more painfully, involved him more deeply, than ever before.

Jerry, when he was a little boy and was often with his father on the farm, could scarcely bear those moments. He would sometimes pick up the object which his father had laid down, and would hold it as though in readiness, as though in encouragement, but there would be a small, sickening congestion in his stomach, and he would avert his face from the scene; and especially as he grew older, this sickness, this confusion, this unformulable distress, might suddenly coagulate into a cold core of hatred, and he would suppress the impulse to hurl the object to the ground and strike out at his father or run away.

At those times he felt as he did the time his setter puppy fell into the old well by a deserted tenant house on the place. For hours he crouched on the crumbling brickwork and the rotting boards, trying to snare the animal with a loop of rope, trying to make it cling to bits of planking tied to the old rope, trying to make it get into the old bucket which he let down, while the sickness rose in him and his whole consciousness was possessed by those thin, mechanical, gargling, accurately timed yelps which, strangely resonant despite their thinness, came up from the deep shaft. Then, involuntarily, he dropped the rope and watched it spin down to the water, and sink. He grubbed an old brick from the sod, and with the icy assurance of hatred, or something like hatred, hard in him now, leaned far over to observe the small target, which was the animal's head, in the middle of the glimmer-fractured blackness of the water. The one brick did it. It struck without a splash, with only a flat, surrendering sound. He leaped up and ran home, across the fields of young corn, while the sunlight rocked giddily over the unfamiliar landscape.

That night he told his father about it. "You did right, son," his father said. "You'd done all a body could do. You couldn't leave the poor little thing down there to be suffering."

He had wanted his father to say that, and his father had said it. But the words, he knew, were a lie.

It was that way, sometimes, when he watched his father. But he felt better when his Uncle Lew, his mother's brother, was standing by and said something, as he never failed to do, about his father's ineptitude. "By God, Jim, by God," he would say, and his small black eyes would sharpen, and his sharp nose and all his bitter, twisted, pale face would seem to concentrate to the malevolency of the eyes, "why don't you put yore arms in a buzz saw and then try to pick yore teeth with what's left?" His father, slowly, would look up, with a sort of smile, and would say: "I reckon I ought to, Lew." Or something like that. Then, with a sense of relief and cleansing, the hatred in the boy would find its focus on Lew. That was all right. Hating Lew was all right. Lew never did anything nice for him, or anybody. Lew was not his father. It was all right to hate Lew.

His mother was dead. She had died at his birth. She had left little tangible record of herself. There was the wedding picture of her and her husband. She was seated, in the picture, wearing a white dress which came up high to the throat, with her hair combed smoothly back from her small intense face. Her husband stood behind her, and a little to one side, big and black-coated, one hand laid cautiously on her shoulder, black-bearded and with the black hair plastered down and parted with an artificial precision. There were a few other pictures of her, too, with that same small face and intense eyes. "She was a quiet sort of girl," his father had once said, "but she moved light on her feet, and nimble, and was clever with her hands. And she had a good voice for singing in the church, didn't she, Lew?"

"I reckon so," Lew had said, grudgingly, "but I never was no hand to take on much over singing."

She had left the pictures and a few objects, which year by year had grown fewer. There had been the set of blue dishes, once referred to as hers and rarely used, but as the years passed, the surviving items, a cream pitcher, a butter dish without its cover, and a few saucers, merged into the nondescript general collection. Once, some time after he had left home and gone to work at Meyers and Murdock, Jerry, on one of his visits home, missed the butter dish. His father, noticing his glance, had said: "The cook broke it." And Jerry had suddenly experienced a startled and inordinate sense of release. His father, years before, had broken the red glass vase, which had stood on the table in the parlor before some of the upstairs rooms had been abandoned and the parlor had been converted into a bedroom for Aunt Ursula. He had come out of the shuttered, never-used parlor one Sunday afternoon, and had closed the door behind him with that awkward carefulness of his, and had announced: "I broke Holly's red vase."

Uncle Lew, hunched before the fire in the living room, had looked up with his air of shrewd and wry triumph and his lips had pulled back as though to speak; but he had said nothing. The pieces of the red vase had been left on the table for a long time. Jerry had seen the smears of the glue with which his father had tried to fit the thing back together, but finally the fragments themselves disappeared; exactly when, or by whose hand, Jerry never knew.

She had left these objects, and had left her brother, Jerry's uncle Lew, and her aunt, Jerry's great-aunt Ursula. At the time of her niece's death, Aunt Ursula had been some sixty-five years old, spry, competent, amiable, and fanatically clean. She had raised her niece, Holly, and nephew, Lew, through years of privation and tight-lipped scrimping, and then she had raised Holly's baby, Jerry. She had never married. She had raised Lew and Holly, the children of her dead brother and of a woman whom she had never seen. She had sweated in summer and had been cold in winter for them. She had lain awake at night, hearing the window sash rattle in whatever draughty house they were lucky enough to have over their heads or hearing the young frogs chirruping from the cattle pond, and had thought of the money which she would need the next month, or the next week, or the next day. She had never known these two children, neither the bitter and quarrelsome club-footed boy nor the silent girl. But the first few years with the baby of her niece had been different, a strong child, affectionate and never sickly. It had been hers more completely than the others. And she had not been forced to worry about the roof over her head or the food on the table. And she had not been aware of, or had shut her mind to, Jim Calhoun's worries; for he never talked of such things. The old Calhoun house which she kept so orderly, the big kitchen where she quarreled at the Negro cook and spied for the slightest spot of old grease or soot, the grassless backyard where the chickens fluffed in the dust or huddled from the rain, the voices about her—it had all been like a late and difficultly won harbor; and the problems and disorders of the life there had rocked her, in that new security, no more than wavelets.

She had loved the child, but as its strength increased, her own diminished, and as the circle of its existence widened, her own contracted, until it was nothing, until the whole world lay outside its periphery. By the time the child was ten years old she was nearly blind, and was confined to her chair. She had fallen against the kitchen stove one day, and had lain on the floor, unconscious, with the flesh of her left arm burned almost to the bone, until the boy had come in and had found her there. When, months later, she had been able to leave her bed and sit in a chair, he had not been able to fit her back into a place in his world. She had never again seemed real to him. "Go and talk to your Aunt Ursula," his father would say to him sometimes. "You ought to talk to her. She was always mighty good to you, son." But he would stand before her and the words would stick in his throat, like dry crumbs. Then, afterwards, when he was alone at night, or when he would be doing something during the day, he would see, suddenly clear before him, the way the flesh sagged off her cheekbones and her eyes lay back in their sockets, or the way the scarred flesh of her left hand seemed to crust off the bones, and he would be overwhelmed by a conviction of guilt and unworthiness.

One fall, after he was in high school and could make a little money of his own, he had saved everything he could for three months so that he could buy her a present. He had paid eleven dollars for a shawl and had given it to her for Christmas. He had put the package on her lap and had stood there to watch while her fingers plucked at the cord and the paper rattled. His father, finally, had opened the package. "Put it on her shoulders, son," he had ordered, and Jerry had obeyed. "It's a present," his father had said, "it's a present Jerry bought for you. He saved his money and bought it for you, Aunt Ursula. It's a shawl, a blue shawl. Feel it. Feel the fringe on it." And his father had picked an edge of the shawl and had dangled it before her as though she could see. Then his father had reached out to take up one of her hands— *Oh, God-a-mighty, God-a-mighty,* Jerry had thought, but his father had picked up her right hand, her good hand. His father's hand had lifted her hand and had guided it, making it stroke the soft woolen texture. "It's a pretty shawl. Jerry got it for you."

Then the boy had seen the tears fill up the hollowish sockets of her eyes and break over, and run unevenly down her cheeks.

"Jerry got it for you, Aunt Ursula. He got it for you because he loves you."

The boy had gone abruptly out of the room, leaving them there, out to the backyard, where the crisp icy crust over the bare ground gave down to the mud under his tread. He had leaned over the fence to the stable lot, and had said, out loud, deliberately, over and over again, the vile words he knew, which reduce everything to the blind, unqualified retch and spasm of the flesh, the twist, the sudden push, the twitch, the pinch of ejection and refusal.

But his feeling toward his Uncle Lew had never changed from the time when he first became aware of the individual qualities of the people around him. Nor had Lew's face changed during these years. The skin on his face pulled back tight from the thin, uncertain mouth and the bridge of the nose, over the sharp angles of the bony structure, which under the skin seemed paper-thin; and the skin itself was pale and delicate, like the skin of a child. The texture and color of that skin never changed, even when the black, too glossy hair had begun to turn gray. His hands were narrow and spidery, deft at small tasks, when he sat by himself. He would hunch down in a chair, or on a bench in the yard when the weather was good, his high shoulder blades cocked up, his elbows sharply cut, the knee of his good leg crooked, and his bad leg thrust out before him, and in the midst of these angles and ineptitudes of bone, the fingers would move flickeringly, a small center of competence and certainty. When there was nothing else for him to do, he often occupied himself with his carving. He carved peach stones, walnuts, and small pieces of oak, hickory, and cedar, into complicated geometrical designs or into grotesque faces, not animal and not quite human. He never seemed to have any desire to show these things to anyone, but kept them in a big box by his bed, and the box had a padlock on it. On rainy days he would sometimes lay the objects out on his bed or on a table and handle them and study them, one by one. His big clasp knife was always sharp as a razor, both the big blade and the little blade, and when he was tired of his carving, he would draw his bad leg up to him, and lean over and hone the steel, with a slow, meditative, caressing motion, against the leather of the shoe sole.

He knew a few coin tricks, too. "Come here, Jerry," he would say, "here's a quarter I'm gonna give you. Look at it good. Here it is. I'm gonna give it to you." Then he would do the tricks. "It's gone. It's done flew away. Ain't that too bad. I'm sure sorry. Naw, here it is again! Here, take it, quick! Aw, durn, it's done gone again."

Finally, Aunt Ursula would say: "Quit pestering the child, Lew. It ain't right."

Then Lew, grinning, would stop. But his father, if he happened to be present, would only watch, saying nothing. But once, after it was over, while the child stood in the middle of the floor, hurt and baffled almost to tears, his father had said: "Come here." Then he had reached into his pocket and had taken out a silver dollar. "Take it," he had said, and had held it out on the humps of his big palm. Slowly, the child had reached for the coin. "It's yours," his father had said. "Don't lose it. And when we go to town Saturday you can buy anything you want." The child had taken the coin.

"I'll be durned," Lew had said, "Mister Astor," and had spat suddenly into the fire.

He had never played the tricks again on Jerry, but Jerry, a long time afterwards, when he was in high school, had seen his uncle call some little nigger child to him: "Hey, little nigger boy, I'm gonna give you a quarter. Come here!"

Jerry never learned much about his mother's people. He had never heard his uncle mention the past but one time, and then only to say: "That nigger Jeff told me today they've done pulled down that little old house on the Moffat place, down toward Hamill's Crossing, putting a road through. I was born in that house." Then his lips had jerked back in a grin. "They oughter burned it down long back. It never was worth a gol-durn." And he had given three or four shrill, constricted cackles of laughter, before subsiding into one of his spells of silence. The old woman had said a little more. She had been born down in Alabama, Jerry knew, and he had heard her say once that down there she had seen Indians. "Indians, and I saw them, I recollect, Indians walking down the big road, just like folks, and me a little sprig of a girl standing in front of our house. Indians, but it was a long time back, and I don't know how come." There had been a big Bible, she said, with names written in it for a long time back, back into the time when her people were in North Carolina before they went down to Georgia, and the last names in it were Holly's and Lew's; but she had lost it, moving around, when the children were little and troubles so thick her mind nigh turned and she was past praying, but she never asked, nor got, mite nor morsel not proper hers, and no hand to stay her.

Georgia, North Carolina, Alabama, Mississippi, Tennessee, Kentucky: these people whose names Jerry did not know had moved, for two hundred years, across the marshes, up the slow rivers where the water was black with rotting vegetation, over ridges where jutting limestone baked white in the glare of sunlight and the oak leaves steamed, through pine flats where the dead needles underfoot masked the sour yellow ground, across the valleys of Alabama and Mississippi and the green slopes and hollows of Tennessee and Kentucky. They had built log cabins, log houses with the logs hewed square, and limestone chimneys, little clapboard houses which they had intended to paint, but they had always left them, and had moved on, and had left the dead in cemeteries at crossroads or in untended plots near the houses where the sassafras and the love-vine took hold. They had always come too late. The best ground had always been taken, the best springs and the good place for the mill dam, or the place near the ford for a tavern. Jerry did not know their names. From them had come his mother, Aunt Ursula, and Uncle Lew. And once or twice, catching sight of Lew's face in repose, he had discovered that that face was the face of his mother in the old pictures, even in the wedding picture.

Jerry had that blood in him, but he looked like his father. Even when he was a child he had the face of his father. As a boy he was rangy and stringy, growing fast, but by the time he was fifteen, when he entered high school, his body was thickening out, and by the time he was eighteen he already had his father's powerful shoulders. His hands were big, and like his father's, were good with animals, when he was handling lambs and chicks and turkey poults, or doctoring a sick horse or breaking a colt. Jerry's hands had the same capacity. By the time he was fourteen he was making a few dollars, now and then, breaking horses in the neighborhood. But his hands, though big and clumsy-looking like his father's, were not clumsy. At the first heart-stopping whirr of the quail from the sage or the brush harbor, the gun would be at his shoulder and the reports of the two barrels would almost merge; and he could lay a fly back under the willows along the creek bank or beside a sunken snag. All his boyhood he had practiced these things, and his father, who had, however, no concern for sport, had never discouraged him. Sometimes, when he practiced casting out in the sideyard on Sunday afternoon, his father would come out and sit there, propped back against the wall of the house, smoking and saying nothing. After he entered high school, another boy would often come out on Sundays, and all afternoon they would pass a football back and forth, until it was too dark to see. His father would watch that, too.

During the first two years when he was in high school, money was very tight with his father, and every penny which went for clothes and books was that much which might have gone to relieve the increasing pressure of debt. Aunt Ursula was completely blind by that time, and often ill; and there were bills for the doctor for her. Mr. Calhoun let the cook go for a while and tried to do for himself, but it was impossible. By the time he had managed to get the simplest breakfast together and had washed the face and hands of the old woman and had settled her in her chair, the morning would be half gone and none of his own work done. Jerry would get home just at the early winter nightfall to find the old woman propped in her chair in the cluttered room, which would be lighted by the fire, and Lew hunched down in his chair, staring into the fire, while the blade of his knife, glintingly, caressingly, moved over the leather sole of the shoe on the bad foot. The whole place would stink of burnt grease and stale food, even the living room. Jerry would go back into the kitchen, which was filthy as a sty, and light the lamp, and after a moment in which the nausea and fury mixed in him, and he gazed wildly about at the disorder, he would begin to clean up as well as he could, hoping to finish before his father got back to the house from the evening chores. After several months, Mr. Calhoun gave up and took the cook back. "I don't reckon it saved much, and me as unhandy as I am, and you having to go to school, and Lew not being able to get about good," he had said.

"I didn't have to go to school," Jerry had retorted angrily, why he did not know.

"Sure you did, boy," his father had said, "don't be talking like that. But I don't reckon a few dollars made all that much difference. I'd taken out the telephone and saved something there if it wasn't for Aunt Ursula, her being porely and maybe needing a doctor any time. And it was hard on Callie, letting her go, with her depending on her work up here to get something for her young ones. And the place here the way it was. It was a mistake, and I made it. It was no way for a man to be living. A man ought to live like a man as long as he can, I reckon."

But at her best, Callie was not a good servant, and as the years passed, she grew more and more incompetent. Later, when Jerry was living in town and would drive out to the house for a visit, he might find his father with a broom and a dust pan trying to clean up the living room or the kitchen, or standing over a pan of dishes. "Callie didn't come this morning," his father would explain defensively.

"You ought to fire her and get somebody who would come."

"It ain't exactly her fault," his father would say. "She's old and ailing, and she's been on the place a long time."

"Ben's no good, either. And he never has been. You ought to have got rid of them both, long ago. They've got children, haven't they? They could go to their children."

"It ain't that easy, son," his father would say, lifting a dish with painful care and swaddling it in the drying cloth. "It just ain't that easy, I reckon."

"Well, you ought to get somebody to come in and help her, some young nigger."

"I can't afford it, son. Not and things the way they are."

"I'll pay it."

"No, no, anything you've got free that-away I want to see put on the place. It'll be yours some day. But you"—the old man would be concentrating all his effort on the dish and the tangled, sodden cloth—"you do plenty as it is, and I'm grateful."

But there had been two or three good years, when Jerry was still in high school, the years of the War, good prices and good crops. His father had paid off the obligation on the place, obligations incurred years before; then, in the fall of 1918, he had bought a tract of fifty acres which lay between his place and the river, which had once belonged to him but which he had been forced to sell off before Jerry's birth.

During the years when that strip of bottom had been out of his possession, he would sometimes take a walk in the late summer evenings along the line. "The corn in the bottom is doing right well," he might announce on his return to the house. "That always was good ground for corn. Not better on the river." He was more excited about the purchase than Jerry had ever seen him about anything, not able to sit still that evening, pacing the room and picking up small objects from the mantel shelf or the table and setting them down, going out in the yard, though it was a cold night, to stand by the gate and look at the frosty, brilliantly starred sky or up the empty road. "Maybe I oughtn't done it," he had said. "Maybe I oughtn't. But it always looked like the place was sort of lopsided the way it was—"

"Lopsided," Lew had said, and had snapped the big blade of his knife shut, "like me."

Then, after Lew's cackle of laughter had stopped short, as though bitten off, Mr. Calhoun had resumed: "That bottom strip went with the place. The place lays natural to the river. It come to me from my folks that-away, and I'd like to be a-leaving it that-away. I hate to be running back into debt, just as I get shed of—"

"You paid too durned much for it," Lew had said, "Mr. Astor."

"Maybe so." Then, after a while: "But it looks like a good place is due some corn bottom. Now, don't it?"

On the evening when Gerald Calhoun was released on bail, his father reached the jail some forty-five minutes after Duckfoot Blake had left to get Kahn. Jerry, sitting on the cot as he had sat before, hunching forward, his elbows on his knees, his wrists drooping forward, did not even look up when he first heard the sound of approaching feet. Even when the sound ceased, and he knew that someone stood before the cell, he did not look up until he heard the chink of metal as the key was applied to the lock.

There, beside the man with the key, was his father, wearing jean pants and an old brown wool coat, and a white shirt, crudely starched but very clean, a button missing at the collar but the collar held almost together by the awkward knot of the black tie, which hung below the slight gap of the collar. Mr. Calhoun, holding his black hat in his hand, stood there, waiting for the manipulation of the lock, looking in through the bars, not saying a word. His breath came with a spasmodic heaviness.

Jerry, looking at him, felt, for the moment, nothing, nothing at all. He stared at him, noting with dispassionate clarity every detail of appearance; but the big old man, with the knotted hands clutching the black hat before him, might have been a stranger getting ready to say, "Mister—mister, I was just wondering if you'd—if you might be wanting to buy—" Or getting ready to say, "Mister, I musta got off the road—I was wondering if—"

The door swung open and Mr. Calhoun stepped into the cell, and stood there, as before, regarding his son but not able, yet, to find the words.

Then, after the door had clicked to behind him, he took one step forward, stopped, and with his face gathering itself for the effort, said: "Son." And then, again, said it: "Son."

Until that moment, the moment when the big old man said, "Son," and again, "Son," Jerry Calhoun had not seen his own situation as related to anything in the world except himself. His confusion, his apathy, his grief, his bitterness, and finally, his single flash of triumphant and releasing ferocity at the thought of Bogan Murdock—Bogan Murdock jailed, Bogan Murdock seized and flung into a cell, Bogan Murdock ruined—had been, simply, his own being, almost absolute in themselves, lacking relationship even to the events and persons of the tangible world which had caused his own situation. For those events and persons, from the time when he had opened a newspaper and seen the photograph of Sue Murdock above the savagely laconic statement *Slain Girl*, had been as shadowy as frosted breath on the air. There had only been the flow of feeling which was himself.

But now, with his father's voice, his father was real, and demanding, demanding to break in upon that privacy of pain, which was himself, in which, now, he was almost jealously, preciously, at home. He looked at his father's face above the white shirt, the buttonless collar with the wisp of thread, the twisted tie. Looking at that wisp of thread, he saw with a horrible precision his father leaning over the open drawer, fumbling for the white shirt, dropping it in his haste, fumbling with the buttons, tearing off the button, his big knotted swollen hands shaking and his breath coming hard. And that scene was there before his eyes clearer than reality, and it was the last indignity, the last assault upon him, the last betrayal. No—it was more—it—

"I came as soon as I could, son," he was saying. "I saw the paper, and soon as I could, soon as I could get hitched up."

—it was more, it was the cause, the very cause of everything, of everything that had happened to him, of Sue Murdock dead, of himself in jail, of everything. And with that blaze of conviction and accusation in him, he stared at the man there before him, who was saying, "Why, son, why didn't you let me know—you ought to let me know, son, you ought—"

With a vindictive delight, he cut in, his voice rising in triumph: "You couldn't have done a thing—not a thing. And you can't do anything now!"

"Maybe not, maybe not, son—maybe I couldn't done a thing, but I could come. And they'd let me in—they let me in now and it late and against the rules, but I told them how I'd come a long piece, and—"

"Oh, God damn it, God damn it!" Jerry burst out, and watched the surprise come on the big, sagging, clay-colored face, as though it had been slapped, and then saw the surprise not there, the face as it had been, looking down at him, saying, "Son."

Mr. Calhoun took a step forward toward the cot.

Oh, God, if he puts his hands on me, if he touches me, Jerry thought, and his muscles went tense as though to brace himself, for that was the one thing, the last thing, which he could not bear.

But Mr. Calhoun did not touch him. He took that single step toward the cot, then stopped, and merely looked at his son, not saying a word.

Then Duckfoot Blake was in the corridor, waiting for the man to unlock, and saying, "Well, Jerry, let's get going. It's all O.K." Then, inside, to Mr. Calhoun: "I'm mighty glad to know you. Jerry's been a buddy of mine for a long time. Yeah, I'm glad you turned up to help me take a hand with that loafer over there. Gawd, look at him, ain't he a sight?" And he wagged a long brittle forefinger toward the cot, where Jerry sat.

Duckfoot drove them out to the Calhoun place, in his car. He had proposed that they spend the night at his house, but Mr. Calhoun had said: "I'm much obliged, Mr. Blake, and I know Jerry's obliged, but I reckon we ought to be getting on home. You know how 'tis on a farm, you got to be getting home."

Home, Jerry had echoed in his mind, *home,* and had seen Lew's face and Aunt Ursula's face and his father's, and had felt the wild impulse to run across the square—for they were standing in front of the jail then —and run down the street under the murky lights, and keep on running, out where it was dark, where there wouldn't be anybody, where they would leave him alone, where everybody, everybody, would leave him alone.

So, over Mr. Calhoun's protest, they went in Duckfoot's car. Mr. Calhoun had said that he couldn't leave his horse and buggy standing out in the street all night. He said it used to be a man could put his horse in a livery stable, but he didn't know as there was one for a man now. But Duckfoot went to the telephone in the all-night restaurant on the square, and got hold of a Negro he knew to get the horse and bring him on out in the morning. They didn't even have to wait for the Negro to come to the square, for the man at the restaurant said he'd attend to it. Duckfoot knew the man at the restaurant, too. Duckfoot knew everybody.

Jerry sat in the back seat of Duckfoot's old car, and his father in front. They rattled across the square, over the tangle of streetcar tracks, out through the wholesale district, out through the suburbs, where the few street lights showed the huddled, paintless houses. There were no lights in the houses. Then they were in the country. On both sides, the fields, stripped, empty, dark, heaved toward the sky. The sky was starless, streaked with dark clouds. The woods beyond the fields were darker than the sky.

Duckfoot was talking to Mr. Calhoun. He was telling him some preposterous, endless tale of the time when he had been an auctioneer at a jewelry joint. He would release the wheel and gesture, and the car would swerve; then he would seize the wheel in the nick of time, and his high, nasal voice would go on and on. But Jerry did not follow the words. His body swayed and lurched with the motion of the car.

They turned off the highway at last, up the lane to the Calhoun place. He observed with some surprise that the house was white now, solid and serene among the leafless trees, under the dark sky. There was a new fence, a white fence. As the car drew up to the gate, he saw that the dead gum by the gate had been cut out. Even the stump had been dug out and the hole sodded over, he could make out even in that light. With a sardonic self-irony, he realized that everything was as he had planned to make it—oh, he had been going to paint the house white some day, oh, he had been going to put up a fence, oh, he had been going to take out that gum, he had been going to do all that when he got a little extra change. Oh, he had been going to fix up the Old Calhoun Place, and drive out Saturday afternoons and look at his herd of pure-bred Herefords—sure, he was going to have them, sure—and see how his setters were doing and maybe go down across the pasture beyond the wood lot, with a gun across his arm and a dog skirting the sage and some friend from town beside him, and knock down a couple of quail, and go back up to the house and sit in front of the fire with a glass in his hand and talk to that anonymous man from town whom he had brought out to the Old Calhoun Place. And where would Lew and Aunt Ursula have been? Gone—dead, perhaps—not in the picture. He had never said to himself, *After they are dead.* They simply were not in the picture. There was no place in the picture for them. Had there been a place in the picture for his father? The question flashed through his mind with its obscene candor. But he refused the question—he hadn't asked the question, nobody had asked the question, it was no question and nobody had a right to ask it. And the spasm of rejection in his mind transmitted itself to his limbs, so that he twitched as at the start of a rigor.

There was his father standing in the road now. So he got out and followed his father and Duckfoot through the white gate and up the brick walk to the glimmeringly white mass of the house beyond the dark trees.

Old Mr. Calhoun fumbled with his keys, found the right one, finally opened the door. "Just a minute," he said, "just a minute and I'll get some light."

The room was almost black dark. Jerry could see a few red chinks on the hearth, where Lew had banked the fire, red coals showing where the ashes had dropped off the chunks of wood. Mr. Calhoun struck a match, peered about with the tiny flame held up, and located the lamp. "We just never got the electricity turned back on since we got back," he said, in a voice of careful explanation, not apology. "And coal oil not costing nothing to speak of."

As the wick caught, the rays of the lamp flickered on the pale walls and on the high white ceiling; then steadied. Jerry stood by the door, staring at the clean room, which was so big and bare, dwarfing and devouring the old pieces of furniture, stripping them of their old meanings and functions, leaving them clearly and pitifully what they were, junk. His gaze traveled slowly around the room, which was familiar and yet so treacherously unfamiliar now, as in a dream.

"Shut the door, Jerry," his father was saying, "and I'll stir up the fire. And you, Mr. Blake, you just have a chair, and I'll get some coffee on. It's a ways for you to be going back in, and the air's got some nip."

"I'm afraid it's no sale, Mr. Calhoun," Duckfoot said. "I'd sure like to have a cup and jaw a little, but it's late. How about fixing me a quart when I come out tomorrow or next day? That is—" he continued, and turned to Jerry, "if you want me to stop by your apartment and bring you anything out here?"

"You might get me some clothes," Jerry said.

"Sure," Duckfoot said, "I'll get your duds. I'll bring you your crate, too, if you'll give me the keys. Then you can drive me as far as the car line when I go back to town."

Jerry took the key pad from his pocket and detached his car keys and held them in his hand.

"You figure on staying out to supper, Mr. Blake," his father was saying, "when you come out with Jerry's stuff. We'd be proud to have you."

"Sure thing," Duckfoot said, and reached over and lifted the keys from Jerry's hand as though he were taking them off a shelf, "sure thing, Mr. Calhoun, and I'll plan on having an appetite. But now I got to shove."

Mr. Calhoun crossed the space toward Duckfoot, stood ponderously in front of him, seemed about to speak, then spoke. "Mr. Blake," he said, "Mr. Blake—you don't know how me and Jerry feel—what you did—" And he thrust out his hand.

"Aw, for Christ's sake," Duckfoot said, almost fretfully. Then he seized the hand and shook it, dropped it suddenly, and said: "I got to shove."

"I'll see you, pal," he called back to Jerry as he stepped out of the door.

Mr. Calhoun had got to the door too late to open it for the guest. Now he held it ajar and looked out. After a moment Jerry heard the sound of the motor, then the grinding of gears. Mr. Calhoun closed the door. He crossed to the hearth, and spread his hands over the embers, which gave forth a little flame now. He seemed to be studying the flame.

Jerry still stood near the door. He stood there like a stranger who, neglected, waits to be asked his errand, and looked at the humped-over figure above the embers and the small flame. That figure would straighten up in a minute, it would straighten up and turn its face toward him. He knew that. He became aware of the ticking of a clock.

He listened to the clock, and knew that in a minute that big, sagging, creased old face would turn toward him, not in accusation, not in rancor, not even in despair, but simply in recognition and acceptance, which would be most horrible of all. For against that there could be no defense.

Mr. Calhoun turned from the fire. "I reckon it's about time we went to bed, son," he said.

Jerry did not answer.

"You can sleep in your room, son," the man said. "The bed's not made up, but there's sheets and stuff up there."

"I'll make it up," Jerry said, and started to move across the room.

"Naw," his father objected, "naw, I'll help you," and followed him into the hall, and up the stairs, carrying the lamp, which threw Jerry's shadow enormously up the stairs ahead of him.

Jerry laid his hand on the iron latch, and in the light the room leaped from the chaos of darkness to its proper proportions, the pale flowered walls, strange to him, the white ceiling here as below, the wide bare floor. The panes of the windows gleamed blackly, with the faintest iridescence, like a film of oil on black water, like a film laid over the coiling immeasurable depth of darkness outside. The single flame of the lamp was reflected winkingly in the black glass.

Mr. Calhoun set the lamp down on the mantel shelf, over the cold black square of the fireplace. Then he went to the walnut wardrobe, which seemed to lean perilously out from the flowered wall. The door of the wardrobe stuck; then, under Mr. Calhoun's uncertain fingers, gave raspingly. He took out two folded sheets, and a blanket and a patchwork quilt, on which the colors had faded and run.

He stood on one side of the bed and Jerry on the other, and they spread the first sheet over the uneven mattress. Then the other sheet, then the blanket and quilt.

Mr. Calhoun went back to the wardrobe, and for some moments, leaning over, fumbled in the interior gloom. Then he straightened up, shaking his head. "A pillow slip," he said. "It looks like I don't find any pillow slip." He stood there, seemingly lost in indecision, marveling and sad, holding in his hand a piece of cloth which was not a pillow slip. "It looks like there'd be a pillow slip," he said. He took a step toward the door. "Maybe," he said, "maybe I could—"

"Let it go," Jerry ordered, and seized a pillow from the chair where the two were piled, and thrust it under the lower sheet. Then he straightened up, and stood by the bed, which was ready.

Mr. Calhoun looked at the bed, then at Jerry, and moved a couple of steps toward the door. "I reckon I better let you get on to bed," he said, but, for the moment, he did not move, looking at his son, who stood by the bed, on the side toward the door, and did not answer. Mr. Calhoun seemed about to approach him; then, as though answering the unphrased impulse in himself, said: "Naw, naw—you better get on to bed, son."

He turned to the door, reached it, and laid his hand on the latch. He opened the door, and about to go out, hesitated on the threshold, again looking at his son's face. "Don't you take on and fret, son. Mr. Blake—" He paused, then continued, "Mr. Blake said he figured it would be all right. It's gonna be all right, son."

"All right, all right," Jerry uttered. "What the hell does he know about it?"

"You go to bed, son," Mr. Calhoun said. "It's gonna be all right." Then he closed the door, and Jerry could hear him feeling his way down the stairs.

"All right," Jerry repeated out loud, bitterly, to the closed door. What the hell did Duckfoot know about it? What the hell did his father know?

He began to undress, flinging his clothes down across the foot of the bed, shivering a little as the air struck his bare flesh. When he had stripped to his underwear, he walked across, barefoot, to the fireplace, and blew out the lamp. Then, in the darkness which was absolute in the moment before his eyes had adjusted themselves, he felt his way to the bed, and laid himself down. The springs creaked painfully with his weight.

The springs had always made that sound when he got into this bed and shifted his body to find the position for comfort, always, ever since he could remember. Then, thinking that, he seemed to be sinking, not into the old mattress, which accepted his body now as it had years ago, but into those years themselves, into the self he had been. What had he been? And what did he share with that Jerry Calhoun who, long ago, had lain here?

He could make out objects now in the gloom—the chair and the table where once he had leaned over his books on Sunday afternoons when his father had come up to sit and watch with the absorbing, pitiless patience, the wardrobe, which was a pile of blackness against the pale paper of the wall. The objects were there in the same old places, waiting, and he had come. Under the paper there was the old wall, secret, aware, with eyes to see the old Jerry Calhoun under the new. And here he was, and they had received him, as the old self had received him, as the mattress had received him, as the past had received him, as he was drawn back into Aunt Ursula, and Lew, and his father, and the mother he had never known, and all the nameless people who were dead. Here he was, and the mattress was like a quicksand into which he would sink, imperceptibly but steadily, forever, drawn down by the number- less, nameless fingers that plucked feebly but inexorably, ceaselessly.

He lay rigid, as though any motion, any struggle, might plunge him deeper. Oh, he had come back. He had come back, all right. *All right, all right,* he thought, and thought how his father had said it would be all right.

All right, all right—what right had his father to say "all right"?

He had stood by the door and had said "All right," and he couldn't even know what *all right* was, for nothing had ever been all right for him, for he had always failed, the cord broke in his hands, the strap twisted in his fingers, the nail bent under his hammer, the dish slipped from his grasp. And he saw his father as he had seen him so many times, leaning over some small thing, some task too precise, breathing heavily, with the sweat on his face; and the old sense of outrage and fury started in him. *All right, all right!* Nothing had ever been all right, and it wouldn't be now, and the old man would be alone in the house, alone with the old woman and Lew, and his son gone to prison and disgraced. Oh, that was part of the picture, that was the perfect ending. Thinking that, Jerry suddenly felt a kind of grim glee, a vindication, a vengeance.

He had come back. He had come back to have the old man stand there and say: "It's gonna be all right." He had come back to find out what he knew now. He had come back to lie in the old bed, in that dark which you couldn't tell from the old darknesses. He had left it for other beds, for other nights. He had gone a long way to come back to it. Something in the old self which had lain here had driven him out, but if you are going to come back, why do you leave?

What had driven him out? What had he wanted? Oh, the crowd had cheered in the autumn sunlight and the band had played and people had slapped him on the back and Bogan Murdock had smiled and money had been in his pocket and Sue Murdock—Sue Murdock had stood in the middle of her apartment that last night and had looked at him and had uttered that small, throaty cry, and he had known that she loved him. He had had those things and he had wanted those things. He had wanted so many things and had had all of them, and had had none of them, for what you had came wrong or too soon or too late, or it wore another face, and your three wishes always came true but the last undid all the rest, and you were where you had begun.

You get your wishes, all right, every one. You wanted to fix up the place that your great-great-uncle had built. It was the Old Calhoun Place. To paint it white and put on new shutters. To paper the walls and get the grime off the floors—oh, what beautiful floors, oh, yes, the original floors, oh, you don't see ten-inch flooring like that any more. To put up the white fence. To take out the dead gum by the gate. And you had your wish, all right. You came home, and found it all the way you had wanted, but it wasn't yours any more, and you had come in the middle of the night. You came home from jail in the middle of the night.

You didn't come home in the middle of the afternoon and go out to look at your pure-bred Herefords and take your gun and your prize setter and go across the back pasture and knock down a couple of birds and sit by the fire with the glass in your hand and the smiling friend and nobody there but the friend and the nigger with the tray and no Aunt Ursula and no Lew and no—

Had you ever wanted your father dead?

No, you had never said that. You never said that. It's just that he isn't in the room. He is out somewhere. But where is he? Damn it, he just isn't here. Damn it, he's just out somewhere. There's nobody here but me and my friend and the nigger, in this beautiful room in the firelight. He just isn't in right now, that's all. And it's not my fault he's not here.

Why, there he is! Coming in the door. See, there is my father, and your suspicions were completely unjustified, but I'll accept your apology. See, there he is, wearing that beautiful new one-hundred-and-twenty-five-dollar gray suit Larkinson made him in New York and looking unusually well and handsome and carrying his stick and smiling hospitably and looking at me with his fine eyes, which have large black pupils ringed with smoky-blue. I want you to meet my father. Father, this is Mr. ———

But your friend stares at your father and bursts into extraordinary laughter. He laughs and laughs, and the terror grows in you. Then he controls his laughter a little, and points at your father, and says: That isn't your father, that's Bogan Murdock!

And you see that it is not your father. It is not your father at all. Where is your father? You better run, you better run quick and find him. Before they say you killed him. Before the police come and dig in the leaves in the woods and drag the river and look in the old well where you hit the drowning puppy with the brick and pry under the hay in the loft.

Jerry Calhoun heaved himself up in bed, and the springs creaked.

Did I want my father dead? he thought.

And said out loud: "No—no—"

He lay back down on the pillow, thinking, *No, no.*

Did I want my father dead?

No, no, he thought, lying there stiff on the mattress, with his eyes closed, and saw his father's face.

Father, Father—I—I—

Yes, son.

Father, I wanted Aunt Ursula dead.

Yes, son.

I didn't really want to give her the blue shawl, Father.

Yes, son.

I wanted Lew dead.

Yes, son.

Father, I wanted to sit by the fire, and they wouldn't be there—they wouldn't be there—and—and you wouldn't be there—

Yes, son.

I wanted you dead—I wanted you dead, Father—I wanted to sit by the fire—

Yes, son.

You knew? Did you know?

Yes, son.

Oh, Father—

Yes, son.

There was frost on the ground when Mr. Calhoun came out of the kitchen door and moved across the backyard to the woodpile. His feet cut through the white frost and left tracks where the dun color of the frozen mud showed through. He leaned above the woodpile, the breath puffing whitely from his mouth, and began to pick up stove-lengths. After he had placed three in the crook of his arm, he had some difficulty in picking more up, for his balance was bad and his hand was cold and unclever. But he finally managed.

While the fire caught and the water for Aunt Ursula's two eggs came slowly to a boil and her pan of milk began to simmer, he laid places for two on the kitchen table. Then he prepared the tray, broke the two eggs into a cup, poured the hot milk into a bowl, and went to feed the old woman, whom he had already propped up in bed on pillows, swathed to the chin in blankets, whose fire he had risen twice in the night to build, and whose face he had, that morning, already wiped with a cloth dipped in water heated in a kettle at her fireplace.

When he came back, Lew was hunched in a chair drawn up almost into contact with the stove.

"Good morning," Mr. Calhoun said.

"Yeah," Lew said, "ain't it, Mr. Astor?"

Mr. Calhoun put a skillet on the stove and in it two thick slices of shoulder meat. While the meat began to uncongeal and the grease to ooze from it onto the black iron, he broke four eggs into a bowl and stirred them. The odor of coffee was already beginning to drift in the air. The breath of the men now did not show white.

"Do you mind setting the bread on?" Mr. Calhoun asked.

"Naw," Lew said, and lurched up, clumping his foot on the hollow boards. He got a plate of cold biscuits and a pat of butter from the safe. As he leaned to place the objects on the table, he observed the plates there. "Ain't Jerry eating?" he demanded, eying Mr. Calhoun's heavy, curved back.

"He'll eat when he wakes up," Mr. Calhoun said, not turning from the stove.

"Yeah, yeah, he'll eat when he wakes up," Lew mimicked. "Yeah, and what'll he eat? Oh, he'll take a morsel of angel-food cake if you please, and a little peach ice cream."

"Being it's the first night," Mr. Calhoun said apologetically, "I figured I'd just not call him."

"Well, I'll call him," Lew announced, "him laying up there sleeping and it broad day. He ain't in no city now, he—"

"Naw, Lew, naw," Mr. Calhoun repeated steadily, occupied with the bowl, the eggs, the frying meat, "don't be bothering him this morning. Just let him sleep now. Tomorrow morning, that'll be different."

"Him laying up there, and work to do!"

"Tomorrow," Mr. Calhoun said. "Jerry, now—he never was no hand to slack, and the need there."

"Laying up there, laying up there!" Lew exulted bitterly, and swung from the table toward the door, and his boot rattled and clumped in victorious tattoo as he lurched and lunged toward the inner door.

"By God!" Mr. Calhoun uttered in a terrible voice.

In the moment of ensuing silence, Lew, his hand already on the knob, turned to confront the powerful, hulking figure, the working face and unsheathed, baleful eyes, the heavy hand lifted to heaven clutching the iron spoon, from which dripped a gout of egg.

He took his hand, almost surreptitiously, from the knob.

CASS MASTERN'S
WEDDING
RING

Long ago Jack Burden was a graduate student, working for his Ph.D. in American History, in the State University of his native State. This Jack Burden (of whom the present Jack Burden, *Me,* is a legal, biological, and perhaps even metaphysical continuator) lived in a slatternly apartment with two other graduate students, one industrious, stupid, unlucky, and alcoholic, and the other idle, intelligent, lucky, and alcoholic. At least they were alcoholic for a period after the first of the month, when they received the miserable check paid them by the University for their miserable work as assistant teachers. The industry and ill luck of one cancelled out against the idleness and luck of the other and they both amounted to the same thing, and they drank what they could get when they could get it. They drank because they didn't really have the slightest interest in what they were doing now and didn't have the slightest hope for the future. They could not even bear the thought of pushing on to finish their degrees, for that would mean leaving the University (leaving the first-of-the-month drunks, the yammer about "work" and "ideas" in smoke-blind rooms, the girls who staggered slightly and giggled indiscreetly on

Text taken from *Partisan Review,* Vol. 11, Fall 1944; became part of *All the King's Men* (1946).

the dark stairs leading to the apartment) to go to some normal school on a sun-baked cross-roads or a junior college long on Jesus and short on funds, to go to face the stark reality of drudgery and dry-rot and prying eyes and the slow withering of the green wisp of dream which had, like some window-plant in an invalid's room, grown out of a bottle. Only the bottle hadn't had water in it. It had had something which looked like water, smelled like kerosene, and tasted like carbolic acid: one-run corn whisky.

Jack Burden lived with them, in the slatternly apartment among the unwashed dishes in the sink and on the table, the odor of stale tobacco smoke, the dirty shirts and underwear piled in corners. He even took a relish in the squalor, in the privilege of letting a last crust of buttered toast fall to the floor to lie undisturbed until the random heel should grind it into the mud-colored carpet, in the spectacle of the fat roach moving across the cracked linoleum of the bathroom floor while he steamed in the tub. Once he had brought his mother to the apartment for tea, and she had sat on the edge of the overstuffed chair, holding a cracked cup and talking with a brittle and calculated charm out of a face which was obviously being held in shape by a profound exercise of will. She saw a roach venture out from the kitchen door. She saw one of Jack Burden's friends crush an ant on the inner lip of the sugar bowl and flick the carcass from his finger. The nail of the finger itself was not very clean. But she kept right on delivering the charm, out of the rigid face. He had to say that for her.

But afterwards, as they walked down the street, she had said: "Why do you live like that?"

"It's what I'm built for, I reckon," Jack Burden said.

"With those people," she said.

"They're all right," he said, and wondered if they were, and wondered if he was.

His mother didn't say anything for a minute, making a sharp, bright clicking on the pavement with her heels as she walked along, holding her small shoulders trimly back, carrying her famished-cheeked, blue-eyed, absolutely innocent face slightly lifted to the pulsing sunset world of April like a very expensive present the world ought to be glad even to have a look at. And back then, fifteen years ago, it was still something to look at, too. Sometimes Jack Burden (who was *Me* or what *Me* was fifteen years ago) would be proud to go into a place with her, and have people stare the way they would, and just for a minute he would be happy. But there is a lot more to everything than just walking into a hotel lobby or restaurant.

Walking along beside him, she said meditatively: "That dark-haired one—if he'd get cleaned up—he wouldn't be bad-looking."

"That's what a lot of other women think," Jack Burden said, and suddenly felt a nauseated hatred of the dark-haired one, the one who had killed the ant on the sugar bowl, who had the dirty nails. But he had to go on, something in him made him go on: "Yes, and a lot of them don't even care about cleaning him up. They'll take him like he is. He's the great lover of the apartment. He put the sag in the springs of that divan we got."

"Don't be vulgar," she said, because she definitely did not like what is known as vulgarity in conversation.

"It's the truth," he said.

She didn't answer, and her heels did the bright clicking. Then she said: "If he'd throw those awful clothes away—and get something decent."

"Yeah," Jack Burden said, "on his seventy-five dollars a month."

She looked at him now, down at his clothes. "Yours are pretty awful, too," she said.

"Are they?" Jack Burden demanded.

"I'll send you money for some decent clothes," she said.

A few days later the check came and a note telling him to get a "couple of decent suits and accessories." The check was for two hundred and fifty dollars. He did not even buy a necktie. But he and the two other men in the apartment had a wonderful blow-out, which lasted for five days, and as a result of which the industrious and unlucky one lost his job and the idle and lucky one got too sociable and, despite his luck, contracted what is quaintly known as a social disease. But nothing happened to Jack Burden, for nothing ever happened to Jack Burden, who was invulnerable. Perhaps that was the curse of Jack Burden: he was invulnerable.

So, as I have said, Jack Burden lived in the slatternly apartment with the two other graduate students, for even after being fired the unlucky, industrious one still lived in the apartment. He simply stopped paying anything but he stayed. He borrowed money for cigarettes. He sullenly ate the food the others brought in and cooked. He lay around during the day, for there was no reason to be industrious any more, ever again. Once at night, Jack Burden woke up and thought he heard the sound of sobs from the living room, where the unlucky, industrious one slept on a wall-bed. Then one day the unlucky, industrious one was not there. They never did know where he had gone, and they never heard from him again.

But before that they lived in the apartment, in an atmosphere of brotherhood and mutual understanding. They had this in common: they were all hiding. The difference was in what they were hiding from. The two others were hiding from the future, from the day when they would get degrees and leave the University. Jack Burden, however, was hiding from the present. The other two took refuge in the present. Jack Burden took refuge in the past. The other two sat in the living room and argued and drank or played cards or read, but Jack Burden was sitting, as like as not, back in his bedroom before a little pine table, with the notes and papers and books before him, scarcely hearing the voices. He might come out and take a drink or take a hand of cards or argue or do any of the other things they did, but what was real was back in that bedroom on the pine table.

What was back in the bedroom on the pine table?

A large packet of letters, eight tattered black-bound account books tied together with faded red tape, a photograph, 5 × 8 inches, mounted on cardboard and stained in its lower half by water, and a plain gold ring, man-sized, with some engraving in it, on a loop of string. The past. Or that part of the past which had gone by the name of Cass Mastern.

Cass Mastern was one of Jack Burden's father's two maternal uncles, a brother of his mother, Lavinia Mastern, a great-uncle to Jack Burden. The other great-uncle was named Gilbert Mastern, who died in 1914, at the age of ninety-four or five, rich, a builder of railroads, a sitter on boards of directors, and left the packet of letters, the black account books, and the photograph, and a great deal of money to a grandson (and not a penny to Jack Burden). Some ten years later the heir of Gilbert Mastern, recollecting that his cousin Jack Burden, with whom he had no personal acquaintance, was a student of history, or something of the sort, sent him the packet of letters, the account books, and the photograph, asking if he, Jack Burden, thought that the enclosures were of any "financial interest," since he, the heir, had heard that libraries sometimes would pay a "fair sum for old papers and ante-bellum relics and keep-sakes." Jack Burden replied that, since Cass Mastern had been of no historical importance as an individual, it was doubtful that any library would pay more than a few dollars, if anything, for the material, and asked for instructions as to the disposition of the parcel. The heir replied that under the circumstances Jack Burden might keep the things for "sentimental reasons."

So Jack Burden made the acquaintance of Cass Mastern, his great-uncle, who had died in 1864 at a military hospital in Atlanta, who had been only a heard but forgotten name to him, and who was the pair of dark, wide-set, deep eyes which burned out of the photograph, through the dinginess and dust and across more than fifty years. The eyes, which were Cass Mastern, stared out of a long, bony face, but a young face with full lips above a rather thin, curly black beard. The lips did not seem to belong to that bony face and the burning eyes.

The young man in the picture, standing visible from the thighs up, wore a loose-fitting, shapeless jacket, too large in the collar, short in the sleeves, to show strong wrists and bony hands clasped at the waist. The thick dark hair, combed sweepingly back from the high brow, came down long and square-cut, after the fashion of time, place, and class, almost to brush the collar of the coarse, hand-me-down-looking jacket, which was the jacket of an infantryman in the Confederate Army.

But everything in the picture, in contrast with the dark, burning eyes, seemed accidental. That jacket, however, was not accidental. It was worn as the result of calculation and anguish, in pride and self-humiliation, in the conviction that it would be worn in death. But death was not to be that quick and easy. It was to come slow and hard, in a stinking hospital in Atlanta. The last letter in the packet was not in Cass Mastern's hand. Lying in the hospital with his rotting wound, he dictated his farewell letter to his brother, Gilbert Mastern. The letter, and the last of the account books in which Cass Mastern's journal was kept, were eventually sent back home to Mississippi, and Cass Mastern was buried somewhere in Atlanta, nobody had ever known where.

It was, in a sense, proper that Cass Mastern—in the gray jacket, sweat-stiffened, and prickly like a hair shirt, which it was for him at the same time that it was the insignia of a begrudged glory—should have gone back to Georgia to rot slowly to death. For he had been born in Georgia, he and Gilbert Mastern and Lavinia Mastern, Jack Burden's grandmother, in the red hills up toward Tennessee. "I was born," the first page of the first volume of the journal said, "in a log cabin in north Georgia, in circumstances of poverty, and if in later years I have lain soft and have supped from silver, may the Lord not let die in my heart the knowledge of frost and of coarse diet. For all men come naked into the world, and in prosperity 'man is prone to evil as the sparks fly upward.' " The lines were written when Cass was a student at Transylvania College, up in Kentucky, after what he called his "darkness and trouble" had given place to the peace of God. For the journal began with an account of the "darkness and trouble"—which was a perfectly real trouble, with a dead man and a live woman and long nail-scratches down Cass Mastern's bony face. "I write this down," he said in the journal, "with what truthfulness a sinner may attain unto that if ever pride is in me, of flesh or spirit, I can peruse these pages and know with shame what evil has been in me, and may be in me, for who knows what breeze may blow upon the charred log and fan up flame again?"

The impulse to write the journal sprang from the "darkness and trouble," but Cass Mastern apparently had a systematic mind, and so he went back to the beginning, to the log cabin in the red hills of Georgia. It was the older brother, Gilbert, some fifteen years older than Cass, who lifted the family from the log cabin. Gilbert, who had run away from home when a boy and gone West to Mississippi, was well on the way to being "a cotton-snob" by the time he was twenty-seven or eight, that is, by 1850. The penniless and no doubt hungry boy walking barefoot onto the black soil of Mississippi was to become, ten or twelve years later, the master sitting the spirited roan stallion (its name was Powhatan—that from the journal) in front of the white veranda. How did Gilbert make his first dollar? Did he cut the throat of a traveller in the canebrake? Did he black boots at an inn? It is not recorded. But he made his fortune, and sat on the white veranda and voted Whig. After the war when the white veranda was a pile of ashes and the fortune was gone, it was not surprising that Gilbert, who had made one fortune with his bare hands, out of the very air, could now, with all his experience and cunning and hardness (the hardness harder now for the four years of riding and short rations and disappointment), snatch another one, much greater than the first. If in later years he ever remembered his brother Cass and took out the last letter, the one dictated in the hospital in Atlanta, he must have mused over it with a tolerant irony. For it said: "Remember me, but without grief. If one of us is lucky, it is I. I shall have rest and I hope in the mercy of the Everlasting and in His blessed election. But you, my dear brother, are condemned to eat bread in bitterness and build on the place where the charred embers and ashes are and to make bricks without straw and to suffer in the ruin and guilt of our dear land and in the common guilt of man. In the next bed to me there is a young man from Ohio. He is dying. His moans and curses and prayers are not different from any others to be heard in this tabernacle of pain. He marched hither in his guilt as I in mine. And in the guilt of his land. May a common Salvation lift us both from the dust. And, dear brother, I pray God to give you strength for what is to come." Gilbert must have smiled, looking back, for he had eaten little bread in bitterness. He had had his own kind of strength. By 1870 he was again well-off. By 1875 he was rich. By 1880 he had a fortune, was living in New York, was a name, a thick, burly man, slow of movement, with a head like a block of bare granite. He had lived out of one world into another. Perhaps he was even more at home in the new than in the old. Or perhaps the Gilbert Masterns are always at home in any world. As the Cass Masterns are never at home in any world.

But to return: Jack Burden came into possession of the papers from the grandson of Gilbert Mastern. When the time came for him to select a subject for his dissertation for his Ph.D., his professor suggested that he edit the journal and letters of Cass Mastern, and write a biographical essay, a social study based on those and other materials. So Jack Burden began his first journey into the past.

It seemed easy at first. It was easy to reconstruct the life of the log cabin in the red hills. There were the first letters back from Gilbert, after he had begun his rise (Jack Burden managed to get possession of the other Gilbert Mastern papers of the period before the Civil War). There was the known pattern of that life, gradually altered toward comfort as Gilbert's affluence was felt at that distance. Then, in one season, the mother and father died, and Gilbert returned to burst, no doubt, upon Cass and Lavinia as an unbelievable vision, a splendid imposter in black broadcloth, varnished boots, white linen, heavy gold ring. He put Lavinia in a school in Atlanta, bought her trunks of dresses, and kissed her goodbye. ("Could you not have taken me with you, dear Brother Gilbert? I would have been ever so dutiful and affectionate a sister," so she wrote to him, in the copybook hand, in brown ink, in a language not her own, a language of schoolroom propriety. "May I not come to you now? Is there no little task which I—" But Gilbert had other plans. When the time came for her to appear in his house she would be ready.) But he took Cass with him, a hobbledehoy now wearing black and mounted on a blooded mare.

At the end of three years Cass was not a hobbledehoy. He had spent three years of monastic rigor at Valhalla, Gilbert's house, under the tuition of a Mr. Lawson and of Gilbert himself. From Gilbert he learned the routine of plantation management. From Mr. Lawson, a tubercular and vague young man from Princeton, New Jersey, he learned some geometry, some Latin, and a great deal of Presbyterian theology. He liked the books, and once Gilbert (so the journal said) stood in the doorway and watched him bent over the table and then said: "At least you may be good for *that*."

But he was good for more than that. When Gilbert gave him a small plantation, he managed it for two years with such astuteness (and such luck, for both season and market conspired in his behalf) that at the end of the time he could repay Gilbert a substantial part of the purchase price. Then he went, or was sent, to Transylvania. It was Gilbert's idea. He came into the house on Cass's plantation one night to find Cass at his books. He walked across the room to the table where the books lay, by which Cass now stood. Gilbert stretched out his arm and tapped the open book with his riding crop. "You might make something out of that," he said. The journal reported that, but it did not report what book it was that Gilbert's riding crop tapped. It is not important what book it was. Or perhaps it is important, for something in our mind, in our imagination, wants to know the fact. We see the red, square, strong hand ("My brother is strong-made and florid") protruding from the white cuff, grasping the crop which in that grasp looks fragile like a twig. We see the flick of the little leather loop on the open page, a flick brisk, not quite contemptuous, but we cannot make out the page.

In any case, it probably was not a book on theology, for it seems doubtful that Gilbert, in such a case, would have used the phrase "make something out of that." It might have been a page of the Latin poets, however, for Gilbert would have discovered that, in small doses, they went well with politics or the law. So Transylvania College it was to be, suggested, it developed, by Gilbert's neighbor and friend, Mr. Davis, Mr. Jefferson Davis, who had once been a student there. Mr. Davis had studied Greek.

At Transylvania, in Lexington, Cass discovered pleasure. "I discovered that there is an education for vice as well as for virtue, and I learned what was to be learned from the gaming table, the bottle, and the racecourse, and from the illicit sweetness of the flesh." He had come out of the poverty of the cabin and the monastic regime of Valhalla and the responsibilities of his own little plantation; and he was tall and strong and, to judge from the photograph, well favored, with the burning dark eyes. It was no wonder that he "discovered pleasure"—or that pleasure discovered him. For, though the journal does not say so, in the events leading up to the "darkness and trouble," Cass seems to have been, in the beginning at least, the pursued rather than the pursuer.

The pursuer is referred to in the journal as "She" and "Her." But I learned the name. "She" was Annabelle Trice, Mrs. Duncan Trice, and Mr. Duncan Trice was a prosperous young banker of Lexington, Kentucky, who was an intimate of Cass Mastern and apparently one of those who led him into the paths of pleasure. I learned the name by going back to the files of the Lexington newspapers for the middle 1850's to locate the story of a death. It was the death of Mr. Duncan

Trice. In the newspaper it was reported as an accident. Duncan Trice had shot himself by accident, the newspaper said, while cleaning a pair of pistols. One of the pistols, already cleaned, lay on the couch where he had been sitting, in his library, at the time of the accident. The other, the lethal instrument, had fallen to the floor. I had known, from the journal, the nature of the case, and when I had located the special circumstances, I had learned the identity of "She." Mr. Trice, the newspaper said, was survived by his widow, née Annabelle Puckett, of Washington, D. C.

Shortly after Cass had come to Lexington, Annabelle Trice met him. Duncan Trice brought him home, for he had received a letter from Mr. Davis, recommending the brother of his good friend and neighbor, Mr. Gilbert Master. (Duncan Trice had come to Lexington from southern Kentucky, where his own father had been a friend of Samuel Davis, the father of Jefferson, when Samuel lived at Fairview and bred racers.) So Duncan Trice brought the tall boy home, who was no longer a hobbledehoy, and set him on a sofa and thrust a glass into his hand and called in his pretty husky-voiced wife, of whom he was so proud, to greet the stranger. "When she first entered the room, in which the shades of approaching twilight were gathering though the hour for the candles to be lit had scarcely come, I thought that her eyes were black, and the effect was most striking, her hair being of such a fairness. I noticed, too, how softly she trod and with a gliding motion which, though she was perhaps of a little less than moderate stature, gave an impression of regal dignity—

> *et avertens rosea cervice refulsit*
> *ambrosiaeque comae divinum vertice odorem*
> *spiravere, pedes vestis defluxit ad imos,*
> *et vera incessu patuit dea.*

So the Mantuan said, when Venus appeared and the true goddess was revealed by her gait. She came into the room and was the true goddess as revealed in her movement, and was, but for Divine Grace (if such be granted to a parcel of corruption such as I), my true damnation. She gave me her hand and spoke with a tingling huskiness which made me think of rubbing my hand upon a soft deep-piled cloth, like velvet, or upon a fur. It would not have been called a musical voice such as is generally admired. I know that, but I can only set down what effect it worked upon my own organs of hearing."

Was she beautiful? Well, Cass set down a very conscientious description of every feature and proportion, a kind of tortured inventory, as though in the midst of the "darkness and trouble," at the very moment of his agony and repudiation, he had to take one last backward look even at the risk of being turned into the pillar of salt. "Her face was not large though a little given to fullness. Her mouth was strong but the lips were red and moist and seemed to be slightly parted or about to part themselves. The chin was short and firmly moulded. Her skin was of a great whiteness, it seemed then before the candles were lit, but afterwards I was to see that it had a bloom of color upon it. Her hair, which was in a remarkable abundance and of great fairness, was drawn back from her face and worn in large coils low down to the neck. Her waist was very small, and her breasts, which seemed naturally high and round and full, were the higher for the corsetting. Her dress, of a dark blue silk, I remember, was cut low to the very downward curve of the shoulders, and in the front showed how the breasts were lifted like twin orbs."

Cass described her that way. He admitted that her face was not beautiful. "Though agreeable in its proportions," he added. But the hair was beautiful, and "of an astonishing softness, upon your hand softer and finer than your thought of silk." So even in that moment, in the midst of the "darkness and trouble," the recollection intrudes into the journal of how that abundant, fair hair had slipped across his fingers. "But," he added, "her beauty was her eyes."

He had remarked how, when she first came in, into the shadowy room, her eyes had seemed black. But he had been mistaken, he was to discover, and that discovery was the first step toward his undoing. After the greeting ("she greeted me with great simplicity and courtesy and bade me again take my seat"), she remarked on how dark the room was and how the autumn always came to take one unawares. Then she touched a bell-pull and a negro boy entered. "She commanded him to bring light and to mend the fire, which was sunk to ash, or near so. He came back presently with a seven-branched candlestick which he put upon the table back of the couch on which I sat. He struck a lucifer but she said 'Let me light the candles.' I remember it as if yesterday. I was sitting on the couch. I had turned my head idly to watch her light the candles. The little table was between us. She leaned over the candles and applied the lucifer to the wicks, one after another. She was leaning over, and I saw how the corset lifted her breasts together, but because she was leaning the eyelids shaded her eyes from my sight. Then she raised her head a little and looked straight at me over the new candle flames, and I saw all at once that her eyes were not black. They were blue, but a blue so deep that I can only compare it to the color of the night sky in autumn when the weather is clear and there is no moon and the stars have just well come out. And I had not known how large they were. I remember saying that to myself with perfect clearness, 'I had not known how large they were,' several times, slowly, like a man marvelling. Then I knew that I was blushing and I felt my tongue dry like ashes in my mouth and I was in the manly state.

"I can see perfectly clearly the expression on her face even now, but I cannot interpret it. Sometimes I have thought of it as having a smiling hidden in it, but I cannot be sure. (I am only sure of this: that man is never safe and damnation is ever at hand, O God and my Redeemer!) I sat there, one hand clenched upon my knee and the other holding an empty glass, and I felt that I could not breathe. Then she said to her husband, who stood in the room behind me, 'Duncan, do you see that Mr. Mastern is in need of refreshment?'"

The year passed. Cass, who was a good deal younger than Duncan Trice, and as a matter of fact several years younger than Annabelle Trice, became a close companion of Duncan Trice and learned much from him, for Duncan Trice was rich, fashionable, clever, and high-spirited ("much given to laughter and full-blooded"). Duncan Trice led Cass to the bottle, the gaming table, and the racecourse, but not to "the illicit sweetness of the flesh." Duncan Trice was passionately and single-mindedly devoted to his wife. ("When she came into a room, his eyes would fix upon her without shame, and I have seen her avert her face and blush for the boldness of his glance when company was present. But I think that it was done by him unawares, his partiality for her was so great.") No, the other young men, members of the Trice circle, led Cass first to the "illicit sweetness." But despite the new interests and gratifications, Cass could work at his books. There was even time for that, for he had great strength and endurance.

So the year passed. He had been much in the Trice house, but no word beyond the "words of merriment and civility" had passed between him and Annabelle Trice. In June, there was a dancing party at the house of some friend of Duncan Trice. Duncan Trice, his wife, and Cass happened to stroll at some moment into the garden and to sit in a little arbor, which was covered with a jasmine vine. Duncan Trice returned to the house to get punch for the three of them, leaving Annabelle and Cass seated side by side in the arbor. Cass commented on the sweetness of the scent of jasmine. All at once, she burst out ("her voice low-pitched and with its huskiness, but in a vehemence which astonished me"), "Yes, yes, it is too sweet. It is suffocating. I shall suffocate." And she laid her right hand, with the fingers spread, across the bare swell of her bosom above the pressure of the corset.

"Thinking her taken by some sudden illness," Cass recorded in the journal, "I asked if she were faint. She said no, in a very low, husky voice. Nevertheless I rose, with the expressed intention of getting a glass of water for her. Suddenly she said, quite harshly and to my amazement, because of her excellent courtesy, 'Sit down, sit down, I don't want water!' So somewhat distressed in mind that unwittingly I might have offended, I sat down. I looked across the garden where in the light of the moon several couples promenaded down the paths between the low hedges. I could hear the sound of her breathing beside me. It was disturbed and irregular. All at once she said, 'How old are you, Mr. Mastern?' I said twenty-two. Then she said, 'I am twenty-nine.' I stammered something, in my surprise. She laughed as though at my confusion, and said, 'Yes, I am seven years older than you, Mr. Mastern. Does that surprise you, Mr. Mastern?' I replied in the affirmative. Then she said, 'Seven years is a long time. Seven years ago you were a child, Mr. Mastern.' Then she laughed, with a sudden sharpness, but quickly stopped herself to add, 'But I wasn't a child. Not seven years ago, Mr. Mastern.' I did not answer her, for there was no thought clear in my head. I sat there in confusion, but in the middle of my confusion I was trying to see what she would have looked like as a child. I could call up no image. Then her husband returned from the house."

A few days later Cass went back to Mississippi to devote some months to his plantation, and, under the guidance of Gilbert, to go once to Jackson, the capital, and once to Vicksburg. It was a busy summer. Now Cass could see clearly what Gilbert intended: to make him rich and to put him into politics. It was a flattering and glittering prospect, and one not beyond reasonable expectation for a young man whose brother was Gilbert Mastern ("My brother is a man of great taciturnity and strong mind, and when he speaks, though he practices no graces and ingratiations, all men, especially those of the sober sort who have responsibility and power, weigh his words with respect.") So the summer passed, under the strong hand and cold eye of Gilbert. But toward the end of the season, when already Cass was beginning to give thought to his return to Transylvania, an envelope came addressed to him from Lexington, in an unfamiliar script. When Cass unfolded the single sheet of paper a small pressed blossom, or what he discovered to be such, slipped out. For a moment he could not think what it was, or why it was in his hand. Then he put it to his nostrils. The odor, now faint and dusty, was the odor of jasmine.

The sheet of paper had been folded twice, to make four equal sections. In one section, in a clean, strong, not large script, he read: "Oh, Cass!" That was all.

It was enough.

One drizzly autumn afternoon, just after his return to Lexington, Cass called at the Trice house to pay his respects. Duncan Trice was not there, having sent word that he had been urgently detained in the town and would be home for a late dinner. Of that afternoon, Cass wrote: "I found myself in the room alone with her. There were shadows, as there had been that afternoon, almost a year before, when I first saw her in that room, and when I had thought that her eyes were black. She greeted me civilly, and I replied and stepped back after having shaken her hand. Then I realized that she was looking at me fixedly, as I at her. Suddenly her lips parted slightly and gave a short exhalation, like a sigh or suppressed moan. As of one accord, we moved toward each other and embraced. No words were passed between us as we stood there. We stood there for a long time, or so it seemed. I held her body close to me in a strong embrace, but we did not exchange a kiss, which upon recollection has since seemed strange. But was it strange? Was it strange that some remnant of shame should forbid us to look each other in the face? I felt and heard my heart racing within my bosom, with a loose feeling as though it were unmoored and were leaping at random in a great cavity within me, but at the same time I scarcely accepted the fact of my situation. I was somehow possessed by incredulity, even as to my identity, as I stood there and my nostrils were filled with the fragrance of her hair. It was not to be believed that I was Cass Mastern, who stood thus in the house of a friend and benefactor. There was no remorse or horror at the turpitude of the act, but only the incredulity which I have referred to. (One feels incredulity at observing the breaking of a habit, but horror at the violation of a principle. Therefore what virtue and honor I had known in the past had been an accident of habit and not the fruit of will. Or can virtue be the fruit of human will? The thought is pride.)

"As I have said, we stood there for a long time in a strong embrace, but with her face lowered against my chest, and my own eyes staring across the room and out a window into the deepening obscurity of the evening. When she finally raised her face, I saw that she had been silently weeping. Why was she weeping? I have asked myself that question. Was it because even on the verge of committing an irremediable wrong she could weep at the consequence of an act which she felt powerless to avoid? Was it because the man who held her was much younger than she and his embrace gave her the reproach of youth and seven years? Was it because he had come seven years too late and could not come in innocence? It does not matter what the cause. If it was the first, then the tears can only prove that sentiment is no substitute for obligation, if the second, then they only prove that pity of the self is no substitute for wisdom. But she shed the tears and finally lifted her face to mine with those tears bright in her large eyes, and even now, though those tears were my ruin, I cannot wish them unshed, for they testify to the warmth of her heart and prove that whatever her sin (and mine) she did not step to it with a gay foot and with the eyes hard with lust and fleshly cupidity.

"The tears were my ruin, for when she lifted her face to me some streak of tenderness was mixed into my feelings, and my heart seemed to flood itself into my bosom to fill that great cavity wherein it had been leaping. She said, 'Cass'—the first time she had ever addressed me by my Christian name. 'Yes,' I replied. 'Kiss me,' she said very simply, 'you can do it now.' So I kissed her. And thereupon in the blindness of our mortal blood and in the appetite of our hearts we performed the act. There in that very room with the servants walking with soft feet somewhere in the house and with the door to the room open and with her husband expected, and not yet in the room the darkness of evening. But we were secure in our very recklessness, as though the lustful heart could give forth a cloud of darkness in which we were shrouded, even as Venus once shrouded Aeneas in a cloud so that he passed unspied among men to approach the city of Dido. In such cases as ours the very recklessness gives security as the strength of the desire seems to give the sanction of justice and righteousness.

"Though she had wept and had seemed to perform the act in a sadness and desperation, immediately afterwards she spoke cheerfully to me. She stood in the middle of the room pressing her hair into place, and I stumblingly ventured some remark about our future, a remark very vague for my being was still confused, but she responded, 'Oh, let us not think about it now,' as though I had broached a subject of no consequence. She promptly summoned a servant and asked for lights. They were brought and thereupon I inspected her face, to find it fresh and unmarked. When her husband came, she greeted him familiarly and affectionately, and as I witnessed it my own heart was wrenched, but not, I must confess, with compunction. Rather with a violent jealousy. When he spoke to me, so great was my disturbance that I was sure that my face could but betray it."

. . .

So began the second phase of the story of Cass Mastern. All that year, as before, he was often in the house of Duncan Trice, and as before he was often with him in field sports, gambling, drinking, and race-going. He learned, he says, to "wear his brow unwrinkled," to accept the condition of things. As for Annabelle Trice, he says that sometimes, looking back, he could scarcely persuade himself that "she had shed tears." She was, he says, "of a warm nature, reckless and passionate of disposition, hating all mention of the future (she would never let me mention times to come), agile, resourceful, and cheerful in devising to gratify our appetites, but with a womanly tenderness such as any man might prize at a sanctified hearthside." She must indeed have been agile and resourceful, for to carry on such a liaison undetected in that age and place must have been a problem. There was a kind of summer house at the foot of the Trice garden, which one could enter unobserved from an alley. Some of their meetings occurred there. A half-sister of Annabelle Trice, who lived in Lexington, apparently assisted the lovers or winked at their relationship, but, it seems, only after some pressure by Annabelle, for Cass hints at "a stormy scene." So some of the meetings were there. But now and then Duncan Trice had to be out of town on business, and on those occasions Cass would be admitted, late at night, to the house, even during a period when Annabelle's mother and father were staying there; so he actually lay in the very bed belonging to Duncan Trice.

There were, however, other meetings, unplanned and unpredictable moments snatched when they found themselves left alone together. "Scarce a corner, cranny, or protected nook or angle of my friend's trusting house did we not at one time or another defile, and that even in the full and shameless light of day," Cass wrote in the journal, and when Jack Burden, the student of history, went to Lexington and went to see the old Trice home he remembered the sentence. The town had grown up around the house, and the gardens, except for a patch of lawn, were gone. But the house was well maintained (some people named Miller lived there and by and large respected the place) and Jack Burden was permitted to inspect the premises. He wandered about the room where the first meeting had taken place and she had raised her eyes to Cass Mastern above the newly lighted candles and where, a year later, she had uttered the sigh, or suppressed moan, and stepped to his arms; and out into the hall, which was finely proportioned and with a graceful stair; and into a small, shadowy library; and to a kind of back hall, which was a well "protected nook or angle" and had, as a matter of fact, furniture adequate to the occasion. Jack Burden stood in the main hall, which was cool and dim, with dully glittering floors, and in the silence of the house, recalled that period, some seventy years before, of the covert glances, the guarded whispers, the abrupt rustling of silk in the silence (the costume of the period certainly had not been designed to encourage casual vice), the sharp breath, the reckless sighs. Well, all of that had been a hell of a long time before, and Annabelle Trice and Cass Mastern were long since deader than mackerel, and Mrs. Miller, who came down to give Jack Burden a cup of tea (she was flattered by the "historical" interest in her house, though she didn't guess the exact nature of the case), certainly was not "agile" and didn't look "resourceful" and probably had used up all her energy in the Ladies Altar Guild of Saint Luke's Episcopal Church and in the D.A.R.

The period of the intrigue, the second phase of the story of Cass Mastern, lasted all of one academic year, part of the summer (for Cass was compelled to go back to Mississippi for his plantation affairs and to attend the wedding of his sister Lavinia, who married a well-connected young man named Willis Burden), and well through the next winter, when Cass was back in Lexington. Then, on March 19, 1854, Duncan died, in his library (which was a "protected nook or angle" of his house), with a lead slug nearly the size of a man's thumb in his chest. It was quite obviously an accident.

The widow sat in church, upright and immobile. When she once raised her veil to touch at her eyes with a handkerchief, Cass Mastern saw that the cheek was "pale as marble but for a single flushed spot, like the flush of fever." But even when the veil was lowered he detected the fixed, bright eyes glittering "within that artificial shadow."

Cass Mastern, with five other young men of Lexington, cronies and boon companions of the dead man, carried the coffin. "The coffin which I carried seemed to have no weight, although my friend had been of large frame and had inclined to stoutness. As we proceeded with it, I marvelled at the fact of its lightness, and once the fancy flitted into my mind that he was not in the coffin at all, that it was empty, and that all the affair was a masquerade or mock-show carried to ludicrous and blasphemous length, for no purpose, as in a dream. Or to deceive me, the fancy came. I was the object of the deception, and all the other people were in league and conspiracy against me. But when that thought came, I suddenly felt a sense of great cunning and a wild exhilaration. I had been too sharp to be caught so. I had penetrated the deception. I had the impulse to hurl the coffin to the ground and see its emptiness burst open and to laugh in triumph. But I did not, and

I saw the coffin sink beneath the level of the earth on which we stood and receive the first clods.

"As soon as the sound of the first clods striking the coffin came to me, I felt a great relief, and then a most overmastering desire. I looked toward her. She was kneeling at the foot of the grave, with what thoughts I could not know. Her head was inclined slightly and the veil was over her face. The bright sun poured over her black-clad figure. I could not take my eyes from the sight. The posture seemed to accentuate the charms of her person and to suggest to my inflamed senses the suppleness of her members. Even the funeral tint of her costume seemed to add to the provocation. The sunshine was hot upon my neck and could be felt through the stuff of my coat upon my shoulders. It was preternaturally bright, so that I was blinded by it and my eyes were blinded and my senses swam. But all the while I could hear, as from a great distance, the scraping of the spades upon the piled earth and the muffled sound of earth falling into the excavation."

That evening Cass went to the summer house in the garden. It was not by appointment, simply on impulse. He waited there a long time, but she finally appeared, dressed in black "which was scarce darker than the night." He did not speak, or make any sign as she approached, "gliding like a shadow among shadows," but remained standing where he had been, in the deepest obscurity of the summer house. Even when she entered, he did not betray his presence. "I can not be certain that any premeditation was in my silence. It was prompted by an overpowering impulse which gripped me and sealed my throat and froze my limbs. Before that moment, and afterwards, I knew that it is dishonorable to spy upon another, but at the moment no such considerations presented themselves. I had to keep my eyes fixed upon her as she stood there thinking herself alone in the darkness of the structure. I had the fancy that since she thought herself alone, I might penetrate into her being, that I might learn what change, what effect, had been wrought by the death of her husband. The passion which had seized me to the very extent of paroxysm that afternoon at the very brink of my friend's grave was gone. I was perfectly cold now. But I had to know, to try to know. It was as though I might know myself by knowing her. (It is the human defect—to try to know oneself by the self of another. One can only know oneself in God and in His great eye.)

"She entered the summer house and sank upon one of the benches, not more than a few feet from my own location. For a long time I stood there, peering at her. She sat perfectly upright and rigid. At last I whispered her name, as low as might be. If she heard it, she gave no sign. So I repeated her name, in the same fashion, and again. Upon the third utterance, she whispered, 'Yes,' but she did not change her posture or turn her head. Then I spoke more loudly, again uttering her name, and instantly, with a motion of wild alarm, she rose, with a strangled cry, and her hands lifted toward her face. She reeled, and it seemed that she would collapse to the floor, but she gained control of herself and stood there staring at me. Stammeringly, I made my apology, saying that I had not wanted to startle her, that I had understood her to answer yes to my whisper before I spoke, and I asked her, 'Did you not answer to my whisper?'

"She replied that she had.

" 'Then why were you distressed when I spoke again?' I asked her.

" 'Because, I did not know that you were here,' she said.

" 'But,' I said, 'you say that you had just heard my whisper and had answered to it, and now you say that you did not know I was here.'

" 'I did not know that you were here,' she repeated, in a low voice, and the import of what she was saying dawned upon me.

" 'Listen,' I said, 'when you heard the whisper—did you recognize it was my voice?'

"She stared at me, not answering.

" 'Answer me,' I demanded, for I had to know.

"She continued to stare, and finally replied hesitantly, 'I do not know.'

" 'You thought it was—' I began, but before I could utter the words she had flung herself upon me, clasping me in desperation like a person frantic with drowning, and ejaculated: 'No, no, it does not matter what I thought, you are here, you are here!' And she drew my face down and pressed her lips against mine to stop my words. Her lips were cold, but they hung upon mine.

"I too was perfectly cold, as of a mortal chill. And the coldness was the final horror of the act which we performed, as though two dolls should parody the shame and filth of man to make it doubly shameful.

"After, she said to me, 'Had I not found you here tonight, it could never have been between us again.'

" 'Why?' I demanded.

" 'It was a sign,' she said.

" 'A sign?' I asked.

" 'A sign that we cannot escape, that we—' and she interrupted herself, to resume, whispering fiercely in the dark, 'I do not want to escape—it is a sign—whatever I have done is done.' She grew quiet for a moment, then she said, 'Give me your hand.'

"I gave her my right hand. She grasped it, dropped it, and said, 'The other, the other hand.'

"I held it out, across my own body, for I was sitting on her left. She seized it with her own left hand, bringing her hand upward from below to press my hand flat against her bosom. Then, fumblingly, she slipped a ring upon my finger, the finger next to the smallest.

" 'What is that?' I asked.

" 'A ring,' she answered, paused, and added, 'It is his ring.'

"Then I recalled that he, my friend, had always worn a wedding ring, and I felt the metal cold upon my flesh. 'Did you take it off of his finger?' I asked, and the thought shook me.

" 'No,' she said.

" 'No?' I questioned.

" 'No,' she said, 'he took it off. It was the only time he ever took it off.'

"I sat beside her, waiting for what, I did not know, while she held my hand pressed against her bosom. I could feel it rise and fall. I could say nothing.

"Then she said, 'Do you want to know how—how he took it off?'

" 'Yes,' I said in the dark, and waiting for her to speak, I moved my tongue out upon my dry lips.

" 'Listen,' she commanded me in an imperious whisper, 'that evening after—after it happened—after the house was quiet again, I sat in my room, in the little chair by the dressing table, where I always sit for Phebe to let down my hair. I had sat there out of habit, I suppose, for I was numb all over. I watched Phebe preparing the bed for the night.' (Phebe was her waiting maid, a comely yellow wench somewhat given to the fits and sulls.) 'I saw Phebe remove the bolster and then look down at a spot where the bolster had lain, on my side of the bed. She picked something up and came toward me. She stared at me—and her eyes, they are yellow, you look into them and you can't see what is in them—she stared at me—a long time—and then she held out her hand, clenched shut, and she watched me—and then—slow, so slow—she opened up the fingers—and there lay the ring on the palm of her hand —and I knew it was his ring but all I thought was, it is gold and it is lying in a gold hand. For Phebe's hand was gold—I had never noticed how her hand is the color of pure gold. Then I looked up and she was still staring at me, and her eyes were gold, too, and bright and hard like gold. And I knew that she knew.'

" 'Knew?' I echoed, like a question, for I knew, too, now. My friend had learned the truth—from the coldness of his wife, from the gossip of servants—and had drawn the gold ring from his finger and carried it to the bed where he had lain with her and had put it beneath her pillow and had gone down and shot himself but under such circumstances that no one save his wife would ever guess it to be more than an accident. But he had made one fault of calculation. The yellow wench had found the ring.

" 'She knows,' she whispered, pressing my hand hard against her bosom, which heaved and palpitated with a new wildness. 'She knows —and she looks at me—she will always look at me.' Then suddenly her voice dropped, and a wailing intonation came into it: 'She will tell. All of them will know. All of them in the house will look at me and know —when they hand me the dish—when they come into the room—and their feet don't make any noise!' She rose abruptly, dropping my hand. I remained seated, and she stood there beside me, her back toward me, the whiteness of her face and hands no longer visible, and to my sight the blackness of her costume faded into the shadow, even in such proximity. Suddenly, in a voice which I did not recognize for its hardness, she said in the darkness above me, 'I will not abide it, I will not abide it!' Then she turned, and with a swooping motion, leaned to kiss me upon the mouth. Then she was gone from my side and I heard her feet running up the gravel of the path. I sat there in the darkness for a time longer, turning the ring upon my finger."

After that meeting in the summer house, Cass did not see Annabelle Trice for some days. He learned that she had gone to Louisville, where, he recalled, she had close friends. She had, as was natural, taken Phebe with her. Then he heard that she had returned, and that night, late, went to the summer house in the garden. She was there, sitting in the dark. She greeted him. She seemed, he wrote later, peculiarly cut off, remote, and vague in manner, like a somnambulist or a person drugged. He asked about her trip to Louisville, and she replied briefly that she had been down the river to Paducah. He remarked that he had not known that she had friends in Paducah, and she said that she had none there. Then, all at once, she turned on him, the vagueness changing to violence, and burst out, "You are prying—you are prying into my affairs—and I will not tolerate it." Cass stammered out some excuse before she cut in to say, "But if you must know, I'll tell you. I took her there."

For a moment Cass was genuinely confused, "Her?" he questioned. "Phebe," she replied, "I took her to Paducah, and she's gone."

"Gone—gone where?"

"Down the river," she answered, repeated, "down the river," and laughed abruptly, and added, "and she won't look at me any more like that."

"You sold her?"

"Yes, I sold her. In Paducah, to a man who was making up a coffle of negroes for New Orleans. And nobody knows me in Paducah, nobody knew I was there, nobody knows I sold her, for I shall say she ran away into Illinois. But I sold her. For thirteen hundred dollars."

"You got a good price," Cass said, "even for a yellow girl as sprightly as Phebe." And, as he reports in the journal, he laughed with some "bitterness and rudeness," though he does not say why.

"Yes," she replied, "I got a good price. I made him pay every penny she was worth. And then do you know what I did with the money, do you?"

"No."

"When I came off the boat at Louisville, there was an old man, a nigger, sitting on the landing stage, and he was blind and picking on a guitar and singing 'Old Dan Tucker.' I took the money out of my bag and walked to him and laid it in his old hat."

"If you were going to give the money away—if you felt the money was defiled—why didn't you free her?" Cass asked.

"She'd stay right here, she wouldn't go away, she would stay right here and look at me. Oh, no, she wouldn't go away, for she's the wife of a man the Motleys have, their coachman. Oh, she'd stay right here and look at me and tell, tell what she knows, and I'll not abide it!"

Then Cass said: "If you had spoken to me, I would have bought the man from Mr. Motley and set him free, too."

"He wouldn't have sold," she said, "the Motleys won't sell a servant."

"Even to be freed?" Cass continued, and she cut in, "I tell you I won't have you interfering with my affairs, do you understand that?" And she rose from his side and stood in the middle of the summer house, and, he reports, he saw the glimmer of her face in the shadow and heard her agitated breathing. "I thought you were fond of her," Cass said.

"I was," she said, "until—until she looked at me like that."

"You know why you got that price for her?" Cass asked, and without waiting for an answer, went on: "Because she's yellow and comely and well-made. Oh, the drovers wouldn't take her down chained in a coffle. They wouldn't wear her down. They'll take her down the river soft. And you know why?"

"Yes, I know why," she said, "and what is it to you? Are you so charmed by her?"

"That is unfair," Cass said.

"Oh, I see, Mr. Mastern," she said, "oh, I see, you are concerned for the honor of a black coachman. It is very delicate sentiment, Mr. Mastern. Why"—and she came to stand above him as he still sat on the bench—"why did you not show some such delicate concern for the honor of your friend? Who is now dead."

According to the journal, there was, at this moment, "a tempest of feeling" in his breast. He wrote: "Thus I heard put into words for the first time the accusation which has ever, in all climes, been that most calculated to make wince a man of proper nurture or natural rectitude. What the hardened man can bear to hear from the still small voice within, may yet be when spoken by any external tongue an accusation dire enough to drain his very cheeks of blood. But it was not only that accusation in itself, for in very truth I had supped full of that horror and made it my long familiar. It was not merely the betrayal of my friend. It was not merely the death of my friend, at whose breast I had leveled the weapon. I could have managed somehow to live with those facts. But I suddenly felt that the world outside of me was shifting and the substance of things, and that the process had only begun of a general disintegration of which I was the center. At that moment of perturbation, when the cold sweat broke on my brow, I did not frame any sentence distinctly to my mind. But I have looked back and wrestled to know the truth. It was not the fact that a slave woman was being sold away from the house where she had had protection and kindness and away from the arms of her husband into debauchery. I knew that such things had happened in fact, and I was no child, for after my arrival in Lexington and my acquaintance with the looser sort of companions, the sportsmen and the followers of the races, I had myself enjoyed such diversions. It was not only the fact that the woman for whom I had sacrificed my friend's life and my honor could, in her new suffering, turn on me with a cold rage and the language of insult so that I did not recognize her. It was, instead, the fact that all of these things —the death of my friend, the betrayal of Phebe, the suffering and rage and great change of the woman I had loved—all had come from my single act of sin and perfidy, as the boughs from the bole and the leaves from the bough. Or to figure the matter differently, it was as though the vibration set up in the whole fabric of the world by my act had spread infinitely and with ever-increasing power and no man could know the end. I did not put it into words in such fashion, but I stood there shaken by a tempest of feeling."

When Cass had somewhat controlled his agitation, he said, "To whom did you sell the girl?"

"What's it to you?" she answered.

"To whom did you sell the girl?" he repeated.

"I'll not tell you," she said.

"I will find out," he said. "I will go to Paducah and find out."

She grasped him by the arm, driving her fingers deep into the flesh, "like talons," and demanded, "Why—why are you going?"

"To find her," he said. "To find her and buy her and set her free." He had not premeditated this. He heard the words, he wrote in the journal, and knew that that was his intention. "To find her and buy her and set her free," he said, and felt the grasp on his arm released and then in the dark suddenly felt the rake of her nails down his cheek, and heard her voice in a kind of "wild sibilance" saying, "If you do—if you do —oh, I'll not abide it—I will not!"

She flung herself from his side and to the bench. He heard her gasp and sob, "a hard dry sob like a man's." He did not move. Then he heard her voice: "If you do—if you do—she looked at me that way, and I'll not abide it—if you do—" Then after a pause, very quietly: "If you do, I shall never see you again."

He made no reply. He stood there for some minutes, he did not know how long, then he left the summer house, where she still sat, and walked down the alley.

The next morning he left for Paducah. He learned the name of the trader, but he also learned that the trader had sold Phebe (a yellow wench who answered to Phebe's description) to a "private party" who happened to be in Paducah at the time but who had gone on downriver. His name was unknown in Paducah. The trader had presumably sold Phebe so that he would be free to accompany his coffle when it had been made up. He had now headed, it was said, into south Kentucky, with a few bucks and wenches, to pick up more. As Cass had predicted, he had not wanted to wear Phebe down by taking her in the coffle. So getting a good figure of profit in Paducah, he had sold her there. Cass went south as far as Bowling Green, but lost track of his man there. So, rather hopelessly, he wrote a letter to the trader, in care of the market at New Orleans, asking for the name of the purchaser and any information about him. Then he swung back north to Lexington.

At Lexington he went down to West Short Street, to the Lewis C.

Robards barracoon, which Mr. Robards had converted from the old Lexington Theatre a few years earlier. He had a notion that Mr. Robards, the leading trader of the section, might be able, through his downriver connections, to locate Phebe, if enough of a commission was in sight. At the barracoon there was no one in the office except a boy, who said that Mr. Robards was downriver but that Mr. Simms was "holding things down" and was over at the "house" at an "inspection." So Cass went next door to the house. (When Jack Burden was in Lexington investigating the life of Cass Mastern, he saw the "house" still standing, a two-storey brick building of the traditional residential type, roof running lengthwise, door in center of front, window on each side, chimney at each end, lean-to in back. Robards had kept his "choice stock" there and not in the coops, to wait for "inspection.")

Cass found the main door unlocked at the house, entered the hall, saw no one, but heard laughter from above. He mounted the stairs and discovered, at the end of the hall, a small group of men gathered at an open door. He recognized a couple of them, young hangers-on he had seen about town and at the track. He approached and asked if Mr. Simms was about. "Inside," one of the men said, "showing." Over the heads, Cass could see into the room. First he saw a short, strongly made man, a varnished-looking man, with black hair, black neckcloth, large bright black eyes, and black coat, with a crop in his hand. Cass knew immediately that he was a French "speculator," who was buying "fancies" for Lousiana. The Frenchman was staring at something beyond Cass's range of vision. Cass moved farther and could see within.

There he saw the man whom he took to be Mr. Simms, a nondescript fellow in a plug hat, and beyond him the figure of a woman. She was a very young woman, some twenty years old perhaps, rather slender, with skin slightly darker than ivory, probably an octoroon, and hair crisp rather than kinky, and deep dark liquid eyes, slightly bloodshot, which stared at a spot above and beyond the Frenchman. She did not wear the ordinary plaid osnaburg and kerchief of the female slave up for sale, but a white, loosely cut dress, with elbow-length sleeves, and skirts to the floor and no kerchief, only a band to her hair. Beyond her, in the neatly furnished room ("quite genteel," the journal called it, while noting the barred windows), Cass saw a rocking chair and little table, and on the table a sewing basket with a piece of fancy needlework lying there with the needle stuck in it, "as though some respectable young lady or householder had dropped it casually aside upon rising to greet a guest." Cass recorded that somehow he found himself staring at the needlework.

"Yeah," Mr. Simms was saying, "yeah." And grasped the girl by the shoulder to swing her slowly around for a complete view. Then he seized one of her wrists and lifted the arm to shoulder level and worked it back and forth a couple of times to show the supple articulation, saying, "Yeah." That done, he drew the arm forward, holding it toward the Frenchman, the hand hanging limply from the wrist which he held. (The hand was, according to the journal, "well moulded, and the fingers tapered.") "Yeah," Mr. Simms said, "look at that-air hand. Ain't no lady got a littler, teensier hand. And round and soft, yeah?"

"Ain't she got nuthen else round and soft?" one of the men at the door called, and the others laughed.

"Yeah," Mr. Simms said, and leaned to take the hem of her dress, which with a delicate flirting motion he lifted higher than her waist, while he reached out with his other hand to wad the cloth and draw it into a kind of "awkward girdle" about her waist. Still holding the wad of cloth, he walked around her, forcing her to turn (she turned "without resistance and as though in a trance") with his motion until her small buttocks were toward the door. "Round and soft, boys," Mr. Simms said, and gave her a good whack on the near buttock to make the flesh tremble. "Ever git yore hand on anything rounder ner softer, boys?" he demanded. "Hit's a cushion, I declare. And shake like sweet jelly."

"God-a-mighty and got on stockings," one of the men said.

While the other men laughed, the Frenchman stepped to the side of the girl, reached out to lay the tip of his riding crop at the little depression just above the beginning of the swell of the buttocks. He held the tip delicately there for a moment, then flattened the crop across the back and moved it down slowly, evenly across each buttock, to trace the fullness of the curve. "Turn her," he said in his foreign voice.

Mr. Simms obediently carried the wad around, and the body followed in the half-revolution. One of the men at the door whistled. The Frenchman laid his crop across the woman's belly as though he were a "carpenter measuring something or as to demonstrate its flatness," and moved it down as before, tracing the structure, until he came to rest across the thighs, below the triangle. Then he let his hand fall to his side, with the crop. "Open your mouth," he said to the girl.

She did so, and he peered earnestly at her teeth. Then he leaned and whiffed her breath. "It is a good breath," he admitted, as though grudgingly.

"Yeah," Mr. Simms said, "yeah, you ain't a-finden no better breath."

"Have you any others?" the Frenchman demanded. "On hand?"

"We got 'em," Mr. Simms said.

"Let me see," the Frenchman said, and moved toward the door with, apparently, the "insolent expectation" that the group there would dissolve before him. He went out into the hall, Mr. Simms following. While Mr. Simms locked the door, Cass said to him, "I wish to speak to you, if you are Mr. Simms."

"Huh?" Mr. Simms said ("grunted," according to the journal), but looking at Cass, became suddenly civil, for he could know from dress and bearing that Cass was not one of the casual hangers-on. So Mr. Simms admitted the Frenchman to the next room to inspect its occupant, and returned to Cass. Cass remarked in the journal that trouble might have been avoided if he had been more careful to speak in private, but he wrote that at the time the matter was so much upon his mind that the men who stood about were as shadows to him.

He explained his wish to Mr. Simms, described Phebe as well as possible, gave the name of the trader in Paducah, and offered a liberal commission. Mr. Simms seemed dubious, promised to do what he could, and then said, "But nine outa ten you won't git her, Mister. And we got sumthen here better. You done seen Delphy, and she's nigh white as airy woman, and a sight more juicy, and that gal you talk about is nuthen but yaller. Now Delphy—"

"But the young gemmun got a hankeren fer yaller," one of the hangers-on said, and laughed, and the others laughed too.

Cass struck him across the mouth. "I struck him with the side of my fist," Cass wrote, "to bring blood. I struck him without thought, and I recollect the surprise which visited me when I saw the blood on his chin and saw him draw a bowie from his shirt-front. I attempted to avoid his first blow, but received it upon my left shoulder. Before he could withdraw, I had grasped his wrist in my right hand, forced it down so that I could also use my left hand, which still had some strength left at that moment, and with a turning motion of my body I broke his arm across my right hip, and then knocked him to the floor. I recovered the bowie from the floor, and with it faced the man who seemed to be the friend of the man who was now prostrate. He had a knife in his hand, but he seemed disinclined to pursue the discussion."

Cass declined the assistance of Mr. Simms, pressed a handkerchief over his wound, walked out of the building and toward his lodgings, and collapsed on West Short Street. He was carried home. The next day he was better. He learned that Mrs. Trice had left the city, presumably for Washington. A couple of days later his wound infected, and for some time he lay in delirium between life and death. His recovery was slow, presumably retarded by what he termed in the journal his "will toward darkness." But his constitution was stronger than his will, and he recovered, to know himself as the "chief of sinners and a plague-spot on the body of the human world." He would have committed suicide except for the fear of damnation for that act, for though "hopeless of Grace, I yet clung to the hope of Grace." But sometimes the very fact of damnation because of suicide seemed to be the very reason for suicide: he had brought his friend to suicide and the friend, by that act, was eternally damned; therefore he, Cass Mastern, should, in justice, insure his own damnation by the same act. "But the Lord preserved me from self-slaughter for ends which are His and beyond my knowledge."

Mrs. Trice did not come back to Lexington.

He returned to Mississippi. For two years he operated his plantation, read the Bible, prayed, and, strangely enough, prospered greatly, almost as though against his will. In the end he repaid Gilbert his debt, and set free his slaves. He had some notion of operating the plantation with the same force on a wage basis. "You fool," Gilbert said to him, "be a private fool if you must, but in God's name, don't be a public one. Do you think you can work them, and them free? One day work, one day loaf. Do you think you can have a passel of free niggers next door to a plantation with slaves? If you did have to set them free, you don't have to spend the rest of your natural life nursing them. Get them out of this country, and take up law or medicine. Or preach the Gospel and at least make a living out of all this praying." Cass tried for more than a year to operate the plantation with his free negroes, but was compelled to confess that the project was a failure. "Get them out of the country," Gilbert said to him. "And why don't you go with them. Why don't you go North?"

"I belong here," Cass replied.

"Well, why don't you preach Abolition right here?" Gilbert demanded. "Do something, do anything, but stop making a fool of yourself trying to raise cotton with free niggers."

"Perhaps I shall preach Abolition," Cass said, "some day. Even here. But not now. I am not worthy to instruct others. Not now. But meanwhile, there is my example. If it is good, it is not lost. Nothing is ever lost."

"Except your mind," Gilbert said, and flung heavily from the room.

There was a sense of trouble in the air. Only Gilbert's great wealth and prestige and scarcely concealed humorous contempt for Cass saved Cass from ostracism, or worse. ("His contempt for me is a shield," Cass wrote. "He treats me like a wayward and silly child who may learn better and who does not have to be taken seriously. Therefore my neighbors do not take me seriously.") But trouble did come. One of Cass's negroes had a broad-wife on a plantation near by. After she had had some minor trouble with the overseer, the husband stole her from the plantation and ran away. Toward the Tennessee border the pair were taken. The man, resisting officers, was shot; the woman was brought back. "See," Gilbert said, "all you have managed to do is get one nigger killed and one nigger whipped. I offer my congratulations." So Cass put his free negroes on a boat bound upriver, and never heard of them again.

"I saw the boat head out into the channel, and watched the wheels churn against the strong current, and my spirit was troubled. I knew that the negroes were passing from one misery to another, and that the hopes they now carried would be blighted. They had kissed my hands and wept for joy, but I could take no part in their rejoicing. I had not flattered myself that I had done anything for them. What I had done I had done for myself, to relieve my spirit of a burden, the burden of their misery and their eyes upon me. The wife of my dead friend had found the eyes of the girl Phebe upon her and had gone wild and had ceased to be herself and had sold the girl into misery. I had found their eyes upon me and had freed them into misery, lest I should do worse. For many cannot bear their eyes upon them, and enter into evil and cruel ways in their desperation. There was in Lexington, a decade and more before my stay in that city, a wealthy lawyer named Fielding L. Turner, who had married a lady of position from Boston. This lady, Caroline Turner, who had never had blacks around her and who had been nurtured in sentiments opposed to the institution of human servitude, quickly became notorious for her abominable cruelties performed in her fits of passion. All persons of the community reprehended her floggings, which she performed with her own hands, uttering meanwhile little cries in her throat, according to report. Once while she was engaged in flogging a servant in an apartment on the second floor of her palatial home, a small negro boy entered the room and began to whimper. She seized him and bodily hurled him through the window of the apartment so that he fell upon a stone below and broke his back to become a cripple for his days. To protect her from the process of law and the wrath of the community, Judge Turner committed her to a lunatic asylum. But later the physicians said her to be of sound mind and released her. Her husband in his will left her no slaves, for to do so would, the will said, be to doom them to misery in life and a speedy death. But she procured slaves, among them a yellow coachman named Richard, mild of manner, sensible, and of plausible disposition. One day she had him chained and proceeded to flog him. But he tore himself from the chains that held him to the wall and seized the woman by the throat and strangled her. Later he was captured and hanged for murder, though many wished that his escape had been contrived. This story was told me in Lexington. One lady said to me: 'Mrs. Turner did not understand negroes.' And another: 'Mrs. Turner did it because she was from Boston where the Abolitionists are.' But I did not understand. Then, much later, I began to understand. I understood that Mrs. Turner flogged her negroes for the same reason that the wife of my friend sold Phebe down the river: she could not bear their eyes upon her. I understand, for I can no longer bear their eyes upon me. Perhaps only a man like my brother Gilbert can in the midst of evil retain enough of innocence and strength to bear their eyes upon him and to do a little justice in the terms of the great injustice."

So Cass, who had a plantation with no one to work it, went to Jackson, the capital of the state, and applied himself to the law. Before he left, Gilbert came to him and offered to take over the plantation and work it with a force of his people from his own great place on a share basis. Apparently he was still trying to make Cass rich. But Cass declined, and Gilbert said: "You object to my working it with slaves, is that it? Well, let me tell you, if you sell it, it will be worked with slaves. It is black land and will be watered with black sweat. Does it make any difference, then, which black sweat falls on it?" And Cass replied that he was not going to sell the plantation. Then Gilbert, in an apopletic rage, bellowed: "My God, man, it is land, don't you understand, it is land, and land cries out for man's hand!" But Cass did not sell. He installed a caretaker in the house, and rented a little land to a neighbor for pasture.

He went to Jackson, sat late with his books, and watched trouble gathering over the land. For it was the autumn of 1858 when he went to Jackson. On January 8, 1861, Mississippi passed the Ordinance of Secession. Gilbert had opposed secession, writing to Cass: "The fools, there is not a factory for arms in the state. Fools not to have prepared themselves if they have foreseen the trouble. Fools, if they have not foreseen it, to act thus in the face of facts. Fools not to temporize now and, if they must, prepare themselves to strike a blow. I have told responsible men to prepare. All fools." To which Cass replied: "I pray much for peace." But later, he wrote: "I have talked with Mr. French, who is, as you know, the Chief of Ordnance, and he says that they have only old muskets for troops, and those but flintlocks. The agents have scraped the state for shotguns, at the behest of Governor Pettus. Shotguns, Mr. French said, and curled his lips. And what shotguns, he added, and then told me of a weapon contributed to the cause, an old musket barrel strapped with metal to a piece of cypress rail crooked at one end. An old slave gave this treasure to the cause, and does one laugh or weep?" (One can guess what Gilbert would have done, reading the letter.) After Jefferson Davis had come back to Mississippi, having resigned from the Senate, and had accepted the command of the troops of Mississippi with the rank of Major-General, Cass called upon him, at the request of Gilbert. He wrote to Gilbert: "The General says that they have given him 10,000 men, but not a stand of modern rifles. But the General also said, they have given me a very fine coat with fourteen brass buttons in front and a black velvet collar. Perhaps we can use the buttons in our shotguns, he said, and smiled."

Cass saw Mr. Davis once more, for he was with Gilbert on the steamboat *Natchez* which carried the new President of the Confederacy on the first stage of his journey from his plantation, "Brierfield," to Montgomery. "We were on old Mr. Tom Leather's boat," Cass wrote in the journal, "which had been supposed to pick up the President at a landing a few miles below Brierfield. But Mr. Davis was delayed in leaving his house and was rowed out to us. I leaned on the rail and saw the little black skiff proceeding toward us over the red water. A man waved from the skiff to us. The captain of the *Natchez* observed the signal, and gave a great blast of his boat's whistle which made our ears tingle and shivered out over the expanse of waters. Our boat stopped and the skiff approached. Mr. Davis was received on board. As the steamboat moved on, Mr. Davis looked back and lifted his hand in salute to the negro servant (Isaiah Montgomery whom I had known at Brierfield) who stood in the skiff, which rocked in the wash of the steamboat, and waved his farewell. Later, as we proceeded upriver toward the bluffs of Vicksburg, he approached my brother, with whom I was standing on the deck. We had previously greeted him. My brother again, and more intimately, congratulated Mr. Davis, who replied that he could take no pleasure in the honor. I have, he said, always looked upon the Union with a superstitious reverence and have freely risked my life for its dear flag on more than one battlefield, and you, gentlemen, can conceive the sentiment now in me that the object of my attachment for many years has been withdrawn from me. And he continued, I have in the present moment only the melancholy pleasure of an easy conscience. Then he smiled, as he did rarely. Thereupon he took his leave of us and retired within. I had observed how worn to emaciation was his face by illness and care, and how thin the skin lay over the bone. I remarked to my brother that Mr. Davis did not look well. He replied, a sick man, it is a fine how-de-do to have a sick man for a president. I responded that there might be no war, that Mr. Davis hoped for peace. But my brother said, make no mistake, the Yankees will fight and they will fight well and Mr. Davis is a fool to hope for peace. I replied, all good men hope for peace. At this my brother uttered an indistinguishable exclamation and said, what we want now that they've got into this is not a good man but a man who can win, and I am not interested in the luxury of Mr. Davis' conscience. Then my brother and I continued our promenade in silence, and I reflected that Mr. Davis was a good man. But the world is full of good men, I reflect as I write these lines, and yet the world drives hard into darkness and the blindness of blood, even as now late at night I sit in this hotel room in Vicksburg, and I am moved to ask the meaning of our virtue. May God hear our prayer!"

Gilbert received a commission as colonel in a cavalry regiment. Cass enlisted as a private in the Second Mississippi Rifles. "You could be a captain," Gilbert said, "or a major. You've got brains enough for that. And," he added, "damned few of them have." Cass replied that he preferred to be a private soldier, "marching with other men." But he could not tell his brother why, or tell his brother that, though he would march with other men and would carry a weapon in his hand, he would never take the life of an enemy. "I must march with these men who march," he wrote in the journal, "for they are my people and I must partake with them of all bitterness, and that more fully. But I cannot take the life of another man. How can I who have taken the life of my friend, take the life of an enemy, for I have used up my right to blood?" So Cass marched away to war, carrying the musket which was, for him, but a meaningless burden, and wearing on a string, against the flesh of his chest, beneath the fabric of the gray jacket, the ring which had once been Duncan Trice's wedding ring and which Annabelle Trice, that night in the summer house, had slipped onto his finger as his hand lay on her bosom.

Cass marched to Shiloh, between the fresh fields, for it was early April, and then into the woods that screened the river. (Dogwood and redbud would have been out then.) He marched into the woods, heard the lead whistle by his head, saw the dead men on the ground, and the next day came out of the woods and moved in the sullen withdrawal toward Corinth. He had been sure that he would not survive the battle. But he had survived, and moved down the crowded road "as in a dream." And he wrote: "And I felt that henceforward I should live in that dream." The dream took him into Tennessee again—Chickamauga, Knoxville, Chattanooga, and the nameless skirmishes, and the bullet for which he waited did not find him. He became known as a man of extreme courage. At Chickamauga, when his company wavered in the enemy fire and seemed about to break in its attack, he moved steadily up the slope and could not understand his own inviolability. And the men regrouped, and followed. "It seemed strange to me," he wrote, "that I who in God's will sought death and could not find it, should in my seeking lead men to it who did not seek." When Colonel Hickman congratulated him, he could "find no words" for answer.

But if he had put on the gray jacket in anguish of spirit and in hope of expiation, he came to wear it in pride, for it was a jacket like those worn by the men with whom he marched. "I have seen men do brave things," he wrote, "and they ask for nothing." More and more into the journals crept the comments of the professional soldier, between the prayers and the scruples—criticism of command (of Bragg after Chickamauga), satisfaction and an impersonal pride in manoeuvre or gunnery ("the practice of Marlowe's battery excellent"), and finally, the admiration for the feints and delays executed by Johnston's virtuosity on the approaches to Atlanta, at Buzzard's Roost, Snake Creek Gap, New Hope Church, Kenesaw Mountain ("there is always a kind of glory, however stained or obscured, in whatever man's hand does well, and General Johnston does well").

Then, outside Atlanta, the bullet found him. He lay in the hospital and rotted slowly to death. But even before the infection set in, when the wound in the leg seemed scarcely serious, he knew that he would die. "I shall die," he wrote in the journal, "and shall be spared the end and the last bitterness of war. I have lived to do no man good, and have seen others suffer for my sin. I do not question the Justice of God, that others have suffered for my sin, for it may be that only by the suffering of the innocent does God affirm that men are brothers, and brothers in His Holy Name. And in this room with me now, men suffer for sins not theirs, as for their own. It is a comfort to know that I suffer only for my own." He knew not only that he was to die, but that the war was over. "It is over. It is all over but the dying, which will go on. Though the boil has come to a head and has burst, yet must the pus flow. Men shall yet come together and die in the common guilt of man and in the guilt that sent them hither from far places and distant firesides. But God in His Mercy has spared me the end. Blessed be His Name."

There was no more in the journal. There was only the letter to Gilbert, written in the strange hand, dictated by Cass after he had grown too weak to write. "Remember me, but without grief. If one of us is lucky, it is I . . ."

Atlanta fell. In the last confusion, the grave of Cass Mastern was not marked. Someone at the hospital, a certain Albert Calloway, kept Cass's papers and the ring which he had carried on the cord around his neck, and much later, after the war in fact, sent them to Gilbert Mastern with a courteous note. Gilbert preserved the journal, the letters from Cass, the picture of Cass, and the ring on its cord, and after Gilbert's death, the heir finally sent the packet to Jack Burden, the student of history and the grand-nephew of Cass and Gilbert Mastern. So they came to rest on the little pine table in Jack Burden's bedroom in the slatternly apartment which he occupied with the two other graduate students, the unlucky, industrious, and alcoholic one, and the lucky, idle, and alcoholic one.

Jack Burden lived with the Mastern papers for a year and a half. He wanted to know all of the facts of the world in which Cass and Gilbert Mastern had lived, and he did know many of the facts. And he felt that he knew Gilbert Mastern. Gilbert Mastern had kept no journal, but he felt that he knew him, the man with the head like the block of bare granite, who had lived through one world into another and had been at home in both. But the day came when Jack Burden sat down at the pine table and realized that he did not know Cass Mastern. He did not have to know Cass Mastern to get the degree; he only had to know the facts about Cass Mastern's world. But without knowing Cass Mastern, he could not put down the facts about Cass Mastern's world. Not that Jack Burden said that to himself. He simply sat there at the pine table, night after night, staring at the papers before him, twisting the ring on its cord, staring at the photograph, and writing nothing. Then he would get up to get a drink of water, and would stand in the dark kitchen, holding an old jelly glass in his hand, waiting for the water to run cold from the tap.

BLACKBERRY
WINTER

To Joseph Warren and Dagmar Beach

It was getting into June and past eight o'clock in the morning, but there was a fire—even if it wasn't a big fire, just a fire of chunks—on the hearth of the big stone fireplace in the living room. I was standing on the hearth, almost into the chimney, hunched over the fire, working my bare toes slowly on the warm stone. I relished the heat which made the skin of my bare legs warp and creep and tingle, even as I called to my mother, who was somewhere back in the dining room or kitchen, and said: "But it's June, I don't have to put them on!"

"You put them on if you are going out," she called.

I tried to assess the degree of authority and conviction in the tone, but at that distance it was hard to decide. I tried to analyze the tone, and then I thought what a fool I had been to start out the back door and let her see that I was barefoot. If I had gone out the front door or the side door, she would never have known, not till dinner time anyway, and by then the day would have been half gone and I would have been all over the farm to see what the storm had done and down to the creek to see the flood. But it had never crossed my mind that they

First published in 1946 by the Cummington Press in a limited edition. In 1947 it was included in *The Circus in the Attic and Other Stories*, from which this text was taken.

would try to stop you from going barefoot in June, no matter if there had been a gully-washer and a cold spell.

Nobody had ever tried to stop me in June as long as I could remember, and when you are nine years old, what you remember seems forever; for you remember everything and everything is important and stands big and full and fills up Time and is so solid that you can walk around and around it like a tree and look at it. You are aware that time passes, that there is a movement in time, but that is not what Time is. Time is not a movement, a flowing, a wind then, but is, rather, a kind of climate in which things are, and when a thing happens it begins to live and keeps on living and stands solid in Time like the tree that you can walk around. And if there is a movement, the movement is not Time itself, any more than a breeze is climate, and all the breeze does is to shake a little the leaves on the tree which is alive and solid. When you are nine, you know that there are things that you don't know, but you know that when you know something you know it. You know how a thing has been and you know that you can go barefoot in June. You do not understand that voice from back in the kitchen which says that you cannot go barefoot outdoors and run to see what has happened and rub your feet over the wet shivery grass and make the perfect mark of your foot in the smooth, creamy, red mud and then muse upon it as though you had suddenly come upon that single mark on the glistening auroral beach of the world. You have never seen a beach, but you have read the book and how the footprint was there.

The voice had said what it had said, and I looked savagely at the black stockings and the strong, scuffed brown shoes which I had brought from my closet as far as the hearth rug. I called once more, "But it's June," and waited.

"It's June," the voice replied from far away, "but it's blackberry winter."

I had lifted my head to reply to that, to make one more test of what was in that tone, when I happened to see the man.

The fireplace in the living room was at the end; for the stone chimney was built, as in so many of the farmhouses in Tennessee, at the end of a gable, and there was a window on each side of the chimney. Out of the window on the north side of the fireplace I could see the man. When I saw the man I did not call out what I had intended, but, engrossed by the strangeness of the sight, watched him, still far off, come along the path by the edge of the woods.

What was strange was that there should be a man there at all. That path went along the yard fence, between the fence and the woods which came right down to the yard, and then on back past the chicken runs and on by the woods until it was lost to sight where the woods bulged out and cut off the back field. There the path disappeared into the woods. It led on back, I knew, through the woods and to the swamp, skirted the swamp where the big trees gave way to sycamores and water oaks and willows and tangled cane, and then led on to the river. Nobody ever went back there except people who wanted to gig frogs in the swamp or to fish in the river or to hunt in the woods, and those people, if they didn't have a standing permission from my father, always stopped to ask permission to cross the farm. But the man whom I now saw wasn't, I could tell even at that distance, a sportsman. And what would a sportsman have been doing down there after a storm? Besides, he was coming from the river, and nobody had gone down there that morning. I knew that for a fact, because if anybody had passed, certainly if a stranger had passed, the dogs would have made a racket and would have been out on him. But this man was coming up from the river and had come up through the woods. I suddenly had a vision of him moving up the grassy path in the woods, in the green twilight under the big trees, not making any sound on the path, while now and then, like drops off the eaves, a big drop of water would fall from a leaf or bough and strike a stiff oak leaf lower down with a small, hollow sound like a drop of water hitting tin. That sound, in the silence of the woods, would be very significant.

When you are a boy and stand in the stillness of woods, which can be so still that your heart almost stops beating and makes you want to stand there in the green twilight until you feel your very feet sinking into and clutching the earth like roots and your body breathing slow through its pores like the leaves—when you stand there and wait for the next drop to drop with its small, flat sound to a lower leaf, that sound seems to measure out something, to put an end to something, to begin something, and you cannot wait for it to happen and are afraid it will not happen, and then when it has happened, you are waiting again, almost afraid.

But the man whom I saw coming through the woods in my mind's eye did not pause and wait, growing into the ground and breathing with the enormous, soundless breathing of the leaves. Instead, I saw him moving in the green twilight inside my head as he was moving at that very moment along the path by the edge of the woods, coming toward the house. He was moving steadily, but not fast, with his shoulders hunched a little and his head thrust forward, like a man who has come a long way and has a long way to go. I shut my eyes for a couple of seconds, thinking that when I opened them he would not be there at all. There was no place for him to have come from, and there was no reason for him to come where he was coming, toward our house. But I opened my eyes, and there he was, and he was coming steadily along the side of the woods. He was not yet even with the back chicken yard.

"Mama," I called.

"You put them on," the voice said.

"There's a man coming," I called, "out back."

She did not reply to that, and I guessed that she had gone to the kitchen window to look. She would be looking at the man and wondering who he was and what he wanted, the way you always do in the country, and if I went back there now, she would not notice right off whether or not I was barefoot. So I went back to the kitchen.

She was standing by the window. "I don't recognize him," she said, not looking around at me.

"Where could he be coming from?" I asked.

"I don't know," she said.

"What would he be doing down at the river? At night? In the storm?"

She studied the figure out the window, then said, "Oh, I reckon maybe he cut across from the Dunbar place."

That was, I realized, a perfectly rational explanation. He had not been down at the river in the storm, at night. He had come over this morning. You could cut across from the Dunbar place if you didn't mind breaking through a lot of elder and sassafras and blackberry bushes which had about taken over the old cross path, which nobody ever used any more. That satisfied me for a moment, but only for a moment. "Mama," I asked, "what would he be doing over at the Dunbar place last night?"

Then she looked at me, and I knew I had made a mistake, for she was looking at my bare feet. "You haven't got your shoes on," she said.

But I was saved by the dogs. That instant there was a bark which I recognized as Sam, the collie, and then a heavier, churning kind of bark which was Bully, and I saw a streak of white as Bully tore round the corner of the back porch and headed out for the man. Bully was a big bone-white bulldog, the kind of dog that they used to call a farm bulldog but that you don't see any more, heavy-chested and heavy-headed, but with pretty long legs. He could take a fence as light as a hound. He had just cleared the white paling fence toward the woods when my mother ran out to the back porch and began calling, "Here you, Bully! Here you!"

Bully stopped in the path, waiting for the man, but he gave a few more of those deep, gargling, savage barks that reminded you of something down a stone-lined well. The red-clay mud, I saw, was splashed up over his white chest and looked exciting, like blood.

The man, however, had not stopped walking even when Bully took the fence and started at him. He had kept right on coming. All he had done was to switch a little paper parcel which he carried from the right hand to the left, and then reach into his pants pocket to get something. Then I saw the glitter and knew that he had a knife in his hand, probably the kind of mean knife just made for devilment and nothing else, with a blade as long as the blade of a frog-sticker, which will snap out ready when you press a button in the handle. That knife must have had a button in the handle, or else how could he have had the blade out glittering so quick and with just one hand?

Pulling his knife against the dogs was a funny thing to do, for Bully was a big, powerful brute and fast, and Sam was all right. If those dogs had meant business, they might have knocked him down and ripped him before he got a stroke in. He ought to have picked up a heavy stick, something to take a swipe at them with and something which they could see and respect when they came at him. But he apparently did not know much about dogs. He just held the knife blade close against the right leg, low down, and kept on moving down the path.

Then my mother had called, and Bully had stopped. So the man let the blade of the knife snap back into the handle, and dropped it into his pocket, and kept on coming. Many women would have been afraid with the strange man who they knew had that knife in his pocket. That is, if they were alone in the house with nobody but a nine-year-old boy. And my mother was alone, for my father had gone off, and Dellie, the cook, was down at her cabin because she wasn't feeling well. But my mother wasn't afraid. She wasn't a big woman, but she was clear and brisk about everything she did and looked everybody and everything right in the eye from her own blue eyes in her tanned face. She had been the first woman in the county to ride a horse astride (that was back when she was a girl and long before I was born), and I have seen her snatch up a pump gun and go out and knock a chicken hawk out of the air like a busted skeet when he came over her chicken yard. She was a steady and self-reliant woman, and when I think of her now after all the years she has been dead, I think of her brown hands, not big, but somewhat square for a woman's hands, with square-cut nails. They looked, as a matter of fact, more like a young boy's hands than a grown woman's. But back then it never crossed my mind that she would ever be dead.

She stood on the back porch and watched the man enter the back gate, where the dogs (Bully had leaped back into the yard) were dancing and muttering and giving sidelong glances back to my mother to see if she meant what she had said. The man walked right by the dogs, almost brushing them, and didn't pay them any attention. I could see now that he wore old khaki pants, and a dark wool coat with stripes in it, and a gray felt hat. He had on a gray shirt with blue stripes in it, and no tie. But I could see a tie, blue and reddish, sticking in his side coat-pocket. Everything was wrong about what he wore. He ought to have been wearing blue jeans or overalls, and a straw hat or an old black felt hat, and the coat, granting that he might have been wearing a wool coat and not a jumper, ought not to have had those stripes. Those clothes, despite the fact that they were old enough and dirty enough for any tramp, didn't belong there in our back yard, coming down the path, in Middle Tennessee, miles away from any big town, and even a mile off the pike.

When he got almost to the steps, without having said anything, my mother, very matter-of-factly, said, "Good morning."

"Good morning," he said, and stopped and looked her over. He did not take off his hat, and under the brim you could see the perfectly unmemorable face, which wasn't old and wasn't young, or thick or thin. It was grayish and covered with about three days of stubble. The eyes were a kind of nondescript, muddy hazel, or something like that, rather bloodshot. His teeth, when he opened his mouth, showed yellow and uneven. A couple of them had been knocked out. You knew that they had been knocked out, because there was a scar, not very old, there on the lower lip just beneath the gap.

"Are you hunting work?" my mother asked him.

"Yes," he said—not "yes, mam"—and still did not take off his hat.

"I don't know about my husband, for he isn't here," she said, and didn't mind a bit telling the tramp, or whoever he was, with the mean knife in his pocket, that no man was around, "but I can give you a few things to do. The storm has drowned a lot of my chicks. Three coops of them. You can gather them up and bury them. Bury them deep so the dogs won't get at them. In the woods. And fix the coops the wind blew over. And down yonder beyond that pen by the edge of the woods are some drowned poults. They got out and I couldn't get them in. Even after it started to rain hard. Poults haven't got any sense."

"What are them things—poults?" he demanded, and spat on the brick walk. He rubbed his foot over the spot, and I saw that he wore a black pointed-toe low shoe, all cracked and broken. It was a crazy kind of shoe to be wearing in the country.

"Oh, they're young turkeys," my mother was saying. "And they haven't got any sense. I oughtn't to try to raise them around here with so many chickens, anyway. They don't thrive near chickens, even in separate pens. And I won't give up my chickens." Then she stopped herself and resumed briskly on the note of business. "When you finish that, you can fix my flower beds. A lot of trash and mud and gravel has washed down. Maybe you can save some of my flowers if you are careful."

"Flowers," the man said, in a low, impersonal voice which seemed to have a wealth of meaning, but a meaning which I could not fathom. As I think back on it, it probably was not pure contempt. Rather, it was a kind of impersonal and distant marveling that he should be on the verge of grubbing in a flower bed. He said the word, and then looked off across the yard.

"Yes, flowers," my mother replied with some asperity, as though she would have nothing said or implied against flowers. "And they were very fine this year." Then she stopped and looked at the man. "Are you hungry?" she demanded.

"Yeah," he said.

"I'll fix you something," she said, "before you get started." She turned to me. "Show him where he can wash up," she commanded, and went into the house.

I took the man to the end of the porch where a pump was and where a couple of wash pans sat on a low shelf for people to use before they went into the house. I stood there while he laid down his little parcel wrapped in newspaper and took off his hat and looked around for a nail to hang it on. He poured the water and plunged his hands into it. They were big hands, and strong-looking, but they did not have the creases and the earth-color of the hands of men who work outdoors. But they were dirty, with black dirt ground into the skin and under the nails. After he had washed his hands, he poured another basin of water and washed his face. He dried his face, and with the towel still dangling in his grasp, stepped over to the mirror on the house wall. He rubbed one hand over the stubble on his face. Then he carefully inspected his face, turning first one side and then the other, and stepped back and settled his striped coat down on his shoulders. He had the movements of a man who has just dressed up to go to church or a party—the way he settled his coat and smoothed it and scanned himself in the mirror.

Then he caught my glance on him. He glared at me for an instant out of the bloodshot eyes, then demanded in a low, harsh voice, "What you looking at?"

"Nothing," I managed to say, and stepped back a step from him.

He flung the towel down, crumpled, on the shelf, and went toward the kitchen door and entered without knocking.

My mother said something to him which I could not catch. I started to go in again, then thought about my bare feet, and decided to go back of the chicken yard, where the man would have to come to pick up the dead chicks. I hung around behind the chicken house until he came out.

He moved across the chicken yard with a fastidious, not quite finicking motion, looking down at the curdled mud flecked with bits of chicken-droppings. The mud curled up over the soles of his black shoes. I stood back from him some six feet and watched him pick up the first of the drowned chicks. He held it up by one foot and inspected it.

There is nothing deader-looking than a drowned chick. The feet curl in that feeble, empty way which back when I was a boy, even if I was a country boy who did not mind hog-killing or frog-gigging, made me feel hollow in the stomach. Instead of looking plump and fluffy, the body is stringy and limp with the fluff plastered to it, and the neck is long and loose like a little string of rag. And the eyes have that bluish membrane over them which makes you think of a very old man who is sick about to die.

The man stood there and inspected the chick. Then he looked all around as though he didn't know what to do with it.

"There's a great big old basket in the shed," I said, and pointed to the shed attached to the chicken house.

He inspected me as though he had just discovered my presence, and moved toward the shed.

"There's a spade there, too," I added.

He got the basket and began to pick up the other chicks, picking each one up slowly by a foot and then flinging it into the basket with a nasty, snapping motion. Now and then he would look at me out of the bloodshot eyes. Every time he seemed on the verge of saying something, but he did not. Perhaps he was building up to say something to me, but I did not wait that long. His way of looking at me made me so uncomfortable that I left the chicken yard.

Besides, I had just remembered that the creek was in flood, over the bridge, and that people were down there watching it. So I cut across the farm toward the creek. When I got to the big tobacco field I saw that it had not suffered much. The land lay right and not many tobacco plants had washed out of the ground. But I knew that a lot of tobacco round the country had been washed right out. My father had said so at breakfast.

My father was down at the bridge. When I came out of the gap in the osage hedge into the road, I saw him sitting on his mare over the heads of the other men who were standing around, admiring the flood. The creek was big here, even in low water; for only a couple of miles away it ran into the river, and when a real flood came, the red water got over the pike where it dipped down to the bridge, which was an iron bridge, and high over the floor and even the side railings of the bridge. Only the upper iron work would show, with the water boiling and frothing red and white around it. That creek rose so fast and so heavy because a few miles back it came down out of the hills, where the gorges filled up with water in no time when a rain came. The creek ran in a deep bed with limestone bluffs along both sides until it got within three quarters of a mile of the bridge, and when it came out from between those bluffs in flood it was boiling and hissing and steaming like water from a fire hose.

Whenever there was a flood, people from half the county would come down to see the sight. After a gully-washer there would not be any work to do anyway. If it didn't ruin your crop, you couldn't plow and you felt like taking a holiday to celebrate. If it did ruin your crop, there wasn't anything to do except to try to take your mind off the mortgage, if you were rich enough to have a mortgage, and if you couldn't afford a mortgage, you needed something to take your mind off how hungry you would be by Christmas. So people would come down to the bridge and look at the flood. It made something different from the run of days.

There would not be much talking after the first few minutes of trying to guess how high the water was this time. The men and kids just stood around, or sat their horses or mules, as the case might be, or stood up in the wagon beds. They looked at the strangeness of the flood for an hour or two, and then somebody would say that he had better be getting on home to dinner and would start walking down the gray, puddled limestone pike, or would touch heel to his mount and start off. Everybody always knew what it would be like when he got down to the bridge, but people always came. It was like church or a funeral. They always came, that is, if it was summer and the flood unexpected. Nobody ever came down in winter to see high water.

When I came out of the gap in the bodock hedge, I saw the crowd, perhaps fifteen or twenty men and a lot of kids, and saw my father sitting his mare, Nellie Gray. He was a tall, limber man and carried himself well. I was always proud to see him sit a horse, he was so quiet and straight, and when I stepped through the gap of the hedge that morning, the first thing that happened was, I remember, the warm feeling I always had when I saw him up on a horse, just sitting. I did not go toward him, but skirted the crowd on the far side, to get a look at the creek. For one thing, I was not sure what he would say about the fact that I was barefoot. But the first thing I knew, I heard his voice calling, "Seth!"

I went toward him, moving apologetically past the men, who bent their large, red or thin, sallow faces above me. I knew some of the men, and knew their names, but because those I knew were there in a crowd, mixed with the strange faces, they seemed foreign to me, and not friendly. I did not look up at my father until I was almost within touching distance of his heel. Then I looked up and tried to read his face, to see if he was angry about my being barefoot. Before I could decide anything from that impassive, high-boned face, he had leaned over and reached a hand to me. "Grab on," he commanded.

I grabbed on and gave a little jump, and he said, "Up-see-daisy!" and whisked me, light as a feather, up to the pommel of his McClellan saddle.

"You can see better up here," he said, slid back on the cantle a little to make me more comfortable, and then, looking over my head at the swollen, tumbling water, seemed to forget all about me. But his right hand was laid on my side, just above my thigh, to steady me.

I was sitting there as quiet as I could, feeling the faint stir of my father's chest against my shoulders as it rose and fell with his breath, when I saw the cow. At first, looking up the creek, I thought it was just another big piece of driftwood steaming down the creek in the ruck of water, but all at once a pretty good-size boy who had climbed part way up a telephone pole by the pike so that he could see better yelled out, "Golly-damn, look at that-air cow!"

Everybody looked. It was a cow all right, but it might just as well have been driftwood; for it was dead as a chunk, rolling and roiling down the creek, appearing and disappearing, feet up or head up, it didn't matter which.

The cow started up the talk again. Somebody wondered whether it would hit one of the clear places under the top girder of the bridge and get through or whether it would get tangled in the drift and trash that had piled against the upright girders and braces. Somebody remem-

bered how about ten years before, so much driftwood had piled up on
the bridge that it was knocked off its foundations. Then the cow hit.
It hit the edge of the drift against one of the girders, and hung there.
For a few seconds it seemed as though it might tear loose, but then we
saw that it was really caught. It bobbed and heaved on its side there in
a slow, grinding, uneasy fashion. It had a yoke around its neck, the kind
made out of a forked limb to keep a jumper behind fence.

"She shore jumped one fence," one of the men said.

And another: "Well, she done jumped her last one, fer a fack."

Then they began to wonder about whose cow it might be. They
decided it must belong to Milt Alley. They said that he had a cow that
was a jumper, and kept her in a fenced-in piece of ground up the creek.
I had never seen Milt Alley, but I knew who he was. He was a squatter
and lived up the hills a way, on a shirt-tail patch of set-on-edge land,
in a cabin. He was pore white trash. He had lots of children. I had seen
the children at school, when they came. They were thin-faced, with
straight, sticky-looking, dough-colored hair, and they smelled something like old sour buttermilk, not because they drank so much buttermilk but because that is the sort of smell which children out of those
cabins tend to have. The big Alley boy drew dirty pictures and showed
them to the little boys at school.

That was Milt Alley's cow. It looked like the kind of cow he would
have, a scrawny, old, sway-backed cow, with a yoke around her neck.
I wondered if Milt Alley had another cow.

"Poppa," I said, "do you think Milt Alley has got another cow?"

"You say 'Mr. Alley,' " my father said quietly.

"Do you think he has?"

"No telling," my father said.

Then a big gangly boy, about fifteen, who was sitting on a scraggly
little old mule with a piece of croker sack thrown across the sawtooth
spine, and who had been staring at the cow, suddenly said to nobody
in particular, "Reckin anybody ever et drownt cow?"

He was the kind of boy who might just as well as not have been the
son of Milt Alley, with his faded and patched overalls ragged at the
bottom of the pants and the mud-stiff brogans hanging off his skinny,
bare ankles at the level of the mule's belly. He had said what he did,
and then looked embarrassed and sullen when all the eyes swung at
him. He hadn't meant to say it, I am pretty sure now. He would have
been too proud to say it, just as Milt Alley would have been too proud.
He had just been thinking out loud, and the words had popped out.

There was an old man standing there on the pike, an old man with a white beard. "Son," he said to the embarrassed and sullen boy on the mule, "you live long enough and you'll find a man will eat anything when the time comes."

"Time gonna come fer some folks this year," another man said.

"Son," the old man said, "in my time I et things a man don't like to think on. I was a sojer and I rode with Gin'l Forrest, and them things we et when the time come. I tell you. I et meat what got up and run when you taken out yore knife to cut a slice to put on the fire. You had to knock it down with a carbeen butt, it was so active. That-air meat would jump like a bullfrog, it was so full of skippers."

But nobody was listening to the old man. The boy on the mule turned his sullen sharp face from him, dug a heel into the side of the mule, and went off up the pike with a motion which made you think that any second you would hear mule bones clashing inside that lank and scrofulous hide.

"Cy Dundee's boy," a man said, and nodded toward the figure going up the pike on the mule.

"Reckin Cy Dundee's young-uns seen times they'd settle fer drownt cow," another man said.

The old man with the beard peered at them both from his weak, slow eyes, first at one and then at the other. "Live long enough," he said, "and a man will settle fer what he kin git."

Then there was silence again, with the people looking at the red, foam-flecked water.

My father lifted the bridle rein in his left hand, and the mare turned and walked around the group and up the pike. We rode on up to our big gate, where my father dismounted to open it and let me myself ride Nellie Gray through. When he got to the lane that led off from the drive about two hundred yards from our house, my father said, "Grab on." I grabbed on, and he let me down to the ground. "I'm going to ride down and look at my corn," he said. "You go on." He took the lane, and I stood there on the drive and watched him ride off. He was wearing cowhide boots and an old hunting coat, and I thought that that made him look very military, like a picture. That and the way he rode.

I did not go to the house. Instead, I went by the vegetable garden and crossed behind the stables, and headed down for Dellie's cabin. I wanted to go down and play with Jebb, who was Dellie's little boy about two years older than I was. Besides, I was cold. I shivered as I walked, and I had gooseflesh. The mud which crawled up between my toes with every step I took was like ice. Dellie would have a fire, but she wouldn't make me put on shoes and stockings.

Dellie's cabin was of logs, with one side, because it was on a slope, set on limestone chunks, with a little porch attached to it, and had a little whitewashed fence around it and a gate with plow-points on a wire to clink when somebody came in, and had two big white oaks in the yard and some flowers and a nice privy in the back with some honeysuckle growing over it. Dellie and Old Jebb, who was Jebb's father and who lived with Dellie and had lived with her for twenty-five years even if they never had got married, were careful to keep everything nice around their cabin. They had the name all over the community for being clean and clever Negroes. Dellie and Jebb were what they used to call "white-folks' niggers." There was a big difference between their cabin and the other two cabins farther down where the other tenants lived. My father kept the other cabins weatherproof, but he couldn't undertake to go down and pick up after the litter they strewed. They didn't take the trouble to have a vegetable patch like Dellie and Jebb or to make preserves from wild plum, and jelly from crab apple the way Dellie did. They were shiftless, and my father was always threatening to get shed of them. But he never did. When they finally left, they just up and left on their own, for no reason, to go and be shiftless somewhere else. Then some more came. But meanwhile they lived down there, Matt Rawson and his family, and Sid Turner and his, and I played with their children all over the farm when they weren't working. But when I wasn't around they were mean sometimes to Little Jebb. That was because the other tenants down there were jealous of Dellie and Jebb.

I was so cold that I ran the last fifty yards to Dellie's gate. As soon as I had entered the yard, I saw that the storm had been hard on Dellie's flowers. The yard was, as I have said, on a slight slope, and the water running across had gutted the flower beds and washed out all the good black woods-earth which Dellie had brought in. What little grass there was in the yard was plastered sparsely down on the ground, the way the drainage water had left it. It reminded me of the way the fluff was plastered down on the skin of the drowned chicks that the strange man had been picking up, up in my mother's chicken yard.

I took a few steps up the path to the cabin, and then I saw that the drainage water had washed a lot of trash and filth out from under Dellie's house. Up toward the porch, the ground was not clean any more. Old pieces of rag, two or three rusted cans, pieces of rotten rope, some hunks of old dog dung, broken glass, old paper, and all sorts of things like that had washed out from under Dellie's house to foul her clean yard. It looked just as bad as the yards of the other cabins, or worse. It was worse, as a matter of fact, because it was a surprise. I had never thought of all that filth being under Dellie's house. It was not anything against Dellie that the stuff had been under the cabin. Trash will get under any house. But I did not think of that when I saw the foulness which had washed out on the ground which Dellie sometimes used to sweep with a twig broom to make nice and clean.

I picked my way past the filth, being careful not to get my bare feet on it, and mounted to Dellie's door. When I knocked, I heard her voice telling me to come in.

It was dark inside the cabin, after the daylight, but I could make out Dellie piled up in bed under a quilt, and Little Jebb crouched by the hearth, where a low fire simmered. "Howdy," I said to Dellie, "how you feeling?"

Her big eyes, the whites surprising and glaring in the black face, fixed on me as I stood there, but she did not reply. It did not look like Dellie, or act like Dellie, who would grumble and bustle around our kitchen, talking to herself, scolding me or Little Jebb, clanking pans, making all sorts of unnecessary noises and mutterings like an old-fashioned black steam thrasher engine when it has got up an extra head of steam and keeps popping the governor and rumbling and shaking on its wheels. But now Dellie just lay up there on the bed, under the patchwork quilt, and turned the black face, which I scarcely recognized, and the glaring white eyes to me.

"How you feeling?" I repeated.

"I'se sick," the voice said croakingly out of the strange black face which was not attached to Dellie's big, squat body, but stuck out from under a pile of tangled bedclothes. Then the voice added: "Mighty sick."

"I'm sorry," I managed to say.

The eyes remained fixed on me for a moment, then they left me and the head rolled back on the pillow. "Sorry," the voice said, in a flat way which wasn't question or statement of anything. It was just the empty word put into the air with no meaning or expression, to float off like a feather or a puff of smoke, while the big eyes, with the whites like the peeled white of hard-boiled eggs, stared at the ceiling.

"Dellie," I said after a minute, "there's a tramp up at the house. He's got a knife."

She was not listening. She closed her eyes.

I tiptoed over to the hearth where Jebb was and crouched beside him. We began to talk in low voices. I was asking him to get out his train and play train. Old Jebb had put spool wheels on three cigar boxes and put wire links between the boxes to make a train for Jebb. The box that was the locomotive had the top closed and a length of broom stick for a smoke stack. Jebb didn't want to get the train out, but I told him I would go home if he didn't. So he got out the train, and the colored rocks, and fossils of crinoid stems, and other junk he used for the load, and we began to push it around, talking the way we thought trainmen talked, making a chuck-chucking sound under the breath for the noise of the locomotive and now and then uttering low, cautious toots for the whistle. We got so interested in playing train that the toots got louder. Then, before he thought, Jebb gave a good, loud *toot-toot*, blowing for a crossing.

"Come here," the voice said from the bed.

Jebb got up slow from his hands and knees, giving me a sudden, naked, inimical look.

"Come here!" the voice said.

Jebb went to the bed. Dellie propped herself weakly up on one arm, muttering, "Come closer."

Jebb stood closer.

"Last thing I do, I'm gonna do it," Dellie said. "Done tole you to be quiet."

Then she slapped him. It was an awful slap, more awful for the kind of weakness which it came from and brought to focus. I had seen her slap Jebb before, but the slapping had always been the kind of easy slap you would expect from a good-natured, grumbling Negro woman like Dellie. But this was different. It was awful. It was so awful that Jebb didn't make a sound. The tears just popped out and ran down his face, and his breath came sharp, like gasps.

Dellie fell back. "Cain't even be sick," she said to the ceiling. "Git sick and they won't even let you lay. They tromp all over you. Cain't even be sick." Then she closed her eyes.

I went out of the room. I almost ran getting to the door, and I did run across the porch and down the steps and across the yard, not caring whether or not I stepped on the filth which had washed out from under the cabin. I ran almost all the way home. Then I thought about my mother catching me with the bare feet. So I went down to the stables.

I heard a noise in the crib, and opened the door. There was Big Jebb, sitting on an old nail keg, shelling corn into a bushel basket. I went in, pulling the door shut behind me, and crouched on the floor near him. I crouched there for a couple of minutes before either of us spoke, and watched him shelling the corn.

He had very big hands, knotted and grayish at the joints, with calloused palms which seemed to be streaked with rust, with the rust coming up between the fingers to show from the back. His hands were so strong and tough that he could take a big ear of corn and rip the grains right off the cob with the palm of his hand, all in one motion, like a machine. "Work long as me," he would say, "and the good Lawd'll give you a hand lak cass-ion won't nuthin' hurt." And his hands did look like cast iron, old cast iron streaked with rust.

He was an old man, up in his seventies, thirty years or more older than Dellie, but he was strong as a bull. He was a squat sort of man, heavy in the shoulders, with remarkably long arms, the kind of build they say the river natives have on the Congo from paddling so much in their boats. He had a round bullet-head, set on powerful shoulders. His skin was very black, and the thin hair on his head was now grizzled like tufts of old cotton batting. He had small eyes and a flat nose, not big, and the kindest and wisest old face in the world, the blunt, sad, wise face of an old animal peering tolerantly out on the goings-on of the merely human creatures before him. He was a good man, and I loved him next to my mother and father. I crouched there on the floor of the crib and watched him shell corn with the rusty cast-iron hands, while he looked down at me out of the little eyes set in the blunt face.

"Dellie says she's mighty sick," I said.

"Yeah," he said.

"What's she sick from?"

"Woman-mizry," he said.

"What's woman-mizry?"

"Hit comes on 'em," he said. "Hit jest comes on 'em when the time comes."

"What is it?"

"Hit is the change," he said. "Hit is the change of life and time."

"What changes?"

"You too young to know."

"Tell me."

"Time come and you find out everthing."

I knew that there was no use in asking him any more. When I asked him things and he said that, I always knew that he would not tell me. So I continued to crouch there and watch him. Now that I had sat there a little while, I was cold again.

"What you shiver fer?" he asked me.

"I'm cold. I'm cold because it's blackberry winter," I said.

"Maybe 'tis and maybe 'tain't," he said.

"My mother says it is."

"Ain't sayen Miss Sallie doan know and ain't sayen she do. But folks doan know everthing."

"Why isn't it blackberry winter?"

"Too late fer blackberry winter. Blackberries done bloomed."

"She said it was."

"Blackberry winter jest a leetle cold spell. Hit come and then hit go away, and hit is growed summer of a sudden lak a gunshot. Ain't no tellen hit will go way this time."

"It's June," I said.

"June," he replied with great contempt. "That what folks say. What June mean? Maybe hit is come cold to stay."

"Why?"

" 'Cause this-here old yearth is tahrd. Hit is tahrd and ain't gonna perduce. Lawd let hit come rain one time forty days and forty nights, 'cause He was tahrd of sinful folks. Maybe this-here old yearth say to the Lawd, Lawd, I done plum tahrd, Lawd, lemme rest. And Lawd say, Yearth, you done yore best, you give 'em cawn and you give 'em taters, and all they think on is they gut, and, Yearth, you kin take a rest."

"What will happen?"

"Folks will eat up everthing. The yearth won't perduce no more. Folks cut down all the trees and burn 'em 'cause they cold, and the yearth won't grow no more. I been tellen 'em. I been tellen folks. Sayen, maybe this year, hit is the time. But they doan listen to me, how the yearth is tahrd. Maybe this year they find out."

"Will everything die?"

"Everthing and everbody, hit will be so."

"This year?"

"Ain't no tellen. Maybe this year."

"My mother said it is blackberry winter," I said confidently, and got up.

"Ain't sayen nuthin' agin Miss Sallie," he said.

I went to the door of the crib. I was really cold now. Running, I had got up a sweat and now I was worse.

I hung on the door, looking at Jebb, who was shelling corn again.

"There's a tramp came to the house," I said. I had almost forgotten the tramp.

"Yeah."

"He came by the back way. What was he doing down there in the storm?"

"They comes and they goes," he said, "and ain't no tellen."

"He had a mean knife."

"The good ones and the bad ones, they comes and they goes. Storm or sun, light or dark. They is folks and they comes and they goes lak folks."

I hung on the door, shivering.

He studied me a moment, then said, "You git on to the house. You ketch yore death. Then what yore mammy say?"

I hesitated.

"You git," he said.

When I came to the back yard, I saw that my father was standing by the back porch and the tramp was walking toward him. They began talking before I reached them, but I got there just as my father was saying, "I'm sorry, but I haven't got any work. I got all the hands on the place I need now. I won't need any extra until wheat thrashing."

The stranger made no reply, just looked at my father.

My father took out his leather coin purse, and got out a half-dollar. He held it toward the man. "This is for half a day," he said.

The man looked at the coin, and then at my father, making no motion to take the money. But that was the right amount. A dollar a day was what you paid them back in 1910. And the man hadn't even worked half a day.

Then the man reached out and took the coin. He dropped it into the right side pocket of his coat. Then he said, very slowly and without feeling, "I didn't want to work on your —— farm."

He used the word which they would have frailed me to death for using.

I looked at my father's face and it was streaked white under the sunburn. Then he said, "Get off this place. Get off this place or I won't be responsible."

The man dropped his right hand into his pants pocket. It was the pocket where he kept the knife. I was just about to yell to my father about the knife when the hand came back out with nothing in it. The man gave a kind of twisted grin, showing where the teeth had been knocked out above the new scar. I thought that instant how maybe he had tried before to pull a knife on somebody else and had got his teeth knocked out.

So now he just gave that twisted, sickish grin out of the unmemorable, grayish face, and then spat on the brick path. The glob landed just about six inches from the toe of my father's right boot. My father looked down at it, and so did I. I thought that if the glob had hit my father's boot, something would have happened. I looked down and saw the bright glob, and on one side of it my father's strong cowhide boots, with the brass eyelets and the leather thongs, heavy boots splashed with good red mud and set solid on the bricks, and on the other side the pointed-toe, broken, black shoes, on which the mud looked so sad and out of place. Then I saw one of the black shoes move a little, just a twitch first, then a real step backward.

The man moved in a quarter circle to the end of the porch, with my father's steady gaze upon him all the while. At the end of the porch, the man reached up to the shelf where the wash pans were to get his little newspaper-wrapped parcel. Then he disappeared around the corner of the house and my father mounted the porch and went into the kitchen without a word.

I followed around the house to see what the man would do. I wasn't afraid of him now, no matter if he did have the knife. When I got around in front, I saw him going out the yard gate and starting up the drive toward the pike. So I ran to catch up with him. He was sixty yards or so up the drive before I caught up.

I did not walk right up even with him at first, but trailed him, the way a kid will, about seven or eight feet behind, now and then running two or three steps in order to hold my place against his longer stride. When I first came up behind him, he turned to give me a look, just a meaningless look, and then fixed his eyes up the drive and kept on walking.

When we had got around the bend in the drive which cut the house from sight, and were going along by the edge of the woods, I decided to come up even with him. I ran a few steps, and was by his side, or almost, but some feet off to the right. I walked along in this position for a while, and he never noticed me. I walked along until we got within sight of the big gate that let on the pike.

Then I said, "Where did you come from?"

He looked at me then with a look which seemed almost surprised that I was there. Then he said, "It ain't none of yore business."

We went on another fifty feet.

Then I said, "Where are you going?"

He stopped, studied me dispassionately for a moment, then suddenly took a step toward me and leaned his face down at me. The lips jerked back, but not in any grin, to show where the teeth were knocked out and to make the scar on the lower lip come white with the tension.

He said, "Stop following me. You don't stop following me and I cut yore throat, you little son-of-a-bitch."

Then he went on to the gate, and up the pike.

. . .

That was thirty-five years ago. Since that time my father and mother have died. I was still a boy, but a big boy, when my father got cut on the blade of a mowing machine and died of lockjaw. My mother sold the place and went to town to live with her sister. But she never took hold after my father's death, and she died within three years, right in middle life. My aunt always said, "Sallie just died of a broken heart, she was so devoted." Dellie is dead, too, but she died, I heard, quite a long time after we sold the farm.

As for Little Jebb, he grew up to be a mean and ficey Negro. He killed another Negro in a fight and got sent to the penitentiary, where he is yet, the last I heard tell. He probably grew up to be mean and ficey from just being picked on so much by the children of the other tenants, who were jealous of Jebb and Dellie for being thrifty and clever and being white-folks' niggers.

Old Jebb lived forever. I saw him ten years ago and he was about a hundred then, and not looking much different. He was living in town then, on relief—that was back in the Depression—when I went to see him. He said to me: "Too strong to die. When I was a young feller just comen on and seen how things wuz, I prayed the Lawd. I said, Oh, Lawd, gimme strength and meke me strong fer to do and to in-dure. The Lawd hearkened to my prayer. He give me strength. I was in-duren proud fer being strong and me much man. The Lawd give me my prayer and my strength. But now He done gone off and fergot me and left me alone with my strength. A man doan know what to pray fer, and him mortal."

Jebb is probably living yet, as far as I know.

That is what has happened since the morning when the tramp leaned his face down at me and showed his teeth and said: "Stop following me. You don't stop following me and I cut yore throat, you little son-of-a-bitch." That was what he said, for me not to follow him. But I did follow him, all the years.

PORTRAIT OF
LA GRAND' BOSSE

*(The time is 1826. The place is Kentucky, an island
in the swampy country near the confluence of the
Ohio and Mississippi. Jeremiah is a young man who
has escaped with his wife Rachel from his death cell
and has fled to the wilderness. Jenkins is a river
bully, late of the keelboats. La Grand' Bosse
is what he is.)*

The light from a fire on the hearth of the cabin fell across the room
toward a great canopied tester bed of mahogany, and a grease lamp
stuck in a chink of the wall beyond the bed supplemented that illumina-
tion. "I stared," Jeremiah says in his journal, "to see that elegant furniture in such a place, for even in that room all other objects were of the
crude make of the backwoods. But I stared again, as my eyes accepted
the dimness and flickering, and as I saw the creature who was master
of that bed and that wild land of swamp and forest. He was propped
in the bed. I saw a large head, bald and swarthy and oily, the face very
wrinkled, and seeming more so for the cast of shadow across it, and on
the shoulders beneath it a scarlet coat with some gold braiding, very
tarnished, which I took to be the coat of a British officer. I say on the
shoulders of the creature, for the coat could not be brought fully across
the chest, having been cut for a smaller person, and I saw some of the
chest (the coat was spliced in the back, I was to learn), which was
sagging and creased like the flesh of an old man.

"But I have not mentioned the aspect of the creature most worthy
of note. The shoulders were very large and the head was thrust forward

Text taken from *The Kenyon Review*, Vol. 12, Winter 1950; became part of *World Enough
and Time* (1950).

from the pillows by a swelling or hump, not unlike the hump of the bull of the buffalo that roamed Kentucky before civil men had conquered the country. Seeing that hump, I suddenly knew what was the name of the creature, what Jenkins and the others had meant by the name Gran Boz. I remembered that in the French tongue the word for hump is *la bosse*, and therefore knew that what they meant to name him was La Grand' Bosse, the Big Hump. He was hump-backed, but in such a way that, by all report, his great strength had never been impaired.

"Now he leaned forward from the pillow, and blinked at us as though in drowsiness. On the far side of the bed stood a woman of dark complexion, but with hair straight rather than kinked, wrapped in a red shawl about the shoulders and with several gold rings to the fingers, which seemed to indicate some position of privilege. She was of middle years and extremely ill favored. Near the fireplace a very large man, also dark, sat on a stool and stared at Rachel. On the floor, by the head of the bed, an old Negro man was squatting with his arms hung forward between his knees. He, too, stared at Rachel.

"All at once, the eyes of La Grand' Bosse ceased to blink, as though he had come full awake, and he lifted his right hand a little in a sign, and said, 'Viens.' The word was to Rachel, but she did not understand, or stood back from fear. Then he said, 'Come—come,' in a husky tone and with a voice not well tuned to the English, and motioned again.

"Again, she did not stir, and Jenkins said, 'Git up thar, he says git up thar.'

"So she slowly approached the bed, and stopped a little back from him. He inspected her in his bleared and drowsy fashion, and I saw that his eyeballs were large and yellowish, streaked with red. He motioned again for Rachel to come closer, and she obeyed by a grudging step. I saw how white her face was and how set as from the strain of the moment.

"Again he motioned, and again she obeyed by a step. He reached up his hand very slowly. It was a large hand, swollen and crooked with age, and it moved with an enormous slowness, like something moving under its own drowsy volition. It came into contact with the cloth of her dress, fixed on a fold and clutched it, and began to draw back, with the same heavy slowness, pulling at the dress. As the strain increased, she again moved a little forward, then stopped, with the fabric straining, for there seemed great strength in that hand. His face blinked up at her.

"The man on the stool by the hearth stirred, and said, 'Il veut you come.'

"Rachel turned her face to him for an instant, like one making an appeal in despair, and he said, 'Attendez! Il veut you bend over.' This he said, too, with a tongue unaccustomed to our language.

"Thereupon Rachel leaned over. La Grand' Bosse continued to blink at her for a moment, then, not releasing the dress, lifted the other hand, a great gold ring and diamond stone glittering on it, and with the same weighted slowness it touched her cropped hair and felt it. Then he drew his hand away. 'Tête de brosse,' he said in his husky voice.

"La Bosse still clung to her dress with one hand, and she still leaned. I saw the other hand move again, but could not be sure of its intent, for the position of Rachel's body somewhat between. Then I saw her jerk a little, then stiffen, and I realized that she had submitted herself to that hand that had entered her bodice, which was low-cut, and had tried her breast.

"At that realization, I started forward and would have plunged at the bed to jerk her back and defend her, but Jenkins grasped me strongly by the wrist and twisted my arm back of a sudden and leaned at me. As I made to jerk from him, he leaned closer and said in a low voice, 'Durn fool—you be a durn fool, with him the Gran Boz,' and I caught the stench of his breath on my face.

"I would have struck him, come what might, but then I saw that Rachel had straightened up, and the gross hand was withdrawn, the diamond glittering on it, though the creature still clung to the fold of the dress, even as he said, 'Va donc, sansnichons!'

"Then, with that insulting word, which would be like naming her Little Tits for the shrunkenness of her breasts, his hand released the dress and Rachel stepped back. As she turned her face to one side I saw that it was white and she looked to be sick. I stepped forward, and supported her with an arm about her waist. Thereupon I found the eyes of La Grand' Bosse upon me. So I stood there and held up my wife, and stared back at that wrinkled and evil and greasy face, and thought how I should have struck it with my fist.

"And the face was saying to me, 'Tu—tu—on me dit che tu—che tu fais du meutre.'

" 'Murder!' I cried, for I had caught his words. 'They lie to say I murdered—I did not murder—I—' And I stumbled for speech, for what could I say to such a creature?

" 'Rien,' he said, and made a gesture with his hand, then let it fall on the cover. 'Rien, ce n'est rien,' he said, and blinked at me.

" 'But I—' I began.

"But he lifted his hand. 'Quelquefois,' he said, 'c'est necessaire.' And he repeated: 'Some time.'

"I began to speak, against my will and common sense, explaining to him, saying that I had not murdered, that if I had taken life, it was done in justice, but he lifted up his hand and said, 'Autrefois—autrefois—you tell me autrefois—how you keel—maintenant j'ai sommeil.'

"Whereupon he let his hand fall, and his eyelids shut to hide the big, bleared old eyes."

La Grand' Bosse—known on the river as Ole Big Hump or Gran Boz—had the legal name of Louis Cadeau. At least, that seems to have been his legal name, if he had any legal name. And one report has it that that name, too, was merely a nickname, and was not Cadeau at all, but Caddo, Louis Caddo, with the name derived from the Caddo tribe of Indians, and that his father was some sort of half-breed Frenchman. All reports agree that his mother was of mixed Indian and Negro blood, with a dash of Spanish or French, probably a slave. In any case, he had been spewed up out of the swamps and jungles of Louisiana, or out of some fetid alley of New Orleans—out of that dark and savage swill of bloods—a sort of monstrous bubble that rose to the surface of the pot, or a sort of great brute of the depth that swagged up from the blind, primal mud to reach the light and wallow in the stagnant flood, festooned with algae and the bright slime, with his scaled, armored, horny back just awash, like a log.

When we first hear of him, he is a trader with the Creeks in Alabama. Ferocity and cunning had already made him a name—if the rumors concerning a certain Cadeau pertain to him. Then he appears among the Cherokees in the towns of Chota and Settico in the late 1760's, when that able people was disputing the passes of the mountains and the waters of the Tennessee River with the push of immigration from the Carolinas. And he stays with the Cherokees, or at least appears and reappears among them, until near the time when Major Ore's Tennesseans fell on them by surprise at Nickajack in the fall of 1794, and broke them forever. During that long period of ambush, treachery and counter-treachery, valor, torture, and endurance, La Bosse survived and prospered. He dealt with the French. During the time of the Revolution he dealt with the British and seems to have acted as their agent to whet the tribes (his tarnished red coat must have dated from that time). He dealt with the colonists. And always during this time he is the friend of chiefs—Double Head, Bloody Fellow, The Breath, Little Owl—a strategist advising in their councils, a diplomatist, a torturer delighting

in the sound of the ritual rattle before the prisoner is put to the stake
and the flames rise. He supports and encourages the irreconcilables of
the party of Dragging Canoe, for what would peace and the penetration
of civilization mean for him? He arranges at least one truce with a white
outpost, and then, when it has been lulled by his gifts and has bought
corn from him, he sits under a tree, at night—a beech tree, according
to the story—and watches the flames rise and hears the screams of the
massacre.

In the end he betrays the Cherokees, too. Or was there any bond, any
allegiance, for him to betray? He was merely La Grand' Bosse, and
himself, and owed nothing to anyone else. Whatever the name for his
act, he threw the Indians off guard, promising to lure the whites into
an ambush, then sold the whites information about the trail over the
mountain to a village fastness guarding the river, himself led the white
party, saw the beginning of the bloody work, when squaw and babe
died beside the warrior, and pocketed his profit and faded westward
into the wilderness. He had, presumably, foreseen the end of the Chero-
kee resistance, and had cashed his investment while the market was still
good.

The Cherokees became peaceful farmers, Christians worshipping the
white man's God and aping the white man's ways, waiting unwitting
for the white man's last great betrayal that would drive them west.
Meanwhile La Grand' Bosse set himself up somewhere in the wilds
south of the Tennessee, gathered about him a few runaway slaves, some
of the white scum of the frontier, and outcast Indians, tribeless outlaws
no longer fighting for their land and their villages but robbing a cabin
or cutting a traveller's throat for the poor loot to be swapped to La
Grande' Bosse for a few sips of whisky and a pinch of powder.

La Grand' Bosse found himself, however, in a kind of backwater
here. So he moved into the country of the Natchez Trace, lingered
briefly (for the heyday of profit in that section had not come), and
struck north. According to one tradition, he built himself two great
"batteaux" on the Tennessee, loaded them with the choicest of his
cut-throats, his several families (black, white, and red, with fine impar-
tiality), his most portable plunder, a few horses, and a small brass
cannon. He drifted down the river toward the Ohio, where a rich traffic
was moving now, broadhorn and ark and galley and keelboat, where
there was no one to say nay to a strong or cunning hand, and a dead
man rotting in the cane or floating slowly toward the Gulf, naked and
swollen and faceless, nibbled by fish, told no tales.

Well before the turn of the century his presence is felt on the river.

Men who start down to New Orleans with a cargo never come back. Cargoes are bought in New Orleans with no questions asked. Possession is ownership. Isolated river settlements are raided. Tales begin of the bald, big-headed creature, with the great shoulders and humped back, more deadly than any chute or snag, an ogre of the swamps terrible enough to give bad dreams to the stoutest bully of the keelboats. Few have seen him and lived, and many have seen him. He is Ole Big Hump. He has a citadel back in the cane, armed with a dozen cannon (so the poor single piece has spawned in the legend). He has raised up a nation out of the mud back there to do his bidding. If every man's hand is against you and you have no refuge, if you are bold-hearted and black-hearted enough, if you are desperate enough to risk your life on Ole Big Hump's whim when you reach him, you may find safety there back in the cane, and a new life.

Then, one day late in 1811, when La Grand' Bosse is, we can guess, about sixty-five, Nicholas Roosevelt runs the falls at the settlement of Louisville with the *City of New Orleans* and starts downriver to the Gulf. In the weeks of waiting before high water allowed Roosevelt to run the falls, had rumor of the contraption reached into the swamps? Or did one of La Grand' Bosse's sentinels, lolling in a skiff under the frost-bitten willows, turn bug-eyed and drop his jaw when he saw the preposterous nightmare thing round a bend above, puffing the black smoke and creaking and clanking? In any case, it was the end of the great day of Ole Big Hump.

Age was already creeping upon him. More and more he had been content to lie at ease in his mud and let the younger men, his sons, slaves, and bullies, venture out for the kill on the river or on the tracks farther east. Civilization, with its rules for making profit, rules too complicated for him to understand, was creeping upon him, too. With the increase in river traffic, the prizes had become richer, dangling there before his eyes, but the risks had increased. He had already lost two sons and six men, trapped by one keelboat while they were plundering another. But it was not age or civilization that undid him in the end. He was simply the victim of technological unemployment.

More steamboats came. There was no end to their coming. They were loaded with richness, all the things that the heart can desire, bright cloths, shining gewgaws, money, women, drink, but he cannot get his hands on them. It is outrageous. It is an outrage, a profound injustice, against La Grand' Bosse, and he will not abide it. He will take a steamboat. He will take it and cut every throat and burn it in the river.

No, he will not burn it, he will take it to New Orleans himself, La Grand' Bosse. Then they will know that he is still La Grand' Bosse. They will know that they cannot flout him, for the river is his. He lies in the swamp and plans. He will make a big barge, will set up his cannon on it and anchor it in the middle of the river, and his men will be in ambush in skiffs along the shore growth. No, he will build a keelboat, no, a galley with oarsmen, the biggest ever seen, with thick walls above water, and set the cannon in that (had he heard of the armed galley that George Rogers Clark had used on this river in the Revolution?) and go out and take the steamboat. He has a thousand plans.

He goes down to the river and lies in his skiff, day after day, spying, waiting for a steamboat to come, that he may study it and perfect his plans. One comes at last, sweeping down the broad water under the black plume of smoke, passes him, strides imperiously away, and is gone. It has not even given him contempt. It has not even known he is there. And he is wild with rage. His breast will burst with rage. He strikes his hands against the edge of the skiff until they bleed. He bites his knuckles until they bleed.

"Je me mords les osselets," he says to Jeremiah, remembering the old time, and leans forward from the pillow and gnaws his knuckles to show the old passion. "They are de sang," he says, "see," and holds up his hand, with the diamond glittering, to show the blood that is not there now. "Je ne peut pas respire—mon coeur—my heart—he se crève —he break—I am insulté—" He heaves on the pillow and gasps, and the old chest swells until it seems that the red coat of a British officer will split off his back and his big, muddy, red-rimmed eyes start from the old face. "A stimbotte," he says, when he can get his breath back. "I weel take heem—I weel burn heem—I am La Grand' Bosse—" and he beats his chest, where the old flesh and muscle sag like shrunk tits, and the diamond glitters on his hand. Then he goes to sleep, and even the shadow of old rage is gone.

He had never taken a steamboat. He had never even tried. Perhaps if he had been a little younger, he would have tried, and we would have our goriest legend of the river. But he had to watch the steamboat pass on the water, and had always to come back to his stronghold in the mud, raging and bitter, to nurse plans that came to nothing, to lie in his big mahogany tester bed under the rotting canopy and drink himself drunk and take one of the women there with him—what woman he did not care, what tint or what relation, for tints and relations had long since become confused in his tribe—and fondle her and have her, if drink or anger or age was not too much for him, and then sleep.

It had been fifteen years now, almost to the month, since Nicholas Roosevelt passed with the *City of New Orleans*. It had been years now since La Grand' Bosse had even seen a steamboat. He had prowled the island, or lain there, torpid or glaring, steeping himself in the outrage, nursing the old passion, revolving the old plans, tyrannizing over his people. The stockade had fallen to ruin. The little cannon was sinking into the earth, rusting away. Some of his nation, even some of his sons or nephews or grandsons, had defied him and fled, or had merely slipped away, not even doing him the respect of defiance. But he remained, lying with his massive stupor and dark twitches amid the massive stupor and dark twitches of the wild land, while the slough steamed and simmered in summer or crusted leprous white with skim ice in the shallows when winter came, and to the north the river, where he went no more, where he was forgotten, slid past, red or green according to season, according to flood or low water, and in his treasure room the loot rotted away, the dresses and ribbons intended for vanity and joy, the silver plate, the rosary and soutane, the books he could not read—all that poor plunder of a world he had never seen and could never have understood.

It is Jeremiah Beaumont who leaves us the last record of Ole Big Hump and his nation. He was there in the last days, and put down the record in his journal. What happened to Ole Big Hump and his people after Jeremiah's departure, there is no knowing. He could not have lived much longer, for he must have been near eighty when Jeremiah saw him. He must soon have been buried there on the island. Some of his people remained there and no doubt fathered some of the breed of later river-folk, malarial, wistful, vindictive, inhabiting shanty-boats or shacks above the mud-flats, scorned by the world and deprived. But some, no doubt, were caught up into the westward sweep of the world that had, in the end, destroyed Ole Big Hump, and entered that world, and raised up sons who learned the rules and tricks of that world, who read the books and wore the clothes of that world, and voted and paid taxes and owned tidy houses with green lawns or subdivision palaces and went to the field or factory or office, and became farmers, storekeepers, statesmen, heroes, mechanics, insurance agents, executives, bankers.

So Ole Big Hump has been forgotten, but more than a century later, lying under the dank earth of his island, he might grin to think that the joke, in the end, was not on him but on the world, for those most respectable descendants, who did not know him and would have denied him with shame and repugnance, still carried under their pink scrubbed hides and double-breasted sack suits (cunningly cut to redeem the sagging paunch) the mire-thick blood of his veins and the old coiling darkness of his heart.

FROM
A PLACE TO COME TO
(1977)

At the end of this novel the middle-aged protagonist and narrator Jed Tewksbury, scholar in classical and medieval literature, after many years of wanderings and vicissitudes, returns to his birthplace, Dugton, Alabama, to visit his mother's grave.

—A.E.

When I drove up to the gate of the house on Jonquil Street, he was already on the porch, and had on his blue Sunday suit—blue serge, as it predictably turned out to be—for my coming, and he must have been watching for hours through a chink in the same front-room lace curtains my mother had nursed through all the years. In any case, as I slowed down my U-Drive-It, rented at the Huntsville Airport, he was already on the front porch, with his right arm waving creakily in welcome. Then, making his way to the gate, his big-boned, liver-spotted, joint-swollen, strong old hand already thrust out on an inadequate wristbone from a too stiffly starched white cuff, he was saying, "I'm Perk Simms, I'm Perk what had the luck to find yore ma in this dark world and I declare I will love her till the day I die."

By this time, forgetting his abortive handshake, he was grappling for my neck like a spookily inept Strangler Lewis returned from the shades, the formidable old hands on their pipestem wrists finally getting a grip, and with both arms around my neck, he pressed one of his great, bony, leathery, and imperfectly shaven cheeks, as raw as a clutch of cockleburs, against my own, all the while saying it was God's blessing to see me, there was so much to tell piling up inside him, and he claimed me like a blood-kin son, with my kind permission, for he had loved her so. And meanwhile I felt the dampness on his cheek.

I muttered what seemed appropriate, and disentangled myself to get my suitcase out of the trunk. Thereupon another struggle ensued, between me and that ectoplasmic version of a man of power, and I won, and after he had opened the gate, I carried the suitcase up to the steps and through the door, one of his bony hands on my shoulder all the way as though he needed to be reassured of my literal presence.

Once we were inside the shadowy house, even as I waited there with the suitcase still in my hand, we both stood in a kind of daze. It was, literally, a daze for me. I kept trying to fix on some small object and claim old familiarity with it—on the black-and-white china bulldog on the mantel shelf that my mother once won in a street carnival raffle, on the crocheted antimacassar-shaped thing she had made to cover the threadbare spot in the headrest of the ritual overstuffed chair in the front room, on the stereopticon viewer and the box of cards I used to spend rainy Sunday afternoons lying on my stomach staring through, on all the wonders of the world beyond Dugton, on Niagara Falls, the Pyramids, and the dynamo of the Chicago World's Fair.

I stood there, clutching the suitcase, which I was afraid to set down, for that action might break the spell, and looked long and hard at each object, until another noiselessly summoned my devotion. Each object seemed to glow with a special assertion of its being—of my being, too, as though only now, after all the years, I was returning to my final self, long lost.

It was the assertion of indestructible and absolute identity, the fullness of being and possibility—the numinousness, one might say with more than etymological whimsy, its "noddingness" at me, its recognition—that gave each object its power to draw me forth from, as it were, the long drowse of my being.

Perk Simms, feet motionlessly planted in the great box-toed, highly polished shoes (polished every Sunday and every funeral) and preternatural Adam's apple tufted with bristly gray hairs sticking out motionless above a blue-and-crimson-striped Christmas tie, seemed to respect the long experience through which I was passing. Perk watched my eyes find each object, now long familiar to him, too, but in a different way, and waited until my mystic transformation was finished. When the last was over, he came to take the suitcase from my woodenly unresisting hand. He had carried it into what had been my mother's (and his) room before I came out of my catatonia and followed him.

"You'll be comfortable here, I bet," he was saying pridefully. "You see, yore ma—now I doan mean she was ever a woman for complaining, she shore-God was not—but lately it got so her back warn't so good—standing all them years leanen over things at the can'ry, and I just went and got her the best mat-ter-ress I could learn about—it's all *or-to-peed-ic,* and it helped her good. You'll sleep good, I'll give you a certified and signed guarantee."

And he pretended to be fumbling for a fountain pen and contract. He grinned, and I grinned back the best I could.

"Much obliged, Perk," I said, "but it'll be wasted on me. I can sleep anywhere." Then, realizing that this was not the most graceful ploy, I said: "You see, Perk, I want to sleep in my old bed tonight. For old times' sake."

At that he nodded, not saying a word. He just picked up the suitcase, beating me to it, and led me to the little room I had occupied so many years and where I had lain laughing my drunk-fool head off while my ma did her work on my nose with the shoe.

"The bed's all made up," Perk said. "I don't mean just for me tonight, though I was going to sleep in here. I mean she always kept it made up. Except when she'd pull it apart for a good airen. I'd catch her at it and I used to laugh at her, before I caught on good how it was a-tween you. I'd say, 'So he's comen tonight!' 'Naw, you clabber-headed hoot owl,' she'd say, she liked to make up names to call me for fun. 'Catch him comen to Dugton, I'll break his durn neck, after all the trouble I taken to git him out. It's only I like to make a bed fer him. It's a way of sayen there's a place fer him in my heart. But he shore better stay out of town.'"

"I guess I'll unpack," I said, and got very busy with the process until he had withdrawn.

Perk said we were going to eat out—at a right new place on the highway, he said—and added he'd be eating enough of his own cooking from now on not to jump at a chance to get some other vittles. My "ma," as he always called her, she had been mighty handy at the stove and liked to see a man eat, he'd say that for her, and said it.

So we went out to the new place on the highway, where, in fact, the steaks were good and the pecan pies homemade. Several people from Dugton came in to get supper, and for each one known to Perk we had a little occasion. Perk introduced the Perfesser, who got told what a fine mother he had had and how sad he must be, and they were sorry for me and glad to see me even on a sad occasion, and were proud of me being from Dugton and being a perfesser at Chicago—or was it Kansas City?

Then we went home, and Perk poked up a coal fire in the grate, before which we drank a quantity of black coffee. Then Perk broke out the bourbon. He carefully poured himself two measured ounces, that being Ma's allowance for Sundays and holidays. He said he knowed I was a grown man and to do what I liked, but I poured myself two ounces.

Perk said that five days after the funeral he was sitting here one night about to go to pieces. Said that with the funeral and all and the next day or two with people talking to you on the street, you sort of forgot how it was going to be. Just sitting in the house at night. Said he tried to pray but he never had no sleight at it. All he could say was "God, God, God," and he felt like something was gonna bust in him. Said he tried to cry but the tears locked up inside. He had slipped, he said, when he seen me that afternoon, and he begged my pardon. But he did have some excuse. Before my mother had died, just before, she said for him to kiss her boy for her.

He said he knew a man had to learn to live by himself, but he said it was a sort of mean joke how the better a man's wife was for him and the more he appreciated her, the worse it was when she left him, you just couldn't win in that raffle. He had had the other kind of wife once, with his kid rotten, his boy shot by the cops in a stolen car, and no trouble getting a divorce the way his wife carried on.

"Then," he said, "yore ma come along and I began to like to open my eyes in the morning, there being something in the world to pleasure 'em. She sort of took me in hand. Give me a way to live and a thing to live for. And me, I'd lay awake sometimes at night trying to figger out something I could fix about the house, build a cabinet or fix a loose step or something, and wondering how she'd grin and what kind of a joke she'd make, her being so long on jokes."

It gave him something to think about now at night, he said, trying to remember the times he'd fixed something she really liked. He'd always been pretty apt with his toolbox, and even now he'd remember something at night and git up. He was trying to hold on to the habit, he said, and keep the house in shape. The house warn't his no ways he said, just for his life, it was mine by will, but he prayed God to keep strength to respect it. She'd always respected the house. No matter how hard she worked at the can'ry, she always was spick-and-span.

He almost let the fire go out, staring at it, having let the conversation die off. Then he put some coal on, and apparently catching sight of himself in a side mirror on the wall, went over there and carefully retied his striped Christmas tie, which had been climbing up his neck and over his Adam's apple like a tropical liana of peculiarly brilliant blossoms.

It was as though he had suddenly heard a voice saying, "Git up, Clabber-Head, and go fix yore tie afore it bites you in yore ear like a spreaden adder."

Having subdued the gaudy spreading adder, he returned to his chair, and downed the last watery dregs in his glass. "She had the gift," he said. "She had the sleight."

"What?" I demanded.

"All her funning and all," he said, "she had the sleight. To make a man always feel like a man. She could stop anything she was doing—washing dishes or anything—and just for a second give you a look that made you feel you and her had a wonderful secret. Sometimes I might be helping her make up a bed on Saturday and she'd give me a wink, and then pretend she hadn't never. She never come home and found me in the house without taking on over me like I was a surprise package—a big fuss, then she'd turn that into a joke, too."

He paused, looking into the fire. "We was married a long time, son. I mean, Perfesser."

"I wish you'd make it son," I said.

"Thank you kindly," he said. "As I was saying, we was married a long time," he repeated, like a lesson, "ever since before you got your growth good, and she never lost the sleight to make a man feel like a man, like she set store by him."

Then: "A man gets old, he ain't what he was. Ain't worth powder and lead to perish. Ain't nothing but spindle bones stuck in a pair of pants. But living with a woman like yore ma"—and here he stopped, twisted in his chair, and seemed to be physically struggling to phrase something just right—"it is like you was living in a—a dream—and time ain't gone by, the way she could make you feel that everything kept on being the truth."

The next pause was a long one. Twice he picked up the empty glass from the floor beside him, tightened his grip on it, and set it back down.

"All she done for me—" he burst out, croakingly.

I waited, for I caught the peculiar inflection.

"And then what she did," he said, "and on her dying bed."

I waited, for I now could tell that whatever it was, it had to come.

"Holding her hand," he said, "setting close to the bed, that's where I was, and she said it. Ast me did I know she loved me. I nodded my head, being a-sudden choked up. Then you know what she said?"

I shook my head.

"She said for me to forgive her," he managed to get out, "she loved me and declared she never knowed a better man and more fitter for her, and she said she prayed God I'd come to know it was not to kick up dirt in my—in my—" He did a few contortions in his chair, then took it head-on: "To kick up dirt in my—in my sweet ole face— No, don't make no mistake, Perfesser, them was the words she spoke, not me." After a little: "Do you know what it was on her mind?"

"No."

"She wanted to be buried out in Heaven's Hope graveyard," he said. "Next to—to you know who." Then: "What kin a man do! You do the best the Lord lets you, and it is like all yore love, it is in vain. All I could do was git out of that hospital chair and git out in the hall, and find a settee in the room at the end. I got there just in time to set."

After a long pause he managed to continue: "When I sort of taken holt, I come back. And she said, did I understand, and I could not say yes, and I could not say no. I was froze. She said, please, to understand, that if something in yore past time was good even a little time, it deserves you not to spit on it, no matter how bad it turned out, and she did not want to see anything good ever happened to her throwed away like dirt. And she said: 'Both the happiness and the miserableness I learned when I was young, it was that that made me ready to set all my heart on you when you come by, Pore Ole Clabber-Head.' "

He turned at me in an awful voice of chill fury, saying: "What's a man to do?"

The nurse, Perk said, had come in by now and she motioned to him. My mother was sure weak by this time, Perk said, and the words faint. But seeing the nurse, she got stronger, Perk said, like a last thing that had to be said. "You'll understand," she said to him, "for I'll be with you in the house, helping you understand all day, and I'll be laying by yore side a-nights."

Then the doctor came and motioned to Perk.

That was the last time except for a minute or two that Perk saw her. They let him go back in to hold her hand. "I understood it was sort of goodbye," Perk said. "Her eyes was closed, but now and then she sort of gripped my hand, and I let her know I felt it. Then I did the foolest thing of my life. I leaned over and said right soft, 'Don't you be afraid. I'm here, and I doan want you afraid.'

"And you know what? The God-durnedest thing happened. Soon as I got them fool words out, her eyes popped wide open, bright and shiny black like when she was excited or full of fun, and her voice was a-sudden strong, almost like usual, and she said: 'Dying—shucks! If you kin handle the living, what's to be afraid of the dying?' "

.   .   .

We sat by the smoldering fire another half-hour or so. Then Perk said he reckoned we might go to bed. So we shook hands good night.

He said if I heard a noise, it was him wandering around. But he'd be as still as he could.

So I said good night again and went into the bathroom to do my duties and on to bed.

My light had been out a time and I was staring up at the dark when the knock came at my door. I called, and Perk entered, turning on the switch by the door to make the top light blaze. He had a great lot of papers under his left arm, various manila files with rubber bands around them and stacks of letters tied in old ribbons of different colors.

"Something I forgot," he said sheepishly.

I sat up in bed and he pulled up a chair. He carefully laid aside the files, which seemed to be of newspaper clippings, and nursed the pile of letters in his lap.

"She set by the fire a-nights," he said, "and read these here letters. I'd be a-reading the paper. Then she'd come acrost something she'd forgot, and she'd slap herself on the thigh and bust out laughing, a-saying, 'Now listen, will ye, ain't he a rooster!' "

So now I sat propped in my bed, while he read, as he said she had done, and listened to some fool insanity of my own, some description of somebody, some joke, some remarks about a dumb class, some lie I had written to please her, now sitting there trying to remember where, when, why I had written each stupid item, feeling my life go by me like a black blast of wind of mounting intensity and from a quarter undefined, until I said, "Excuse me," and took my suitcase and went to the bathroom and exhumed my private supply and took three long gulps of whiskey, and came back, and got propped in bed to resume the inquisitorial infliction.

Superfluously inquisitorial, I may add, for I was long since prepared to confess to anything whatsoever. But I did not know what the Inquisitor wanted me to confess to in particular.

The only thing I could think of confessing was that I was I.

It had flurried snow during the night, and though my rented car was parked out there by a road of blacktop shiny in the sun, here in Heaven's Hope graveyard the snow was still powdery white on fallen leaves, like sugar sprinkled on cornflakes. The last time I had traveled this road, I had been a little snot-nose sprig lost in the world, on a wagon stuffed with our meager household gear, and the iron tires of

the wagon wheels had seemed to grind the gravel on forever on the way
to Dugton and the shadowy future. Now, standing in the graveyard,
I remembered how the snot-nose sprig had stolen one look, like crime
or not-yet-developed masturbation, toward the spot of heaped raw
ground where lay the father he would never see again.

This return trip had taken only twenty-five minutes on blacktop, and
a quarter of a mile up the road toward Dugton there was already a real
development started—two split-level ranch-type houses glittering with
new and untarnished mortgages; and the kind of people who used to
sweat and moan in anguish for their salvation in the little goods-box-
sized church, and bury their dead in the Heaven's Hope graveyard,
were long since gone, or had transmogrified themselves into another
kind of people.

I knew what the church was like now. I had just inspected it. The
steeple, never too steady on its pins, had long back definitively collapsed, and the bell had been made off with. Wind, weather, and
wandering fowl of the air now made entrance and exit at will through
apertures once covered by colored paper on window glass to shed a dim
religious light. The little pump-organ, which had suffered some random mayhem from hands of the ungodly, had now taken a thirty-five-
degree header at the corner where the floor had finally rotted out. The
scene was the same as that of one of the more famous photographs by
Walker Evans, but a generation of damage later. Walker Evans should
have hung on to take the valedictory view, for now the last soul had
been saved here and the last flesh committed to the process of nature.

No—my mother's body might not be the last thus consigned. I had
that very morning promised Perk that when he died and got cremated,
I would personally see that his ashes got stuck in the ground out here.
"Just anywheres, not too unhandy to Ma," he had said. "And no stone
—no funeral, no nothing. Whatever my life was, there warn't nothing
to brag on but her, and that don't belong on no stone. Just here, it
belongs—here—" he had burst out, and struck himself on the chest
with such vigor as to upset his coffee cup.

After a moment, having wiped up the coffee and replenished the cup,
he had said: "What's writing for, no ways, on a stone in a place like
this, all ruint. Nothing but common folks to begin with, and now who
comes? I say, let folks lay with what's in they hearts."

Later, having extracted my solemn promise, he added that when the
time came, I would find a spade in the cellar with his garden tools. He
was one, he said, always believed in keeping a man's tools in order.

So now I wandered around and idly tried to decide on a good, not too unhandy place for Perk's ashes, Perk not having come with me, saying he believed a man sometimes wanted to be by himself.

Yes, I had wanted to be alone. And now I was. I was alone with what Perk Simms had told me: "You know, she said she done the best she knowed to raise you right and git you out of Dugton, and keep you out."

And: "She kept that bed fresh ever night. Said it was the least she could do."

And: "When that photo-shot of yore boy Eph—that's what we calls him—come, she kiss it ever night, and say, 'Now, ain't he a rooster?' And she'd grin. And one time she said she'd give a million dollars to have holt of him in her arms not more'n five minutes."

And: "Gittin on later, when come a photo-shot of Eph sort of growed up, she kept looking at it, a-saying, 'You know, if I could only be behind a post or something or in a crowd and only look at him to the content of my heart and him not know! That would be enough,' she said."

And: "Time that letter come about you and Eph's mother split up, looked like she couldn't believe it. That night, us in bed, she put her head on my shoulder to cry, a-saying, 'Don't my boy ever have no luck? Gits his name in the papers, makes good money, but don't he know nothing's no good when the lonesome time come?' "

Ah, but I knew about the lonesome time!

I sat on a moss-grown, fallen tombstone, and thought how all things I did to ward off the lonesome time seemed to come to nothing. I had not been found worthy to sit on the placeless, sunlit lawn of Dante's vision and listen to the blessèd music that was the language uttered by the saints and sages—or, at least, I had brought back no fair report to open the ears of others. I was no citizen, after all, of the *imperium intellectus*. My naturalization papers were forged. And as for the kindly thought that Dr. Stahlmann had long ago held out to me—the hope that out of my anger, my innocence, what he called my *sancta simplicitas*, I might write a worthy thing—what a comedy!

The mysterious anger was there, and unannealed, God knew. But my *simplicitas* was not *sancta*. My *simplicitas* had lost the blessèdness of knowing that men were real, and brothers in their reality. And all I had in place of that was a vast number of cards that measured three by five inches, with notes in my large and legible script. But could not a man pray?

Was all too late? Was all too late, after all?

I had the wild impulse to lie on the earth between the two graves, the old and the new, and stretch out a hand to each. I thought that if I could do that, I might be able to weep, and if I could weep, something warm and blessèd might happen. But I did not lie down. The trouble was, I was afraid that nothing might happen, and I was afraid to take the risk.

And I had the notion of coming back when Perk died—that shouldn't be too long now and I'd be getting toward retirement. I would come back and live alone in that house on Jonquil Street, that Perk, handy with tools as he was, would have left in good shape, and at night, in winter, I would sit by the fire and try to figure out why things had all turned out the way they had. And later, not being able to sleep, I might get up and wander about with a dimming flashlight in my hand to touch familiar objects.

Well, I couldn't stay here all day. I had a plane to catch. After a last look at the graves, I went and started up the car. All very businesslike, with squared shoulders.

Then it came to mind that I had one further piece of business. To see the spot where Buck Tewksbury had taken his lethal header with the noble dong in clutch. It was just beyond the old iron bridge, "t'other side o' the church." That was what a man had said, standing under the chinaberry tree, long ago, but the voice was clear in my ear.

I was at the church now, so that meant toward Dugton. The trouble was, there wasn't any old iron bridge. There wasn't even a creek now. Podmore Creek, I suddenly remembered its name—the creek my mother had thrown the saber into. Now only a couple of big culverts went under the road, and so it must have been along here before they drained for the new development and the untarnished mortgages. But there was no marker, nothing to inform the tourist that at this spot Buck Tewksbury—remarkable man that he was—did so-and-so.

I drove on and thought that the only thing wrong with Buck was he was born out of phase. If he had been born in 1840, he would have been just ripe for sergeant in a troop of Alabama cavalry. You could see him, high in stirrups, black mustaches parted to expose white teeth and emit the great yell, the saber, light as a toy in his big hand, flashing like flame. Buck leading the charge, Buck breveted rank by rank, Buck the darling of his tattered wolfish crew, Buck in some last action under Forrest—say, in the last breakthrough into Tennessee—meeting lead as the saber flashes and the yell fades from his throat.

Poor Buck, I thought.
Then I said out loud: "Poor Buck."

A month later, back in Chicago, I wrote the letter:

Dear Dauphine:
   You have known me a long time and know what I am, too, for it
is unlikely that we change much. But perhaps, in what little growth
of wisdom is granted us, I am wiser than when, a thousand years ago,
in our ignorance, we quarreled over politics, or even a little wiser
than when years later you said everything was wrong and wept in
despair. And we do have Ephraim. And his gloriousness may give
some indication that his father may not be entirely without worth.
   It would be disingenuous of me to appeal to your feelings by
saying that you and I should be together to rejoice in him. I ask for
your company because it is what I feel myself most deeply craving.

At this point I laid down my pen and stared into distance for a long
time. Then I resumed:

   It is not that I cannot stand solitude. Perhaps I stand it all too easily,
   and have been, far beyond my own knowing, solitary all my life.
   I ask for your company for what blessèdness it is. But I say also
   that in it I may learn, even as the light fails, a little of what I need
   to know.
                              In all hope,
                              Your (whether you like it or not) JED

   It was night, but I did not want to wait until morning to post the
letter. I went out, found a mailbox, and then walked for a long time.
In the course of my wanderings, I fell into the fantasy that someday
—perhaps on the mission to put the ashes of Pore Ole Perk in the
ground, unmarked, but not too unhandy to the spot where Ma lay—
I would be accompanied by Ephraim, and I could point out to him all
the spots that I had dreamed of pointing out to him.

NONFICTION

PURE AND
IMPURE POETRY

Critics are rarely faithful to their labels and their special strategies. Usually the critic will confess that no one strategy—the psychological, the moralistic, the formalistic, the historical—or combination of strategies, will quite work the defeat of the poem. For the poem is like the monstrous Orillo in Boiardo's *Orlando Innamorato*. When the sword lops off any member of the monster, that member is immediately rejoined to the body, and the monster is as formidable as ever. But the poem is even more formidable than the monster, for Orillo's adversary finally gained a victory by an astonishing feat of dexterity: he slashed off both the monster's arms and quick as a wink seized them and flung them into the river. The critic who vaingloriously trusts his method to account for the poem, to exhaust the poem, is trying to emulate this dexterity: he thinks that he, too, can win by throwing the lopped-off arms into the river. But he is doomed to failure. Neither fire nor water will suffice to prevent the rejoining of the mutilated members to the monstrous torso. There is only one way to conquer the monster: you must eat it, bones, blood, skin, pelt, and gristle. And even then the monster is not dead, for it lives in you, is assimilated into you, and you

First published in *The Kenyon Review*, Spring 1943. In 1958 it was included in *Selected Essays*, from which this text was taken.

are different, and somewhat monstrous yourself, for having eaten it.

So the monster will always win, and the critic knows this. He does not want to win. He knows that he must always play stooge to the monster. All he wants to do is to give the monster—the poem—a chance to exhibit again its miraculous power, which is poetry.

With this fable, I shall begin by observing that poetry wants to be pure. And it always succeeds in this ambition. In so far as we have poetry at all, it is always pure poetry; that is, it is not non-poetry. The poetry of Shakespeare, the poetry of Pope, the poetry of Herrick, is pure, in so far as it is poetry at all. We call the poetry "higher" or "lower," we say "more powerful" or "less powerful" about it, and we are, no doubt, quite right in doing so. The souls that form the great rose of Paradise are seated in banks and tiers of ascending blessedness, but they are all saved, they are all perfectly happy; they are all "pure," for they have all been purged of mortal taint. This is not to say, however, that if we get poetry from only one source, say Shakespeare, such a single source ought to suffice us, in as much as we can always appeal to it; or that, since all poetry is equally pure, we engage in a superfluous labor in trying to explore or create new sources of poetry. No, for we can remember that every soul in the great rose is precious in the eyes of God. No soul is the substitute for another.

Poetry wants to be pure, but poems do not. At least, most of them do not want to be too pure. The poems want to give us poetry, which is pure, and the elements of a poem, in so far as it is a good poem, will work together toward that end, but many of the elements, taken in themselves, may actually seem to contradict that end, or be neutral toward the achieving of that end. Are we then to conclude that neutral or recalcitrant elements are simply an index to human frailty, and that in a perfect world there would be no dross in poems, which would, then, be perfectly pure? No, it does not seem to be merely the fault of our world, for the poems include, deliberately, more of the so-called dross than would appear necessary. They are not even as pure as they might be in this imperfect world. They mar themselves with cacophonies, jagged rhythms, ugly words and ugly thoughts, colloquialisms, clichés, sterile technical terms, headwork and argument, self-contradictions, clevernesses, irony, realism—all things which call us back to the world of prose and imperfection.

Sometimes a poet will reflect on this state of affairs, and grieve. He will decide that he, at least, will try to make one poem as pure as possible. So he writes:

Now sleeps the crimson petal, now the white;
Nor waves the cypress in the palace walk;
Nor winks the gold fin in the porphyry font.
The fire-fly wakens; waken thou with me.

We know the famous garden—the garden in Tennyson's "Princess."
We know how all nature conspires here to express the purity of the
moment: how the milk-white peacock glimmers like a ghost, and how
like a ghost the unnamed "she" glimmers on to her tryst; how earth lies
"all Danaë to the stars," as the beloved's heart lies open to the lover;
and how, in the end, the lily folds up her sweetness, "and slips into the
bosom of the lake," as the lovers are lost in the sweet dissolution of love.

And we know another poet and another garden. Or perhaps it is the
same garden, after all, viewed by a different poet, Shelley.

I arise from dreams of thee
In the first sweet sleep of night,
When the winds are breathing low,
And the stars are shining bright.
I arise from dreams of thee,
And a spirit in my feet
Hath led me—who knows how?
To thy chamber window, Sweet!

We remember how, again, all nature conspires, how the wandering airs
"faint," how the Champak's odors "pine," how the nightingale's complaint "dies upon her heart," as the lover will die upon the beloved's
heart. Nature here strains out of nature, it wants to be called by another
name, it wants to spiritualize itself by calling itself another name. How
does the lover get to the chamber window? He refuses to say how, in
his semi-somnambulistic daze, he got there. He blames, he says, "a spirit
in my feet," and hastens to disavow any knowledge of how that spirit
operates. In any case, he arrives at the chamber window. Subsequent
events and the lover's reaction toward them are somewhat hazy. We
know only that the lover, who faints and fails at the opening of the last
stanza and who asks to be lifted from the grass by a more enterprising
beloved, is in a condition of delectable passivity, in which distinctions
blur out in the "purity" of the moment.

Let us turn to another garden: the place, Verona; the time, a summer
night, with full moon. The lover speaks:

> *But, soft! what light through yonder*
> *window breaks?*
> *It is the east . . .*

But we know the rest, and know that this garden, in which nature for the moment conspires again with the lover, is the most famous of them all, for the scene is justly admired for its purity of effect, for giving us the very essence of young, untarnished love. Nature conspires benefi-cently here, but we may remember that beyond the garden wall strolls Mercutio, who can celebrate Queen Mab, but who is always aware that nature has other names as well as the names the pure poets and pure lovers put upon her. And we remember that Mercutio, outside the wall, has just said:

> *. . . 'twould anger him*
> *To raise a spirit in his mistress' circle*
> *Of some strange nature, letting it there stand*
> *Till she had laid it and conjured it down.*

Mercutio has made a joke, a bawdy joke. That is bad enough, but worse, he has made his joke witty and, worst of all, intellectually complicated in its form. Realism, wit, intellectual complication—these are the ene-mies of the garden purity.

But the poet has not only let us see Mercutio outside the garden wall. Within the garden itself, when the lover invokes nature, when he spiritualizes and innocently trusts her, and says,

> *Lady, by yonder blessed moon I swear,*

the lady herself replies,

> *O! swear not by the moon, the inconstant moon,*
> *That monthly changes in her circled orb.*

The lady distrusts "pure" poems, nature spiritualized into forgetful-ness. She has, as it were, a rigorous taste in metaphor, too; she brings a logical criticism to bear on the metaphor which is too easy; the metaphor must prove itself to her, must be willing to subject itself to scrutiny beyond the moment's enthusiasm. She injects the impurity of an intellectual style into the lover's pure poem.

And we must not forget the voice of the nurse, who calls from within, a voice which, we discover, is the voice of expediency, of half-measures, of the view that circumstances alter cases—the voice of prose and imperfection.

It is time to ask ourselves if the celebrated poetry of this scene, which as poetry is pure, exists despite the impurities of the total composition, if the effect would be more purely poetic were the nurse and Mercutio absent and the lady a more sympathetic critic of pure poems. I do not think so. The effect might even be more vulnerable poetically if the impurities were purged away. Mercutio, the lady, and the nurse are critics of the lover, who believes in pure poems, but perhaps they are necessary. Perhaps the lover can be accepted only in their context. The poet seems to say: "I know the worst that can be said on this subject, and I am giving fair warning. Read at your own risk." So the poetry arises from a recalcitrant and contradictory context; and finally involves that context.

Let us return to one of the other gardens, in which there is no Mercutio or nurse, and in which the lady is more sympathetic. Let us mar its purity by installing Mercutio in the shrubbery, from which the poet was so careful to banish him. You can hear his comment when the lover says:

> *And a spirit in my feet*
> *Hath led me—who knows how?*
> *To thy chamber window, Sweet!*

And we can guess what the wicked tongue would have to say in response to the last stanza.

It may be that the poet should have made early peace with Mercutio, and appealed to his better nature. For Mercutio seems to be glad to co-operate with a poet. But he must be invited; otherwise, he is apt to show a streak of merry vindictiveness about the finished product. Poems are vulnerable enough at best. Bright reason mocks them like sun from a wintry sky. They are easily left naked to laughter when leaves fall in the garden and the cold winds come. Therefore, they need all the friends they can get, and Mercutio, who is an ally of reason and who himself is given to mocking laughter, is a good friend for a poem to have.

On what terms does a poet make his peace with Mercutio? There are about as many sets of terms as there are good poets. I know that I have loaded the answer with the word *good* here, that I have implied a scale of excellence based, in part at least, on degree of complication. I shall return to this question. For the moment, however, let us examine an anonymous sixteenth-century poem whose apparent innocence and simple lyric cry should earn it a place in any anthology of "pure poetry."

> *Western wind, when will thou blow,*
> *The small rain down can rain?*
> *Christ, if my love were in my arms*
> *And I in my bed again!*

The lover, grieving for the absent beloved, cries out for relief. Several kinds of relief are involved in the appeal to the wind. First, there is the relief that would be had from the sympathetic manifestation of nature. The lover, in his perturbation of spirit, invokes the perturbations of nature. He invokes the beneficent perturbation,

> *Western wind, when will thou blow,*

as Lear invokes the destructive,

> *Blow, winds, and crack your cheeks! rage! blow!*

Second, there is the relief that would be had by the fulfillment of grief —the frost of grief, the drought of grief broken, the full anguish expressed, then the violence allayed in the peace of tears. Third, there is the relief that would be had in the excitement and fulfillment of love itself. There seems to be a contrast between the first two types of relief and the third type; speaking loosely, we may say that the first two types are romantic and general, the third type realistic and specific. So much for the first two lines.

In the last two lines, the lover cries out for the specific solace of his case: reunion with his beloved. But there is a difference between the two lines. The first is general, and romantic. The phrase "in my arms" does not seem to mean exactly what it says. True, it has a literal meaning, if we can look close at the words, but it is hard to look close because of the romantic aura—the spiritualized mist about them.[1] But

---

[1] It may be objected here that I am reading the phrase "in my arms" as a twentieth-century reader. I confess the fact. Certainly, several centuries have passed since the composition of the little poem, and those centuries have thickened the romantic mist about the words, but it is scarcely to be believed that the sixteenth century was the clear, literal Eden dawn of poetry when words walked without the fig leaf.

with the last line the perfectly literal meaning suddenly comes into sharp focus. The mist is rifted and we can look straight at the words, which, we discover with a slight shock of surprise, do mean exactly what they say. The last line is realistic and specific. It is not even content to say,

And I in bed again!

It is, rather, more scrupulously specific, and says,

And I in my *bed again!*

All of this does not go to say that the realistic elements here are to be taken as canceling, or negating, the romantic elements. There is no ironical leer. The poem is not a celebration of carnality. It is a faithful lover who speaks. He is faithful to the absent beloved, and he is also faithful to the full experience of love. That is, he does not abstract one aspect of the experience and call it the whole experience. He does not strain nature out of nature; he does not overspiritualize nature. This nameless poet would never have said, in the happier days of his love, that he had been led to his Sweet's chamber window by "a spirit in my feet"; and he certainly would not have added the coy disavowal, "who knows how?" But because the nameless poet refused to overspiritualize nature, we can accept the spirituality of the poem.

Another poem gives us another problem.

Ah, what avails the sceptered race!
    Ah, what the form divine!
What every virtue, every grace!
    Rose Aylmer, all were thine.

Rose Aylmer, whom these wakeful eyes
    May weep, but never see,
A night of memories and of sighs
    I consecrate to thee.

This is another poem about lost love: a "soft" subject. Now, to one kind of poet the soft subject presents a sore temptation. Because it is soft in its natural state, he is inclined to feel that to get at its poetic essence he must make it softer still, that he must insist on its softness, that he must render it as "pure" as possible. At first glance, it may seem that Landor is trying to do just that. What he says seems to be emphatic, unqualified, and open. Not every power, grace, and virtue could avail to preserve his love. That statement insists on the pathetic contrast. And in the next stanza, wakefulness and tearfulness are mentioned quite unashamedly, along with memories and sighs. It is all blurted out, as pure as possible.

But only in the paraphrase is it "blurted." The actual quality of the first stanza is hard, not soft. It is a chiseled stanza, in which formality is insisted upon. We may observe the balance of the first and second lines; the balance of the first half with the second half of the third line, which recapitulates the structure of the first two lines; the balance of the two parts of the last line, though here the balance is merely a rhythmical and not a sense balance as in the preceding instances; the binders of discreet alliteration, repetition, and assonance. The stanza is built up, as it were, of units which are firmly defined and sharply separated, phrase by phrase, line by line. We have the formal control of the soft subject, ritual and not surrender.

But in the second stanza the rigor of this formality is somewhat abated, as the more general, speculative emphasis (why cannot pomp, virtue, and grace avail?) gives way to the personal emphasis, as though the repetition of the beloved's name had, momentarily, released the flood of feeling. The first line of the second stanza spills over into the second; the "wakeful eyes" as subject find their verb in the next line, "weep," and the *wake-weep* alliteration, along with the pause after *weep*, points up the disintegration of the line, just as it emphasizes the situation. Then with the phrase "but never see" falling away from the long thrust of the rhetorical structure to the pause after *weep*, the poem seems to go completely soft, the frame is broken. But, even as the poet insists on "memories and sighs," in the last two lines he restores the balance. Notice the understatement of "A night." It says: "I know that life is a fairly complicated affair, and that I am committed to it and to its complications. I intend to stand by my commitment, as a man of integrity, that is, to live despite the grief. Since life is complicated, I cannot, if I am to live, spare too much time for indulging grief. I can give *a* night, but not all nights." The lover, like the hero of Frost's poem "Stopping by Woods on a Snowy Evening," tears himself from the temptation of staring into the treacherous, delicious blackness, for he, too, has "promises to keep." Or he resembles the Homeric heroes who, after the perilous passage is made, after their energy has saved their lives, and after they have beached their craft and eaten their meal, can then set aside an hour before sleep to mourn the comrades lost by the way—the heroes who, as Aldous Huxley says, understand realistically a whole truth as contrasted with a half-truth.

Is this a denial of the depth and sincerity of the grief? The soft reader, who wants the poem pure, may be inclined to say so. But let us look at the last line to see what it gives us in answer to this question. The answer seems to lie in the word *consecrate*. The meter thrusts this word at us; we observe that two of the three metrical accents in the line fall on syllables of this word, forcing it beyond its prose emphasis. The word is important and the importance is justified, for the word tells us that the single night is not merely a lapse into weakness, a trivial event to be forgotten when the weakness is overcome. It is, rather, an event of the most extreme and focal importance, an event formally dedicated, "set apart for sacred uses," an event by which other events are to be measured. So the word *consecrate* formalizes, philosophizes, ritualizes the grief; it specifies what in the first stanza has been implied by style.

But here is another poem of grief, grief at the death of a child. It is "Bells for John Whiteside's Daughter," by John Crowe Ransom.[2]

> There was such speed in her little body,
> And such lightness in her footfall,
> It is no wonder her brown study
> Astonishes us all.
>
> Her wars were bruited in our high window.
> We looked among orchard trees and beyond,
> Where she took arms against her shadow,
> Or harried unto the pond
>
> The lazy geese, like a snow cloud
> Dripping their snow on the green grass,
> Tricking and stopping, sleepy and proud,
> Who cried in goose, Alas,
>
> For the tireless heart within the little
> Lady with rod that made them rise
> From their noon apple-dreams, and scuttle
> Goose-fashion under the skies!
>
> But now go the bells, and we are ready;
> In one house we are sternly stopped
> To say we are vexed at her brown study,
> Lying so primly propped.

2 From *Selected Poems*, by John Crowe Ransom. Copyright, 1924, 1945, by Alfred A. Knopf, Inc. Used by permission.

Another soft subject, softer, if anything, than the subject of "Rose Aylmer," and it presents the same problem. But the problem is solved in a different way.

The first stanza is based on two time-honored clichés: first, "Heavens, won't that child ever be still, she is driving me distracted"; and second, "She was such an active, healthy-looking child, who would've ever thought she would just up and die?" In fact, the whole poem develops these clichés, and exploits, in a backhand fashion, the ironies implicit in their interrelation. And in this connection, we may note that the fact of the clichés, rather than more original or profound observations at the root of the poem, is important; there is in the poem the contrast between the staleness of the clichés and the shock of the reality. Further, we may note that the second cliché is an answer, savagely ironical in itself, to the first: the child you wished would be still *is* still, despite all that activity which had interrupted your adult occupations.

But such a savage irony is not the game here. It is too desperate, too naked, in a word, too pure. And ultimately, it is, in a sense, a meaningless irony if left in its pure state, because it depends on a mechanical, accidental contrast in nature, void of moral content. The poem is concerned with modifications and modulations of this brute, basic irony, modulations and modifications contingent upon an attitude taken toward it by a responsible human being, the speaker of the poem. The savagery is masked, or ameliorated.

In this connection, we may observe, first, the phrase "brown study." It is not the "frosted flower," the "marmoreal immobility," or any one of a thousand such phrases which would aim for the pure effect. It is merely the brown study which astonishes—a phrase which denies, as it were, the finality of the situation, underplays the pathos, and merely reminds one of those moments of childish pensiveness into which the grownup cannot penetrate. And the phrase itself is a cliché—the common now echoed in the uncommon.

Next, we may observe that stanzas two, three, and four simply document, with a busy yet wavering rhythm (one sentence runs through the three stanzas), the tireless naughtiness which was once the cause of rebuke, the naughtiness which disturbed the mature goings-on in the room with the "high window." But the naughtiness is now transmuted into a kind of fanciful story-book dream world, in which geese are whiter than nature, and the grass greener, in which geese speak in goose language, saying "Alas," and have apple-dreams. It is a drowsy, delicious world, in which the geese are bigger than life, and more important. It is an unreal (now unreal because lost), stylized world. Notice how the phrase "the little lady with rod" works: the detached primness of "little lady"; the formal, stiff effect gained by the omission of the article before *rod;* the slightly unnatural use of the word *rod* itself, which sets some distance between us and the scene (perhaps with the hint of the fairy story, a magic wand, or a magic rod—not a common, everyday stick). But the stanzas tie back into the premises of the poem in other ways. The little girl, in her excess of energy, warred against her shadow. Is it crowding matters too hard to surmise that the shadow here achieves a sort of covert symbolic significance? The little girl lost her war against her "shadow," which was always with her. Certainly the phrase "tireless heart" has some rich connotations. And the geese which say "Alas" conspire with the family to deplore the excessive activity of the child. (They do not conspire to express the present grief, only the past vexation—an inversion of the method of the pastoral elegy, or of the method of the first two garden poems.)

The business of the three stanzas, then, may be said to be twofold. First, they make us believe more fully in the child and therefore in the fact of the grief itself. They "prove" the grief, and they show the deliciousness of the lost world which will never look the same from the high window. Second, and contrariwise, they "transcend" the grief, or at least give a hint of a means for transcending immediate anguish: the lost world is, in one sense, redeemed out of time; it enters the pages of the picture book where geese speak, where the untrue is true, where the fleeting is fixed. What was had cannot, after all, be lost. (By way of comparison—a comparison which, because extreme, may be helpful —we may think of the transcendence in *La Recherche du Temps Perdu.*) The three stanzas, then, to state it in another way, have validated the first stanza and have prepared for the last.

The three stanzas have made it possible for us to say, when the bell tolls, "we are ready." Some kind of terms, perhaps not the best terms possible but some kind, has been made with the savage underlying irony. But the terms arrived at do not prevent the occasion from being a "stern" one. The transcendence is not absolute, and in the end is possible only because of an exercise of will and self-control. Because we control ourselves, we can say "vexed" and not some big word. And the word itself picks up the first of the domestic clichés on which the poem is based—the outburst of impatience at the naughty child who, by dying, has performed her most serious piece of naughtiness. But now the word comes to us charged with the burden of the poem, and further, as re-echoed here by the phrase "brown study," charged by the sentence in which it occurs: we are gathered formally, ritualistically, sternly together to say the word *vexed*. [3] *Vexed* becomes the ritualistic, the summarizing word.

I have used the words *pure* and *impure* often in the foregoing pages, and I confess that I have used them rather loosely. But perhaps it has been evident that I have meant something like this: the pure poem tries to be pure by excluding, more or less rigidly, certain elements which might qualify or contradict its original impulse. In other words, the pure poems want to be, and desperately, all of a piece. It has also been evident, no doubt, that the kinds of impurity which are admitted or excluded by the various little anthology pieces which have been presented, are different in the different poems. This is only to be expected, for there is not one doctrine of "pure poetry"—not one definition of what constitutes impurity in poems—but many.

And not all of the doctrines are recent. When, for example, one cites Poe as the father of *the* doctrine of pure poetry, one is in error; Poe simply fathered a particular doctrine of pure poetry. One can find other doctrines of purity long antedating Poe. When Sir Philip Sidney, for example, legislated against tragicomedy, he was repeating a current doctrine of purity. When Ben Jonson told William Drummond that Donne, for not keeping of accent, deserved hanging, he was defending another kind of purity; and when Dryden spoke to save the ear of the fair sex from metaphysical perplexities in amorous poems, he was defending another kind of purity, just as he was defending another when he defined the nature of the heroic drama. The eighteenth century had a doctrine of pure poetry, which may be summed up under the word *sublimity*, but which involved two corollary doctrines, one concerning diction and the other concerning imagery. But at the same time that this century, by means of these corollary doctrines, was tidying up and purifying the doctrine derived from Longinus, it was admitting into the drama certain impurities which the theorists of the heroic drama would not have admitted.

---

[3] It might be profitable, in contrast with this poem, to look at "After the Burial," by James Russell Lowell, a poem which is identical in situation. But in Lowell's poem the savagery of the irony is unqualified. In fact, the whole poem insists, quite literally, that qualification is impossible: the scheme of the poem is to set up the brute fact of death against possible consolations. It insists on "tears," the "thin-worn locket," the "anguish of deathless hair," "the smallness of the child's grave," the "little shoe in the corner." It is a poem which, we might say, does not progress, but ends where it begins, resting in savage irony from which it stems; or we might say that it is a poem without any "insides," for the hero of the poem is not attempting to do anything about the problem which confronts him—it is a poem without issue, without conflict, a poem of unconditional surrender. In other words, it tries to be a pure poem, pure grief, absolutely inconsolable. It is a strident poem, and strident in its rhythms. The fact that we know this poem to be an expression of a bereavement historically real makes it an embarrassing poem, as well. It is a naked poem.

But when we think of the modern doctrine of pure poetry, we usually think of Poe, as critic and poet, perhaps of Shelley, of the Symbolists, of the Abbé Bremond, perhaps of Pater, and certainly of George Moore and the Imagists. We know Poe's position: the long poem is "a flat contradiction in terms," because intense excitement, which is essential in poetry, cannot be long maintained; the moral sense and the intellect function more satisfactorily in prose than in poetry, and, in fact, "Truth" and the "Passions," which are for Poe associated with the intellect and the moral sense, may actually be inimical to poetry; vagueness, suggestiveness are central virtues, for poetry has for "its object an *indefinite* instead of a *definite* pleasure"; poetry is not supposed to undergo close inspection, only a cursory glance, for it, "above all things, is a beautiful painting whose tints, to minute inspection, are confusion worse confounded, but start out boldly to the cursory glance of the connoisseur"; poetry aspires toward music, since it is concerned with "indefinite sensations, to which music is an *essential*, since the comprehension of sweet sound is our most indefinite conception"; melancholy is the most poetical effect and enters into all the higher manifestations of beauty. We know, too, the Abbé Bremond's mystical interpretation, and the preface to George Moore's anthology, and the Imagist manifesto.

But these views are not identical. Shelley, for instance, delights in the imprecision praised and practiced by Poe, but he has an enormous appetite for "Truth" and the "Passions," which are, except for purposes of contrast, excluded by Poe. The Imagist manifesto, while excluding ideas, endorses precision rather than vagueness in rendering the image, and admits diction and objects which would have seemed impure to Poe and to many poets of the nineteenth century, and does not take much stock in the importance of verbal music. George Moore emphasizes the objective aspect of his pure poetry, which he describes as "something which the poet creates outside his own personality," and this is opposed to the subjective emphasis in Poe and Shelley; but he shares with both an emphasis on verbal music, and with the former a distaste for ideas.

But more recently, the notion of poetic purity has emerged in other contexts, contexts which sometimes obscure the connection of the new theories with the older theories. For instance, Max Eastman has a theory. "Pure poetry," he says in *The Literary Mind*, "is the pure effort to heighten consciousness." Mr. Eastman, we discover elsewhere in his book, would ban idea from poetry, but his motive is different from, say, the motive of Poe, and the difference is important: Poe would kick out the ideas because the ideas hurt the poetry, and Mr. Eastman would kick out the ideas because the poetry hurts the ideas. Only the scientist, he tells us, is entitled to have ideas on any subject, and the rest of the citizenry must wait to be told what attitude to take toward the ideas which they are not permitted to have except at second-hand. Literary truth, he says, is truth which is "uncertain or comparatively unimportant." But he does assign the poet a function—to heighten consciousness. In the light of this context we would have to rewrite his original definition: pure poetry is the pure effort to heighten consciousness, but the consciousness which is heightened must not have any connection with ideas, must involve no attitude toward any ideas.

Furthermore, to assist the poet in fulfilling the assigned function, Mr. Eastman gives him a somewhat sketchy doctrine of "pure" poetic diction. For instance, the word *bloated* is not admissible into a poem because it is, as he testifies, "sacred to the memory of dead fish," and the word *tangy* is, though he knows not exactly how, "intrinsically poetic." The notion of a vocabulary which is intrinsically poetic seems, with Mr. Eastman, to mean a vocabulary which indicates agreeable or beautiful objects. So we might rewrite the original definition to read: pure poetry is the pure effort to heighten consciousness, but the consciousness which is heightened must be a consciousness exclusively of agreeable or beautiful objects—certainly not a consciousness of any ideas.

In a recent book, *The Idiom of Poetry*, Frederick Pottle has discussed the question of pure poetry. He distinguishes another type of pure poetry in addition to the types already mentioned. He calls it the "Elliptical," and would include in it symbolist and metaphysical poetry (old and new) and some work by poets such as Collins, Blake, and Browning. He observes—without any pejorative implication, for he is a critical relativist and scarcely permits himself the luxury of evaluative judgments—that the contemporary product differs from older examples of the elliptical type in that "the modern poet goes much farther in employing private experiences or ideas than would formerly have been thought legitimate." To the common reader, he says, "the prime characteristic of this kind of poetry is not the nature of its imagery but its obscurity; its urgent suggestion that you add something to the poem without telling you what that something is." This omitted "something" he interprets as the prose "frame"—to use his word—the statement of the occasion, the logical or narrative transitions, the generalized application derived from the poem, etc. In other words, this type of pure poetry contends that "the effect would be more powerful if we could somehow manage to feel the images fully and accurately without having the effect diluted by any words put in to give us a 'meaning'—that is, if we could expel all the talk *about* the imaginative realization and have the pure realization itself."[4]

For the moment I shall pass the question of the accuracy of Mr. Pottle's description of the impulse of Elliptical Poetry and present the question which ultimately concerns him. How pure does poetry need to be in practice? That is the question which Mr. Pottle asks. He answers by saying that a great degree of impurity *may* be admitted, and cites our famous didactic poems, *The Faerie Queene, An Essay on Man, The Vanity of Human Wishes, The Excursion*. That is the only answer which the relativist, and nominalist, can give. Then he turns to what he calls the hardest question in the theory of poetry: What kind of prosaism is acceptable and what is not? His answer, which he advances very modestly, is this:

> . . . the element of prose is innocent and even salutary when it appears as—take your choice of three metaphors—a background on which the images are projected, or a frame in which they are shown, or a thread on which they are strung. In short, when it serves a *structural* purpose. Prose in a poem seems offensive to me when . . . the prosaisms are sharp, obvious, individual, and ranked co-ordinately with the images.

At first glance this looks plausible, and the critic has used the sanctified word *structural*. But at second glance we may begin to wonder what the sanctified word means to the critic. It means something rather mechanical—background, frame, thread. The structure is a showcase, say a jeweler's showcase, in which the little jewels of poetry are exhibited, the images. The showcase shouldn't be ornamental itself ("sharp, obvious, individual," Mr. Pottle says), for it would then distract us from the jewels; it should be chastely designed, and the jewels should repose

---

[4] F. W. Bateson, in *English Poetry and the English Language,* discusses the modern elliptical practice in poetry. Tennyson, he points out in connection with "The Sailor Boy," dilutes his poetry by telling a story as well as writing a poem, and "a shorter poem would have spoilt his story." The claims of prose conquer the claims of poetry. Of the Victorians in general: "The dramatic and narrative framework of their poems, by circumventing the disconcerting plunges into *medias res* which are the essence of poetry, brings it down to a level of prose. The reader knows where he is; it serves the purpose of introduction and note." Such introduction and notes in the body of the poem itself are exactly what Mr. Pottle says is missing in Elliptical Poetry. Mr. Bateson agrees with Poe in accepting intensity as the criterion of the poetic effect, and in accepting the corollary that a poem should be short. But he, contradicting Poe, seems to admire precise and complicated incidental effects.

on black velvet and not on flowered chintz. But Mr. Pottle doesn't ask what the relation among the bright jewels should be. Not only does the showcase bear no relation to the jewels, but the jewels, apparently, bear no relation to each other. Each one is a shining little focus of heightened interest, and all together they make only such a pattern, perhaps, as may make it easier for the eye to travel from one little jewel to the next, when the time comes to move on. Structure becomes here simply a device of salesmanship, a well-arranged showcase.

It is all mechanical. And this means that Mr. Pottle, after all, is himself an exponent of pure poetry. He locates the poetry simply in the images, the nodes of "pure realization." This means that what he calls the "element of prose" includes definition of situation, movement of narrative, logical transition, factual description, generalization, ideas. Such things, for him, do not participate in the poetic effect of the poem; in fact, they work against the poetic effect, and so, though necessary as a frame, should be kept from being "sharp, obvious, individual."[5]

I have referred to *The Idiom of Poetry*, first, because it is such an admirable and provocative book, sane, lucid, generous-spirited, and second, because, to my mind, it illustrates the insidiousness with which a doctrine of pure poetry can penetrate into the theory of a critic who is suspicious of such a doctrine. Furthermore, I have felt that Mr. Pottle's analysis might help me to define the common denominator of the various doctrines of pure poetry.

That common denominator seems to be the belief that poetry is an essence that is to be located at some particular place in a poem, or in some particular element. The exponent of pure poetry persuades himself that he has determined the particular something in which the poetry inheres, and then proceeds to decree that poems shall be composed, as nearly as possible, of that element and of nothing else. If we add up the things excluded by various critics and practitioners, we get a list about like this:

[5]Several other difficulties concerning Pottle's statement may suggest themselves. First, since he seems to infer that the poetic essence resides in the image, what view would he take of meter and rhythm? His statement, strictly construed, would mean that these factors do not participate in the poetic effect, but are simply part of the frame. Second, what view of dramatic poetry is implied? It seems again that a strict interpretation would mean that the story and the images bear no essential relation to each other, that the story is simply part of the frame. That is, the story, characters, rhythms, and ideas are on one level, and the images, in which the poetry inheres, are on another. But Caroline Spurgeon, G. Wilson Knight, and other critics have given us some reason for holding that the images do bear some relation to the business of the other items. In fact, all of the items, as Jacques Maritain has said, "feelings, ideas, representations, are for the artist merely materials and means, still symbols." That is, they are all elements in a single expressive structure.

1. ideas, truths, generalizations, "meaning"
2. precise, complicated, "intellectual" images
3. unbeautiful, disagreeable, or neutral materials
4. situation, narrative, logical transition
5. realistic details, exact descriptions, realism in general
6. shifts in tone or mood
7. irony
8. metrical variation, dramatic adaptations of rhythm, cacophony, etc.
9. meter itself
10. subjective and personal elements

No one theory of pure poetry excludes all of these items, and, as a matter of fact, the items listed are not on the same level of importance. Nor do the items always bear the same interpretation. For example, if one item seems to be central to discussions of pure poetry, it is the first: "ideas," it is said, "are not involved in the poetic effect, and may even be inimical to it." But this view can be interpreted in a variety of ways. If it is interpreted as simply meaning that the paraphrase of a poem is not equivalent to the poem, that the poetic gist is not to be defined as the statement embodied in the poem with the sugar-coating as bait, then the view can be held by opponents as well as exponents of any theory of pure poetry. We might scale down from this interpretation to the other extreme interpretation that the poem should merely give the sharp image in isolation. But there are many complicated and confused variations possible between the two extremes. There is, for example, the interpretation that "ideas," though they are not involved in the poetic effect, must appear in poems to provide, as Mr. Pottle's prosaisms do, a kind of frame, or thread, for the poetry—a spine to support the poetic flesh, or a Christmas tree on which the baubles of poetry are hung.[6] T. S. Eliot has said something of this sort:

> The chief use of the "meaning" of a poem, in the ordinary sense, may be (for here again I am speaking of some kinds of poetry and not all) to satisfy one habit of the reader, to keep his mind diverted and quiet, while the poem does its work upon him: much as the imaginary burglar is always provided with a bit of nice meat for the house-dog.

[6]Such an interpretation seems to find a parallel in E. M. Forster's treatment of plot in fiction. Plot in his theory becomes a mere spine and does not really participate, except in a narrow, formal sense, in the fictional effect. By his inversion of the Aristotelian principle the plot becomes merely a necessary evil.

Here, it would seem, Mr. Eliot has simply inverted the old sugar-coated-pill theory: the idea becomes the sugar-coating and the "poetry" becomes the medicine. This seems to say that the idea in a poem does not participate in the poetic effect, and seems to commit Mr. Eliot to a theory of pure poetry. But to do justice to the quotation, we should first observe that the parenthesis indicates that the writer is referring to some sort of provisional and superficial distinction and not to a fundamental one, and second observe that the passage is out of its context. In the context, Mr. Eliot goes on to say that some poets "become impatient of this 'meaning' [explicit statement of ideas in logical order] which seems superfluous, and perceive possibilities of intensity through its elimination." This may mean either of two things. It may mean that ideas do not participate in the poetic effect, or it may mean that, though they do participate in the poetic effect, they need not appear in the poem in an explicit and argued form. And this second reading would scarcely be a doctrine of pure poetry at all, for it would involve poetic casuistry and not poetic principle.

We might, however, illustrate the second interpretation by glancing at Marvell's "Horatian Ode" on Cromwell. Marvell does not give us narrative; he does not give us an account of the issues behind the Civil War; he does not state the two competing ideas which are dramatized in the poem, the idea of "sanction" and the idea of "efficiency." But the effect of the poem does involve those two factors; and the reserved irony, scarcely resolved, which emerges from the historical situation, is an irony derived from unstated materials and ideas. It is, to use Mr. Pottle's term again, a pure poem in so far as it is elliptical in method, but it is anything but a pure poem if by purity we mean the exclusion of idea from participation in the poetic effect. And Mr. Eliot's own practice implies that he believes that ideas do participate in the poetic effect. Otherwise, why did he put the clues to his ideas in the notes at the end of *The Waste Land* after so carefully excluding any explicit statement of them from the body of the poem? If he is regarding those ideas as mere bait—the "bit of nice meat for the house-dog"—he has put the ideas in a peculiar place, in the back of the book, like giving the dog the meat on the way out of the house with the swag, or giving the mouse the cheese after he is in the trap.

All this leads to the speculation that Marvell and Mr. Eliot have purged away statement of ideas from their poems, not because they wanted the ideas to participate less in the poetry, but because they wanted them to participate more fully, intensely, and immediately. This impulse, then, would account for the characteristic types of image, types in which precision, complication, and complicated intellectual relation to the theme are exploited; in other words, they are trying—whatever may be their final success—to carry the movement of mind to the center of the process. On these grounds they are the exact opposite of poets who, presumably on grounds of purity, exclude the movement of mind from the center of the poetic process—from the internal structure of the poem—but pay their respects to it as a kind of footnote, or gloss, or application coming at the end. Marvell and Eliot, by their cutting away of frame, are trying to emphasize the participation of ideas in the poetic process. Then Elliptical Poetry is not, as Mr. Pottle says it is, a pure poetry at all; the elliptical poet is elliptical for purposes of inclusion, not exclusion.

But waiving the question of Elliptical Poetry, no one of the other theories does—or could—exclude all the items on the list above. And that fact may instruct us. If all of these items were excluded, we might not have any poem at all. For instance, we know how some critics have pointed out that even in the strictest Imagist poetry, idea creeps in—when the image leaves its natural habitat and enters a poem, it begins to "mean" something. The attempt to read ideas out of the poetic party violates the unity of our being and the unity of our experience. "For this reason," as Santayana puts it, "philosophy, when a poet is not mindless, enters inevitably into his poetry, since it has entered into his life; or rather, the detail of things and the detail of ideas pass equally into his verse, when both alike lie in the path that has led him to his ideal. To object to theory in poetry would be like objecting to words there; for words, too, are symbols without the sensuous character of the things they stand for; and yet it is only by the net of new connections which words throw over things, in recalling them, that poetry arises at all. Poetry is an attenuation, a rehandling, an echo of crude experience; it is itself a theoretic vision of things at arm's length."

Does this not, then, lead us to the conclusion that poetry does not inhere in any particular element but depends upon the set of relationships, the structure, which we call the poem?

Then the question arises: what elements cannot be used in such a structure? I should answer that nothing that is available in human experience is to be legislated out of poetry. This does not mean that anything can be used in *any* poem, or that some materials or elements may not prove more recalcitrant than others, or that it might not be easy to have too much of some things. But it does mean that, granted certain contexts, any sort of material, a chemical formula for instance, might appear functionally in a poem. It also may mean that, other things being equal, the greatness of a poet depends upon the extent of the area of experience which he can master poetically.

Can we make any generalizations about the nature of the poetic structure? First, it involves resistances, at various levels. There is the tension between the rhythm of the poem and the rhythm of speech (a tension which is very low at the extreme of free verse and at the extreme of verse such as that of "Ulalume," which verges toward a walloping doggerel); between the formality of the rhythm and the informality of the language; between the particular and the general, the concrete and the abstract; between the elements of even the simplest metaphor; between the beautiful and the ugly; between ideas (as in Marvell's poem); between the elements involved in irony (as in "Bells for John Whiteside's Daughter" or "Rose Aylmer"); between prosaisms and poeticisms (as in "Western Wind").

This list is not intended to be exhaustive; it is intended to be merely suggestive. But it may be taken to imply that the poet is like the jujitsu expert; he wins by utilizing the resistance of his opponent—the materials of the poem. In other words, a poem, to be good, must earn itself. It is a motion toward a point of rest, but if it is not a resisted motion, it is motion of no consequence. For example, a poem which depends upon stock materials and stock responses is simply a toboggan slide, or a fall through space. And the good poem must, in some way, involve the resistances; it must carry something of the context of its own creation; it must come to terms with Mercutio.

This is another way of saying that a good poem involves the participation of the reader; it must, as Coleridge puts it, make the reader into "an active creative being." Perhaps we can see this most readily in the case of tragedy: the determination of good or evil is not a "given" in tragedy, it is something to be earned in the process, and even the tragic villain must be "loved." We must kill him, as Brutus killed Caesar, not as butchers but as sacrificers. And all of this adds up to the fact that the structure is a dramatic structure, a movement through action toward rest, through complication toward simplicity of effect.

In the foregoing discussion, I have deliberately omitted reference to another type of pure poetry, a type which tends to become dominant in an age of political crisis and social disorientation. Perhaps the most sensible description of this type can be found in an essay by Herbert Muller:

If it is not the primary business of the poet to be eloquent about these matters [faith and ideals], it still does not follow that he has more dignity or wisdom than those who are, or that he should have more sophistication. At any rate the fact is that almost all poets of the past did freely make large, simple statements, and not in their prosy or lax moments.

Mr. Muller then goes on to illustrate by quoting three famous large, simple statements:

> *E'n la sua volontade è nostra pace*

and

> *We are such stuff*
> *As dreams are made on; and our little life*
> *Is rounded with a sleep.*

and

> *The mind is its own place, and in itself*
> *Can make a heaven of hell, a hell of heaven.*

Mr. Muller is here attacking the critical emphasis on ironic tension in poetry. His attack really involves two lines of argument. First, the poet is not wiser than the statesman, philosopher, or saint, people who are eloquent about faith and ideals and who say what they mean, without benefit of irony. This Platonic line of argument is, I think, off the point in the present context. Second, the poets of the past have made large, simple affirmations, have said what they meant. This line of argument is very much on the point.

Poets *have* tried very hard, for thousands of years, to say what they mean. Not only have they tried to say what they mean, they have tried to prove what they mean. The saint proves his vision by stepping cheerfully into the fires. The poet, somewhat less spectacularly, proves his vision by submitting it to the fires of irony—to the drama of his structure—in the hope that the fires will refine it. In other words, the poet wishes to indicate that his vision has been earned, that it can survive reference to the complexities and contradictions of experience. And irony is one such device of reference.

In this connection let us look at the first of Mr. Muller's exhibits. The famous line occurs in Canto III of the *Paradiso*. It is spoken by Piccarda Donati, in answer to Dante's question as to why she does not desire to rise higher than her present sphere, the sphere of the moon. But it expresses, in unequivocal terms, a central theme of the *Commedia,* as of Christian experience. On the one hand, it may be a pious truism, fit for sampler work, and on the other hand, it may be a burning conviction, tested and earned. Dante, in his poem, sets out to show how it has been earned and tested.

One set of ironic contrasts which centers on this theme concerns, for instance, the opposition between the notion of human justice and the notion of divine justice. The story of Paolo and Francesca is so warm, appealing, and pathetic in its human terms, and their punishment so savage and unrelenting, so incommensurable, it seems, with the fault, that Dante, torn by the conflict, falls down as a dead body falls. Or Farinata, the enemy of Dante's house, is presented by the poet in terms of his human grandeur, which now, in Hell, is transmuted into a superhuman grandeur,

com' avesse l'inferno in gran dispitto.

Ulysses remains a hero, a hero who should draw special applause from Dante, who defined the temporal end of man as the conquest of knowledge. But Ulysses is damned, as the great Brutus is damned, who hangs from the jaws of the fiend in the lowest pit of traitors. So divine justice is set over against human pathos, human dignity, human grandeur, human intellect, human justice. And we recall how Virgil, more than once, reminds Dante that he must not apply human standards to the sights he sees. It is this long conflict, which appears in many forms, this ironic tension, which finally gives body to the simple eloquence of the line in question; the statement is meaningful, not for what it says, but for what has gone before. It is earned. It has been earned by the entire poem.

I do not want to misrepresent Mr. Muller. He does follow his quotations by the sentence: "If they are properly qualified in the work as a whole, they may still be taken straight, they *are* [he italicizes the word] taken so in recollection as in their immediate impact." But how can we take a line "straight," in either "recollection" or "immediate impact," unless we ignore what "properly qualified" the line in "the work as a whole"? And if we do take it so, are we not violating, very definitely, the poet's meaning, for the poet means the *poem,* he doesn't mean the line.

It would be interesting to try to develop the contexts of the other passages which Mr. Muller quotes. But in any case, he is simply trying, in his essay, to guard against what he considers to be, rightly or wrongly, a too narrow description of poetry; he is not trying to legislate all poetry into the type of simple eloquence, the unqualified statement of "faith and ideas." But we have also witnessed certain, probably preliminary, attempts to legislate literature into becoming a simple, unqualified, "pure" statement of faith and ideal. We have seen the writers of the 1920's called the "irresponsibles." We have seen writers such as Proust, Eliot, Dreiser, and Faulkner called writers of the "death drive." Why are these writers condemned? Because they have tried, within the limits of their gifts, to remain faithful to the complexities of the problems with which they are dealing, because they have refused to take the easy statement as solution, because they have tried to define the context in which, and the terms by which, faith and ideals may be earned.

This method, however, will scarcely satisfy the mind which is hot for certainties; to that mind it will seem merely an index to lukewarmness, indecision, disunity, treason. The new theory of pure purity would purge out all complexities and all ironies and all self-criticism. And this theory will forget that the hand-me-down faith, the hand-me-down ideals, no matter what the professed content, is in the end not only meaningless but vicious. It is vicious because, as parody, it is the enemy of all faith.

LOVE AND SEPARATENESS IN EUDORA WELTY

He could understand God's giving Separateness
first and then giving Love to follow and heal in its
wonder; but God had reversed this, and given Love
first and then Separateness, as though it did not
matter to Him which came first.
—"A STILL MOMENT"

If we put *The Wide Net*, Eudora Welty's second collection of stories, up against her first collection, *A Curtain of Green*, we can immediately observe a difference: the stories of *The Wide Net* represent a specializing, an intensifying, of one of the many strains which were present in *A Curtain of Green*. All of the stories in *A Curtain of Green* bear the impress of Miss Welty's individual talent, but there is a great variety among them in subject matter and method and, more particularly, mood. It is almost as if the author had gone at each story as a fresh start in the business of writing fiction, as if she had had to take a new angle each time out of a joy in the pure novelty of the perspective. We find the vindictive farce of "The Petrified Man," the nightmare of "Clytie," the fantasy and wit of "Old Mr. Marblehall," the ironic self-revelation of "Why I Live at the P.O.," the nearly straight realism of "The Hitch-Hikers," the macabre comedy and pathos of "Keela, the Outcast Indian Maiden." The material of many of the stories was sad, or violent, or warped, and even the comedy and wit were not straight, but if read from one point of view, if read as a performance, the book was exhilarating, even gay, as though the author were innocently delighted

First published in *The Kenyon Review*, Spring 1944. In 1958 it was included in *Selected Essays*, from which this text was taken.

not only with the variety of the world but with the variety of ways in which one could look at the world and the variety of things that stories could be and still be stories. Behind the innocent delight of the craftsman, and of the admirer of the world, there was also a seriousness, a philosophical cast of mind, which gave coherence to the book, but on the surface, there was the variety, the succession of surprises. In *The Wide Net* we do not find the surprises. The stories are more nearly cut to one pattern.

We do not find the surprises. Instead, on the first page, with the first sentence of the first story, "First Love," we enter a special world: "Whatever happened, it happened in extraordinary times, in a season of dreams . . ." And that is the world in which we are going to live until we reach the last sentence of the last story. "Whatever happened," the first sentence begins, as though the author cannot be quite sure what did happen, cannot quite undertake to resolve the meaning of the recorded event, cannot, in fact, be too sure of recording all of the event. This is coyness, of course; or a way of warning the reader that he cannot expect quite the ordinary direct light on the event. For it is "a season of dreams"—and the faces and gestures and events often have something of the grave retardation, the gnomic intensity, the portentous suggestiveness of dreams. The logic of things here is not quite the logic by which we live, or think we live, our ordinary daylight lives. In "The Wide Net," for example, the young husband, who thinks his wife has jumped into the river, goes out with a party of friends to dredge for the body, but the sad occasion turns into a saturnalian fish-fry which is interrupted when the great King of the Snakes raises his hoary head from the surface of the river. But usually, in *The Wide Net,* the wrenching of logic is not in terms of events themselves, though "The Purple Hat" is a fantasy, and "Asphodel" moves in the direction of fantasy. Usually the events as events might be given a perfectly realistic treatment (Dreiser could take the events of "The Landing" for a story). But in these cases where the events and their ordering are "natural" and not supernatural or fantastic, the stories themselves finally belong to the "season of dreams" because of the special tone and mood, the special perspective, the special sensibility with which they are rendered.

Some readers, in fact, who are quite aware of Miss Welty's gifts, have recently reported that they are disturbed by the recent development of her work. Diana Trilling, in her valuable and sobering comments on current fiction, which appear regularly in the *Nation,* says that the author "has developed her technical virtuosity to the point where it outweighs the uses to which it is put, and her vision of horror to the point of nightmare." There are two ideas in this indictment, and let us take the first one first and come to the second much later. The indictment of the technique is developed along these lines: Miss Welty has made her style too fancy—decorative, "falsely poetic" and "untrue," "insincere." ("When an author says 'look at me' instead of 'look at it,' there is insincerity. . . .") This insincerity springs from "the extreme infusion of subjectivism and private sensibility." But the subjectivism, Mrs. Trilling goes on to say, leads not only to insincerity and fine writing but to a betrayal of the story's obligation to narrative and rationality. Miss Welty's stories take off from a situation, but "the stories themselves stay with their narrative no more than a dance, say, stays with its argument." That is the summary of the indictment.

The indictment is, no doubt, well worth the close attention of Miss Welty's admirers. There is, in fact, a good deal of the falsely poetic in Miss Welty's present style, metaphors that simply pretend to an underlying logic, and metaphors (and descriptions) that, though good themselves, are irrelevant to the business in hand. And sometimes Miss Welty's refusal to play up the objective action—her attempt to define and refine the response rather than to present the stimulus—does result in a blurred effect. But the indictment treats primarily not of such failures to fulfill the object the artist has set herself but of the nature of that object. The critic denies, in effect, that Miss Welty's present kind of fiction is fiction at all: "It is a book of ballets, not of stories."

Now, is it possible that the critic is arguing from some abstract definition of "story," some formalistic conception which does not accommodate the present exhibit, and is not concerning herself with the question of whether or not the present exhibit is doing the special job which it proposes for itself, and, finally, the job which we demand of all literature? Perhaps we should look at a new work first in terms of its effect and not in terms of a definition of type, because every new work is in some degree, however modest, wrenching our definition, straining its seams, driving us back from the formalistic definition to the principles on which the definition was based. Can we say this, therefore, of our expectation concerning a piece of literature, new or old: that it should intensify our awareness of the world (and of ourselves in relation to the world) in terms of an idea, a "view." This leads us to what is perhaps the key statement by Diana Trilling concerning *The Wide Net:* she grants that the volume "has tremendous emotional impact, despite its obscurity." In other words, she says, unless I misinterpret her, that the book does intensify the reader's awareness—but *not* in terms of a presiding idea.

This has led me to reread Miss Welty's two volumes of stories in the attempt to discover the issues which are involved in the "season of dreams." To begin with, almost all of the stories deal with people who, in one way or another, are cut off, alienated, isolated from the world. There is the girl in "Why I Live at the P.O."—isolated from her family by her arrogance, meanness, and sense of persecution; the half-witted Lily Daw, who, despite the efforts of "good" ladies, wants to live like other people; the deaf-mutes of "The Key," and the deaf-mute of "First Love"; the people of "The Whistle" and "A Piece of News," who are physically isolated from the world and who make their pathetic efforts to re-establish something lost; the traveling salesman and the hitch-hikers of "The Hitch-Hikers," who, for their different reasons, are alone, and the traveling salesman of "Death of a Traveling Salesman," who, in the physically and socially isolated backwoods cabin, discovers that he is the one who is truly isolated; Clytie, isolated in family pride and madness and sexual frustration, and Jennie of "At the Landing," and Mrs. Larkin of "A Curtain of Green," the old women of "A Visit of Charity" and the old Negro woman of "A Worn Path"; the murderer of "Flowers for Marjorie," who is cut off by an economic situation and the pressure of a great city; Mr. Marblehall in his secret life; Livvie, who, married to an old man and trapped in his respectable house, is cut off from the life appropriate to her years; Lorenzo, Murrell, and Audubon in "A Still Moment," each alone in his dream, his obsession; the old maids of "Asphodel," who tell the story of Miss Sabina and then are confronted by the naked man and pursued by the flock of goats. In some of the cases, the matter is more indirectly presented. For instance, in "Keela, the Outcast Indian Maiden," we find, as in *The Ancient Mariner,* the story of a man who, having committed a crime, must try to re-establish his connection with humanity; or in the title story of *The Wide Net,* William Wallace, because he thinks his wife has drowned herself, is at the start of the story cut off from the world of natural joy in which he had lived.

We can observe that the nature of the isolation may be different from case to case, but the fact of isolation, whatever its nature, provides the basic situation of Miss Welty's fiction. The drama which develops from this basic situation is of either of two kinds: first, the attempt of the isolated person to escape into the world; or second, the discovery by the isolated person, or by the reader, of the nature of the predicament.

As an example of the first type, we can remember Clytie's obsessed inspection of faces ("Was it possible to comprehend the eyes and the mouth of other people, which concealed she knew not what, and secretly asked for still another unknown thing?") and her attempt to escape, and to solve the mystery, when she lays her finger on the face of the terrified barber who has come to the ruinous old house to shave her father. Or there is Jennie, of "At the Landing," or Livvie, or the man of "Keela." As an example of the second type, there is the new awareness on the part of the salesman in "The Hitch-Hikers," or the new awareness on the part of the other salesman in the back-country cabin.

Even in "A Still Moment" we have this pattern, though in triplicate. The evangelist Lorenzo, the outlaw Murrell, and the naturalist and artist Audubon stand for a still moment and watch a white heron feeding. Lorenzo sees a beauty greater than he can account for (he had earlier "accounted for" the beauty by thinking, "Praise God, His love has come visible"), and with the sweat of rapture pouring down from his forehead, shouts into the marshes, "Tempter!" He has not been able to escape from his own obsession, or in other words, to make his definition of the world accommodate the white heron and the "natural" rapture which takes him. Murrell, looking at the bird, sees "only whiteness ensconced in darkness," and thinks that "if it would look at him a dream penetration would fill and gratify his heart"—the heart which Audubon has already defined as belonging to the flinty darkness of a cave. Neither Lorenzo nor Murrell can "love" the bird, and so escape from their own curse as did, again, the Ancient Mariner. But there remains the case of Audubon himself, who does "love" the bird, who can innocently accept nature. There is, however, an irony here. To paint the bird he must "know" the bird as well as "love" it, he must know it feather by feather, he must have it in his hand. And so he must kill it. But having killed the bird, he knows that the best he can make of it now in a painting would be a dead thing, "never the essence, only a sum of parts," and that "it would always meet with a stranger's sight, and never be one with beauty in any other man's head in the world." Here, too, the fact of the isolation is realized: as artist and lover of nature, he had aspired to a communication, a communion, with other men in terms of the bird, but now "he saw his long labor most revealingly at the point where it met its limit" and he is forced back upon himself.

"A Still Moment," however, may lead us beyond the discussion of the characteristic situation, drama, and realization in Miss Welty's stories. It may lead us to a theme which seems to underlie the stories. For convenience, though at the risk of incompleteness, or even distortion, we may call it Innocence and Experience. Let us take Audubon in relation to the heron. He loves the bird, innocently, in its fullness of being. But he must subject this love to knowledge; he must kill the bird if he is to commemorate its beauty, if he is to establish his communion with other men in terms of the bird's beauty. There is in the situation an irony of limit and contamination.

Let us look at this theme in relation to other stories. "A Memory," in *A Curtain of Green*, gives a simple example. Here we have a young girl lying on a beach and looking out at the scene through a frame made by her fingers, for the girl can say of herself, "To watch everything about me I regarded grimly and possessively as a need." (As does Audubon, in "A Still Moment.") And further: "It did not matter to me what I looked at; from any observation I would conclude that a secret of life had been nearly revealed to me. . . ." Now the girl is cherishing a secret love, a love for a boy at school about whom she knows nothing, to whom she has never even spoken, but whose wrist her hand had once accidentally brushed. The secret love had made her watching of the world more austere, had sharpened her demand that the world conform to her own ideas, and had created a sense of fear. This fear had seemed to be realized one day when, in the middle of a class, the boy had a fit of nosebleed. But that is in the past. This morning she suddenly sees between the frame of her fingers a group of coarse, fat, stupid, and brutal people disporting themselves on the sand with a maniacal, aimless vigor which comes to a climax when the fat woman, into the front of whose bathing suit the man had poured sand, bends over and pulls down the cloth so that the lumps of mashed and folded sand empty out. "I felt a peak of horror, as though her breasts themselves had turned to sand, as though they were of no importance at all and she did not care." Over against this defilement (a defilement which implies that the body, the breasts which turn to sand, has no meaning), there is the refuge of the dream, "the undefined austerity of my love."

"A Memory" presents the moment of the discovery of the two poles —the dream and the world; the idea and nature; innocence and experience; individuality and the anonymous, devouring life-flux; meaning and force; love and knowledge. It presents the contrast in terms of horror (as do "The Petrified Man" and "Why I Live at the P.O." when taken in the context of Miss Welty's work) and with the issue left in suspension, but other stories present it with different emphases and tonalities.

For instance, when William Wallace, in "The Wide Net," goes out to dredge the river, he is presumably driven by the fear that his wife has jumped in, but the fear is absorbed into the world of the river, and in a saturnalian revel he prances about with a great catfish hung on his belt, like a river-god laughing and leaping. But he had also dived deep down into the water: "Had he suspected down there, like some secret, the real true trouble that Hazel had fallen into, about which words in a letter could not speak . . . how (who knew?) she had been filled to the brim with that elation that they all remembered, like their own secret, the elation that comes of great hopes and changes, sometimes simply of the harvest time, that comes with a little course of its own like a tune to run in the head, and there was nothing she could do about it, they knew—and so it had turned into this? It could be nothing but the old trouble that William Wallace was finding out, reaching and turning in the gloom of such depths."

This passage comes clear when we recall that Hazel, the wife who is supposed to have committed suicide by drowning, is pregnant: she had sunk herself in the devouring life-flux, has lost her individuality there, just as the men hunting for the body have lost the meaning of their mission. For the river is simply force, which does not have its own definition; in it are the lost string of beads to wind around the little Negro boy's head, the catfish for the feast, the baby alligator that looks "like the oldest and worst lizard," and the great King of the Snakes. As Doc, the wise old man who owns the net, says: "The outside world is full of endurance." And he also says: "The excursion is the same when you go looking for your sorrow as when you go looking for your joy." Man has the definition, the dream, but when he plunges into the river he runs the risk of having it washed away. But it is important to notice that in this story, there is not horror at the basic contrast, but a kind of gay acceptance of the issue: when William Wallace gets home he finds that his wife had fooled him, and spanks her, and then she lies smiling in the crook of his arm. "It was the same as any other chase in the end."

As "The Wide Net," unlike "A Memory," does more than merely present the terms of contrast, so do such stories as "Livvie" and "At the Landing." Livvie, who lives in the house of wisdom (her infirm husband's name is Solomon) and respectability (the dream, the idea, which has withered) and Time (there is the gift of the silver watch), finally crosses into the other world, the world of the black buck, the field hand, in his Easter clothes—another god, not a river-god but a field god. Just after Solomon's death, the field hand in his gorgeous Easter clothes takes Livvie in his arms, and she drops the watch which Solomon had given her, while outside "the redbirds were flying and crisscrossing, the sun was in all the bottles on the prisoned trees, and the young peach was shining in the middle of them with the bursting light of spring."

If Livvie's crossing into the world of the field god is joyous, the escape of Jennie, in "At the Landing," is rendered in a different tonality. This story assimilates into a new pattern many of the elements found in "A Memory," "The Wide Net," "Livvie," and "Clytie." As in the case of Clytie, Jennie is caught in the house of pride, tradition, history, and as in the case of Livvie, in a house of death. The horror which appears in "A Memory," in "Clytie," reappears here. The basic symbolism of "Livvie" and of "The Wide Net" is again called into play. The river, as in "The Wide Net," is the symbol of that world from which Jennie is cut off. The grandfather's dream at the very beginning sets up the symbolism which is developed in the action:

> "The river has come back. That Floyd came to tell me. The sun was shining full on the face of the church, and that Floyd came around it with his wrist hung with a great long catfish. . . . That Floyd's catfish has gone loose and free. . . . And all of a sudden, my dears—my dears, it took its river life back, and shining so brightly swam through the belfry of the church, and downstream."

Floyd, the untamed creature of uncertain origin, is like William Wallace, the river-god dancing with the great catfish at his belt. But he is also, like the buck in "Livvie," a field god, riding the red horse in a pasture full of butterflies. He is free and beautiful, and Jennie is drawn after him, for "she knew that he lived apart in delight." But she also sees him scuffling playfully with the hideous old Mag: the god does not make nice distinctions. When the flood comes over the Landing (upsetting the ordered lives, leaving slime in the houses), Floyd takes her in his boat to a hill (significantly, the cemetery hill where her people are buried), violates her, feeds her wild meat and fish (field and river), and when the flood is down, leaves her. She has not been able to talk to him, and when she does say, "I wish you and I could be far away. I wish for a little house," he only stares into the fire as though he hasn't heard a word. But after he has gone she cannot live longer in the Landing; she must find him.

Her quest leads her into the dark woods (which are like an underwater depth) and to the camp of the wild river people, where the men are throwing knives at a tree. She asks for Floyd, but he is not there. The men put her in a grounded houseboat and come in to her. "A rude laugh covered her cry, and somehow both the harsh human sounds could easily have been heard as rejoicing, going out over the river in the dark night." Jennie has crossed into the other world to find violence and contamination, but there is not merely the horror as in "Clytie" and "A Memory." Jennie has acted out a necessary role: she has moved from the house of death, like Livvie, and there is "gain" as well as "loss." We must not forget the old woman who looks into the dark houseboat, at the very end of the story, and understands when she is told that the strange girl is "waiting for Billy Floyd." The old woman nods "out to the flowing river, with the firelight following her face and showing its dignity."

If this general line of interpretation is correct, we find that the stories represent variations on the same basic theme, on the contrasts already enumerated. It is not that there is a standard resolution for the contrasts which is repeated from story to story; rather, the contrasts, being basic, are not susceptible of a single standard resolution, and there is an implicit irony in Miss Welty's work. But if we once realize this, we can recognize that the contrasts are understood not in mechanical but in vital terms: the contrasts provide the terms of human effort, for the dream must be carried to, submitted to, the world, innocence to experience, love to knowledge, knowledge to fact, individuality to communion. What resolution is possible is, if I read the stories with understanding, in terms of the vital effort. The effort is a "mystery," because it is in terms of the effort, doomed to failure but essential, that the human manifests itself as human. Again and again, in different forms, we find what we find in Joel of "First Love": "Joel would never know now the true course, or the true outcome of any dream: this was all he felt. But he walked on, in the frozen path into the wilderness, on and on. He did not see how he could ever go back and still be the boot-boy at the Inn."

It is possible that in trying to define the basic issue and theme of Miss Welty's stories, I have made them appear too systematic, too mechanical. I do not mean to imply that her stories should be read as allegories, with a neat point-to-point equating of image and idea. It is true that a few of her stories, such as "The Wide Net," do approach the limit of allegory, but even in such cases we find rather than the system of allegory a tissue of symbols which emerge from, and disappear into, a world of scene and action which, once we discount the author's special perspective, is recognizable in realistic terms. The method is similar to the method of much modern poetry, and to that of much modern fiction and drama, but at the same time it is a method as old as fable, myth, and parable. It is a method by which the items of fiction (scene, action, character, etc.) are presented not as document but as comment, not as a report but as a thing made, not as history but as idea. Even in the most realistic and reportorial fiction, the social picture, the psychological analysis, and the pattern of action do not rest at the level of mere report; they finally operate as expressive symbols as well.

Fiction may be said to have two poles, history and idea, and the emphasis may be shifted very far in either direction. In the present collection the emphasis has been shifted very far in the direction of idea, but at the same time there remains a sense of the vividness of the actual world: the picnic of "The Wide Net" is a real picnic as well as a "journey," Cash of "Livvie" is a real field hand in his Easter clothes as well as a field god. In fact, it may be said that when the vividness of the actual world is best maintained, when we get the sense of one picture superimposed upon another, different and yet somehow the same, the stories are most successful.

The stories which fail are stories like "The Purple Hat" and "Asphodel," in which the material seems to be manipulated in terms of an idea, in which the relation between the image and the vision has become mechanical, in which there is a strain, in which we do find the kind of hocus-pocus deplored by Diana Trilling.

And this brings us back to the criticism that the volume "has tremendous emotional impact, despite its obscurity," that the "fear" it engenders is "in inverse ratio to its rational content." Now, it seems to me that this description does violence to my own experience of literature, that we do not get any considerable emotional impact unless we sense, at the same time, some principle of organization, some view, some meaning. This does not go to say that we have to give an abstract formulation to that principle or view or meaning before we can experience the impact of the work, but it does go to say that it is implicit in the work and is having its effect upon us in immediate aesthetic terms. Furthermore, in regard to the particular work in question, I do not feel that it is obscure. If anything, the dreamlike effect in many of the stories seems to result from the author's undertaking to squeeze meaning from the item which, in ordinary realistic fiction, would be passed over with a casual glance. Hence the portentousness, the retardation, the otherworldliness. For Miss Welty is like the girl in "A Memory":

. . . from any observation I would conclude that a secret of life had been nearly revealed to me, and from the smallest gesture of a stranger I would wrest what was to me a communication or a presentiment.

In many cases, as a matter of fact, Miss Welty has heavily editorialized her fiction. She wants us to get that smallest gesture, to participate in her vision of things as intensely meaningful. And so there is almost always a gloss to the fable.

One more word: It is quite possible that Miss Welty has pushed her method to its most extreme limit. It is also possible that the method, if pursued much further, would lead to monotony and self-imitation and merely decorative elaboration. Perhaps we shall get a fuller drama when her vision is submitted more daringly to fact, when the definition is plunged into the devouring river. But meanwhile Miss Welty has given us stories of brilliance and intensity; and as for the future, Miss Welty is a writer of great resourcefulness, sensitivity, and intelligence, and can probably fend for herself.

WILLIAM
FAULKNER

At the age of fifty-three, William Faulkner has written nineteen books which for range of effect, philosophical weight, originality of style, variety of characterization, humor, and tragic intensity are without equal in our time and country. Let us grant, even so, that there are grave defects in Faulkner's work. Sometimes the tragic intensity becomes mere sensationalism, the technical virtuosity mere complication, the philosophical weight mere confusion of mind. Let us grant that much, for Faulkner is a very uneven writer. The unevenness is, in a way, an index to his vitality, his willingness to take risks, to try for new effects, to make new explorations of material and method. And it is, sometimes at least, an index to a very important fact about Faulkner's work. The fact is that he writes of two Souths: he reports one South and he creates another. On one hand he is a perfectly straight realistic writer, and on the other he is a symbolist.

Let us speak first of that realistic South, the South which we can recognize by its physical appearance and its people. In this realistic way we can recognize that county which Faulkner calls Yoknapatawpha County, the county in which most of his stories occur and most of his

First published in *The New Republic*, August 12 and August 26, 1946, as "Cowley's Faulkner," parts I and II. In 1958 it was included in *Selected Essays*, from which this text was taken.

people live. Jefferson, the county seat of Yoknapatawpha County, is already the most famous county seat in the nation, and is as solidly recognizable as anybody's home town. There is Miss Emily's house, the big squarish frame house, once white, decorated with cupolas and spires and scrolled balconies, in the heavily lightsome style of the seventies, once on the most select street but now surrounded by garages and cotton gins, lifting its stubborn and coquettish decay above the cotton wagons and gasoline pumps. There is Uncle Gavin's law office. There is the cedar-bemused cemetery. There is the jail where a hundred years ago, or near, the jailer's daughter, a young girl, scratched her name with a diamond on a windowpane. There are the neat small new one-story houses designed in Florida and California, set with matching garages in their neat plots of clipped grass and tedious flower beds. Then beyond that town where we recognize every item, the country stretches away, the plantation houses, the cotton fields, the back country of Frenchman's Bend, where Snopeses and Varners live, the Beat Four section, where the Gowrie clan holds the land and brawls and makes whiskey in the brush.

We know everything about Yoknapatawpha County. Its 2,400 square miles lie between the hills of north Mississippi and the rich black bottom lands. No land in all fiction lives more vividly in its physical presence than this county of Faulkner's imagination—the pine-winey afternoons, the nights with a thin sickle of moon like the heel print of a boot in wet sand, the tremendous reach of the big river in flood, yellow and sleepy in the afternoon, and the little piddling creeks, that run backward one day and forward the next and come busting down on a man full of dead mules and hen houses, the ruined plantation which was Popeye's hangout, the swamps and fields and dusty roads, the last remnants of the great original forests, "green with gloom" in summer, "if anything actually dimmer than they had been in November's gray dissolution, where even at noon the sun fell only in windless dappling upon earth which never completely dried." A little later I shall speak of what the physical world means to Faulkner, but for the moment I wish only to insist on its vividness, its recognizability.

This county has a population of 15,611 persons, who spill in and out of Faulkner's books with the startling casualness of life, not explaining themselves or asking to be explained, offering their being with no apology, as though we, the readers, were the intruders on their domain. They compose a society with characters as various as the Bundrens of *As I Lay Dying;* the Snopeses of *The Hamlet* and several stories; the Gowries of *Intruder in the Dust;* Ike McCaslin of "The Bear" and

"Delta Autumn"; Percy Grimm, the gun-mad Nazi prototype of *Light in August;* Temple Drake, the dubious little heroine of *Sanctuary;* the Compsons, the ruined great family; Christmas, the tortured and self-torturing mulatto of *Light in August;* Dilsey, the old Negro woman, heroic and enduring, who stands at the center of *The Sound and the Fury;* Wash, the no-good poor white; and Sutpen, the violent bearer of the great design which the Civil War had brought to nothing, in *Absalom, Absalom!;* and the tall convict of *The Wild Palms.* No land in all fiction is more painstakingly analyzed from the sociological point of view. The descendants of the old families, the descendants of bush-whackers and carpetbaggers, the swamp rats, the Negro cooks and farm hands, the bootleggers and gangsters, tenant farmers, college boys, county-seat lawyers, country storekeepers, peddlers—all are here in their fullness of life and their complicated interrelations. The marks of class, occupation, and history are fully rendered, and we know completely their speech, food, dress, houses, manners, and attitudes.

Faulkner not only gives us the land and the people as we can see them today; he gives us glimpses of their history. His stories go back to the time when the Indians occupied Yoknapatawpha County and held slaves, and the first Compson came with a small, light-waisted, strong-hocked mare that could do two furlongs in under a half-minute, and won all the races from Ikkemotubbe's young braves until Ikkemotubbe swapped him a square mile of that land for the little mare. We know how Sartorises, the aristocrats, and Sutpens, nameless, driven, rancorous, ambitious men, seized the land, created a society, fought a war to defend that society, lost the war, and watched their world change and the Snopeses arise. The past is dramatized in situation after situation, in its full complication. It is a recognizable past, not a romanticized past, though we find many characters in Faulkner who are themselves romantics about that past, Quentin of *The Sound and the Fury* or High-tower of *Light in August.*

The land, the people, and their history—they come to us at a realistic level, at the level of recognition. This realistic, recognizable world is one of the two Souths about which Faulkner writes. As a realist he knows this world; it is the world he lives in and carries on his daily business in. To represent this world with full fidelity is in itself a great achievement, and I would not underrate it. But this achievement is not Faulkner's claim to our particular attention. That claim is the world he creates out of the materials of the world he presents. Yoknapatawpha County, its people and its history, is also a parable—as Malcolm Cowley has called it, a legend.

We can approach the significance of this legend by thinking of the land and its history as a fate or doom—words that are often on Faulkner's page. From the land itself, from its rich soil yearning to produce, and from history, from an error or sin committed long ago and compounded a thousand times over, the doom comes. That is, the present is to be understood, and fully felt, only in terms of the past.

The men who seized the land from the Indians were determined to found an enduring and stable order. They brought to this project imagination and rectitude and strength and integrity and cunning and endurance, but their project—or their great "design," to use Sutpen's word from *Absalom, Absalom!*—was doomed from the first. It was "accurst"—to use one of Faulkner's favorite words—by chattel slavery. There is a paradox here. The fact of slavery itself was not a single, willed act. It was a natural historical growth. But it was an evil, and all its human and humane mitigations and all its historical necessity could not quiet the bad conscience it engendered. The Civil War began the fulfillment of the doom. The war was fought with courage and fortitude and strength but with divided conscience. Not that the enemy was the bearer of light—the enemy was little better than a blind instrument of doom or fate. After the Civil War the attempt to rebuild according to the old plan and for the old values was defeated by a combination of forces: the carpetbaggers, the carriers of Yankee exploitation—or better, a symbol of it, for the real exploiters never left their offices fifteen hundred miles away—and the Snopeses, a new exploiting indigenous class descended from the bushwhackers and landless whites.

Meanwhile, most of the descendants of the old order are in various ways incompetent. For one thing, in so far as they carry over into the new world the code of behavior prescribed by the old world, some sense of honor and honesty, they are at a disadvantage in dealing with the Snopeses, who have no code, who are pure pragmatists. But often the descendant of the old order clings to the letter of his tradition and forgets the spirit. George Marion O'Donnell, in one of the first perceptive essays ever published on Faulkner, pointed out the story "There Was a Queen" as an example of this. The heroine, in order to get possession of certain obscene and insulting letters written her by a Snopes, gives herself to a detective who has blackmailed her. That is, to protect her reputation, she is willing to perform the act which will render the reputation a mere sham.

We find something of the same situation with the whining Mrs. Compson, the mother in *The Sound and the Fury,* who with her self-pity and insistence on her "tradition" surrenders all the decency which the tradition would have prescribed, the honor and courage. Or the exponents of the tradition may lose all contact with reality and escape into a dream world of alcohol or rhetoric or madness or sexual dissipation. Or they fall in love with defeat and death, like Quentin Compson, who commits suicide at Harvard. Or they lose nerve and become cowardly drifters. Or, worst of all, they try to come to terms with reality by adopting Snopesism, like the last Jason of *The Sound and the Fury,* whose portrait is one of the most terrifying in all literature—the paranoidal self-deceiver, who plays the cotton market and when he loses, screams about those "kikes" in New York who rob him, who himself robs the daughter of his sister Caddy over the years and in the end makes her into the desperate and doomed creature she becomes, who under the guise of responsibility for his family—the ailing mother, the idiot brother, the wild niece—tortures them all with an unflagging sadistic pleasure.

The point to insist on here is that you do not characteristically have noble examples of antique virtue beset by little and corrupt men. There are a few such examples of the antique virtue—old Ike McCaslin, for example, whom we shall come to later—but the ordinary situation is to find the descendant of the old order contributing, actively or passively, to his own ruin and degradation. He is not merely a victim, and he frequently misunderstands his own tradition.

Over against these people there stand, as we have said, the forces of "modernism," embodied in various forms. There are, of course, the Snopeses, the pure exploiters, descendants of barn-burners and bushwhackers, of people outside of society, belonging to no side, living in a kind of limbo, not even having the privilege of damnation, reaching their apotheosis in Flem Snopes, who becomes a bank president in Jefferson. But there is also Popeye, the gangster of *Sanctuary,* with eyes like "rubber knobs," a creature with "that vicious depthless quality of stamped tin," the man who "made money and had nothing he could do with it, spend it for, since he knew that alcohol would kill him like poison, who had no friends and had never known a woman." Popeye is a kind of dehumanized robot, a mere mechanism, an abstraction, and as such he is a symbol for what Faulkner thinks of as modernism, for the society of finance capitalism.

It is sometimes said that Faulkner's theme is the disintegration of the Southern traditional life. For instance, Malcolm Cowley, in his fine introduction to the *Portable Faulkner,* says that the violence of Faulkner's work is "an example of the Freudian method turned backward, being full of sexual nightmares that are in reality social symbols.

It is somehow connected in the author's mind with what he regards as the rape and corruption of the South." And Maxwell Geismar, whose lack of comprehension of Faulkner strikes me as monumental, interprets Faulkner's work as merely Southern apologetics, as "the extreme hallucinations" of a "cultural psychosis."

It is true that Faulkner deals almost exclusively with the Southern scene, it is true that the conflict between past and present is a constant concern for him, it is true that the Civil War is always behind his work as a kind of backdrop, and it is true, or at least I think it is true, that in Faulkner's work there is the implication that Northern arms were the cutting edge of modernism. But granting all this, I should put the emphasis not in terms of South and North, but in terms of issues common to our modern world.

The Faulkner legend is not merely a legend of the South but of a general plight and problem. The modern world is in moral confusion. It does suffer from a lack of discipline, of sanction, of community of values, of a sense of mission. We don't have to go to Faulkner to find that out—or to find that it is a world in which self-interest, workableness, success provide the standards of conduct. It was a Yankee who first referred to the bitch goddess Success. It is a world in which the individual has lost his relation to society, the world of the power state in which man is a cipher. It is a world in which man is the victim of abstraction and mechanism, or at least, at moments, feels himself to be. It can look back nostalgically upon various worlds of the past, Dante's world of the Catholic synthesis, Shakespeare's world of Renaissance energy, or the world of our grandfathers who lived before Shiloh and Gettysburg, and feel loss of traditional values and despair in its own aimlessness and fragmentation. Any of those older worlds, so it seems now, was a world in which, as one of Faulkner's characters puts it, men "had the gift of living once or dying once instead of being diffused and scattered creatures drawn blindly from a grab bag and assembled"—a world in which men were, "integer for integer," more simple and complete.

At this point we must pause to consider an objection. Someone will say, and quite properly, that there never was a golden age in which man was simple and complete. Let us grant that. But we must grant that even with that realistic reservation, man's conception of his own role and position has changed from time to time. It is unhistorical to reduce history to some dead level, and the mere fact that man in the modern world is worried about his role and position is in itself significant.

Again, it may be objected, and quite properly, that any old order that had satisfied human needs would have survived; that it is sentimental to hold that an old order is killed from the outside by certain wicked people or forces. But when this objection is applied to Faulkner it is based on a misreading of his work. The old order, he clearly indicates, did *not* satisfy human needs, did *not* afford justice, and therefore was "accurst" and held the seeds of its own ruin. But the point is this: the old order, even with its bad conscience and confusion of mind, even as it failed to live up to its ideal, cherished the concept of justice. Even in terms of the curse, the old order as opposed to the new order (in so far as the new order is equated with Snopesism) allowed the traditional man to define himself as human by setting up codes, ideas of virtue, however mistaken; by affirming obligations, however arbitrary; by accepting the risks of humanity. But Snopesism has abolished the concept, the very possibility of entertaining the idea of virtue. It is not a question of one idea and interpretation. It is simply that no idea of virtue is conceivable in the world in which practical success is the criterion.

Within the traditional world there had been a notion of truth, even if man in the flow of things could not readily define or realize his truth. Take, for instance, a passage from "The Bear."

'All right,' he said. 'Listen,' and read again, but only one stanza this time and closed the book and laid it on the table. 'She cannot fade, though thou has not thy bliss,' McCaslin said: 'Forever wilt thou love, and she be fair.'
'He's talking about a girl,' he said.
'He had to talk about something,' McCaslin said. Then he said, 'He was talking about truth. Truth is one. It doesn't change. It covers all things which touch the heart—honor and pride and pity and justice and courage and love. Do you see now?'

The important thing, then, is the presence of the concept of truth—that covers all things which touch the heart and define the effort of man to rise above the mechanical process of life.

When it is said, as it is sometimes said, that Faulkner is "backward-looking," the answer lies, I think, in the notion expressed above. The "truth" is neither of the past nor of the future. Or rather, it is of both. The constant ethical center of Faulkner's work is to be found in the glorification of human effort and human endurance, which are not confined to any one time. It is true that Faulkner's work contains a savage attack on modernity, but the values he admires *are* found in our time. The point is that they are found most often in people who are outside the stream of the dominant world, the "loud world," as it is called in *The Sound and the Fury*. Faulkner's world is full of "good" people—Byron Bunch, Lucas Beauchamp, Dilsey, Ike McCaslin, Uncle Gavin, Benbow, the justice of the peace in *The Hamlet*, Ratliff of the same book, Hightower of *Light in August*—we could make an impressive list, probably a longer list from Faulkner than from any other modern writer. "There are good men everywhere, at all times," Ike McCaslin says in "Delta Autumn."

It is not ultimately important whether the traditional order (Southern or other) as depicted by Faulkner fits exactly the picture which critical historical method provides. Let it be granted that Faulkner does simplify the matter. What remains important is that his picture of the traditional order has a symbolic function in contrast to the modern world which he gives us. It is a way of embodying his values—his "truth."

In speaking of the relation of the past to the present, I have mentioned the curse laid upon the present, the Southern present at least, by slavery. But also, as I have said, Faulkner is not concerned ultimately with the South, but with a general philosophical view. Slavery merely happens to be the particular Southern curse. To arrive at his broader philosophical view, we can best start with his notions of nature.

For one thing, one of the most impressive features of Faulkner's work is the vivid realization of the natural background. It is accurately observed, as accurately as in Thoreau, but observation provides only the stuff from which Faulkner's characteristic effects are gained. It is the atmosphere that counts, the infusion of feeling, the symbolic weight. Nature provides a backdrop—of lyric beauty, as in the cow episode of *The Hamlet*; of homely charm, as in the trial scene after the spotted horses episode of the same book; of sinister, brooding force, as in the river episodes from *The Wild Palms*—a backdrop for the human action and passion.

Nature is, however, more than a backdrop. There is an interrelation between man and nature, something not too unlike the Wordsworthian communion. At least, at moments, there is the communion, the interrelation. The indestructible beauty is there, beyond man's frailty. "God created man," Ike McCaslin says in "Delta Autumn," "and He created the world for him to live in and I reckon He created the kind of world He would have wanted to live in if He had been a man."

Ideally, if man were like God, as Ike McCaslin puts it, man's attitude toward nature would be one of pure contemplation, pure participation in nature's great forms and appearances, pure communion. The appropriate attitude for this communion is love, for with Ike McCaslin, who is as much Faulkner's spokesman as any other character, the moment of love is equated with godhood. But since man "wasn't quite God himself," since he lives in the world of flesh, he must be a hunter, user, and violator. To return to McCaslin's words: God "put them both here: man and the game he would follow and kill, foreknowing it. I believe He said, 'So be it.' I reckon He even foreknew the end. But He said, 'I will give him his chance. I will give him warning and foreknowledge too, along with the desire to follow and the power to slay. The woods and the fields he ravages and the game he devastates will be the consequence and signature of his crime and guilt, and his punishment.' "

There is, then, a contamination implicit in the human condition— a kind of Original Sin, as it were—the sin of use, exploitation, violation. So slavery is but one of the many and constant forms of that Original Sin. But it is possible—and necessary if man is to strive to be human —to achieve some measure of redemption through love. For instance, in "The Bear," the great legendary beast which is pursued from year to year to the death is also an object of love and veneration, and the symbol of virtue; and the deer hunt of "Delta Autumn" is for old Ike McCaslin a ritual of renewal. Those who have learned the right relationship to nature—"the pride and humility" which Ike as a boy learns from the half-Negro, half-Indian Sam Fathers (he learns it appropriately from an outcast)—are set over against those who do not have it. In "The Bear," General Compson speaks up to Cass McCaslin to defend the wish of the boy Ike McCaslin to stay an extra week in the woods:

> "You've got one foot straddled into a farm and the other foot straddled into a bank; you aint even got a good hand-hold where this boy was already an old man long before you damned Sartorises and Edmondses invented farms and banks to keep yourselves from having to find out what this boy was born knowing and fearing too maybe but without being afraid, that could go ten miles on a compass because he wanted to look at a bear none of us had ever got near enough to put a bullet in and looked at the bear and came the ten miles back on the compass in the dark; maybe by God that's the why and the wherefore of farms and banks."

The Sartorises and Edmondses, according to General Compson, have in their farms and banks something of the contamination, they have cut themselves off from the fundamental truth which young Ike already senses. But the real contamination is that of the pure exploiters, the apostles of abstractionism, those who have the wrong attitude toward nature and therefore toward other men.

We have a nice fable of this in the opening of *Sanctuary*, in the contrast between Benbow, the traditional man, and Popeye, the symbol of modernism. While the threat of Popeye keeps Benbow crouching by the spring, he hears a Carolina wren sing, and even under these circumstances, tries to recall the local name for it. And he says to Popeye: "And of course you don't know the name of it. I dont suppose you'd know a bird at all, without it was singing in a cage in a hotel lounge, or cost four dollars on a plate." Popeye, as we may remember, spits in the spring (he hates nature and must foul it), is afraid to go through the woods ("Through all them trees?" he demands when Benbow points out the shortcut), and when an owl whisks past them in the twilight, he claws at Benbow's coat with almost hysterical fear. "It's just an owl," Benbow explains. "It's nothing but an owl."

The pure exploiters are, however, caught in a paradox. Though they may gain ownership and use of a thing, they never really have it. Like Popeye, they are impotent. For instance, Flem Snopes, the central character and villain of *The Hamlet*, who brings the exploiter's mentality to the quiet country of Frenchman's Bend, finally marries Eula Varner, a kind of fertility goddess or earth goddess; but his ownership is meaningless, for she never refers to him as anything but "that man" —she does not even have a name for him—and he had got her only after she had given herself willingly to one of the hot-blooded boys of the neighborhood. In fact, nothing can, in one sense, be "owned." Ike McCaslin, in "The Bear," says of the land which had come down to him:

'It was never Father's and Uncle Buddy's to bequeath to me to repudiate because it was never Grandfather's to bequeath them to bequeath me to repudiate because it was never old Ikkemotubbe's to sell to Grandfather for bequeathment and repudiation. Because it was never Ikkemotubbe's fathers' fathers' to bequeath Ikkemotubbe to sell to Grandfather or any man because on the instant when Ikkemotubbe discovered, realized, that he could sell it for money, on that instant it ceased ever to have been his forever, father to father to father, and the man who bought it bought nothing.'

In other words, reality cannot be bought. It can only be had by love. The right attitude toward nature and man is love. And love is the opposite of the lust for power over nature or over other men, for God gave the earth to man, we read in "The Bear," not "to hold for himself and his descendants inviolable title forever, generation after generation, to the oblongs and squares of the earth, but to hold the earth mutual and intact in the communal anonymity of brotherhood, and all the fee He [God] asked was pity and humility and sufferance and endurance and the sweat of his face for bread." It is the failure of this pity that curses the earth and brings on the doom. For the rape of nature and the rape of man are always avenged. Mere exploitation without love is always avenged because the attitude which commits the crime in itself leads to its own punishment, so that man finally punishes himself. It is along this line of reasoning that we can read the last page of "Delta Autumn":

> *This land which man has deswamped and denuded and derivered in two generations so that white men can own plantations and commute every night to Memphis and black men own plantations and ride in jim crow cars to Chicago to live in millionaires' mansions on Lakeshore Drive, where white men rent farms and live like niggers and niggers crop on shares and live like animals, where cotton is planted and grows man-tall in the very cracks of the sidewalks, and usury and mortgage and bankruptcy and measureless wealth, Chinese and African and Aryan and Jew, all breed and spawn together until no man has time to say which one is which nor cares. . . .* No wonder the ruined woods I used to know dont cry for retribution! he thought: The people who have destroyed it will accomplish its revenge.

Despite the emphasis on the right relation to nature, and the communion with nature, the attitude toward nature in Faulkner's work does not involve a sinking into nature. In Faulkner's mythology man has "suzerainty over the earth," he is not of the earth, and it is the human virtues that count—"pity and humility and endurance." If we take even the extreme case of the idiot Snopes and his fixation on the cow in *The Hamlet* (a scene whose function in the total order of the book is to show that even the idiot pervert is superior to Flem), a scene in which the human being appears as close as possible to the "natural" level, we find that the scene is the most lyrical in Faulkner's work: even the idiot is human and not animal, for only human desires, not animal desires, must clothe themselves in poetry. I think that George Marion O'Donnell is right in pointing to the humanism-naturalism opposition in Faulkner's work, and over and over again we find that the point of some story or novel has to do with the human effort to break out of the mechanical round of experience at the merely "natural" level—"not just to eat and evacuate and sleep warm," as Charlotte Rittenmeyer says in *The Wild Palms*, "so we can get up and eat and evacuate in order to sleep warm again," or not just to raise cotton to buy niggers to raise cotton to buy niggers, as it is put in another place. Even when a character seems to be caught in the iron ring of some compulsion, of some mechanical process, the effort may be discernible. And in Quentin's attempt in *The Sound and the Fury* to persuade his sister Caddy, who is pregnant by one of the town boys of Jefferson, to confess that she has committed incest with him, we find among other things the idea that "the horror" of the crime and the "clean flame" of guilt would be preferable to the meaninglessness of the "loud world." More is at stake in Quentin's attitude than the snobbery of a Compson, which would prefer incest to the notion that his sister has had to do with one of the underbred town boys.

And that leads us to the question of class and race. There is a current misconception on this point, the notion that Faulkner's Snopesism is a piece of snobbery. It is true that the Snopeses are poor whites, descendants of bushwhackers (those who had no side in the Civil War but tried to make a good thing out of it), but any careful reader should realize that a Snopes is not to be equated with a poor white. For instance, the book most fully about the poor white, *As I Lay Dying*, is charged with sympathy and poetry. There are a hundred touches like that in Cash's soliloquy about the phonograph:

I reckon it's a good thing we ain't got ere a one of them. I reckon I wouldn't never get no work done a-tall for listening to it. I don't know if a little music ain't about the nicest thing a fellow can have. Seems like when he comes in tired of a night, it ain't nothing could rest him like having a little music played and him resting.

Or like the long section devoted to Addie Bundren, a section full of eloquence like that of this paragraph:

And then he died. He did not know he was dead. I would lie by him in the dark, hearing the dark land talking of God's love and His beauty and His sin; hearing the dark voicelessness in which the words are the deeds, and the other words that are not deeds, that are just the gaps in people's lacks, coming down like the cries of geese out of the wild darkness in the old terrible nights, fumbling at the deeds like orphans to whom are pointed out in a crowd two faces and told, That is your father, your mother.

The whole of *As I Lay Dying* is based on the heroic effort of the Bundren family to fulfill the promise to the dead mother to take her body to Jefferson; and the fact that Anse Bundren, after the effort is completed, immediately gets him a new wife, "the duck-shaped woman," does not negate the heroism of the effort or the poetry in which it is clothed. We are told by one critic that "what should have been the drama of the Bundrens thus becomes in the end a sort of brutal farce," and that we are "unable to feel the tragedy because the author has refused to accept the Bundrens, as he did accept the Compsons, as tragic." Rather, I should say, the Bundrens come off a little better than the latter-day Compsons, the whining, self-deluding mother, the promiscuous Caddy, the ineffectual Quentin, and the rest, including the vile Jason. The Bundrens at least are capable of the heroic effort. What the conclusion indicates is that even such a fellow as Anse Bundren, in the grip of an idea, in terms of promise or code, can rise above his ordinary level; Anse falls back at the end, but only after the prop of the obligation has been removed. And we can recall that Wash Jones has been capable of some kind of obscure dream, as his attachment to Sutpen indicates, and that in the end, in his murder of Sutpen, he achieves dignity and manhood.

The final evidence that the Snopeses are not to be equated with "poor white" comes in *The Hamlet*. The point of the book is the assault made by the Snopes family on a community of plain, hard-working small farmers. And if the corruption of Snopesism does penetrate into the community, there is no one here, not even Flem Snopes, who can be compared to Jason of *The Sound and the Fury*, the Compson who has embraced Snopesism.

As for the poor white, there has been a grave misconception in some quarters concerning the Negro in Faulkner's work. In one of Faulkner's books it is said that every white child is born crucified on a black cross, and remarks like this have led to the notion that Faulkner "hates" Negroes—or at least all Negroes except the favored black servitors. For instance, we find Maxwell Geismar exclaiming what a "strange inversion" it is to take the Negro, who is the "tragic consequence," and to exhibit him as the "evil cause" of the failure of the old order in the South. But all this is to misread the text. It is slavery, not the Negro, which is defined quite flatly as the curse, and the Negro is the black cross in so far as he is the embodiment of the curse, the reminder of the guilt, the incarnation of the problem. The black cross is, then, the weight of the white man's guilt, the white man who now sells salves and potions to "bleach the pigment and straighten the hair of Negroes that they might resemble the very race which for two hundred years had held them in bondage and from which for another hundred years not even a bloody civil war would have set them completely free." The curse is still operative, as the crime is still compounded.

The actual role of the Negro in Faulkner's fiction is consistently one of pathos or heroism. There is Dilsey, under whose name in the Compson genealogy Faulkner writes, "They endured," and whose role in *The Sound and the Fury* is to be the very ethical center of the book, the vessel of virtue and compassion. Then there is the Negro in "Red Leaves," the slave held by Indians who is hunted down to be killed at the funeral of the chief. When he is overtaken, one of the Indians says to him, "You ran well. Do not be ashamed," and when he walks among the Indians, he is "the tallest there, his high, close, mud-caked head looming above them all." And old Sam Fathers is the fountain of the wisdom which Ike McCaslin, Faulkner's philosopher, finally gains, and the repository of the virtues central for Faulkner—"an old man, son of a Negro slave and an Indian king, inheritor on the one hand of the long chronicle of a people who had learned humility through suffering and learned pride through the endurance which survived the suffering, and on the other side the chronicle of a people even longer in the land than the first, yet who now existed there only in the solitary brotherhood of an old and childless Negro's alien blood and the wild and invincible spirit of an old bear." Even Christmas in *Light in August* is a mixture of pathos and heroism. With his mixed blood, he is the lost, suffering, enduring creature, and even the murder he commits at the end is a fumbling attempt to define his manhood, an attempt to break out of the iron ring of mechanism, for the woman whom he kills has become a figure of the horror of the human which has surrendered human attributes.

Or for a general statement let us take a passage from "The Bear":

'Because they will endure. They are better than we are. Stronger than we are. Their vices are vices aped from white men or that white men and bondage have taught them: improvidence and intemperance and evasion—not laziness: evasion: of what white men had set them to, not for their aggrandisement or even comfort but his own—' and McCaslin

'All right. Go on: Promiscuity. Violence. Instability and lack of control. Inability to distinguish between mine and thine—' and he

'How distinguish, when for two hundred years mine did not even exist for them?' and McCaslin

'All right. Go on. And their virtues—' and he

'Yes. Their own. Endurance—' and McCaslin

'So have mules:' and he

'—and pity and tolerance and forbearance and fidelity and love of children—' and McCaslin

'So have dogs:' and he

'—whether their own or not or black or not. And more: what they got not only from white people but not even despite white people because they had it already from the old free fathers a longer time free than us because we have never been free—'

It is in *Intruder in the Dust,* however, that his views of the Negro are most explicit and best dramatized. Lucas Beauchamp, the stiff-necked and high-nosed old Negro man, is accused on good evidence of having shot a white man in the back, and is lodged in the Jefferson jail with a threat of lynching. The lynching is averted and Lucas's innocence established by a boy and an old lady. But what is important about the book is twofold: First, there is the role of Lucas as hero, the focus of dignity and integrity. Second, there is the quite explicit and full body of statement, which comes to us through the lips of Gavin, the lawyer-uncle of the boy who saves Lucas. To quote Gavin:

'. . . the postulate that Sambo is a human being living in a free country and hence must be free. That's what we are really defending [against the North]: the privilege of setting him free ourselves: which we will have to do for the reason that nobody else can since going on a century ago now the North tried it and have been admitting for seventy-five years now that they failed. So it will have to be us. Soon now this sort of thing [the lynching] wont even threaten anymore. It shouldn't now. It should never have. Yet it did last Saturday and it probably will again, perhaps once more, perhaps twice more. But then no more, it will be finished; the shame will still be there of course but then the whole chronicle of man's immortality is in the suffering he has endured, his struggle toward the stars in the stepping-stones of his expiations. Someday Lucas Beauchamp can shoot a white man in the back with the same impunity to lynch-rope or gasoline as a white man; in time he will vote anywhen and anywhere a white man can and send his children to the same school anywhere the white man's children go and travel anywhere the white man travels as the white man does it. But it won't be next Tuesday. . . .'

This is not the whole passage, or even the burden of the whole passage, but it merits our lingering. The motive behind the notion of "defending" against the North is not merely resentment at easy Phariseeism. It is something else, two other things in fact. First, the realization that legislation in itself never solves a really fundamental question. Legislation can only reflect a solution already arrived at. Second, the problem is finally one of understanding and, in a sense, conversion: conversion and, as the passage puts it, expiation. That is, the real problem is a spiritual and moral one. The story of *Intruder in the Dust* is, in a sense, the education of the boy, and the thing he learns is a lesson in humanity. This can be brought to focus on two parallel episodes. He sees Lucas on the street one day, and Lucas walks past him without recognition. Later he realizes that Lucas had been grieving for his dead wife. Again, in the cemetery where the body of a Gowrie had been exhumed, he sees old Stub Gowrie, the father of the man Lucas had presumably killed, and realizes that this head of the brawling, mean, lawless Gowrie clan is grieving, too. The recognition of grief, the common human bond, that is his education.

That is the central fact in Faulkner's work, the recognition of the common human bond, a profound respect for the human. There are, in one way, no villains in his work, except those who deny the human bond. Even some of the Snopes family are, after all, human: the son of the barn-burner in the story "Barn-Burning," or Mink in *The Hamlet*. The point about the Gowries in *Intruder in the Dust* is the same: the Gowries seem to be the enemy, the pure villains, but in the end there is the pure grief on old Stub's face, and he is human, after all.

If respect for the human is the central fact of Faulkner's work, what makes that fact significant is that he realizes and dramatizes the difficulty of respecting the human. Everything is against it, the savage egotism, the blank appetite, stupidity and arrogance, even virtues sometimes, the misreading of our history and tradition, our education, our twisted loyalties. That is the great drama, however, the constant story. His hatred of "modernism"—and we must quote the word to give it his special meaning—arises because he sees it as the enemy of the human, as abstraction, as mechanism, as irresponsible power, as the cipher on the ledger or the curve on a graph.

And the reference to modernism brings us back to the question of the past and the present. But what of the future? Does Faulkner come to a dead end, setting up traditional virtues against the blank present, and let the matter stand there? No, he does not. But he holds out no easy solutions for man's "struggle toward the stars in the stepping-stones of his expiations." He does, however, give a sense of the future, though as a future of struggle in working out that truth referred to in "The Bear." We can remember that old Ike McCaslin, at the end of "Delta Autumn," gives General Compson's hunting horn to the mu-latto girl who has been deserted by his young kinsman, saying, "We will have to wait." And *The Sound and the Fury,* which is Faulkner's *Waste Land,* ends with Easter and the promise of resurrection.

INTRODUCTION TO
THE MODERN LIBRARY EDITION OF
ALL THE KING'S MEN

Sometime in the winter of 1937–38, when I was teaching at the Louisiana State University, in Baton Rouge, I got the notion of doing a verse play about a Southern politician who achieved the power of a dictator, at least in his home state, and who was assassinated in the Capitol which had been the scene of his triumphs. As well as I can recall, the notion began to take on some shape when, sitting one afternoon on the porch of a friend's cottage, I began to describe my intentions.

Very often it is in conversation during the germinal stage of a project that I stumble on my meanings, or they stumble on me, and I recall this particular conversation rather vividly because it was then that I hit on the idea that the politician—then unnamed—would not simply be a man who by force or fraud rises to absolute power, offends the principles of decency and democracy, and then is struck down by a self-appointed Brutus. There would be no drama to such a story—no "insides," no inner tensions, no involvement of the spectator's own deep divisions. My politician would be—or at least I was groping toward some such formulation—a man whose personal motivation had been, in one sense, idealistic, who in many ways was to serve the cause of social betterment, but who was corrupted by power, even by power exercised against corruption. That is, his means defile his ends. But more than that, he was to be a man whose power was based on the fact that somehow he could vicariously fulfill some secret needs of the people about him. The choruses—and it was in talking about the place of the choruses in the proposed verse play that the notion came—were to develop this in a subsidiary way—a chorus of builders, a chorus of highway patrolmen, a chorus of surgeons, etc. And, naturally, each of the main characters should bear such a relation to the politician, even the Brutus assassin. But over against his power to fulfill, in some degree, a secret need of those about him, the politician was to discover, more and more, his own emptiness and his own alienation. So much for that conversation in the unseasonable sunshine of a Louisiana winter day.

The play did get written. I wrote a couple of choruses in the next few months. In Italy, the next summer, the summer of 1938, I got a little more done, beginning the process, I recall, in the late afternoon, in a wheat field outside of Perugia. The thing dragged on all the next winter and spring, in Louisiana, with a bit done after classes and on week-ends, but the bulk of the play was written in Rome, in the fall and winter of 1939, with the news of the war filling the papers and the boot heels of Mussolini's legionaries clanging on the stones. During that time I was deep in Machiavelli and Dante. Later, in the novel *All the King's Men*, Machiavelli found a place in the musings of Jack Burden, and Dante provided the epigraph.

When the play was finished, it was somewhat different from the thing dreamed up in the conversation with my friend. For instance, another theme had crept in—the theme of the relation of science (or pseudo-science) and political power, the theme of the relation of the science-society and the power-state, the problem of naturalistic determinism and responsibility, etc. At least, if such grand topics did not find explicit place in the play, and if I did not pretend to wisdom about them, they were casting a shade over the meditations of composition. The play, by the way, had the title *Proud Flesh*. I was rather pleased with the double significance of the phrase.

I mailed off the play to some friends back home. I knew that it was not finished, but I would postpone the rewriting for the benefit of the judgment of my first readers and my own more detached contemplation. Back in America, in the summer of 1940, I did do some rewriting, with the subtle criticism and inspiring instruction of Francis Fergusson. But still the play was not, to my mind or taste, finished. And besides, I had already begun a novel, to appear as *At Heaven's Gate*, which was drawing on some of the feelings and ideas involved in the play.

It was not until the spring of 1943 that I began again on the play. I had taken the manuscript out of its cupboard with the intention of revising it, but immediately I found myself thinking of the thing as a novel. That idea wasn't entirely new. Now and then I had entertained the possibility of making a novel of the story. But now, all at once, a novel seemed the natural and demanding form for it, and for me.

This new impulse was, I suppose, a continuation of the experience of writing *At Heaven's Gate,* just as that novel had been, in a way, a continuation of *Proud Flesh.* Despite important contrasts, there were some points of essential similarity between my businessman hero, Bogan Murdock, in *At Heaven's Gate,* and the politician hero of the play. And even some of the contrasts between them were contrasts in terms of the same thematic considerations. For example, if Bogan Murdock was supposed to embody, in one of his dimensions, the desiccating abstraction of power, to be a violator of nature, a usurer of Dante's Seventh Circle,* and to try to fulfill vicariously his natural emptiness by exercising power over those around him, so the politician rises to power because of the faculty of fulfilling vicariously the secret needs of others, and in the process, as I have already said, discovers his own emptiness. But beyond such considerations, the effort of *At Heaven's Gate* had whetted my desire to compose a highly documented picture of the modern world—at least, as the modern world manifested itself in the only region I knew well enough to write about.

There was, however, another consideration, if one can use such a term of scruple and calculation to describe the coiling, interfused forces that go into such a "literary" decision. This consideration was a technical one—the necessity for a character of a higher degree of self-consciousness than my politician, a character to serve as a kind of commentator and *raisonneur* and chorus. But since in fiction one should never do a thing for merely a single reason (not if he hopes to achieve that feeling of a mysterious depth which is one of the chief beauties of the art), I wanted to give that character a dynamic relation to the general business, to make him the chief character among those who were to find their vicarious fulfillment in the dynamic and brutal, yet paradoxically idealistic, drive of the politician. There was, too, my desire to avoid writing a straight naturalistic novel, the kind of novel that the material so readily invited. The impingement of that material, I thought, upon a special temperament would allow another perspec-

---

*It was this Circle that provided, with some liberties of interpretation and extension, the basic scheme and metaphor for the whole novel. All of the main characters are violators of nature.

tive than the reportorial one, and would give a basis for some range of style. So Jack Burden entered the scene.

But that is not quite a complete account of his origin. In *Proud Flesh*, at the time when Dr. Adam Stanton is waiting in the lobby of the Capitol to kill the Governor, and is meditating his act to come, an old friend, now a newspaperman, approaches him, and for one instant the assassin turns to him with a sense of elegiac nostalgia for the innocence and simplicity of the shared experiences of boyhood. This character, who appears so fleetingly in the last act of the play to evoke the last backward look of the dedicated assassin, gave me Jack Burden. And the story, in a sense, became the story of Jack Burden, the teller of the tale.

The composition of the novel moved slowly, in Minneapolis, in 1943 and through the spring of 1944; in Washington, through the rest of the year and up till June of 1945; in Connecticut, in the summer of 1945. The work was constantly interrupted, by teaching, by some traveling, by the duties of my post in Washington, by the study for and the writing of a long essay on Coleridge. The interruptions were, in some way, welcome, for they meant that the pot had to be pushed to the back of the stove to simmer away at its own pace. The book was finished in the fall of 1945, back in Minneapolis, the last few paragraphs being written in a little room in the upper reaches of the Library of the University of Minnesota. The book, after a good deal of revision along the way, with the perceptive criticism of Lambert Davis of Harcourt, Brace and Company, was published in August, 1946.

One of the unfortunate characteristics of our time is that the reception of a novel may depend on its journalistic relevance. It is a little graceless of me to call this characteristic unfortunate, and to quarrel with it, for certainly the journalistic relevance of *All the King's Men* had a good deal to do with what interest it evoked. My politician hero, whose name, in the end, was Willie Stark, was quickly equated with the late Senator Huey P. Long, whose fame, even outside of Louisiana, was yet green in pious tears, anathema, and speculation.

This equation led, in different quarters, to quite contradictory interpretations of the novel. On one hand, there were those who took the thing to be a not-so-covert biography of, and apologia for, Senator Long, and the author to be not less than a base minion of the great man. There is really nothing to reply to this kind of innocent boneheadedness or gospel-bit hysteria. As Louis Armstrong is reported to have said, there's some folks that if they don't know, you can't tell 'em.

But on the other hand, there were those who took the thing to be

a rousing declaration of democratic principles and a tract for the assassi-
nation of dictators. This view, though somewhat more congenial to my
personal political views, was almost as wide of the mark. For better or
for worse, Willie Stark was not Huey Long. Willie was only himself,
whatever that self turned out to be, a shadowy wraith or a blundering
human being.

This disclaimer, whenever I was callow enough to make it, was
almost invariably greeted by something like a sardonic smile or a con-
spiratorial wink, according to what the inimical smiler or the friendly
winker took my motives to be—either I wanted to avoid being called
a fascist or I wanted to avoid a lawsuit. Now, in making the disclaimer
again, I do not mean to imply that there was no connection between
Governor Stark and Senator Long. Certainly, it was the career of Long
and the atmosphere of Louisiana that suggested the play that was to
become the novel. But suggestion does not mean identity, and even if
I had wanted to make Stark a projection of Long, I should not have
known how to go about it. For one reason, simply because I did not,
and do not, know what Long was like, and what were the secret forces
that drove him along his violent path to meet the bullet in the Capitol.
And in any case, Long was but one of the figures that stood in the
shadows of imagination behind Willie Stark. Another one of that company was the scholarly and benign figure of William James.

Though I did not profess to be privy to the secret of Long's soul, I
did have some notions about the phenomenon of which Long was but
one example, and I tried to put some of those notions into my book.
Something about those notions, and something of what I felt to be the
difference between the person Huey P. Long and the fiction Willie
Stark, may be indicated by the fact that in the verse play the name of
the politician was Talos—the name of the brutal, blank-eyed "iron
groom" of Spenser's *Faerie Queene,* the pitiless servant of the knight of
justice. My conception grew wider, but that element always remained,
and Willie Stark remained, in one way, Willie Talos. In other words,
Talos is the kind of doom that democracy may invite upon itself. The
book, however, was never intended to be a book about politics. Politics
merely provided the framework story in which the deeper concerns,
whatever their final significance, might work themselves out.

New York City, March, 1953

SEGREGATION

THE INNER CONFLICT
IN THE SOUTH

"I'm glad it's you going," my friend, a Southerner, long resident in New York, said, "and not me." But I went back, for going back this time, like all the other times, was a necessary part of my life. I was going back to look at the landscapes and streets I had known—Kentucky, Tennessee, Arkansas, Mississippi, Louisiana—to look at the faces, to hear the voices, to hear, in fact, the voices in my own blood. A girl from Mississippi had said to me: "I feel it's all happening inside of me, every bit of it. It's all there."

I know what she meant.

To the right, the sun, cold and pale, is westering. Far off, a little yellow plane scuttles down a runway, steps awkwardly into the air, then climbs busily, learning grace. Our big plane trundles ponderously forward, feeling its weight like a fat man, hesitates, shudders with an access of sudden, building power, and with a new roar in my ears, I see the ground slide past, then drop away, like a dream. I had not been aware of the instant we had lost that natural contact.

Memphis is behind me, and I cannot see it, but yonder is the river,

Published in 1956.

glittering coldly, and beyond, the tree-sprigged flats of Arkansas. Still climbing, we tilt eastward now, the land pivoting away below us, the tidy toy farms, white houses, silos the size of a spool of white thread, or smaller, the stock ponds bright like little pieces of gum wrapper dropped in brown grass, but that brown grass is really trees, the toy groves with shadows precise and long in the leveling light.

Arkansas has pivoted away. It is Mississippi I now see down there, the land slipping away in the long light, and in my mind I see, idly, the ruined, gaunt, classic clay hills, with the creek bottoms throttled long since in pink sand, or the white houses of Holly Springs, some of them severe and beautiful, or Highway 61 striking south from Memphis, straight as a knife edge through the sad and baleful beauty of the Delta country, south toward Vicksburg and the Federal cemeteries, toward the fantasia of Natchez.

It seems like a thousand years since I first drove that road, more than twenty-five years ago, a new concrete slab then, dizzily glittering in the August sun-blaze, driving past the rows of tenant shacks, Negro shacks set in the infinite cotton fields, and it seems like a hundred years since I last drove it, last week, in the rain, then toward sunset the sky clearing a little, but clouds solid and low on the west like a black range of mountains frilled upward with an edge of bloody gold light, quickly extinguished. Last week I noticed that more of the shacks were ruinous, apparently abandoned. More, but not many, had an electric wire running back from the road. But when I caught a glimpse, in the dusk, of the interior of a lighted shack, I usually saw the coal-oil lamp. Most shacks were not lighted. I wondered if it was too early in the evening. Then it was early no longer. Were that many of the shacks abandoned?

Then we would pass in the dark some old truck grudging and clanking down the concrete, and catch, in the split-second flick of our headlamps, a glimpse of the black faces and the staring eyes. Or the figure, sudden in our headlight, would rise from the roadside, dark and shapeless against the soaked blackness of the cotton land: the man humping along with the croker sack on his shoulders (containing what?), the woman with a piece of sacking or paper over her head against the drizzle now, at her bosom a bundle that must be a small child, the big children following with the same slow, mud-lifting stride in the darkness. The light of the car snatches past, and I think of them behind us in the darkness, moving up the track beside the concrete, seeing another car light far yonder toward Memphis, staring at it perhaps, watching it grow, plunge at them, strike them, flick past. They will move on, at their pace. Yes, they are still here.

I see a river below us. It must be the Tennessee. I wonder on which side of us Shiloh is, and guess the right, for we must have swung far enough north for that. I had two grandfathers at Shiloh, that morning of April 6, 1862, young men with the other young men in gray uniforms stepping toward the lethal spring thickets of dogwood and redbud, to the sound of bird song. "One hundred and sixty men we took in the first morning, son. Muster the next night, and it was sixteen answered." They had fallen back on Corinth, into Mississippi.

The man in the seat beside me on the plane is offering me a newspaper. I see the thumb of the hand clutching the paper. The nail is nearly as big as a quarter, split at the edges, grooved and horny, yellowish, with irrevocable coal-black grime deep under the nail and into the cuticle. I look at the man. He is a big man, very big, bulging over the seat, bulging inside his blue serge. He is fiftyish, hair graying. His face is large and raw-looking, heavy-jowled, thick gray eyebrows over small, deep-set, appraising eyes. His name, which he tells me, sounds Russian or Polish, something ending in -ski.

I begin to read the paper, an article about the riots at the University of Alabama. He notices what I am reading. "Bet you thought I was from down here," he said. "From the way I talk. But I ain't. I was born and raised in New York City, but I been in the scrap business down here ten years. Didn't you think I was from down here?"

"Yes," I say, for that seems the sociable thing to say.

He twists his bulk in the blue serge and reaches and stabs a finger at the headline about Alabama. "Folks could be more gen'rous and fair-thinking," he says. "Like affable, you might say, and things would work out. If folks get affable and contig'ous, you might say, things sort of get worked out in time, but you get folks not being affable-like and stirring things up and it won't work out. Folks on both sides the question."

He asks me if I don't agree, and I say, sure, I agree. Sure, if folks were just affable-like.

I am thinking of what a taxi driver had said to me in Memphis: "Looks like the Lucy girl wouldn't want to go no place where people throw eggs at her and sich. But if they'd jist let her alone, them Goodrich plant fellers and all, it would blow over. What few niggers come would not have stayed no duration. Not when they found she couldn't git the social stuff, and all."

And what the school superintendent, in middle Tennessee, had said:

"You take a good many people around here that I know, segregationists all right, but when they read about a thousand to one, it sort of makes them sick. It is the unfairness in that way that gets them."

And an organizer of one of the important segregation groups, a lawyer, when I asked him if Autherine Lucy wasn't acting under law, he creaked his swivel chair, moved his shoulders under his coat, and touched a pencil on his desk, before saying: "Yes—yes—but it was just the Federal Court ruled it."

And a taxi driver in Nashville, a back-country man come to the city, a hard, lean, spare face, his lean, strong shoulders humped forward over the wheel so that the clavicles show through the coat: "A black-type person and a white-type person, they ain't alike. Now, the black-type person, all they think about is fighting and having a good time and you know what. Now, the white-type person is more American-type, he don't mind fighting but he don't fight to kill for fun. It's that cannibal blood you caint git out."

Now, on the plane, my companion observes me scribbling something in a notebook.

"You a writer or something?" he asks. "A newspaper fellow, maybe?"

I say yes.

"You interested in that stuff?" he asks, and points to the article. "Somebody ought to tell 'em not to blame no state, not even Alabam' or Mississippi, for what the bad folks do. Like stuff in New York or Chicago. Folks in Mississippi got good hearts as any place. They always been nice and good-hearted to me, for I go up to a man affable. The folks down here is just in trouble and can't claw out. Don't blame 'em, got good hearts but can't claw out of their trouble. It is hard to claw out from under the past and the past way."

He asks me if I have been talking to a lot of people.

I had been talking to a lot of people.

I had come to the shack at dusk, by the brimming bayou, in the sea of mud where cotton had been. The cold drizzle was still falling. In the shack, on the hickory chair, the yellow girl, thin but well made, wearing a salmon sweater and salmon denim slacks, holds the baby on her knee and leans toward the iron stove. On the table beyond her is an ivory-colored portable radio and a half-full bottle of Castoria. On the other side of the stove are her three other children, the oldest seven. Behind me, in the shadowy background, I know there are faces peering in from the other room of the shack, black faces, the half-grown boys, another girl I had seen on entering. The girl in the salmon sweater is telling me how she heard her husband had been killed. "Livin in town then, and my sister, she come that night and tole me he was shot. They had done shot him dead. So I up and taken out fer heah, back to the plantation. Later, my sister got my chillen and brought 'em. I ain't gonna lie, mister. I tell you, I was scairt. No tellin if that man what done it was in jail or no. Even if they had arrest him, they might bon' him out and he come and do it to me. Be mad because they 'rest him. You caint never tell. And they try him and 'quit him, doan know as I kin stay heah. Even they convick him, maybe I leave. Some good folks round heah and they helpin me, and I try to appreciate and be a prayin chile, but you git so bore down on and nigh ruint and sort of brain-washed, you don't know what. Things git to goin round in yore head. I could run out or somethin, but you caint leave yore chillen. But look like I might up and leave. He git 'quitted, that man, and maybe I die, but I die goin."

This is the cliché. It is the thing the uninitiate would expect. It is the cliché of fear. It is the cliché come fresh, and alive.

There is another image. It is morning in Nashville. I walk down Union Street, past the Negro barbershops, past the ruinous buildings plastered over with placards of old circuses and rodeos, buildings being wrecked now to make way for progress, going into the square where the big white stone boxlike, ugly and expensive Davidson County Court House now stands on the spot where the old brawling market once was. Otherwise, the square hasn't changed much, the same buildings, wholesale houses, liquor stores, pawnshops, quick lunches, and the same kind of people stand on the corners, countrymen, in khaki pants and mackinaw coats, weathered faces and hard, withdrawn eyes, usually pale eyes, lean-hipped men ("narrow-assted" in the country phrase) like the men who rode with Forrest, the farm wives, young with a baby in arms, or middle-aged and work-worn, with colored cloths over the head, glasses, false teeth, always the shopping bag.

I walk down toward the river, past the Darling Display Distribution show window, where a wax figure stands in skirt and silk blouse, the fingers spread on one uplifted hand, the thin face lifted with lips lightly parted as though in eternal, tubercular expectation of a kiss. I see the power pylons rising above the river mist. A tug is hooting upriver in the mist.

I go on down to the right, First Street, to the replica of Fort Nash-borough, the original settlement, which stands on the riverbank under the shadow of warehouses. The stockade looks so child-flimsy and jerry-built jammed against the massive, soot-stained warehouses. How could the settlers have ever taken such protection seriously? But it was enough, that and their will and the long rifles and the hunting knives and the bear-dogs they unleashed to help them when they broke the Indians at the Battle of the Bluffs. They took the land, and remain.

I am standing in the middle of the empty stockade when a boy enters and approaches me. He is about fifteen, strongly built, wearing a scruffed and tattered brown leather jacket, blue jeans, a faded blue stocking cap on the back of his head, with a mop of yellow hair hanging over his forehead. He is a fine-looking boy, erect, manly in the face, with a direct, blue-eyed glance. "Mister," he said to me, "is this foh't the way it was, or they done remodeled it?"

I tell him it is a replica, smaller than the original and not on the right spot, exactly.

"I'm glad I seen it, anyway," he says. "I like to go round seeing things that got history, and such. It gives you something to think about. Helps you in a quiz sometimes, too."

I ask him where he goes to school.

"Atlanta," he says. "Just come hitchhiking up this a-way, looking at things for interest. Like this here foh't."

"You all been having a little trouble down your way," I ask, "haven't you?"

He looks sharply at me, hesitates, then says: "Niggers—you mean niggers?"

"Yes."

"I hate them bastards," he says, with a shuddering, automatic violence, and averts his face and spits through his teeth, a quick, viperish, cut-off expectoration.

I say nothing, and he looks at me, stares into my face with a dawning belligerence, sullen and challenging, and suddenly demands: "Don't you?"

"I can't say that I do," I reply. "I like some and I don't like some others."

He utters the sudden obscenity, and removes himself a couple of paces from me. He stops and looks back over his shoulder. "I'm hitching on back to Atlanta," he declares in a flat voice, "this afternoon," and goes on out of the fort.

This, too, is a cliché. The boy, standing on the ground of history and heroism, his intellect and imagination stirred by the fact, shudders with that other, automatic emotion which my question had evoked. The

cliché had come true: the cliché of hate. And somehow the hallowed-
ness of the ground he stood on had vindicated, as it were, that hate.

The boy in the fort was the only person to turn from me, but occasionally there would be a stiffening, a flicker of suspicion, an evasion or
momentary refusal of the subject, even in the casual acquaintance of
lobby or barroom. At one of the new luxurious motels near Clarksdale
(the slick motels and the great power stations and booster stations,
silver-glittering by day and jewel-glittering by night, are the most
obvious marks of the new boom), a well-dressed young man is talking
about a movie being made down near Greenville. The movie is something about cotton, he says, by a fellow named Williams. Anyway, they
had burned down a gin in the middle of the night, just for the movie.
The woman at the desk (a very good blue dress that had cost money,
a precise, respectable middle-aged mouth, pince-nez) speaks up: "Yes,
and they say it's the only movie ever made here didn't criticize Mississippi."

"Criticize?" I ask. "Criticize how?"

She turns her head a little, looks at the man with her behind the desk,
then back at me. "You know," she says, "just criticize."

I see the eyes of the man behind the desk stray to the license of our
car parked just beyond the glass front. It has a Tennessee license, a
U-Drive-It from Memphis.

"Criticize?" I try again.

The man had been busy arranging something in the drawer behind
the desk. Suddenly, very sharply, not quite slamming, he shoves the
drawer shut. "Heck, you know," he says.

"Didn't they make another movie over at Oxford?" I ask.

The man nods, the woman says yes. I ask what that one had been
about. Nobody has seen it, not the woman, neither of the men. "It was
by that fellow Faulkner," the woman says. "But I never read anything
he ever wrote."

"I never did either," the man behind the desk says, "but I know what
it's like. It's like that fellow Hemingway. I read some of his writings.
Gory and on the seedy side of life. I didn't like it."

"That's exactly right," the woman says, and nods. "On the seedy side
of life. That fellow Faulkner, he's lost a lot of friends in Mississippi.
Looking at the seedy side."

"Does he criticize?" I ask.

She turns away. The man goes into a door behind the desk. The

well-dressed young man has long since become engrossed in a magazine.

My Tennessee license, and Tennessee accent, hadn't been good enough
credentials in Clarksdale, Mississippi. But on one occasion, the accent
wasn't good enough even in Tennessee, and I remember sitting one
evening in the tight, tiny living room (linoleum floor, gas heater, couch,
one chair, small table with TV) of an organizer of a new important
segregation group (one-time official of the Klan, this by court record)
while he harangues me. He is a fat but powerful man, face fat but not
flabby, the gray eyes squinty, set deep in the flesh, hard and sly by turns,
never genial, though the grin tries to be when he has scored a point and
leans forward at me, creaking the big overstuffed chair, his big hands
crossed on his belly. He is a hill-man, come to town from one of the
counties where there aren't too many Negroes, but he's now out to
preserve, he says, "what you might name the old Southern way, what
we was raised up to."

He is not out for money. ("I just git one dollar ever fellow I sign,
the other two goes to Mr. Perkins at headquarters, for expense. Hell,
I lose money on hit, on my gasoline.") No, he's not out for money, but
something else. He is clearly a man of force, force that somehow has
never found its way, and a man of language and leadership among his
kind, the angry and ambitious and disoriented and dispossessed. It is
language that intoxicates him now. He had been cautious at first, had
thought I was from the FBI (yes, he had had a brush with them once,
a perjury indictment), but now it seems some grand vista is opening
before him and his eyes gleam and the words come.

He is talking too much, tangling himself. All the while his wife (very
handsome, almost beautiful, in fact, bobbed, disordered black hair
around a compact, smooth-chiseled, tanned face, her body under a
flimsy dress tight and compact but gracefully made) has been standing
in the deep shadow of the doorway to a room beyond, standing patiently, hands folded but tense, with the fingers secretly moving, standing like the proper hill-wife while the menfolks talk.

"Excuse me," she suddenly says, but addressing me, not the husband,
"excuse me, but didn't you say you were born down here, used to live
right near here?"

I say yes.

She takes a step forward, coming out of the shadow. "Yes," she says, "yes," leaning at me in vindictive triumph, "but you never said where you're living now!"

And I remember sitting with a group of college students, and one of them, a law student it develops, short but strong-looking, dark-haired and slick-headed, dark bulging eyes in a slick, rather handsome, arrogant—no, bumptious—face, breaks in: "I just want to ask one question before anything starts. I just want to ask where you're from."

Suspicion of the outlander, or of the corrupted native, gets tangled up sometimes with suspicion of the New York press, but this latter suspicion may exist quite separately, on an informed and reasoned basis. For instance, I have seen a Southern newspaperman of high integrity and ability (an integrationist, by the way) suddenly strike down his fist and exclaim: "Well, by God, it's just a fact, it's not in them not to load the dice in a news story!" And another, a man publicly committed to maintaining law and order, publicly on record against the Citizens Councils and all such organizations: "*Life* magazine's editorial on the Till case, that sure fixed it. If Till's father had died a hero's death fighting for liberty, as *Life* said, that would have been as irrelevant as the actual fact that he was executed by the American army for rape-murder. It sure makes it hard."

There is the Baptist minister, an educated and intelligent man, who, when I show him an article in the *Reader's Digest,* an article mentioning that the Southern Baptist Convention had voted overwhelmingly for support of the Supreme Court decision, stiffens and says to me: "Look —look at that title!"

I didn't need to look. I knew what it was: "The Churches Repent."

But there is another suspicion story. A Negro told me this. A man from New Haven called on him, and upon being asked politely to take a chair, said: "Now, please, won't you tell me about the race problem."

To which the Negro replied: "Mister, I can't tell you a thing about that. There's nothing I could tell to you. If you want to find out, you better just move down here and live for a while."

That is the something else—the instinctive fear, on the part of black or white, that the massiveness of experience, the concreteness of life, will be violated; the fear of abstraction. I suppose it is this fear that made one man, a subtle and learned man, say to me: "There's something you can't explain, what being a Southerner is." And when he said that, I remembered a Yankee friend saying to me: "Southerners and Jews, you're exactly alike, you're so damned special."

"Yes," I said, "we're both persecuted minorities."

I had said it for a joke.

But had I?

In the end people talked, even showed an anxiety to talk, to explain something. Even the black Southerners, a persecuted minority, too, would talk, for over and over, the moment of some sudden decision would come: "All right—all right—I'll tell it to you straight. All right, there's no use beating around the bush."

But how fully can I read the words offered in the fullest efforts of candor?

It is a town in Louisiana, and I am riding in an automobile driven by a Negro, a teacher, a slow, careful man, who puts his words out in that fashion, almost musingly, and drives his car that way, too. He has been showing me the Negro business section, how prosperous some of it is, and earlier he had said he would show me a section where the white men's cars almost line up at night. Now he seems to have forgotten that sardonic notion in the pleasanter, more prideful task. He has fallen silent, seemingly occupied with his important business of driving, and the car moves deliberately down the street. Then, putting his words out that slow way, detachedly as though I weren't there, he says: "You hear some white men say they know Negroes. Understand Negroes. But it's not true. No white man ever born ever understood what a Negro is thinking. What he's feeling."

The car moves on down the empty street, negotiates a left turn with majestic deliberation.

"And half the time that Negro," he continues, "he don't understand, either."

I know that the man beside me had once, long back, had a bright-skinned, pretty wife. She had left him to be set up by a well-off white man (placée is the old word for it). The Negro man beside me does not know that I know this, but I have known it a long time, and now I wonder what this man is thinking as we ride along, silent again.

Just listening to talk as it comes is best, but sometimes it doesn't come, or the man says, "You ask me some questions," and so, bit by bit, a certain pattern of questions emerges, the old obvious questions, I suppose—the questions people respond to or flinch from.

What are the white man's reasons for segregation?

The man I am talking to is a yellow man, about forty years old, shortish, rather fat, with a very smooth, faintly Mongolian face, eyes very shrewd but ready to smile. When the smile really comes, there is a gold tooth showing, to become, in that gold face, part of the sincerity of the smile. His arms seem somewhat short, and as he sits very erect in a straight chair, he folds his hands over his stomach. He gives the impression of a man very much at home in himself, at peace in himself, in his dignity, in his own pleasant, smooth-skinned plumpness, in some sustaining humorousness of things. He owns a small business, a shoe-shop with a few employees.

"What does the white man do it for?" he rephrases the question. He pauses, and you can see he is thinking, studying on it, his smooth yellow face compressing a little. All at once the face relaxes, a sort of humorous ripple, humorous but serious too, in a sort of wry way, before the face settles to its blandness. "You know," he says, "you know, years and years I look at some white feller, and I caint never figure him out. You go long with him, years and years, and all of a sudden he does something. I caint figure out what makes him do the way he does. It is like a mystery, you might say. I have studied on it."

Another Negro, a very black man, small-built and intense, leans forward in his chair. He says it is money, so the white man can have cheap labor, can make the money. He is a bookish man, has been to a Negro college, and though he has never been out of the South, his speech surprises me the way my native ear used to be surprised by the speech of a Negro born and raised, say, in Akron, Ohio. I make some fleeting, tentative association of his speech, his education, his economic interpretation of things; then let the notion slide.

"Yeah, yeah," the yellow man is saying, agreeing, "but—" He stops, shakes his head.

"But what?" I ask.

He hesitates, and I see the thumbs of the hands lightly clasped across his belly begin to move, ever so slowly, round and round each other. "All right," he says, "I might as well say it to you."

"Say what?"

"Mongrelization," he says, "that's what a white man will say. You ask him and he'll say that. He wants to head it off, he says. But—" He grins, the skin crinkles around his eyes, the grin shows the gold tooth. "But," he says, "look at my face. It wasn't any black man hung it on me."

The other man doesn't seem to think this is funny. "Yes," he says, "yes, they claim they don't want mongrelization. But who has done it? They claim Negroes are dirty, diseased, that that's why they want segregation. But they have Negro nurses for their children, they have Negro cooks. They claim Negroes are ignorant. But they won't associate with the smartest and best-educated Negro. They claim . . ." And his voice goes on, winding up the bitter catalogue of paradoxes. I know them all. They are not new.

The smooth-faced yellow man is listening. But he is thinking, too, the yellow blandness of his face creaming ever so little with his slow, humorous intentness. I ask him what he is thinking.

He grins, with philosophic ruefulness. "I was just studying on it," he says. "It's all true, what Mr. Elmo here says. But there must be something behind it all. Something he don't ever say, that white feller. Maybe . . ." He pauses, hunting for the formulation. "Maybe it's just pridefulness," he says, "him being white."

Later, I am talking with the hill-man organizer, the one with the handsome wife who asks me where I live now, and he is telling me why he wants segregation. "The Court," he says, "hit caint take no stick and mix folks up like you swivel and swull eggs broke in a bowl. Naw," he says, "you got to raise 'em up, the niggers, not bring the white folks down to nigger level." He illustrates with his pudgy, strong hands in the air before him, one up, one down, changing levels. He watches the hands, with fascination, as though he has just learned to do a complicated trick.

How would you raise the level? I ask.

"Give 'em good schools and things, yeah. But"—and he warms to the topic, leaning at me—"I'd 'bolish common-law marriage. I'd put 'em in jail fer hit, and make 'em learn morals. Now, a nigger don't know how to treat no wife, not even a nigger wife. He whup her and beat her and maybe carve on her jaw with a pocketknife. When he ought to trick and pet her, and set her on his knee like a white man does his wife."

Then I talk with a Negro grade-school teacher, in the country, in Tennessee. She is a mulatto woman, middle-aged, with a handsome aquiline face, rather Indian-looking. She is sitting in her tiny, pridefully clean house, with a prideful bookcase of books beyond her, talking with slow and detached tones. I know what her story has been, years of domestic service, a painfully acquired education, marriage to a professional man, no children ("It was a cross to bear, but maybe that's why I love 'em so and like to teach 'em not my own").

I ask her why white people want to keep segregation.

"You ought to see the schoolhouse I teach in," she says, and pauses, and her lips curl sardonically, "set in the mud and hogs can come under it, and the privies set back in the mud. And see some of the children that come there, out of homes with nothing, worse than the school-house, no sanitation or cleanness, with disease and dirt and no manners. You wouldn't blame a white person for not wanting the white child set down beside them." Then with a slow movement of the shoulders, again the curl of the lips: "Why didn't the Federal government give us money ten years ago for our school? To get ready, to raise us up a little to integrate. It would have made it easier. But now—"

But now? I ask.

"You got to try to be fair," she says.

I am talking with an official of one of the segregation outfits, late at night, in his house, in a fringe subdivision, in a small living room, with red velvet drapes at the one window, a TV set, new, on a table, a plastic or plaster bas-relief of a fox hunter hung on the wall, in color, the hunting coat very red and arrogant. My host is seventy-five years old, bald except for a fringe of gray hair, sallow-skinned, very clean and scrubbed-looking, white shirt but no tie, a knife-edge crease to his hard-finish gray trousers. He smokes cigarettes, one after another, with nervous, stained fingers.

He was born in North Kentucky, romantically remembers the to-bacco nightriders ("Yeah, it was tight, nobody talked tobacco much, you might get shot"), remembers the Civil War veterans ("even the GAR's") sitting round, talking to the kids ("Yeah, they talked their war, they had something to remember and be proud of, not like these veterans we got nowadays, nothing to be proud of"), started out to be a lawyer ("But Blackstone got too dry, but history now, that's different, you always get something out of it to think about"), but wound up doing lots of things, finally, for years, a fraternal organizer.

Yes, he is definitely a pro, and when he talks of Gerald L. K. Smith he bursts out, eyes a-gleam: "Lord, that man's mailing list would be worth a million dollars!" He is not the rabble-rouser, the crusader, but the persuader, the debater, the man who gives the reasons. He is, in fact, a very American type, the old-fashioned, self-made, back-country intel-lectual—the type that finds apotheosis in Mark Twain and Abraham Lincoln. If he is neither of them, if he says "gondorea" and "enviro-mental" and "ethnolology," if something went wrong, if nothing ever came out quite right for him along the long way, you can still sense the old, unappeased hungers, the old drives of a nameless ambition. And he is sadly contemptuous of his organizers, who "aren't up to it," who "just aren't posted on history and ethnolology," who just haven't got "the old gray matter."

I ask him why the white man wants segregation.

"He'll say one thing and another," he says, "he knows in his bones it ain't right to have mixing. But you got to give him the reasons, explain it to him. It is the ethnolology of it you got to give. You got to explain how no *Negroes*"—he pronounces it with the elaborate polemical correctness, but not for polemics, just to set himself off intellectually, I suppose, from the people who might say *nigger*— "explain how no Negroes ever created a civilization. They are parasites. They haven't got the stuff up here." And he taps his forehead. "And explain how there is just two races, white and black, and—"

"What about the Bible," I ask, "doesn't the Bible say three?"

"Yes, but you know, between you and me, I don't reckon you have to take much stock in the Bible in this business. I don't take much stock in Darwin in some ways, either. He is too enviromental, he don't think enough about the blood. Yes, sir, I'll tell you, it's hard to come by good books on ethnolology these days. Got a good one from California the other day, though. But just one copy. Been out of print a long time. But like I was saying, the point is there's just two races, black and white, and the rest of them is a kind of mixing. You always get a mess when the mixing starts. Take India. They are a pure white people like you and me, and they had a pretty good civilization, too. Till they got to shipping on a little Negro blood. It don't take much to do the damage. Look at 'em now."

That is his argument. It is much the same argument given me by another official of another segregation group, whom I sit with a week later in another state, a lawyer, forty-five or -six, of strong middle height, sandy blond, hands strong, with pale hairs and square-cut, scrubbed-looking nails. He is cagey at first, then suddenly warm, in an expanding, sincere, appealing way. He really wants to explain himself, wants to be regarded as an honest man, wants to be liked. I do like him, as he tells about himself, how he had gone to college, the hard way I gather, had prepared to be a teacher of history in high school, had given that up, had tried business in one way or another, had given that up, had studied law. "You ought to know my politics, too," he says. He was New Deal till the Court-packing plan. "That disgusted me," he says, and you believe him. Then he was for Willkie, then for Dewey, then Dixiecrat, then for Eisenhower. (I remember another lawyer, hired by another group: "Hell, all Southerners are Republicans at heart, conservative, and just don't know they're Republican.")

But Eisenhower doesn't satisfy my friend now. "We'll elect our own President. Our organization isn't just Southern. We're going national.

Plenty of people in Chicago and other places feel like we do. And afraid of a big central government, too. We'll elect our own President and see how Chief Justice Warren's decision comes out."

I ask if the main point is the matter of States' rights, of local integrity.

"Yes, in a way," he says, "but you got to fight on something you can rouse people up about, on segregation. There's the constitutional argument, but your basic feeling, that's what you've got to trust—what you feel, not your reasons for it. But we've got argument, reasons."

He hesitates, thumps the desk top in a quick tattoo of his strong, scrubbed-looking fingers (he isn't a nervous man in the ordinary sense, but there are these sudden bursts), twists himself in his chair, then abruptly leans forward, jerks a drawer open (literally jerks it), and thrusts an envelope at me. "Heck, you might as well see it," he says.

I look at it. The stuff is not new. I have seen it before, elsewhere. It was used in the last gubernatorial campaign in Tennessee, it was used in the march on the Capitol at Nashville a few weeks ago. There are the handbills showing "Harlem Negro and White Wife," lying abed, showing "Crooner Roy Hamilton & Teenage Fans," who are white girls, showing a schoolyard in Baltimore with Negro and white children, "the new look in education." On the back of one of the handbills is a crudely drawn valentine-like heart, in it the head of a white woman who (with feelings not indicated by the artist) is about to be kissed by a black man of the most primitive physiognomy. On the heart two vultures perch. Beneath it is the caption: "The Kiss of Death."

Below are the "reasons": "While Russia makes laws to protect her own race she continues to prod us to accept 14,000,000 Negroes as social equals and we are doing everything possible to please her. . . . Segregation is the law of God, not man. . . . Continue to rob the white race in order to bribe the Asiatic and Negro and these people will overwhelm the white race and destroy all progress, religion, invention, art, and return us to the jungle. . . . Negro blood destroyed the civilization of Egypt, India, Phoenicia, Carthage, Greece, and it will destroy America!"

I put the literature into my pocket, to join the other samples. "If there's trouble," I ask, "where will it begin?"

"We don't condone violence," he says.

"But if—just suppose," I say.

He doesn't hesitate. "The redneck," he says, "that's what you call 'em around here. Those fellows—and I'm one of them myself, just a redneck that got educated—are the ones who will feel the rub. He is the one on the underside of the plank with nothing between him and the bare black ground. He's got to have something to give him pride. Just to be better than something."

To be better than something: so we are back to the pridefulness the yellow man had talked about. But no, there is more, something else.

There is the minister, a Baptist, an intellectual-looking man, a man whose face indicates conscience and thoughtfulness, pastor of a good church in a good district in a thriving city. "It is simple," he says. "It is a matter of God's will and revelation. I refer you to Acts 17—I don't remember the verse. This is the passage the integrationists are always quoting to prove that integration is Christian. But they won't quote it all. It's the end that counts."

I looked it up: *And hath made of one blood all nations of men for to dwell on all the face of the earth, and hath determined the times before appointed, and the bounds of their habitation.*

There is the very handsome lady of forty-five, charming and witty and gay, full of dramatic mimicry, a wonderful range of phrase, a quick sympathy, a totally captivating talker of the kind you still occasionally find among women of the Deep South, but never now in a woman under forty. She is sitting before the fire in the fine room, her brother, big and handsome but barefoot and rigid drunk, opposite her. But she gaily overrides that small difficulty ("Oh, don't mind him, he's just had a whole bottle of brandy. Been on a high-lonesome all by himself. But poor Jack, he feels better now"). She has been talking about the Negroes on her plantation, and at last, about integration, but that only in one phrase, tossed off as gaily and casually as any other of the evening, so casual as to permit no discussion: "But of course we have to keep the white race intact."

But the husband, much her senior, who has said almost nothing all evening, lifts his strong, grizzled old face, and in a kind of *sotto voce* growl, not to her, not to me, not to anybody, utters: "In power—in power—you mean the white race in power."

And I think of another Southerner, an integrationist, saying to me: "You simply have to recognize a fact. In no county where the Negroes are two to one is the white man going to surrender political power, not with the Negroes in those counties in their present condition. It's not a question of being Southern. You put the same number of Yankee liberals in the same county and in a week they'd be behaving the same way. Living with something and talking about it are two very different things, and living with something is always the slow way."

And another, not an integrationist, from a black county, saying: "Yeah, let 'em take over and in six months you'd be paying the taxes but a black sheriff would be collecting 'em. You couldn't walk down the sidewalk. You'd be communized, all right."

But is it power. Merely power? Or any of the other things suggested thus far?

I think of a college professor in a section where about half the population is Negro. The college has no Negro students, but—"The heat is on," he says. "But listen, brother," he says, "lots of our boys don't like it a bit. Not a bit."

I ask would it be like the University of Alabama.

"It would be something, brother. I'll tell you that, brother. One of our boys—been fooling around with an organization uptown—he came to me and asked me to be sure to let him know when a nigger was coming, he and some friends would stop that clock. But I didn't want to hear student talk. I said, son, just don't tell me."

I asked what the faculty would do.

"Hide out, brother, hide out. And, brother, I would, too."

Yes, he was a segregationist. I didn't have to ask him. Or ask his reasons, for he was talking on, in his rather nasal voice—leaning happily back in his chair in the handsome office, a spare, fiftyish man, dark-suited, rather dressy, sharp-nosed, with some fringe-remnants of sandy hair on an elongated, slightly freckled skull, rimless glasses on pale eyes: "Yeah, brother, back in my county there was a long ridge running through the county, and one side the ridge was good land, river bottom, and folks put on airs there and held niggers, but on the other side of the ridge the ground so pore you couldn't grow peas and nothing but pore white trash. So when the Civil War came, the pore white trash, as the folks who put on airs called them, just picked down the old rifle off the deer horns over the fireplace and joined the Federals coming down, just because they hated those fellows across the ridge. But don't get me wrong, brother. They didn't want any truck with niggers, either. To this day they vote Republican and hate niggers. It is just they hate niggers."

Yes, they hate niggers, but I am in another room, the library of a plantation house, in Mississippi, and the planter is talking to me, leaning his length back at ease, speaking deliberately from his high-nosed, commanding face, the very figure of a Wade Hampton or Kirby Smith, only the gray uniform and cavalry boots not there, saying: "No, I don't hate Negroes. I never had a minute's trouble with one in my life, and never intend to. I don't believe in getting lathered up, and I don't intend to get lathered up. I simply don't discuss the question with anybody. But I'll tell you what I feel. I came out of the university with a lot of ideals and humanitarianism, and I stayed by it as long as I could. But I tell you now what has come out of thirty years of experience and careful consideration. I have a deep contempt for the Negro race as it exists here. It is not so much a matter of ability as of character. Character."

He repeats the word. He is a man of character, it could never be denied. Of character and force. He is also a man of fine intelligence and good education. He reads Roman history. He collects books on the American West. He is widely traveled. He is unusually successful as a planter and businessman. He is a man of human warmth and generosity, and eminent justice. I overhear his wife, at this moment, talking to a Negro from the place, asking him if she can save some more money for him, to add to the hundred dollars she holds, trying to persuade him.

The husband goes on: "It's not so much the hands on my place, as the lawyers and doctors and teachers and insurance men and undertakers—oh, yes, I've had dealings all around, or my hands have. The character just breaks down. It is not dependable. They pay lip service to the white man's ideals of conduct. They say, yes, I believe in honesty and truth and morality. But it is just lip service. Most of the time. I don't intend to get lathered up. This is just my private opinion. I believe in segregation, but I can always protect myself and my family. I dine at my club and my land is my own, and when I travel, the places I frequent have few if any Negroes. Not that I'd ever walk out of a restaurant, for I'm no professional Southerner. And I'd never give a nickel to the Citizens Council or anything like that. Nor have any of my friends, that I know of. That's townspeople stuff, anyway."

Later on, he says: "For years, I thought I loved Negroes. And I loved their humor and other qualities. My father—he was a firster around here, first man to put glass windows in for them, first to give them a written monthly statement, first to do a lot to help them toward financial independence—well, my father, he used to look at me and say how it would be. He said, son, they will knock it out of you. Well, they did. I learned the grimness and the sadness."

And later, as we ride down the long row of the houses of the hands, he points to shreds of screening at windows, or here and there a broken screen door. "One of my last experiments," he says, dourly. "Three months, and they poked it out of the kitchen window so they could throw slops on the bare ground. They broke down the front door so they could spit tobacco juice out on the porch floor."

We ride on. We pass a nicely painted house, with a fenced dooryard, with flower beds, and flower boxes on the porch, and good bright-painted porch furniture. I ask who lives there. "One of the hands," he says, "but he's got some energy and character. Look at his house. And he loves flowers. Has only three children, but when there's work he gets it done fast, and then finds some more to do. Makes $4,500 to $5,000 a year." Some old pride, or something from the lost days of idealism, comes back into his tone.

I ask what the other people on the place think of the tenant with the nice house.

"They think he's just lucky." And he mimics, a little bitterly, without any humor: "Boss, looks lak Jefferson's chillen, they jes picks faster'n mine. Caint he'p it, Boss."

I ask what Jefferson's color is.

"A real black man, a real Negro, all right. But he's got character."

I look down the interminable row of dingy houses, over the interminable flat of black earth toward the river.

Now and then, I encounter a man whose argument for segregation, in the present context, has nothing to do with the Negro at all. At its simplest level its spokesman says: "I don't give a durn about the niggers, they never bother me one way or another. But I don't like being forced. Ain't no man ever forced me."

But the law always carries force, you say.

"Not this law. It's different. It ain't our law."

At another level, the spokesman will say it is a matter of constitutionality, pure and simple. He may even be an integrationist. But this decision, he will say, carries us one more step toward the power state, a cunningly calculated step, for this decision carries a moral issue and the objector to the decision is automatically put in the role of the enemy of righteousness. "But wait till the next decision," he will say. "This will be the precedent for it, and the next one won't have the moral façade."

Precedent for what? you ask.

"For government by sociology, not law," he will say.

"Is it government by law," one man asks me, "when certain members of the Supreme Court want to write a minority decision, and the great conciliator conciliates them out of it, saying that the thing is going to be controversial enough without the Court splitting? Damn it, the Court should split, if that's the honest reading of the law. We want the reading of the law, not the conciliation by sociology. Even if we don't happen to like the kind of law it turns out to be in a particular case."

And another man: "Yes, government by sociology not law is a two-edged business. The next guy who gets in the saddle just picks another brand of sociology. And nothing to stop him, for the very notion of law is gone."

Pridefulness, money, level of intelligence, race, God's will, filth and disease, power, hate, contempt, legality—perhaps these are not all the words that get mentioned. There is another thing, whatever the word for it. An eminent Negro scholar, is, I suppose, saying something about that other thing. "One thing," he says, "is that a lot of people down here just don't like change. It's not merely desegregation they're against so much, it's just the fact of any change. They feel some emotional tie to the way things are. A change is disorienting, especially if you're pretty disoriented already."

Yes, a lot of them are disoriented enough already, uprooted, driven from the land, drawn from the land, befuddled by new opportunities, new ambitions, new obligations. They have entered the great anonymity of the new world.

And I hear a college student in the Deep South: "You know, it's just that people don't like to feel like they're spitting on their grandfather's grave. They feel some connection they don't want to break. Something would bother them if they broke it."

The young man is, I gather, an integrationist. He adds: "And sometimes something bothers them if they don't break it."

Let us give a name now to whatever it is that the eminent Negro scholar and the young white college boy were talking about. Let us, without meaning to be ironical, call it piety.

What does the Negro want?

The plump yellow man, with his hands folded calmly over his belly, the man who said it is the white man's "pridefulness," thinks, and answers the new question. "Opportunity," he says. "It's opportunity a man wants."

For what? I ask.

"Just to get along and make out. You know, like anybody."

"About education, now. If you got good schools, as good as anybody's, would that satisfy you?"

"Well—" the yellow man begins, but the black, intense-faced man breaks in. "We never had them, we'd never have them!"

"You might get them now," I say, "under this pressure."

"Maybe," the yellow man agrees, "maybe. And it might have satisfied once. But"—and he shakes his head—"not now. That doctrine won't grip now."

"Not now," the intense-faced man says. "Not after the Supreme Court decision. We want the law."

"But when?" I ask. "Right now? Tomorrow morning?"

"The Supreme Court decision says—" And he stops.

"It says deliberate speed," I say, "or something like that."

"If a Negro wants to study medicine, he can't study it. If he wants to study law, he can't study it. There isn't any way in this state for him to study it."

"Suppose," I say, "suppose professional and graduate schools got opened. To really qualified applicants, no funny business either way. Then they began some sort of staggered system, a grade or two at a time, from either top or bottom. Would something like that satisfy you? Perhaps not all over the state at the same time, some place serving as a sort of pilot for others where the going would be rougher."

The yellow man nods. The intense-faced man looks down at his new and newly polished good black shoes. He looks across at the wall. Not looking at me, he says: "Yes, if it was in good faith. If you could depend on it. Yes."

He hates to say it. At least, I think he hates to say it. It is a wrench, grudging.

I sit in another room, in another city, in the Deep South, with several men, two of them Negroes. One Negro is the local NAACP secretary, a man in build, color and quality strangely like the black, intense-faced man. I am asking again what will satisfy the Negroes. Only this time the intense-faced man does not as readily say, yes, a staggered system would be satisfactory. In fact, he doesn't say it at all. I ask him what his philosophy of social change is, in a democracy. He begins to refer to the law, to the Court, but one of the white men breaks in.

This white man is of the Deep South, born, bred and educated there. He is a middle-aged man, tall, rather spare but not angular, the impression of the lack of angularity coming, I suppose, from a great deliberation in voice and movement, a great calmness in voice and face. The face is an intellectual's face, a calm, dedicated face, but not a zealot's. His career, I know, has been identified with various causes of social reform. He has sat on many committees, has signed many things, some of them things I personally take to be nonsense. What he says now, in his serene voice, the words and voice being really all that I know of him, is this: "I know that Mr. Cranford here"—and he nods toward this black, intense-faced man—"doesn't want any change by violence. He knows—we know—that change will take time. He wants a change in a Christian way that won't aggravate to violence. We have all got to live together. It will take time."

Nobody says anything. After a moment I go back to my question about the philosophy of social change. Wearily the intense-faced man says something, something not very relevant, not evasive, just not relevant. I let the matter drop. He sits with his head propped on his right hand, brow furrowed. He is not interested in abstractions. Why should he be?

Again, it is the Deep South, another town, another room, the bright, new-sparkling living room of the house of a Negro business-man, new furniture, new TV, new everything. There are several white men present, two journalists, myself (I've just come along to watch, I'm not involved), some technicians, and about ten Negroes, all in Sunday best, at ease but slightly formal, as though just before going in to a church service. Some of the Negroes, I have heard, are in the NAACP.

The technicians are rigging up their stuff, lights and cameras, etc., moving arrogantly in their own world superior to human concerns. In the background, in the dining room, the wife of our host, a plump fortyish mulatto, an agreeable-looking woman wearing a new black dress with a discreet white design on it, stands watching a big new electric percolator on a silver tray. Another silver tray holds a bottle of Canadian whiskey, a good whiskey, and glasses. When someone comes out of the kitchen, I catch a glimpse of a gray-haired Negro woman wearing a maid's uniform.

It is a bright, sunny, crisp day outside. The coffee is bubbling cheer-fully. Out the window I see a little Negro girl, about ten years old, with a pink bow in her hair, an enormous bow, come out of a small pink house with aquamarine trim and shutters, and a dull blue roof. She stands a moment with the pink bow against the aquamarine door, then moves through the opening in the clipped privet hedge, a very tidy, persnickety hedge, and picks her way down the muddy street, where there is no sidewalk.

One of the journalists is instructing a Negro who is to be inter-viewed, a tall, well-set-up, jut-nosed, good-looking dark-brown man in a blue suit. He has a good way of holding his head. "Now, you're supposed to tell them," the journalist is saying, "what a lot of hogwash this separate but equal stuff is. What you said to me last night."

Pedagogical and irritable, one of the technicians says: "Quiet, quiet!"

They take a voice level. The dark-brown man is very much at ease, saying: "Now is the time for all good men to come to the aid of their country."

The interview begins. The dark-brown man, still very much at ease, is saying: ". . . and we're not disturbed. The only people disturbed are those who have not taken an unbiased look. We who have taken our decision, we aren't disturbed." He goes on to say the Negroes want an interracial discussion on the "how" of desegregation—but with the background understanding that the Court decision is law.

The journalist cuts in: "Make it simple and direct. Lay it on the line."

The tall brown man is unruffled. There is sweat on his face now, but from the lamps. He wipes his face, and patiently, condescendingly, smiles at the journalist. "Listen," he says, "you all are going back to New York City. But we stay here. We aren't afraid, but we live here. They know what we think, but it's a way of putting it we got to think about."

He says it is going to take some time to work things out, he knows that, but there is a chorus from the Negroes crowded back out of range of the camera: "Don't put no time limit—don't put any time on it— no ten or fifteen years!"

The dark-brown man doesn't put any time on it. He says all they want is to recognize the law and to sit down in a law-abiding way to work out the "how" and the "when."

"That's good, that's all right!" the chorus decides.

Leave the "how" in detail up to the specialists in education. As for the "when"—the dark-brown, jut-nosed man hesitates a second: "Well, Negroes are patient. We can wait a little while longer."

The dark-brown man gets up to his considerable height, wipes the sweat off his face, asks the journalist: "You got your playback?"

The chorus laughs. It is indulgent laughter of human vanity and such. Sure, any man would like to hear his voice played back, hear himself talking.

There is no playback. Not now, anyway.

The dark-brown man is receiving the handshakes, the shoulder-slaps, of his friends. They think he did well. He did do well. He looks back over his shoulder at the white men, grins. "When I got to leave," he says, "who's going to give me that job as chauffeur? I see that nice Cadillac sitting out front there."

There are the quick, deep-throated giggles.

I turn to a Negro beside me. "Ten years ago," I ask, "would this have been possible?"

"No," he says.

. . .

Then there is another house, the tangle of wires, the jumble of rig and lights, and another Negro being arranged for an interview. There is no air of decorous festivity here, just a businesslike bustle, with the Negro waiting. This one will be knocked off quick. It's getting on to lunch.

This one, one of the journalists told me, is supposed to be the Uncle Tom. He is a middle-aged man, fair-sized, tallish, medium brown, with a balding, rather high forehead. He is wearing a good dark suit. His manner is dignified, slow, a little sad. I have known him before, know something about him. He had begun life as waterboy on a plantation, back in the times when "some folks didn't think a thing of bloodying a Negro's head, just for nothing, and I have seen their heads bloodied." But a white man on the plantation had helped him. ("Noticed I was sort of quick and took an interest in things, trying to learn"), and now he is a preacher. For a voice level, he does not say: "Now is the time for all good men to come to the aid of their country." He says: "Jesus wept, Jesus wept, Jesus wept."

The journalist tells him he is supposed to say some good things for segregation.

The Negro doesn't answer directly to that. "If you have some opinions of your own," he says, "your own people sometimes call you a son-of-a-gun, and sometimes the white people call you a son-of-a-gun."

Your own people. And I remember that the men at the last house had said: "Don't tell him you've seen us, don't tell him that or you won't get him to talk."

Is integration a good thing? the journalist asks him, and he says: "Till Negro people get as intelligent and self-sustaining they can't mix." But he flares up about discrimination along with segregation: "That's what makes Negroes bitter, wage differentials, no good jobs, that and the ballot." As for the Court decision, he says: "It's something for people to strive for, to ascertain their best."

I break in—I don't think the machinery is going yet—and ask about humiliation as a bar to Negro fulfillment.

"Segregation did one thing," he says. "No other race but the Negroes could build up as much will to go on and do things. To get their goals."

What goals? I ask.

"Just what anybody wants, just everything people can want to be a citizen," he says.

This isn't what the journalist has come for.

Things aren't promising too well. Uncle Tom is doing a disappearing act, Old Black Joe is evaporating, the handkerchief-head, most inconveniently, isn't there. The genie has got out of the bottle clearly labeled: *Negro* segregationist.

But maybe the genie can be coaxed back into the bottle. The sad-mannered man is, the journalist suggests, a pro-segregationist in that he thinks segregation built a will to achieve something.

The machinery gets going, the mike is lifted on its rod, the slow, sad voice speaks: "For segregation has test steel into the Negro race and this is one valuable point of segregation—segregation has proven that Negroes in the South, where it's practiced most, have done a fine job in building an economic strength beyond that of many other sections in the United States of America. Negroes own more farmland in Mississippi than any other state in the United States that is engaged in agriculture."

He goes along, he says, "with the idea you should have a moderate approach. You will never be able to integrate children on the school campus, the mothers holding a lot of bitterness in their hearts against each other white and colored."

It will take time, he says. "It is absurd otherwise, it's just foolish thinking for people to believe you can get the South to do in four or five years what they have been doing in the North for one hundred years. These people are emotional about their tradition, and you've got to have an educational program to change their way of thinking and this will be a slow process."

Yes, the genie is safely back in the labeled bottle. Or is he?

For the slow, sad voice is saying: ". . . has got to outthink the white man, has got to outlive the white man . . ."

Is saying: ". . . no need of saying that the South won't ever integrate . . ."

Is saying: ". . . not ultimate goal just to go to white schools and travel with white people on conveyances over the country. No, the Negro, he is a growing people and he will strive for all the equalities belonging to any American citizen. He is a growing people."

Yes, Uncle Tom is gone again, and gone for good. Too bad for the program. I wondered if they got this last part on tape.

The Negro turns to the journalist and asks if he has interviewed other people around.

"Yes, saw Mr. So-and-so of the Citizens Council."

Had we interviewed any other Negroes?

"Oh, some," after a shade of hesitation.

Had we seen So-and-so and So-and-so?

"No—why, no. Well, we want to thank you . . ."

We leave the sad-mannered, slow man and we know that he knows. He isn't a big enough fool not to know. White men have lied to him before. What is one more time after all the years?

Besides, what if you do tell him a lie?

There are, as a matter of fact, in Arkansas, Negroes who go from door to door collecting money to fight integration. There *are* Uncle Toms.

So it all evens out.

I ask my question of the eminent Negro scholar. His reply is immediate: "It's not so much what the Negro wants as what he doesn't want. The main point is not that he has poor facilities. It is that he must endure a constant assault on his ego. He is denied human dignity."

And I think of the yellow girl wearing the salmon sweater and slacks, in the shack in the sea of mud, at dusk, the girl whose husband has been shot, and she says: "It's how yore feelings git tore up all the time. The way folks talk, sometimes. It ain't what they say sometimes, if they'd jes say it kind."

She had gone to a store, in another town, for some dress goods, and had requested a receipt for the minister who manages the fund raised in her behalf. By the receipt the saleswoman identifies her and asks if "that man up yonder is still in jail for killing a nigger."

"Well," the girl had said, "if you want to put it that a-way."

"They can't do anything to a man for something he does drunk," the saleswoman has said.

The girl has laid the package down on the counter. "If you want it that a-way," she has said, "you kin take back yore dress goods. They's other places to buy."

She tells me the story.

And I think of another woman, up in Tennessee, middle-aged, precise, the kind of woman who knows her own competent mind, a school inspector for county schools, a Negro. "We don't want to socialize. That's not what we want. We do everything the white folks do already, even if we don't spend as much money doing it. And we have more fun. But I don't want to be insulted. If somebody has to tell you something, about some regulation or other, they could say it in a low, kind voice, not yell it out at you. And when I go to a place to buy something, and have that dollar bill in my hand, I want to be treated right. And I won't ride on a bus. I won't go to a restaurant in a town where there's just one. I'll go hungry. I won't be insulted at the front door and then crawl around to the back. You've got to try to keep some respect."

And in Tennessee again, the Negro at the biracial committee meeting says: "My boy is happy in the Negro school where he goes. I don't want him to go to the white school and sit by your boy's side. But I'd die fighting for his right to go." "We don't want to socialize," the woman in Tennessee says.

The college student, a Negro, in Tennessee, says: "The Negro doesn't want social equality. My wife is my color. I'm above wanting to mix things up. That's low class. Low class of both races."

The Negro man in Mississippi says: "Take a Negro man wanting a white woman. A man tends to want his own kind, now. But the white folks make such an awful fuss about it. They make it seem so awful special-like. Maybe that's what makes it sort of prey on some folks' mind."

And I remember the gang rape by four Negroes of a white woman near Memphis last fall, shortly after the Till killing. "One of our boys was killed down in Mississippi the other day and we're liable to kill you," one of the Negroes said as they bludgeoned the man who was with the woman and told him to get going.

This is a question for Negroes only. *Is there any difference between what the Negro feels at the exclusions of segregation, and what a white man feels at the exclusions which he, any man, must always face at some point?*

"Yes, it's different," the Negro college administrator says, "when your fate is on your face. Just that. It's the unchangeableness. But a white man, even if he knows he can't be President, even if he knows the chances for his son are one in many millions—long odds—still there's an idea there."

And the Negro lawyer: "Yes, it's different. But it's not easy to name it. Take how some unions come in and make some plant build nice rest rooms, one for white, one for Negroes, but same tile, same fixtures and all. But off the white ones, there's a little lounge for smoking. To make 'em feel superior to somebody. You see what I mean, how it's different?"

He thinks some more. "Yes," he says, "I got my dreams and hopes and aspirations, but me, I have to think what is sort of possible in the possibilities and probabilities. Some things I know I can't think on because of the circumstances of my birth."

And he thinks again, looking out of the window, over Beale Street. "Yes, there's a difference," he says. "A Negro, he doesn't really know some things, but he just goes walking pregnant with worries, not knowing their name. It's he's lost his purpose, somewhere. He goes wandering and wondering, and no purpose."

I look out the window, too, over Beale Street. It is late afternoon. I hear the pullulation of life, the stir and new tempo toward evening, the babble of voices, a snatch of laughter. I hear the remorseless juke boxes. They shake the air.

What's coming?

"Whatever it is," the college student in the Deep South says, "I'd like to put all the Citizens Council and all the NAACP in one room and give every man a baseball bat and lock 'em in till it was over. Then maybe some sensible people could work out something."

What's coming? I say it to the country grade-school superintendent. He is a part-time farmer, too, and now he is really in his role as farmer, not teacher, as we stand, at night, under the naked light of a flyspecked 200-watt bulb hanging from the shed roof, and he oversees two Negroes loading sacks of fertilizer on a truck. "I know folks round here," he says, and seeing his hard, aquiline, weathered face, with the flat, pale, hard eyes, I believe him.

"They aren't raised up to it," he says. "Back in the summer now, I went by a lady's house to ask about her children starting to school. Well, she was a real old-timey gal, a gant-headed, barefoot, snuff-dipping, bonnet-wearing, hard-ankled old gal standing out in the to-bacco patch, leaning on her hoe, and she leaned at me and said, 'Done hear'd tell 'bout niggers gonna come in,' and before I could say anything, she said, 'Not with none of my young 'uns,' and let out a stream of ambeer."

"Would you hire a Negro teacher?" I asked.

"I personally would, but folks wouldn't stand for it, not now, mostly those who never went much to school themselves. Unless I could prove I couldn't get white." He paused. "And it's getting damned hard to get white, I tell you," he says.

I ask if integration will come.

"Sure," he says, "in fifty years. Every time the tobacco crop is reduced, we lose just that many white sharecroppers and Negroes. That eases the pain."

What's coming? And the Methodist minister, riding with me in the

dusk, in the drizzle, by the flooded bayou, says: "It'll come, desegregation and the vote and all that. But it will be twenty-five, thirty years,
a generation. You can preach love and justice, but it's a slow pull till
you get the education." He waves a hand toward the drowned black
cotton fields, stretching on forever, toward the rows of shacks mar-
shaled off into the darkening distance, toward the far cypresses where
dusk is tangled. "You can see," he says. "Just look, you can see."

What's coming? I ask the young lawyer in a mid-South city, a lawyer
retained by one of the segregation outfits. "It's coming that we got to
fight this bogus law," he says, "or we'll have a lot of social dis-tensions.
The bogus law is based on social stuff and progress and just creates
dis-tension. But we're gaining ground. Some upper-class people, I
mean a real rich man, is coming out for us. And we get rolling, a
Southern President could repack the Court. But it's got so a man can't
respect the Supreme Court. All this share-the-wealth and Communist
stuff and progress. You can't depend on law any more."

What can you depend on? I ask.

"Nothing but the people. Like the Civil War."

I suggest that whatever the constitutional rights and wrongs of the
Civil War were, we had got a new Constitution out of it.

"No," he said, "just a different type of dog saying what it is."

I ask if, in the end, the appeal would be to violence.

"No, I don't believe in violence. I told Mr. Perkins, when we had
our mass meeting, to keep the in-ci-dents down. But you get a lot of
folks and there's always going to be in-ci-dents."

I ask if at Tuscaloosa the mob hadn't dictated public policy.

"Not dictate exactly." And he smiles his handsome smile. "But it was
a lot of people."

He has used the word *progress,* over and over, to damn what he does
not like. It is peculiar how he uses this laudatory word—I can imagine
how he would say it in other contexts, on public occasions, rolling it
on his tongue—as the word now for what he hates most. I wonder how
deep a cleavage the use of that word indicates.

What's coming? I ask the handsome, aristocratic, big gray-haired man,
sitting in his rich office, high over the city, an ornament of the vestry,
of boards of directors, of club committees, a man of exquisite simplicity
and charm, and a member of a segregation group.

"We shall exhaust all the legal possibilities," he says.

I ask if he thinks his side will win. The legal fight, that is.

He rolls a cigarette fastidiously between the strong, white, waxy
forefinger and thumb. "No," he says. "But it is just something you have

to do." He rolls the cigarette, looking out the window over the city, a city getting rich now, "filthy rich," as somebody has said to me. There is the undertone and unceasing susurrus of traffic in the silence of his thoughts.

"Well," he says at last, "to speak truth, I think the whole jig is up. We'll have desegregation right down the line. And you know why?"

I shake my head.

"Well, I'll tell you. You see those girls in my office outside, those young men. Come from good lower-middle-class homes, went to college a lot of them. Well, a girl comes in here and says to me a gentleman is waiting. She shows him in. He is as black as the ace of spades. It just never crossed that girl's mind, what she was saying, when she said a gentleman was waiting." He pauses. "Yes, sir," he says, "I just don't know why I'm doing it."

I am thinking of walking down Canal Street, in New Orleans, and a man is saying to me: "Do you know how many millions a year the Negroes spend up and down this street?"

No, I had said, I didn't know.

He tells me the figure, then says: "You get the logic of that, don't you?"

What's coming? And the college student says: "I'll tell you one thing that's coming, there's not going to be any academic freedom or any other kind around here if we don't watch out. Now, I'm a segregationist, that is, the way things are here right now, but I don't want anybody saying I can't listen to somebody talk about something. I can make up my own mind."

What's coming? And a state official says: "Integration sure and slow. A creeping process. If the NAACP has got bat sense, not deliberately provoking things as in the University of Alabama deal. They could have got that girl in quiet and easy, but that wouldn't satisfy them. No, they wanted the bang. As for things in general, grade schools and high schools, it'll be the creeping process. The soft places first, and then one county will play football or basketball with Negroes on the team. You know how it'll be. A creeping process. There'll be lots of court actions, but don't let court actions fool you. I bet you half the superintendents over in Tennessee will secretly welcome a court action in their county. Half of 'em are worried morally and half financially, and a court action just gets 'em off the hook. They didn't initiate it, they can always claim, but it gets them off the hook. That's the way I would feel, I know."

What's coming? I ask the taxi driver in Memphis. And he says: "Lots of dead niggers round here, that's what's coming. Look at Detroit, lots of dead niggers been in the Detroit River, but it won't be a patch on the Ole Mississippi. But hell, it won't stop nothing. Fifty years from now everybody will be gray anyway, Jews and Germans and French and Chinese and niggers, and who'll give a durn?"

The cab has drawn to my destination. I step out into the rain and darkness. "Don't get yourself drownded now," he says. "You have a good time now. I hope you do."

What's coming? And a man in Arkansas says: "We'll ride it out. But it looked like bad trouble one time. Too many outsiders. Mississippians and all. They come back here again, somebody's butt will be busted."

And another man: "Sure, they aim for violence, coming in here. When a man gets up before a crowd and plays what purports to be a recording of an NAACP official, an inflammatory sex thing, and then boasts of having been in on a lynching himself, what do you call it? Well, they got him on the witness stand, under oath, and he had to admit he got the record from Patterson, of the Citizens Council, and admitted under oath the lynching statement. He also admitted under oath some other interesting facts—that he had once been indicted for criminal libel but pleaded guilty to simple libel, that he has done sixty days for contempt of court on charges of violating an injunction having to do with liquor. Yeah, he used to run a paper called *The Rub Down* —that's what got him into the libel business. What's going to happen if a guy like that runs things? I ask you."

What's coming? And the planter leans back with the glass in his hand. "I'm not going to get lathered up," he says, "because it's no use. Why is the country so lathered up to force the issue one way or the other? Democracy—democracy has just come to be a name for what you like. It has lost responsibility, no local integrity left, it has been bought off. We've got the power state coming on, and communism or socialism, whatever you choose to call it. Race amalgamation is inevitable. I can't say I like any of it. I am out of step with the times."

What's coming? I ask the Episcopal rector, in the Deep South, a large handsome man, almost the twin of my friend sitting in the fine office overlooking the rich city. He has just told me that when he first came down from the North, a generation back, his bishop had explained it all to him, how the Negroes' skull capacity was limited. But, as he has said, brain power isn't everything, there's justice, and not a member of his congregation wasn't for conviction in the Till case.

"But the Negro has to be improved before integration," he says. "Take their morals, we are gradually improving the standard of morality and decency."

The conversation veers, we take a longer view. "Well, anthropologically speaking," he says, "the solution will be absorption, the Negro will disappear."

I ask how this is happening.

"Low-class people, immoral people, libertines, wastrels, prostitutes and such," he says.

I ask if, in that case, the raising of the moral level of the Negro does not prevent, or delay, what he says is the solution.

The conversation goes into a blur.

What's coming? And the young man from Mississippi says: "Even without integration, even with separate but pretty good facilities for the Negro, the Negro would be improving himself. He would be making himself more intellectually and socially acceptable. Therefore, as segregationists, if we're logical, we ought to deny any good facilities to them. Now, I'm a segregationist, but I can't be that logical."

What's coming? And the officer of the Citizens Council chapter says: "Desegregation, integration, amalgamation—none of it will come here. To say it will come is defeatism. It won't come if we stand firm."

And the old man in north Tennessee, a burly, full-blooded, red-faced, raucous old man, says: "Hell, son, it's easy to solve. Just blend 'em. Fifteen years and they'll all be blended in. And by God, I'm doing my part!"

Out of Memphis, I lean back in my seat on the plane, and watch the darkness slide by. I know what the Southerner feels going out of the South, the relief, the expanding vistas. Now, to the sound of the powerful, magnanimous engines bearing me through the night, I think of that, thinking of the new libel laws in Mississippi, of the academic pressures, of academic resignations, of the Negro facing the shotgun blast, of the white man with a nice little hard-built business being boycotted, of the college boy who said: "I'll just tell you, everybody is *scairt.*"

I feel the surge of relief. But I know what the relief really is. It is the relief from responsibility.

Now you may eat the bread of the Pharisee and read in the morning paper, with only a trace of irony, how out of an ultimate misery of rejection some Puerto Rican schoolboys—or is it Jews or Negroes or Italians?—who call themselves something grand, the Red Eagles or the Silver Avengers, have stabbed another boy to death, or raped a girl, or trampled an old man into a bloody mire. If you can afford it, you will, according to the local mores, send your child to a private school, where there will be, of course, a couple of Negro children on exhibit. And that delightful little Chinese girl who is so good at dramatics. Or is it finger painting?

Yes, you know what the relief is. It is the flight from the reality you were born to.

But what is that reality you have fled from?

It is the fact of self-division. I do not mean division between man and man in society. That division is, of course, there, and it is important. Take, for example, the killing of Clinton Melton, in Glendora, Mississippi, in the Delta, by a man named Elmer Kimbell, a close friend of Milam (who had been acquitted of the murder of Till, whose car was being used by Kimbell at the time of the killing of Melton, and to whose house Kimbell returned after the deed).

Two days after the event, twenty-one men—storekeepers, planters, railroad men, schoolteachers, preachers, bookkeepers—sent money to the widow for funeral expenses, with the note: "Knowing that he was outstanding in his race, we the people of this town are deeply hurt and donate as follows." When the Lions Club met three days after the event, a resolution was drawn and signed by all members present: "We consider the taking of the life of Clinton Melton an outrage against him, against all the people of Glendora, against the people of Mississippi as well as against the entire human family. . . . We humbly confess in repentance for having so lived as a community that such an evil occurrence could happen here, and we offer ourselves to be used in bringing to pass a better realization of the justice, righteousness and peace which is the will of God for human society."

And the town began to raise a fund to realize the ambition of the dead man, to send his children to college; the doctor of Glendora offered employment in his clinic to the widow; and the owner of the plantation where she had been raised offered to build for her and her children a three-room house.

But, in that division between man and man, the jury that tried Elmer Kimbell acquitted him.

But, in that same division between man and man, when the newspaper of Clarksdale, Mississippi, in the heart of the Delta, ran a front-page story of the acquittal, that story was bracketed with a front-page editorial saying that there had been some extenuation for acquittal in the Till case, with confusion of evidence and outside pressures, but that in the

Melton case, there had been no pressure and "we were alone with ourselves and we flunked it."

Such division between man and man is important. As one editor in Tennessee said to me: "There's a fifth column of decency here, and it will, in the end, betray the extremists, when the politicians get through." But such a division between man and man is not as important in the long run as the division within the individual man.

Within the individual there are, or may be, many lines of fracture. It may be between his own social idealism and his anger at Yankee Phariseeism. (Oh, yes, he remembers that in the days when Federal bayonets supported the black Reconstruction state governments in the South, not a single Negro held elective office in any Northern state.) It may be between his social views and his fear of the power state. It may be between his social views and his clan sense. It may be between his allegiance to organized labor and his racism—for status or blood purity. It may be between his Christianity and his social prejudice. It may be between his sense of democracy and his ingrained attitudes toward the Negro. It may be between his own local views and his concern for the figure America cuts in the international picture. It may be between his practical concern at the money loss to society caused by the Negro's depressed condition and his own personal gain or personal prejudice. It may be, and disastrously, between his sense of the inevitable and his emotional need to act against the inevitable.

There are almost an infinite number of permutations and combinations, but they all amount to the same thing: a deep intellectual rub, a moral rub, anger at the irremediable self-division, a deep exacerbation at some failure to find identity. That is the reality.

It expresses itself in many ways. I sit for an afternoon with an old friend, a big, weather-faced, squarish man, a farmer, an intelligent man, a man of good education, of travel and experience, and I ask him questions. I ask if he thinks we can afford, in the present world picture, to alienate Asia by segregation here at home. He hates the question. "I hate to think about it," he says. "It's too deep for me," he says, and moves heavily in his chair. We talk about Christianity—he is a church-going man—and he says: "Oh, I know what the Bible says, and Christianity, but I just can't think about it. My mind just shuts up."

My old friend is an honest man. He will face his own discomfort. He will not try to ease it by passing libel laws to stop discussion or by firing professors.

There are other people whose eyes brighten at the thought of the new unity in the South, the new solidarity of resistance. These men are idealists, and they dream of preserving the traditional American values of individualism and localism against the anonymity, irresponsibility, and materialism of the power state, against the philosophy of the ad-man, the morality of the Kinsey report, and the gospel of the bitch-goddess. *To be Southern again:* to re-create a habitation for the values they would preserve, to achieve in unity some clarity of spirit, to envisage some healed image of their own identity.

Some of these men are segregationists. Some are desegregationists, but these, in opposing what they take to be the power-state implications of the Court decision, find themselves caught, too, in the defense of segregation. And defending segregation, both groups are caught in a paradox: in seeking to preserve individualism by taking refuge in the vision of a South redeemed in unity and antique virtue, they are fleeing from the burden of their own individuality—the intellectual rub, the moral rub. To state the matter in another way, by using the argument of *mere* social continuity and the justification by mere *mores,* they think of a world in which circumstances and values are frozen; but the essence of individuality is the willingness to accept the rub which the flux of things provokes, to accept one's fate in time. What heroes would these idealists enshrine to take the place of Jefferson and Lee, those heroes who took the risk of their fate?

Even among these people some are in discomfort, discomfort because the new unity, the new solidarity, once it descends from the bright new world of Idea, means unity with some quite concrete persons and specific actions. They say: "Yes—yes, we've got to unify." And then: "But we've got to purge certain elements."

But who will purge whom? And what part of yourself will purge another part?

"Yes, it's our own fault," the rich businessman, active in segregation, says. "If we'd ever managed to bring ourselves to do what we ought to have done for the Negro, it would be different now, if we'd managed to educate them, get them decent housing, decent jobs."

So I tell him what a Southern Negro professor had said to me. He had said that the future now would be different, would be hopeful, if there could just be "one gesture of graciousness" from the white man —even if the white man didn't like the Supreme Court decision, he might try to understand the Negro's view, not heap insult on him.

And the segregationist, who is a gracious man, seizes on the word. "Graciousness," he says, "that's it, if we could just have managed some graciousness to the race. Sure, some of us, a lot of us, could manage some graciousness to individual Negroes, some of us were grateful to individuals for being gracious to us. But you know, we couldn't manage it for the race." He thinks a moment, then says: "There's a Negro woman buried in the family burial place. We loved her."

I believe him when he says it. And he sinks into silence, feeling the rub, for the moment anyway, between the man who can talk in terms of graciousness, in whatever terms that notion may present itself to him, and the man who is a power for segregation.

This is the same man who has said to me, earlier, that he knows integration to be inevitable, doesn't know why he is fighting it. But such a man is happier, perhaps, than those men, destined by birth and personal qualities to action and leadership, who in the face of what they take to be inevitable feel cut off from all action. "I am out of step with the times," one such man says to me, and his wife says, "You know, if we feel the way we do, we ought to do something about it," and he, in some deep, inward, unproclaimed bitterness, says, "No, I'm not going to get lathered up about anything."

Yes, there are many kinds of rub, but I suppose that the commonest one is the moral one—the Christian one, in fact, for the South is still a land of faith. There is, of course, the old joke that after the Saturday night lynching, the congregation generally turns up a little late for church, and the sardonic remark a man made to me about the pro-integration resolution of the Southern Baptist Convention: "They were just a little bit exalted. When they got back with the home folks a lot of 'em wondered how they did it."

But meanwhile, there are the pastors at Glendora and Hoxie and Oxford and other nameless places. And I remember a pastor, in Tennessee, a Southerner born and bred, saying to me: "Yes, I think the Court decision may have set back race equality—it was coming fast, faster than anybody could guess, because so quiet. But now some people get so put out with the idea of Negroes in church, they stop me on the street and say if I ever let one in, they won't come to church. So I ask about Heaven, what will they do in Heaven?

" 'Well,' one woman said, 'I'll just let God segregate us.'

" 'You'll *let* God segregate you?' I said, and she flounced off. But I ask, where is Christianity if people can't worship together? There's only one thing to try to preach, and that is Christ. And there's only one question to ask, and that is what would Christ do?"

Will they go with him? I ask.

"They are good Christian people, most of them," he says. "It may be slow, but they are Christians."

And in a town in south Kentucky, in a "black county," a Confederate county, where desegregation is now imminent in the high schools, the superintendent says to me: "The people here are good Christian people, trying to do right. When this thing first came up, the whole board said they'd walk out. But the ministers got to preaching, and the lawyers to talking on it, and they came around."

I asked how many were influenced by moral, how many by legal, considerations.

About half and half, he reckons, then adds: "I'm a Rebel myself, and I don't deny it, but I'm an American and a law-abiding citizen. A man can hate an idea but know it's right, and it takes a lot of thinking and praying to bring yourself around. You just have to uncover the un-recognized sympathy in the white man for the Negro humiliation."

Fifty miles away I shall sit in a living room and hear some tale of a Negro coming to somebody's front door—another house—and being admitted by a Negro servant and being found by the master of the house, who says: "I don't care if Susie did let you in. I don't care if Jesus Christ let you in. No black son-of-a-bitch is coming to my front door."

After the tale, there is silence. All present are segregationist, or I think they are.

Then one woman says: "Maybe he did take a lot on himself, coming to the front door. But I can't stand it. He's human."

And another woman: "I think it's a moral question, and I suffer, but I can't feel the same way about a Negro as a white person. It's born in me. But I pray I'll change."

The successful businessman in Louisiana says to me: "I have felt the moral question. It will be more moral when we get rid of segregation. But I'm human enough—I guess it's human to be split up—to want things just postponed till my children are out of school. But I can't lift my finger to delay things."

But this man, privately admitting his division of feeling, having no intention of public action on either side, is the sort of man who can be trapped, accidentally, into action.

There is the man who got the letter in the morning mail, asking him to serve as chairman of a citizens committee to study plans for desegre-gation in his county. "I was sick," he says, "and I mean literally sick. I felt sick all day. I didn't see how I could get into something like that. But next morning, you know, I did it."

That county now has its schedule for desegregation.

There is another man, a lawyer, who has been deeply involved in a desegregation action. "I never had much feeling of prejudice, but hell, I didn't have any theories either, and I now and then paid some lip service to segregation. I didn't want to get mixed up in the business. But one night a telephone call came. I told the man I'd let him know next day. You know, I was sick. I walked on back in the living room, and my wife looked at me. She must have guessed what it was. 'You going to do it?' she asked me. I said, hell, I didn't know, and went out. I was plain sick. But next day I did it. Well," he says, and grins, and leans back under the shelves of lawbooks, "and I'm stuck with it. But you know, I'm getting damned tired of the paranoiacs and illiterates I'm up against."

Another man, with a small business in a poor county, "back in the shelf country," he calls it, a short, strong-looking, ovoidal kind of man, with his belt cutting into his belly when he leans back in his office chair. He is telling me what he has been through. "I wouldn't tell you a lie," he says. "I'm Southern through and through, and I guess I got every prejudice a man can have, and I certainly never would have got mixed up in this business if it hadn't been for the Court decision. I wouldn't be out in front. I was just trying to do my duty. Trying to save some money for the county. I never expected any trouble. And we might not have had any if it hadn't been for outsiders, one kind and another.

"But what nobody understands is how a man can get cut up inside. You try to live like a Christian with your fellowman, and suddenly you find out it is all mixed up. You put in twenty-five years trying to build up a nice little business and raise up a family, and it looks like it will all be ruined. You get word somebody will dynamite your house and you in it. You go to lawyers and they say they sympathize, but no-body'll take your case. But the worst is, things just go round and round in your head. Then they won't come a-tall, and you lay there in the night. You might say, it's the psychology of it you can't stand. Getting all split up. Then, all of a sudden, somebody stops you on the street and calls you something, a so-and-so nigger-lover. And you know, I got so mad, not a thing mattered any more. I just felt like I was all put back together again."

He said he wished he could write it down, how awful it is for a man to be split up.

Negroes, they must be split up, too, I think. They are human, too. There must be many ways for them to be split up. I remember asking a Negro schoolteacher if she thought Negro resentment would be a bar to integration. "Some of us try to teach love," she says, "as well as we can. But some of us teach hate. I guess we can't help it."

Love and hate, but more than that, the necessity of confronting your own motives: *Do we really want to try to work out a way to live with the white people or do we just want to show them, pay off something, show them up, rub their noses in it?*

And I can imagine the grinding anger, the sense of outrage of a Negro crying out within himself: *After all the patience, after all the humility, after learning and living those virtues, do I have to learn magnanimity, too?*

Yes, I can imagine the outrage, the outrage as some deep, inner self tells him, yes, he must.

I am glad that white people have no problem as hard as that.

The taxi drew up in front of the apartment house, and I got out, but the driver and I talked on for a moment. I stood there in the rain, then paid him, and ran for the door. It wasn't that I wanted to get out of the rain. I had an umbrella. I wanted to get in and write down what he had said.

He was a local man, born near Nashville, up near Goodlettsville, "raised up with niggers." He had been in the army, with lots of fighting, Africa, Sicily, Italy, but a lot of time bossing work gangs. In Africa, at first, it had been Arabs, but Arabs weren't "worth a durn." Then they got Negro work battalions.

But here are the notes:

Niggers a lot better than Arabs, but they didn't hurt themselves—didn't any of 'em git a hernia for Uncle Sam—race prejudice—but it ain't our hate, it's the hate hung on us by the old folks dead and gone. Not I mean to criticize the old folks, they done the best they knew, but that hate, we don't know how to shuck it. We got that God-damn hate stuck in our craw and can't puke it up. If white folks quit shoving the nigger down and calling him a nigger, he could maybe get to be a asset to the South and the country. But how stop shoving?

We are the prisoners of our history.

Or are we?

There is one more interview I wish to put on record. I shall enter it by question and answer.

Q. You're a Southerner, aren't you?

A. Yes.

Q. Are you afraid of the power state?

A. Yes.

Q. Do you think the Northern press sometimes distorts Southern news?

A. Yes.

Q. Assuming that they do, why do they do it?

A. They like to feel good.

Q. What do you think the South ought to do about that distortion?

A. Nothing.

Q. Nothing? What do you mean, nothing?

A. The distortion—that's the Yankees' problem, not ours.

Q. You mean they ought to let the South work out a way to live with the Negro?

A. I don't think the problem is to learn to live with the Negro.

Q. What is it, then?

A. It is to learn to live with ourselves.

Q. What do you mean?

A. I don't think you can live with yourself when you are humiliating the man next to you.

Q. Don't you think the races have made out pretty well, considering?

A. Yes. By some sort of human decency and charity, God knows how. But there was always an image of something else.

Q. An image?

A. Well, I knew an old lady who grew up in a black county, but a county where relations had been, as they say, good. She had a fine farm and a good brick house, and when she got old she sort of retired from the world. The hottest summer weather and she would lock all the doors and windows at night, and lie there in the airless dark. But sometimes she'd telephone to town in the middle of the night. She would telephone that somebody was burning the Negroes out there on her place. She could hear their screams. Something was going on in her old head which in another place and time would not have been going on in her old head. She had never, I should think, seen an act of violence in her life. But something was going on in her head.

Q. Do you think it is chiefly the redneck who causes violence?

A. No. He is only the cutting edge. He, too, is a victim. Responsibility is a seamless garment. And the northern boundary of that garment is not the Ohio River.

Q. Are you for desegregation?

A. *Yes.*

Q. When will it come?

A. Not soon.

Q. When?

A. When enough people, in a particular place, a particular county or state, cannot live with themselves any more. Or realize they don't have to.

Q. What do you mean, don't have to?

A. When they realize that desegregation is just one small episode in the long effort for justice. It seems to me that that perspective, suddenly seeing the business as little, is a liberating one. It liberates you from yourself.

Q. Then you think it is a moral problem?

A. Yes, but no moral problem gets solved abstractly. It has to be solved in a context for possible solution.

Q. Can contexts be changed?

A. Sure. We might even try to change them the right way.

Q. Aren't you concerned about possible racial amalgamation?

A. I don't even think about it. We have to deal with the problem our historical moment proposes, the burden of our time. We all live with a thousand unsolved problems of justice all the time. We don't even recognize a lot of them. We have to deal only with those which the moment proposes to us. Anyway, we can't legislate for posterity. All we can do for posterity is to try to plug along in a way to make them think we— the old folks—did the best we could for justice, as we could understand it.

Q. Are you a gradualist on the matter of segregation?

A. If by gradualist you mean a person who would create delay for the sake of delay, then no. If by gradualist you mean a person who thinks it will take time, not time as such, but time for an educational process, preferably a calculated one, then yes. I mean a process of mutual education for whites and blacks. And part of this education should be in the actual beginning of the process of desegregation. It's a silly question, anyway, to ask if somebody is a gradualist. Gradualism is all you'll get. History, like nature, knows no jumps. Except the jump backward, maybe.

Q. Has the South any contribution to make to the national life?

A. It has made its share. It may again.

Q. How?

A. If the South is really able to face up to itself and its situation, it may achieve identity, moral identity. Then in a country where moral identity is hard to come by, the South, because it has had to deal concretely with a moral problem, may offer some leadership. And we need any we can get. If we are to break out of the national rhythm, the rhythm between complacency and panic.

This is, of course, an interview with myself.

THE LEGACY OF
THE CIVIL WAR

MEDITATIONS ON
THE CENTENNIAL

The Civil War is, for the American imagination, the great single event of our history. Without too much wrenching, it may, in fact, be said to *be* American history. Before the Civil War we had no history in the deepest and most inward sense. There was, of course, the noble vision of the Founding Fathers articulated in the Declaration and the Constitution—the dream of freedom incarnated in a more perfect union. But the Revolution did not create a nation except on paper; and too often in the following years the vision of the Founding Fathers, which men had suffered and died to validate, became merely a daydream of easy and automatic victories, a vulgar delusion of manifest destiny, a conviction of being a people divinely chosen to live on milk and honey at small expense.

The vision had not been finally submitted to the test of history. There was little awareness of the cost of having a history. The anguished scrutiny of the meaning of the vision in experience had not become a national reality. It became a reality, and we became a nation, only with the Civil War.

The Civil War is our only "felt" history—history lived in the national imagination. This is not to say that the War is always, and by

Published in 1961.

all men, felt in the same way. Quite the contrary. But this fact is an index to the very complexity, depth, and fundamental significance of the event. It is an overwhelming and vital image of human, and national, experience.

Many clear and objective facts about America are best understood by reference to the Civil War. The most obvious fact is that, for better or worse, and despite any constitutional theorizing by Governor Almond of Virginia, we are a united nation. Before the War there had been, of course, a ferocious love of the Union, but the Union sometimes seemed to exist as an idea, an ideal, rather than as a fact. There was a sense that it had to be struggled for, to be won and re-won against many kinds of enemies—not only the Burrs and Wilkinsons and Houstons and the conventioneers of Hartford, Connecticut, and the nullifiers of South Carolina, but also distance, sprawling space, apathy, selfishness, ignorance, the westward slope of the watershed beyond the Appalachians.

This unionism was, we remember, particularly ferocious in the South, as the old Jackson, the young Calhoun, and many a Whig planter, even in 1860, would testify. We can recall with what reluctance Jefferson Davis or Stonewall Jackson took the step toward dis-union, and lately some historians find the corrosive of a crypto-unionism deep in many a Confederate breast less eminent than that of General Lee. When General Pickett, leading his division on the road to Gettysburg, passed a little Dutch girl defiantly waving the Federal flag, he took off his hat and bowed to her. Asked why he had saluted the flag of the enemy, he replied: "I did not salute the enemy's flag. I saluted the heroic womanhood in the heart of that brave little girl, and the glorious old banner under which I won my first laurels." True or not, the tale, reported by LaSalle Corbell Pickett, points to a truth. Shared experiences of the past and shared hopes for the future could not easily be expunged; and I myself have heard an old man who had ridden three years with Forrest, and never regretted that fact, say that he would have sadly regretted the sight of this country "Balkanized."

That old unionism was, however, very different from the kind we live with now. We do not live with an ideal, sometimes on the defensive, of union. We live with the overriding, overwhelming fact, a fact so technologically, economically, and politically validated that we usually forget to ask how fully this fact represents a true community, the spiritually significant communion which the old romantic unionism had envisaged. In any case, the "Union"—which we rarely refer to as a union any more, so obvious is the fact—gives us our most significant sense of identity, limited as that may be, and the best and most inclusive hope for our future, and that of mankind.

A second clear and objective fact is that the Civil War abolished slavery, even if it did little or nothing to abolish racism; and in so doing, removed the most obvious, if perhaps not the most important, impediment to union. However we may assess the importance of slavery in the tissue of "causes" of the Civil War—in relation to secession, the mounting Southern debt to the North, economic rivalry, Southern fear of encirclement, Northern ambitions, and cultural collisions—slavery looms up mountainously and cannot be talked away. It was certainly a necessary cause, to use the old textbook phrase, and provided the occasion for all the mutual vilification, rancor, self-righteousness, pride, spite, guilt, and general exacerbation of feeling that was the natural atmosphere of the event, the climate in which the War grew. With slavery out of the way, a new feeling about union was possible. Despite bumbling and vindictiveness and deprivation, many a Southerner, in one part of the soul at least, must have felt much as did the planter's wife who referred to the War as the time Mr. Lincoln set her free. As there had been crypto-unionism in the Confederate psyche, so there had been a crypto-emancipationism, or at least a deep moral, logical, and economic unease. After 1865 the terms of life were a little clearer, and one of the things clearer was the possibility of another kind of relation to the Union.

The new nation came not merely from a military victory. It came from many circumstances created or intensified by the War. The War enormously stimulated technology and productivity. Actually, it catapulted America from what had been in considerable part an agrarian, handicraft society into the society of Big Technology and Big Business. "Parallel with the waste and sorrows of war," as Allan Nevins puts it, "ran a stimulation of individual initiative, a challenge to large-scale planning, and an encouragement of co-operative effort, which in combination with new agencies for developing natural resources amounted to a great release of creative energy." The old sprawling, loosely knit country disappeared into the nation of Big Organization.

It is true that historians can debate the question whether, in the long run and in the long perspective, war—even wars of that old pre-atomic age—can stimulate creativity and production. And it is true that there had been a surge of technological development in the decade or so before 1861, followed, some maintain, by an actual decline in inventiveness during the War. But the question is not how many new inventions were made but how the existing ones were used. The little device of the "jig," which, back in 1798, had enabled Eli Whitney to make firearms with interchangeable parts led now to the great mass-production factories of the Civil War—factories used not merely for firearms but for all sorts of products. The Civil War demanded the great American industrial plant, and the industrial plant changed American society.

To take one trivial fact, the ready-made clothing industry was an offshoot of the mass production of blue uniforms—and would not this standardization of fashion, after the sartorial whim, confusion, fantasy, and individualism of an earlier time, have some effect on man's relation to man? But to leap from the trivial to the grand, the War prepared the way for the winning of the West. Before the War a transcontinental railroad was already being planned, and execution was being delayed primarily by debate about the route to take, a debate which in itself sprang from, and contributed something to, the intersectional acrimony. After the War, debate did not long delay action. But the War did more than remove impediment to this scheme. It released enormous energies, new drives, and know-how for the sudden and massive occupation of the continent. And for the great adventure, there was a new cutting edge of profit.

Not only the industrial plant but the economic context in which industry could thrive came out of the War. The Morril tariff of 1861 actually preceded the firing on Sumter, but it was the mark of Republican victory and an omen of what was to come; and no session of Congress for the next four years failed to raise the tariff. Even more importantly, came the establishment of a national banking system in place of the patchwork of state banks, and the issuing of national greenbacks to rationalize the crazy currency system of the state-bank notes. The new system, plus government subsidy, honed the cutting edge of profit. "The fact is that people have the money and they are looking around to see what to do with it," said the New York magnate William E. Dodge in a speech in Baltimore in 1865. At last, he said, there was indigenous capital to "develop the natural interests of the country." And he added, enraptured: "The mind staggers as we begin to contemplate the future."

The mind staggered, and the bookkeeping in New York by the new breed of businessmen fostered by the Civil War was as potent a control for the centrifugal impulses of the South and West as ever bayonet or railroad track. The pen, if not mightier than the sword, was very effective in consolidating what the sword had won—when the pen was wielded by the bookkeeper.

Not only New York bookkeeping but Washington bookkeeping was a new force for union. The war had cost money. Hamilton's dream of a national debt to insure national stability was realized, by issuing the bonds so efficiently peddled by Jay Cooke, to a degree astronomically beyond Hamilton's rosiest expectations. For one thing, this debt meant a new tax relation of the citizen to the Federal government, including the new income tax; the citizen had a new and poignant sense of the reality of Washington. But the great hand that took could also give, and with pensions and subsidies, the iron dome of the Capitol took on a new luster in the eyes of millions of citizens.

Furthermore, the War meant that Americans saw America. The farm boy of Ohio, the trapper of Minnesota, and the pimp of the Mackerel-ville section of New York City saw Richmond and Mobile. They not only saw America, they saw each other, and together shot it out with some Scot of the Valley of Virginia or ducked hardware hurled by a Louisiana Jew who might be a lieutenant of artillery, CSA. By the War, not only Virginia and Louisiana were claimed for the Union. Ohio and Minnesota were, in fact, claimed too—claimed so effectively that for generations the memory of the Bloody Shirt and the GAR would prompt many a Middlewestern farmer to vote almost automatically against his own interests.

The War claimed the Confederate States for the Union, but at the same time, paradoxically, it made them more Southern. Even during the War itself, there had been great and disintegrating tensions within the Confederacy. The doctrine of States' rights did more to wreck Confederate hopes than the Iron Brigade of Minnesota and the Twentieth of Maine put together, and split the South as effectively as Sherman's March to the Sea. But once the War was over, the Confederacy became a City of the Soul, beyond the haggling of constitutional lawyers, the ambition of politicians, and the jealousy of localisms.

In defeat the Solid South was born—not only the witless automatism of fidelity to the Democratic Party but the mystique of prideful "difference," identity, and defensiveness. The citizen of that region "of the Mississippi the bank sinister, of the Ohio the bank sinister," could now think of himself as a "Southerner" in a way that would have defied the imagination of Barnwell Rhett—or of Robert E. Lee, unionist-emancipationist Virginian. We may say that only at the moment when Lee

handed Grant his sword was the Confederacy born; or to state matters
another way, in the moment of death the Confederacy entered upon
its immortality.

But let us leave the Southerner and his War, and return to the more
general effects of the War on American life. It formed, for example, the
American concept of war, and since the day when Grant tried his bold
maneuver in the Wilderness and Lee hit him, military thinking at
Washington has focused as much on problems of supply, transport,
matériel, and attrition, as it ever did on problems of slashing tactics and
grand strategy.

Furthermore, on land and sea, the Civil War was a war waged under
new conditions and in a new economic, technological, political, and
moral context. The rules in the textbooks did not help very much. The
man whose mind could leap beyond the book was apt to win. It was
a war fought, on both sides, with the experimental intelligence, the
experimental imagination, not only in the arena of lethal contact, but
in the very speculations about the nature of war. Out of the Civil War
came the concept of total war, the key to Northern Victory.

A people's way of fighting reflects a people's way of thinking, and
the lessons of the fighting are very apt, in a kind of dialectical progres-
sion, to modify and refine the thinking. So it may be argued that the
pragmatic bias of American philosophy is not without significant relation to the encounter between the *Monitor* and the *Merrimac,* the
Confederate submarine, the earthworks of Petersburg or Atlanta, the
observation balloon and field telegraph, General Herman Haupt's use
of the railroad at Gettysburg, the new use of mounted riflemen, Grant's
systematically self-nurtured gift for problem-solving, or Sherman's theory of war.

Not that the War created pragmatism, which, in one sense, has
always existed as an aspect of the human intelligence; William James
called it, as a matter of fact, a new name for an old way of thinking.
Some scholars have claimed that it even bears a relationship to Tran-
scendentalism; and it developed, of course, in the new atmosphere of
science in the Western world. The War did something, however, to
create a climate peculiarly favorable to the formulation of this aspect of
intelligence as a philosophy.

More than one historian has found in Lincoln the model of the
pragmatic mind. David Donald, in "Lincoln and the Pragmatic Tradition," says that no man ever distinguished more carefully between "is"

and "ought to be," and on another aspect of pragmatism, quotes him: "I concluded that it was better to make a rule for the practical matter in hand than to decide a general question." And T. Harry Williams says: "One of the keys to his thinking is his statement that few things in this world are wholly good or wholly bad. Consequently the position he took on specific political issues was always a pragmatic one. His personal or inner opinions were based on principle; his public or outer opinions were tempered by empiricism."

The philosopher Sidney Hook has found in much of Lincoln's thinking and action the essential doctrines of pragmatism; for instance, in the message to Congress of 1862: "The dogmas of the quiet past are inadequate to the stormy present. . . . As our case is new, we must think anew, and act anew." But in Lincoln's whole course of action, even more fully than in his words, this modern pragmatist finds the core of his philosophy: "To be principled without being fanatical, and flexible without being opportunistic, summarizes the logic and ethics of pragmatism in action."

We may turn to a man who, young, fought in the Civil War and was thrice wounded, and who, old, modified American life by his "pragmatism in action." Justice Holmes held that the locus of law is not in the stars or in the statute book, but on the lips of the judge making the particular ruling; that "the life of law is not logic but experience," that is, "the felt necessities of the time"; that law is "predictive" of the way the force of society will act against those who would violate custom or those who would obstruct demanded change; that the document, say the Constitution (which he said is "an experiment as all life is an experiment"), cannot envisage the future contexts of applicability; that the process of seeking truth through the free collision, coil, and jar of ideas is more important than any particular "truth" found, for truth must be understood in the ever-unfolding context of needs and the *I-can't-help* of believing.

The War, we know, had made a profound impression on Holmes, nourishing his tragic sense of life and his soldierly ethic. Even granting the clear influence of Darwin and the new science, can we see Holmes' philosophy as being a reaction from two types of absolutes, the collision of which was an essential part of the picture of the War?

We may call these two opposing absolutes "higher law" and "legalism."

The Abolitionist exponent of the "higher law" claimed a corner on truth by reason of divine revelation. The man who is privy to God's will cannot long brook argument, and when one declines the arbitrament of reason, even because one seems to have all the reason and virtue on one's side, one is making ready for the arbitrament of blood. So we have the saddening spectacle of men courageously dedicated to a worthy cause letting their nobility grow so distempered by impatience that sometimes it is difficult to distinguish love of liberty from lust for blood. And we find by their charismatic arithmetic that "if all the slaves in the United States—men, women and helpless babes—were to fall on the field or become the victims of vengeance . . . if only one man survived to enjoy the freedom they had won, the liberty of that solitary negro . . . would be cheaply purchased by the universal slaughter of his people and their oppressors."

James Redpath, the author of the above calculation, was not alone. The Reverend George B. Cheever preached that it would be "infinitely better that three hundred thousand slaveholders were abolished, struck out of existence," than that slavery should continue. The Reverend Theodore Parker welcomed the prospect of "the White Man's blood." And William Lloyd Garrison, in his characteristic style which a fellow Abolitionist, Theodore Dwight Weld, described as "the vibration of serpents' tongues," proclaimed that the career of a typical Southern planter "from the cradle to the grave is one of unbridled lust, of filthy amalgamation, of swaggering braggadocio, of haughty domination, of cowardly ruffianism, of boundless dissipation, of matchless insolence, of infinite self-conceit, of unequalled oppression, of more than savage cruelty." More succinctly, he declared that "every slaveholder has forfeited his right to live." John Brown, of course, summed it all up when, with the fervor of an Old Testament prophet pronouncing on the Canaanite the bloodbath of the *cherim,* he would mutter his favorite text: "Without the shedding of blood there is no remission of sins."

One can entertain the possibility that Cornelius C. Felton, eminent Harvard Latinist and friend of Senator Charles Sumner of Massachusetts, struck the heart of the matter when he said that it seemed "as if the *love of man* meant the *hatred of men.*" What had begun as a "gnawing sense of responsibility for the ills of society at large," to take Stanley M. Elkins' formulation, "became a more and more intolerable burden of guilt" charged by all the secret confusions, frustrations, and vainglorious dreams, until, in its intolerableness, guilt was "transformed into implacable moral aggression: hatred of both the sinner and the sin." And then, to compound matters, came the longing for the apocalyptic moment, the "total solution," to purge in violence the unacknowledged, the even unrecognized, tension.

The cause for which the Abolitionists labored was just. Who can deny that, or deny that often they labored nobly? But who can fail to be disturbed and chastened by the picture of the joyful mustering of the darker forces of our nature in that just cause?

It did not matter that Theodore Weld, one of the most effective of the Abolitionists, withdrew from active propagandizing because, as he said to an admirer, he found that "he himself needed reforming," and that he "had been laboring to destroy evil in the same spirit as his antagonists." Nor did it matter that Julia Ward Howe, the author-to-be of "The Battle Hymn of the Republic," could write in 1858, after a trip to South Carolina: "Moral justice dissents from the habitual sneer, denunciation, and malediction, which have become consecrated forms of piety in speaking of the South." Nor did it matter that Lincoln could take a reasonable tone about John Brown's raid on Harpers Ferry: "Old John Brown has been executed for treason against a State. We cannot object, even though he agreed with us in thinking slavery wrong. That cannot excuse violence, bloodshed and treason. It could avail him nothing that he might think himself right."

It was certainly too late for anything to matter when, in 1862, in the *Atlantic Monthly*, Hawthorne said of Emerson's famous pronouncement on John Brown that he had never expected to "shrink so unutterably from any apothegm of a sage whose happy lips have uttered a hundred golden sentences as from that saying (perhaps falsely attributed to so honored a source) that the death of this blood-stained fanatic has 'made the Gallows as venerable as the Cross!' Nobody was ever more justly hanged." And it was far, far too late for anything to matter when James Russell Lowell, looking back, after the War, on the reformism that had flowered in that event, wrote, in his essay on Thoreau, that every form of "intellectual dyspepsia brought forth its gospel," and the reformers "stood ready at a moment's notice to reform everything but themselves." And with melancholy hindsight he added that this comic side of the period had been "the whistle and trailing fuse of the shell, but there was a very solid and serious kernel, full of the most deadly explosiveness."

Despite Theodore Weld and Julia Ward Howe and Abraham Lincoln, love of liberty and lust for blood continued to conspire to forbid much self-scrutiny or meditation on the social effects of inspired rhetoric.

The mood that prevailed did not, to say the least, cement the bonds of society. The exponent of the "higher law" was, furthermore, quite prepared to dissolve the society in which he lived, and say, with Garrison, "Accursed be the American Union." The word treason, according to the Reverend Fales H. Newhall of Roxbury, Massachusetts, had become "holy in the American language," and according to the Reverend Edwin M. Wheelock of Boston, "sacred" and "radiant." And Emerson lectured that John Brown would make the "gallows glorious like the cross." So the exponent of the "higher law" was, like Garrison, ready to burn the Constitution as a "covenant with death" and an "agreement with Hell."

But the higher-law man, in any time and place, must always be ready to burn any constitution, for he must, ultimately, deny the very concept of society. These "higher-law men" did indeed deny the very concept of society. The Transcendentalists, who had given the pattern of gospel in this matter, were men who, in a period of social change, had lost what they took to be their natural and deserved role. The country was losing leadership to the city. The banker, the lawyer, the "Lords of the loom," were taking over power from the preacher and teacher. The new business values were supplanting those of the past age. "Too distinguished a family, too gentle an education, too nice a morality," David Donald points out, "were handicaps in a bustling world of business"; and he sums up the Transcendentalists as "an elite without function, a displaced class." Henry Adams, himself an example of the elite without function, says that the Puritan in this new age "thought his thought higher and his moral standards better than those of his successors," and could not be satisfied "that utilitarian morality was good enough for him, as it was for the graceless."

Having lost access to power and importance in the world of affairs, these men repudiated all the institutions in which power is manifested —church, state, family, law, business. Men pursue and paw the individual, says Thoreau in *Walden*, "with their dirty institutions, and if they can, constrain him to belong to their desperate odd-fellow society." For all things were equally besmirched and besmirching to the ineffable and quivering purity. As Emerson says in "Man the Reformer," there is no place where the danger of besmirchment does not enter as long as one is in contact with society: "The trail of the serpent reaches into all the lucrative professions and practices of men. . . . Inextricable seem to be the twinings and tendrils of this evil, and we all involve ourselves in it the deeper by forming connections, by wives and children, by benefits and debts."

These men were reformers, but the impulse to shrink away from the besmirchment of the new society was so great that they could not bring themselves to face, practically, the most obvious abuse in that society. They railed against the values of the society, against State Street in

Boston and investment banking, but to grapple with the concrete, immediate problem of poverty and exploitation would have been, for any except Orestes Brownson, too befouling, too full of the danger of involvement. So we find Garrison accusing labor leaders of trying to "inflame the minds of the working class against the more opulent." We find Samuel Gridley Howe, who had fought for liberty in Greece, had seen the inside of a German jail, and was one of the backers of John Brown, declaring that a law limiting the work day to ten hours would "emasculate" the people. And we find Emerson fretfully saying that he did not want to hear of any "obligation to put all poor men in good situations. Are they *my* poor? I tell thee, thou foolish philanthropist, that I begrudge the dollar, the dime, the cent I give to such men."

Not only would one dirty oneself by trying to reform the local system. One would have to deal practically and by piecemeal; one would, clearly, have to work out compromise solutions. But with slavery, all was different. One could demand the total solution, the solution of absolute morality; one could achieve the apocalyptic *frisson*. Furthermore, since the slave grew cotton, the cotton came to the New England mills, and the mills made the new "Lords of the loom" rich, the attack on slavery had the gratifying side-effect of being, consciously or unconsciously, an attack on the new order from which the Transcendentalist had withdrawn.

He had withdrawn, and all that was left was "the infinitude of the individual"—with no "connections," with no relation to "dirty institutions," and ideally, with none of the tarnishing affections of wives and children. The Transcendentalist rejoiced, as Octavius Frothingham puts it, "in the production of the 'mountainous Me' fed at the expense of life's sweetest humanities." Harold Laski, seeing even now the residual effect of this "fallacy of abstraction," describes it in *The American Democracy:* "The individual is not seen in his context as a member of a particular society at a particular time; he is seen as an individual standing outside society who can by an act of will . . . assure his own regeneration." In other words, man as a total abstraction, in the pure blinding light of total isolation, alone with the Alone, narcissism raised to the infinite power.

This is one perspective in which we can regard the Transcendentalists. In another perspective we can be grateful not only for some of their insights and the aura of personal genius which clings about the work of some of them, but also for their role as defenders of the right to dissent, as keepers of conscience. They have most eloquently defined, we happily grant, one pole of our moral and political life. We

can grant, too, that for social problems to be diagnosed, some detachment from society is necessary. Their detachment, perhaps, made their
diagnosis possible.

But social problems are rarely to be solved by men totally outside of
society—certainly not by men not merely outside of a particular society
but outside of the very concept of society. For if all institutions are
"dirty," why really bother to amend them? Destruction is simpler,
purer, more logical, and certainly more exciting. Conscience without
responsibility—this is truly the last infirmity of noble mind.

Nor are all social problems best solved by an abstract commitment
to virtue. Before delivering his famous speech on "The Crime Against
Kansas," Senator Sumner might have meditated on a passage from
Aristotle's *Ethics*, with which, in his great learning, he was certainly
familiar: "In discussions on subjects of moral action, universal statements are apt to be too vague, but particular ones are more consistent
with truth; for actions are conversant with particulars; and it is necessary that the statements should agree with these." Or as Lincoln said:
"I concluded that it was better to make a rule for the practical matter
in hand . . . than to decide a general question." But to Sumner, the
angry Platonist, too many "particulars" about the situation in Kansas,
or too much concern for "the practical matter," might embarrass
Truth; and might lower the rhetorical temperature.

Ethics should be, indeed, the measure of politics, but there is an ethic
which is somewhat different from that of individual absolutism—an
ethic that demands scrutiny of motive, context, and consequences,
particularly the consequences to others. This kind of ethic, laborious,
fumbling, running the risk of degenerating into expediency, finds its
apotheosis in Lincoln—whom Wendell Phillips felt impelled to call
"the slave-hound of Illinois."

The other kind of ethic, that of personal absolutism, gives us the
heroic, charged images that our hearts and imaginations strenuously
demand—for instance, that of the Abolitionist Elijah Lovejoy rushing
out from the warehouse in Alton, Illinois, to meet his death at the hands
of the lynch mob. It even gives us the image of John Brown, abstracted
from his life and from history, standing on the scaffold and drawing a
pin from the lapel of his coat and offering it to the executioner to use
in adjusting the hood. Such images survive everything—logic, criticism, even fact if fact stands in the way. They generate their own
values. For men need symbols for their aspirations.

To return to the immediate, practical effects of higher-law-ism, the
conviction, proclaimed by Wendell Phillips, that "one with God is

always a majority," does not lend encouragement to the ordinary democratic process. With every man his own majority as well as his own law, there is, in the logical end, only anarchy, and anarchy of a peculiarly tedious and bloodthirsty sort, for every drop is to be spilled in God's name and by His explicit directive.

The Southern constitutionalists and philosophical defenders of slavery did not deny the concept of society. But the version of society which these egregious logicians deduced so logically from their premises denied, instead, the very concept of life. It denied life in its defense, anachronistic and inhuman, of bondage. It denied life also, and in a sense more viciously, in its refusal to allow, through the inductive scrutiny of fact, for change, for the working of the life process through history.

This is not to say that under the impact of experience the actual South might not have been capable of change. Men are often wiser than their philosophers, and in the desperate last season the Confederate government authorized, ironically enough, the enlisting and arming of slaves, with emancipation; and at the end of March 1865, only a week before its fall, the populace of Richmond was heartened by a public drill of Negro troops in Capitol Square, Negro troops in new gray uniforms about to go forth and repel the invaders. But despite what practical modifications the exigencies of war forced upon the Confederacy (or the exigencies of peace and developing technology might later have forced, had the Confederacy survived), the apologists offered a philosophy of marmoreal rigidity, proper to the rigidity of that society.

After the debates in the Virginia legislature in 1831, when, from a variety of motives, the question of slavery was subjected to a searching scrutiny, public discussion was at an end. It does not matter whether the end came from panic at the Nat Turner insurrection, from resentment at the attacks of Abolitionists, or from the new profits to be had from the slave system. The sad fact was that the possibility of criticism —criticism from the inside—was over. There could be no new Jefferson, the type of critic whose mind, to take the words of Stanley Elkins, "operated under the balanced tensions created not only by a repugnance to the system but also by a commitment to it." This kind of informed and morally based self-criticism, which could aim at practical solutions, was gone. If in the North the critic had repudiated society, in the South society repudiated the critic; and the stage was set for trouble.

It is one of the paradoxes of our history that the South, which in the years before 1861 had become a closed society suppressing all criticism, should seem to become, with the firing of the first shot, extremely open. Individual rights were allowed to a degree which was, from the military point of view, disastrous. The Southerner was a first-class fighting man but a very poor soldier, and the chief reason was that he had not, as a Confederate congressman proudly pointed out, "lost the identity of the citizen in the soldier." Further, in the jealous regard for political democracy and civil rights—freedom of speech, freedom from arbitrary arrest, and due process of law—the Confederacy persisted to the point of mania. Disloyalty, sedition, profiteering, and exploitation could all take refuge behind the barricade of civil rights. Despite the most violent, and sometimes venal, attacks on the government, not one newspaper in the Confederacy was ever suppressed, or even censored. The suspension of the writ of habeas corpus was, indeed, allowed three times, but only in moments of grave crisis and only with strict limitations of time and place; and when in the last desperate months Davis, who had been extremely tender in such matters, asked for a renewal of the power, he was refused by his Congress on the ground that it might encourage a dictatorial encroachment on democratic rights.

Over against this, we may remember that more than 300 newspapers were, at one time or another, suppressed in the North; that Lincoln, without any by-your-leave from Congress, acting on what he termed a "popular necessity," suspended the writ of habeas corpus; that in the North upward of 15,000 persons were arrested on the presidential warrant to be held indefinitely, under presidential order, without any shadow of due process of law.

The point here is not that Lincoln was a dictator and Davis was not. One point is clearly that Lincoln was a realist and Davis was not. But there is another point—the point that interests us here. When the South, as a minority section of the Union, was acting defensively, with acute pathological suspiciousness, the legalistic and deductive bias of mind had been developed for the justification of slavery and of a society based on slavery. But as soon as, by the act of secession, the South changed its role from that of a defensive minority in the Union to that of an independent nation, the same legalistic and deductive bias of mind was free—or felt itself free—to operate on another premise, that of the individual's rights within the newly created state.

It may be that the inner motive was not basically libertarian, after all, merely an extension of the old minority psychology, with the theory of States' rights and a very untheoretical individualism now directed against Richmond rather than Washington. And certainly, behind the legal scrupulosity, there was a good deal of folk pressure against dissidence, a pressure not always mild. But whatever the motive, in the new situation and new emotional climate, the old legalistic bias of mind fulfilled itself in an apparent libertarianism so extreme and doctrinaire that even the obvious necessities of victory could not contain it. The habit of mind that had worked to precipitate the War, now worked, with equal efficacy, to lose it.

But to return to the situation before 1861, the only function then left open to intellect in the South was apologetics for the closed society, not criticism of it; and in those apologetics, there was little space for the breath of life, no recognition of the need for fluidity, growth, and change which life is. The philosophy of the Southern apologists did, however, offer space in its finely wrought interstices, for the bravado, arrogance, paranoid suspiciousness, and reckless or ignorant disregard for consequences that marked the Southern "fire-eater." It offered space for the anachronistic idiocy of Preston Brooks, who, on May 22, 1856, caned Charles Sumner in the Senate chamber and spilled what has been called the first blood of the Civil War. And a little later it offered space, too, for the folly of Governor Wise and his fellow Virginians, who, instead of committing John Brown to an asylum, where all the medical evidence, even then available to the court, clearly indicated that he should be, hanged him—and thereby proved again what is never in much need of proof, that a crazy man is a large-scale menace only in a crazy society.

In setting up the contrast between the "higher law" and legalism, I have not intended to imply that the Civil War was "caused" by the extremists on both sides. That is far too simple a notion of cause, and far too simple a description of the situation. In fact, both "higher law" and legalism were reactions to a situation already in existence. But they did aggravate the situation and they did poison thinking about it; and it is not hard to see how the revulsion from the two absolutes of "higher law" and legalism—or revelation and deduction—which had, in their unresolvable antinomy, helped to drench the country in blood, could condition, not only for Holmes but for others, the tentative, experimental, "open" approach to the life process which was given the name of pragmatism. We may go even further, and hazard that the philosophy of pragmatism represented an attempt to establish the right relation between intellect and society—the relation which had been violated by the Transcendentalist repudiation of society, and Southern society's repudiation of criticism.

But to return to the notion of pragmatism as a reaction from the disastrous absolutes of "higher law" and legalism, it is not hard to see how the revulsion from the two absolutes conditions, to this day, our attitude toward our political system.

I am not referring to the fact, already noted, of Southern Democracy and Middlewestern Republicanism as results of the War. Nor to another fact, equally a result of the War: the long tradition of the Republican Party as the party of Eastern business (captured from the Middlewestern farmers who had founded it, just as the old Democratic Party had been captured by the Southern planters from the Jacksonian farmer-labor voter), and the tradition of the new Democratic Party as the party of protest. What I am referring to is the fact that, despite the neat balance and opposition between the traditional roles of our two parties, there is an apparent illogicality in the way the system operates.

This illogicality, which appalls most foreign observers, is a logical product of the Civil War—or rather, the Civil War deeply confirmed us in a system which had gradually developed. The logic-bit foreigner, especially from a country like France or Italy, where scrupulous logicality produces some dozens of parties and where political street-fighting goes almost as unremarked as the appearance of the street-sweeper with his broom, says that our parties do not represent the real forces operating in society. In a sense the foreigner is right; if our parties do represent fundamentally opposing forces, they represent them in so muzzled and domesticated a fashion that once Election Day is over, business, no matter who wins, is resumed as usual. Good business sense, as well as innate prudery, forbids that we look upon the logicality of History in all its beauty bare.

The election in which social, sectional, moral, and philosophical forces found logical projection into the party setup was that of 1860; and when the votes were counted, business was not resumed as usual. Somewhere in their bones most Americans learned their lesson from this election. They learned that logical parties may lead logically to logical shooting, and they had had enough of that. The American feels that logicality, when not curbed and channeled by common sense, is a step toward fanaticism; it tends to sharpen controversy to some exclusive and vindictive point. Chesterton said that logic is all that is left to the insane; the American is almost prepared to go him one better and say that logic is the mark of the insane, at least of the politically insane. Illogicality, like apathy (which, according to David Reisman, has "its positive side as a safeguard against the overpoliticization of the country"), makes life possible; it guarantees continuity. From the Civil War the American emerged confirmed in his tendency to trust some un-defined sense of a social compact which undergirds and overarches mere political activity.

America has been full of reformers promoting everything from bloomers and Dr. Graham's bread to Prohibition and Technocracy, and perhaps in this age of complacency we should look back on them with a new nostalgic fondness; but Americans have a more and more ambivalent attitude toward such fanaticisms, however high-minded or holy. Americans freely admit that such single-minded citizens may be noble and even socially valuable; but they also feel them somewhat inconvenient. Americans don't mind enshrining a few martyrs in text-books or naming a few high schools after them, but they do have an instinctive distaste for being made martyrs themselves to the admirable convictions of a politician who happens to have won an election. And Americans have had reason to congratulate themselves that even in the "logical" election of 1860 the successful candidate was not a "logical" politician—even though, as a result of his illogicality, he was regarded as sadly unprincipled by the logical and high-minded segment of the electorate.

The result of all this is that now a political party is a very complicated menagerie, and logically considered, the wildebeest on the extreme left of the Democratic tent looks more like the wildebeest on the extreme left of the Republican tent than like the hypocritically drowsy lion facing him from the extreme right of his own show. But to drop our metaphor, the struggle for power conducted along logical lines is much more likely to occur in smoke-filled rooms than at the polls. The party system is a grid, a filter, a meat chopper, through which issues are processed for the consuming public. The Civil War confirmed our preference for this arrangement. We like the fog of politics, with the occasional drama of the flash of a lightning bolt that, happily, is usually nothing more than a near-miss.

Union, the abolition of slavery, the explosion of the westward expan-sion, Big Business and Big Technology, style in war, philosophy, and politics—we can see the effects of the Civil War in all of these things. In a sense they all add up to the creation of the world power that America is today. Between 1861 and 1865, America learned how to mobilize, equip, and deploy enormous military forces—and learned the will and confidence to do so. For most importantly, America emerged with a confirmed sense of destiny, the old sense of destiny confirmed by a new sense of military and economic competence. The Civil War was the secret school for 1917–18 and 1941–45. Neither the Kaiser nor the Führer had read the right history book of the United States.

Perhaps we ourselves shall not have read the right history book if we think we can stop here and complacently cast our accounts with the past. Every victory has a price tag; every gain entails a loss, not merely the price of effort and blood to achieve the victory but the rejection, or destruction, of values which are incommensurable with the particular victory. All victories carry with them something of the irony of the fairy story of the three wishes; and even if we willingly settle for our victory, we should, if we are wise, recognize that, as William James in "Pragmatism and Religion" puts it, "something permanently drastic and bitter always remains at the bottom of the cup."

With the War the old America, with all its virtues and defects, was dead. With the War the new America, with its promise of realizing the vision inherited from the old America, was born. But it was born, too, with those problems and paradoxes which Herman Melville, during the War, could already envisage when he wrote that the wind of History "spins *against* the way it drives," and that with success, "power unanointed" may come to corrupt us,

> And the Iron Dome,
> Stronger for stress and strain,
> Fling her huge shadow athwart the main;
> But the Founders' dream shall flee.

The War made us a new nation, and our problem, because of the very size and power of that new nation and the nobility of the promise which it inherits, remains that of finding in our time and in our new terms a way to recover and reinterpret the "Founders' dream." Is it possible for the individual, in the great modern industrial state, to retain some sense of responsibility? Is it possible for him to remain an individual? Is it possible, in the midst of all the forces making for standardization and anonymity, for society to avoid cultural starvation—to retain, and even develop, cultural pluralism and individual variety, and foster both social and individual integrity? Can we avoid, in its deep and more destructive manifestations, the tyranny of the majority, and at the same time keep a fruitful respect for the common will? We sense that one way, however modest, to undertake this mandatory task of our time is to contemplate the Civil War itself, that mystic cloud from which emerged our modernity.

. . .

We are right to see power, prestige, and confidence as conditioned by the Civil War. But it is a very easy step to regard the War, therefore, as a jolly piece of luck only slightly disguised, part of our divinely instituted success story, and to think, in some shadowy corner of the mind, of the dead at Gettysburg as a small price to pay for the development of a really satisfactory and cheap compact car with decent pick-up and road-holding capability. It is to our credit that we survived the War and tempered our national fiber in the process, but human decency and the future security of our country demand that we look at the costs. What are some of the costs?

Blood is the first cost. History is not melodrama, even if it usually reads like that. It was real blood, not tomato catsup or the pale ectoplasm of statistics, that wet the ground at Bloody Angle and darkened the waters of Bloody Pond. It modifies our complacency to look at the blurred and harrowing old photographs—the body of the dead sharpshooter in the Devil's Den at Gettysburg or the tangled mass in the Bloody Lane at Antietam.

But beyond this shock and pathos of the death of 600,000 men, men who really died and in ways they would scarcely have chosen, what has the loss of blood meant, if anything, in the development of the country? The answer is, apparently, not simple. Economists calculate the potential population increase that was cut off ninety-five years ago and try to convert this into dollars and cents, but they do not come up with the same answer. Some even say that the massive immigration which more than compensated for the slaughter was in itself a product of the War, and that the War, therefore, occasioned a net gain in population and consequent productivity.

Not only men, with their debatable cash value, are expended in war; property, with its more clear-cut price tag, is destroyed. Between April 1861 and April 1865, millions of dollars were shot away and otherwise used up in non-productive pursuits. Now, it is quite clear that during the War the North enjoyed a boom. Almost everybody had reason for pocketbook-and-belly rejoicing. Quite the contrary was, of course, true in that foreign country across the Mason and Dixon Line, and as soon as the War was concluded and had established that that foreign country couldn't be foreign after all, the barren fields, ruined cities, and collapsed economy of the South became a national liability.

Everyone agrees that the chronic poverty and social retardation of the South have, in fact, been a national liability ever since, with only such gleams as William Faulkner's prose and Al Capp's cartoons to compensate for the drain. But the experts do not agree about the relation of the Civil War to the chronic poverty and social retardation. Some see the loss of capital and the massive debt structure consequent upon the War as riveting the economy to an obsolescent crop (the crop varying from one region to another) and a semi-feudal sharecropping system. But others, in denying the deleterious effects of the War, point out that twenty years after the War the South was producing more bales of cotton than ever before, that the cities had been rebuilt, and that life had, in general, returned to its old unpromising normalcy.

Some argue that the extinction of property in slaves to the value of some $4,000,000,000, to take the figure of Charles and Mary Beard, had no significant economic effect, that the change of the status from bondage to freedom did not lower, but rather enhanced, the economic value of the Negro. Some maintain, further, that even without the War the South would have run the same course—perhaps even more disastrously, stubbornly raising, with the help of uneconomic black hands, more and more bales of the fatally stultifying cotton, and that aside from any psychological or ethical considerations, the War, by breaking up the static and throttling feudal structure of slavery, did the South an economic favor and made possible what poor progress did occur.

Let us leave in suspension such debates about the economic costs of the War and look at another kind of cost, a kind more subtle, pervasive, and continuing, a kind that conditions in a thousand ways the temper of American life today. This cost is psychological, and it is, of course, different for the winner and the loser. To give things labels, we may say that the War gave the South the Great Alibi and gave the North the Treasury of Virtue.

By the Great Alibi the South explains, condones, and transmutes everything. By a simple reference to the "War," any Southern female could, not too long ago, put on the glass slipper and be whisked away to the ball. Any goose could dream herself (or himself) a swan—surrounded, of course, by a good many geese for contrast and devoted hand-service. Even now, any common lyncher becomes a defender of the Southern tradition, and any rabble-rouser the gallant leader of a thin gray line of heroes, his hat on saber-point to provide reference by which to hold formation in the charge. By the Great Alibi, pellegra, hookworm, and illiteracy are all explained, or explained away, and mortgages are converted into badges of distinction. Laziness becomes the aesthetic sense, blood-lust rising from a matrix of boredom and resentful misery becomes a high sense of honor, and ignorance becomes divine revelation. By the Great Alibi the Southerner makes his Big Medicine. He turns defeat into victory, defects into virtues. Even more pathetically, he turns his great virtues into absurdities—sometimes vicious absurdities.

It may, indeed, be arguable that in economic matters the Southerner (like the Westerner) is entitled to some grievance, and an alibi—there was, for instance, such a thing as the unfavorable freight-rate differential. But the Southerner isn't nearly as prompt to haul out the Great Alibi for economic as for social and especially racial matters. And the most painful and costly consequences of the Great Alibi are found, of course, in connection with race. The race problem, according to the Great Alibi, is the doom defined by history—by New England slavers, New England and Middlewestern Abolitionists, cotton, climate, the Civil War, Reconstruction, Wall Street, the Jews. Everything flows into the picture.

Since the situation is given by history, the Southerner therefore is guiltless; is, in fact, an innocent victim of a cosmic conspiracy. At the same time, the Southerner's attitude toward the situation is frozen. He may say, in double vision of self-awareness, that he wishes he could feel and act differently, but cannot. I have heard a Southerner say: "I pray to feel different, but so far I can't help it." Even if the Southerner prays to feel different, he may still feel that to change his attitude would be a treachery—to that City of the Soul which the historical Confederacy became, to blood spilled in hopeless valor, to the dead fathers, and even to the self. He is trapped in history.

As he hears his own lips parroting the sad clichés of 1850, does the Southerner sometimes wonder if the words are his own? Does he ever, for a moment, feel the desperation of being caught in some great Time-machine, like a treadmill, and doomed to an eternal effort without progress? Or feel, like Sisyphus, the doom of pushing a great stone up a hill only to have the weight, like guilt, roll back over him, over and over again? When he lifts his arm to silence protest, does he ever feel, even fleetingly, that he is lifting it against some voice deep in himself?

Does he ever realize that the events of Tuscaloosa, Little Rock, and New Orleans are nothing more than an obscene parody of the meaning of his history? It is a debasement of his history, with all that was noble, courageous, and justifying bleached out, drained away. Does the man who in the relative safety of mob anonymity stands howling vituperation at a little Negro girl being conducted into a school building, feel himself at one with those gaunt, barefoot, whiskery scarecrows who fought it out, breast to breast, to the death, at the Bloody Angle at Spotsylvania, in May 1864? Can the man howling in the mob imagine General R. E. Lee, CSA, shaking hands with Orval Faubus, Governor of Arkansas?

Does that man in the mob ever wonder why his own manly and admirable resentment at coercion should be enlisted, over and over again, in situations which should, and do, embarrass the generosity and dignity of manhood, including his own? Does he ever consider the possibility that whatever degree of dignity and success a Negro achieves actually enriches, in the end, the life of the white man and enlarges his own worth as a human being?

There are, one must admit, an impressive number of objective difficulties in the race question in the South—difficulties over and beyond those attributable to Original Sin and Confederate orneriness; but the grim fact is that the Great Alibi rusts away the will to confront those difficulties, at either a practical or an ethical level. All is explained—and transmuted.

The whole process of the Great Alibi resembles the neurotic automatism. The old trauma was so great that reality even now cannot be faced. The automatic repetition short-circuits clear perception and honest thinking. North as well as South (for the North has its own mechanism for evading reality), we all seem to be doomed to re-enact, in painful automatism, the errors of our common past.

The Treasury of Virtue, which is the psychological heritage left to the North by the Civil War, may not be as comic or vicious as the Great Alibi, but it is equally unlovely. It may even be, in the end, equally corrosive of national, and personal, integrity. If the Southerner, with his Great Alibi, feels trapped by history, the Northerner, with his Treasury of Virtue, feels redeemed by history, automatically redeemed. He has in his pocket, not a papal indulgence peddled by some wandering pardoner of the Middle Ages, but an indulgence, a plenary indulgence, for all sins past, present, and future, freely given by the hand of history.

The Northerner feels redeemed, for he, being human, tends to rewrite history to suit his own deep needs; he may not, in fact, publish this history, but it lies open on a lectern in some arcane recess of his being, ready for his devotional perusal. He knows, as everybody knows, that the War saved the Union. He knows, as everybody knows—and as Lincoln, with sardonic understatement, said—that slavery was the *sine qua non* of the War. But that *sine qua non* is not enough for the deep need for justification. Even "almost all," if the all is salted with psychological and historical realism, is not enough. The *sine qua non* has to become a secretly enshrined ikon of a boy in blue striking off, with one hand, iron shackles from a grizzle-headed Uncle Tom weeping in gratitude, and with the other, passing out McGuffey's First Reader to a rolypoly pickaninny laughing in hope.

When one is happy in forgetfulness, facts get forgotten. In the happy contemplation of the Treasury of Virtue it is forgotten that the Republican platform of 1860 pledged protection to the institution of slavery where it existed, and that the Republicans were ready, in 1861, to guarantee slavery in the South, as bait for a return to the Union. It is forgotten that in July, 1861, both houses of Congress, by an almost unanimous vote, affirmed that the War was waged not to interfere with the institutions of any state but only to maintain the Union. The War, in the words of the House resolution, should cease "as soon as these objects are accomplished." It is forgotten that the Emancipation Proclamation, issued on September 23, 1862, was limited and provisional: slavery was to be abolished *only* in the seceded states and *only if* they did not return to the Union before the first of the next January. It is forgotten that the Proclamation was widely disapproved and even contributed to the serious setbacks to Republican candidates for office in the subsequent election. It is forgotten that, as Lincoln himself freely admitted, the Proclamation itself was of doubtful constitutional warrant and was forced by circumstances; that only after a bitter and prolonged struggle in Congress was the Thirteenth Amendment sent, as late as January 1865, to the states for ratification; and that all of Lincoln's genius as a horse trader (here the deal was Federal patronage swapped for Democratic votes) was needed to get Nevada admitted to statehood, with its guaranteed support of the Amendment. It is forgotten that even *after* the Fourteenth Amendment, not only Southern states, but most Northern ones, refused to adopt Negro suffrage, and that Connecticut had formally rejected it as late as July 1865. It is forgotten that it was not until 1870 that the Negro finally won his vote —or rather, that very different thing, the right to vote.

It is forgotten that Sherman, and not only Sherman, was violently opposed to arming Negroes against white troops. It is forgotten that, as Bell Irvin Wiley has amply documented in *The Life of Billy Yank*, racism was all too common in the liberating army. It is forgotten that only the failure of Northern volunteering overcame the powerful prejudice against accepting Negro troops, and allowed "Sambo's Right to be Kilt"—as the title of a contemporary song had it.

It is forgotten that racism and Abolitionism might, and often did, go hand in hand. This was true even in the most instructed circles, and so one is scarcely surprised to find James T. Ayers, a clergyman and a committed Abolitionist acting as recruiting officer for Negro troops, confiding to his diary his fear that freed Negroes would push North and "soon they will be in every whole and Corner, and the Bucks will be wanting to galant our Daughters Round." It is forgotten that Lincoln, at Charlestown, Illinois, in 1858, formally affirmed: "I am not, nor ever have been, in favor of bringing about in any way the social and political equality of the white and black races." And it is forgotten that as late as 1862 he said to Negro leaders visiting the White House: "Even when you cease to be slaves, you are yet far removed from being placed on an equality with the white race. . . . It is better for us both to be separated."

It is forgotten, in fact, that history is history.

Despite all this, the War appears, according to the doctrine of the Treasury of Virtue, as a consciously undertaken crusade so full of righteousness that there is enough overplus stored in Heaven, like the deeds of the saints, to take care of all small failings and oversights of the descendants of the crusaders, certainly unto the present generation. From the start America had had adequate baggage of self-righteousness and Phariseeism, but with the Civil War came grace abounding, for the least of sinners.

The crusaders themselves, back from the wars, seemed to feel that they had finished the work of virtue. Their efforts had, indeed, been almost superhuman, but they themselves were, after all, human. "God has given us the Union, let us enjoy it," they said, in a paraphrase of the first Medici pope entering upon his pontificate. Men turned their minds outward, for external victory always seems to signify for the victor that he need spend no more effort on any merely internal struggle. Few shared the moral qualms expressed by Brooks Adams in an oration pronounced at Taunton, Massachusetts, on the great centennial of July 4, 1876. He demanded: "Can we look over the United States and honestly tell ourselves that all things are well within us?" And he answered: "We cannot conceal from ourselves that all things are not well."

Brooks Adams, with his critical, unoptimistic mind, could not conceal it from himself, but many could; and a price was paid for the self-delusion. As Kenneth Stampp, an eminent Northern historian and the author of a corrosive interpretation of slavery, puts it: "The Yankees went to war animated by the highest ideals of the nineteenth-century middle classes. . . . But what the Yankees achieved—for their generation at least—was a triumph not of middle-class ideals but of middle-class vices. The most striking products of their crusade were the shoddy aristocracy of the North and the ragged children of the South. Among the masses of Americans there were no victors, only the vanquished." And Samuel Eliot Morison has written of his own section, New England: "In the generation to come that region would no longer furnish the nation with teachers and men of letters, but with a mongrel breed of politicians, sired by abolition out of profiteering."

Perhaps the eminent historians have overstated the case. Perhaps, as some other historians say, the gusty vigor of the heroes of the period from Grant to McKinley is a tribute to the American character; and in the great a-moral economy of history their a-moral rapacity has contributed something to our present power and glory. But the process, however much it may have contributed to our advantage, was not a pretty one. James Russell Lowell, in his "Ode" for the 1876 Centennial, looked about him and addressed his countrymen:

> Show your new bleaching process, cheap and brief,
> To wit; a jury chosen by the thief;
> Show your State Legislatures; show your Rings,
> And challenge Europe to produce such things
> As high officials sitting half in sight
> To share the plunder and to fix things right . . .

We find, in the North, the Gilded Age, when a father could say: "Where Vanderbilt sits is the head of the table. I shall make my son rich." We find the apotheosis of what William James called the "bitch-goddess Success," and the heirs of the "sybarites of shoddy," and Jim Fisk and all the rest, including no self-reconstruction whatsoever. And in the South we find a confused and aimless Reconstruction ending in the Big Sell-Out of 1876, with the deal to make the Republican Hayes President in return for the end of any Reconstruction whatever in the South. The Republican Party, writes L. D. Reddick in *The Journal of Negro History*, "found the Negro a highly useful instrument to consolidate the gains made through the Civil War. Accordingly, he was abandoned as soon as the so-called 'New South' acquiesced in the *fait accompli.*"

The Negro didn't get his forty acres and a mule, or anything else except a shadowy freedom, and even such erstwhile doughty crusaders as Carl Shurz, Charles Francis Adams, and Thomas Wentworth Higginson, who, besides being the staunchest of the secret backers of John Brown, had commanded the first Negro regiment in the Federal army, thought that the Negro was best left to his own devices and the ministrations of his late masters. In any case, could any such near-socialism as the settlement of Negroes on expropriated lands—even Southern land—have been really acceptable to sound Northern business sense in that heyday of rambunctious young capitalism?

But the Big Sell-Out gets forgotten—except, of course, by Negroes. There was, apparently, enough virtue stored up to redeem even that, for the West was won, money poured out of the plains, hills, factories, and brokerage offices, and prosperity was clearly a reward for virtue. In fact, prosperity *was* virtue—and the equation was supported not only by the old belief that virtue is rewarded by prosperity, but by the new market-mentality conviction that high price in the market (i.e., prosperity) is the only criterion of worth (i.e., virtue). The dollars in the bank were in themselves a Treasury of Virtue; and poverty, especially Southern poverty, became a vice to be severely reprobated.

It takes little reflection or imagination to see the effect on American life of belief in the Treasury of Virtue. For one thing, as Harold Faulkner and other historians have pointed out, the reforming impulse burned itself out in the slavery controversy, and it was another generation "before the nation again turned seriously to the quest for social justice." But the effects of belief in the Treasury of Virtue are with us yet. For instance, the spiritual *rentier* in the North, living on the income of the Treasury of Virtue, casts a far more tender—or at least morally more myopic—eye on the South Side in Chicago or on a Harlem slum than he does on Little Rock, Arkansas, and when possible, insulates himself from democratic hurly-burly by withdrawing into penthouse, suburb, or private school.

From 1899, when W. E. B. Du Bois published his *Philadelphia Negro*, anatomizing Northern race prejudice, up to some of the articles of Carl Rowan, Negroes have found some grim comedy in the social effects of the Treasury of Virtue. There is another kind of comedy, equally grim and more complex, in seeing the unregenerate Southerner join the Negro in the good laugh at Yankee Phariseeism. But others, too, have had a right to join in the grisly hilarity—all those spooky tribes of immigrants, from the early Irish and German through the Jews and Scots and Poles and Italians, to the late-arriving Puerto Ricans.

Not only foreigners who emigrated to America, but foreigners who stayed at home, have sometimes availed themselves of the opportunity for sardonic mirth. From the first, Americans had a strong tendency to think of their land as the Galahad among nations, and the Civil War, with its happy marriage of victory and virtue, has converted this tendency into an article of faith nearly as sacrosanct as the Declaration of Independence.

Most Americans are ready to echo the sentiment of Woodrow Wilson that "America is the only idealist country in the world." As Reinhold Niebuhr has put it, we live in the illusions of our national infancy, the illusions of innocence and virtue. We have not grown up enough to appreciate the difficulty of moral definition, the doubleness of experience—what he calls "the irony of history."

All this is not to say that America has not characteristically demonstrated generosity, sometimes even informed generosity, in dealing with other peoples, or has not, in the course of its history, struggled to define and realize certain worthy ideals. But moral narcissism is a peculiarly unlovely and unlovable trait. Even when the narcissist happens to possess the virtues which he devotes his time to congratulating himself upon, the observer is less apt to regard the virtues than their context of pathology. Certainly, moral narcissism is a poor basis for national policy; but we have our crusades of 1917–18 and 1941–45 and our diplomacy of righteousness, with the slogan of unconditional surrender and universal spiritual rehabilitation—for others.

Even if moral narcissism did not get us into the wars, even if we should have been in the wars, the narcissism certainly did have a great deal to do with the spirit and method by which they were conducted. And it contributed no little to the sad, embarrassing, and even perilous consequences. Furthermore, in our moments of victory it is hard for us to remember the full implications of William James' remark that "the victory to be philosophically prayed for is that of the more inclusive side—of the side which even in the hour of triumph will to some degree do justice to the ideals in which the vanquished interests lay."

In all our victories the United States has, I am confident, been the "more inclusive side." And we can look at our history and see examples of the attempt "to do justice to the ideals in which the vanquished interests lay." To take a trivial and sentimental example, we can think of the glorification by Northern publishers and public of the idyl of the Southern plantation as presented by the school of Thomas Nelson

Page. To take a more serious and sophisticated example, we can think of the use Melville, Henry Adams, and Henry James made, as Vann Woodward has pointed out, of Confederate characters to serve as ironical critics of the values of the Gilded Age—Ungar in Melville's epic *Clarel*, John Carrington in Adams' novel *Democracy*, and Basil Ransom in James' *Bostonians*. But Melville, Adams, and James stood outside their age, and the age swept past them oblivious of their criticism, with little concern to do justice to anything except the demands of double-entry bookkeeping. In our subsequent victories we have, I trust, done better. But have we fully accepted the obligations of our "inclusiveness"?

Wrapped in our righteousness, we sometimes feel that our solitude is, as Henry Adams said of the righteous solitude of Charles Sumner, "glacial." We are isolated in righteousness, beleaguered by lesser breeds without the law whose heads of state incline to secret diplomacy, back-stairs agreements, imperialistic exploitation, and espionage, and in general lack the missionary spirit. Not that the foreigner himself minds too much being credited with professional savvy. He rather likes that. What he finds funny is the incorruptibly automatic gleam of righteousness in the American eye.

The man of righteousness tends to be so sure of his own motives that he does not need to inspect consequences. Therefore, says Abraham Kaplan in "American Ethics and Public Policy," "any debate on principle offers the incomparable advantage of irresponsibility." He proceeds to quote Max Weber: "There is an abysmal contrast between conduct that follows the maxim of an ethic of ultimate ends—that is, in religious terms, 'The Christian does rightly and leaves the results with the Lord' —and conduct that follows the maxim of an ethic of responsibility, in which case one has to give an account of the foreseeable results of one's action." The American, in his conviction of righteousness, may be, on some occasions, morally unassailable, but for reasons that may also make him politically irresponsible.

Righteousness is our first refuge and our strength—even when we have acted on the grounds of calculated self-interest, and have got caught red-handed, and have to admit, a couple of days later, to a great bumbling horse-apple of a lie. In such a case, the effect of the conviction of virtue is to make us lie automatically and awkwardly, with no élan of artistry and no forethought; and then, in trying to justify the lie, lie to ourselves and transmute the lie into a kind of superior truth.

The Great Alibi and the Treasury of Virtue—they are maiming liabilities we inherit from the Civil War. But at the same time they may contribute—how unworthily—to the attraction the War holds for us. The Great Alibi and the Treasury of Virtue both serve deep needs of poor human nature; and if, without historical realism and self-criticism, we look back on the War, we are merely compounding the old inherited delusions which our weakness craves. We fear, in other words, to lose the comforting automatism of the Great Alibi or the Treasury of Virtue, for if we lose them, we may, at last, find ourselves nakedly alone with the problems of our time and with ourselves. Where would we find our next alibi and our next assurance of virtue?

Despite all the costs, however, most Americans are prepared to see the Civil War as a fountainhead of our power and prestige among the nations. They are right; and even the most disgruntled Southerner, no matter how much he may damn the Yankee and his works, loves as well as the next man to bask in the beams of power and prestige. But is it our delight in power and prestige that gives the War its grip on the American imagination? No, and it is not even the fact that the effects of the War, for better and worse, permeate American life and culture —for we are so accustomed to breath that we are unaware of the air we breathe. It is not even the comfort we get from the Great Alibi and the Treasury of Virtue.

No one thing accounts for the appeal of the Civil War, certainly not the simple piety of family or region, which once was so important in the matter. We see the marks of that old piety in the sad little monument on the village green in Vermont or in the square in East Texas. But for a long time America has been on the move, and local pieties wear thin. Family pieties and family ties, they thin, too, with time. Relatively few Americans now alive once sat by the grandfather's knee to hear how the men of Pickett and Pettigrew held formation up the ridge at Gettysburg, or how dogwood bloomed white in the dark woods of Shiloh.

It is not merely that few men now alive can, chronologically, have known the grandfather who had been in the War; the grandfather, or great-grandfather, of a high proportion of our population was not even in this country when the War was being fought. Not that this disqualifies the grandson from experiencing to the full the imaginative appeal of the Civil War. To experience this appeal may be, in fact, the very ritual of being American. A man with an Italian name may don eighteenth-century garb and mount a horse to commemorate the Ride of Paul Revere, and a man with a Swedish name is the author of the most popular biography of Abraham Lincoln. To be American is not, as the Pole Adam Gurowski pointed out more than a hundred years ago, a matter of blood; it is a matter of an idea—and history is the image of that idea.

No, simple piety and blood connection do not account for the appeal, and certainly not for the fact that the popular interest has been steadily rising, and rising for nearly twenty years before the natural stir about the approaching centennial. We can remember that during World War II, the Civil War, not the Revolution, was characteristically used in our propaganda, and that it was the image of Lincoln, not that of Washington or Jefferson, that flashed ritualistically on the silver screen after the double feature; and in classrooms for young Air Force specialists (and perhaps elsewhere), it was sometimes pointed out that the Founding Fathers were not really "democratic," that democracy stemmed from the Civil War.

The turning to the Civil War is, however, a more significant matter than the manipulations of propaganda specialists, and their sometimes unhistorical history. When a people enters upon a period of crisis it is only natural that they look back upon their past and try to find therein some clue to their nature and their destiny—as the kingdom of Judah looked back to the Mosaic period when King Josiah, ensnared in the imperialist struggles of Egypt, Assyria, and Babylon, instituted the Deuteronomic Reformation, or as the English, under Elizabeth I, first undertook the study of their own origins and the origins of their church.

World War II merely initiated the period of crisis through which we are passing, and it is only natural that the Civil War looms larger now than ever before. There was a time when the custody of the War was for the most part relegated to the Southerners, but now things are different. We can see this quite simply from the enormous number and sale of books on the War and from the dense population at the Civil War Round Tables.

In any case, the War grows in our consciousness. The event stands there larger than life, massively symbolic in its inexhaustible and sibylline significance. Significances, rather, for it is an image of life, and as such, is a condensation of many kinds of meanings. There is no one single meaning appropriate to our occasion, and that portentous richness is one of the things that make us stare at the towering event. We shall not be able to anatomize this portentous richness, but we feel that we must try. We must try because it is a way of understanding our own deeper selves, and that need to understand ourselves is what takes us, always, to the deeper contemplations of art, literature, religion, and history.

To begin with, the Civil War offers a gallery of great human images for our contemplation. It affords a dazzling array of figures, noble in proportion yet human, caught out of Time as in a frieze, in stances so profoundly touching or powerfully mythic that they move us in a way no mere consideration of "historical importance" ever could. We can think of Lincoln alone at night in the drafty corridors of the White House, the shawl on his shoulders; of Jackson's dying words; of Lee coming out of the McLean farmhouse at Appomattox to stare over the heads of his waiting men, who crowded around, and strike his gauntleted hands deliberately together; of Sam Davis, with the rope around his neck, giving the Federal soldiers the order for his own execution, the order which General Dodge was too overcome by emotion to give; of Colonel Robert Gould Shaw, Harvard '60, who led his black Fifty-fourth Massachusetts in its first test of manhood, died with the cry "Forward, my boys!" and was buried under the heaps of his own men in the ditch before Fort Wagner; of Grant, old, discredited, dying of cancer, driving pen over paper, day after day, to tell his truth and satisfy his creditors. That was our Homeric period, and the figures loom up only a little less than gods, but even so, we recognize the lineaments and passions of men, and by that recognition of common kinship, share in their grandeur.

Their appeal, and that of their war, is, however, deeper than that. Perhaps we can best understand this by asking why the Civil War appeals so much more strongly to the imagination than does the Revolution. We can start our answer by saying that the Revolution is too simple. That is, it comes to our imagination as white against black, good against bad. It is comfortable, of course, to think that way of the Revolution, even if somewhat unhistorical; but it is not very interesting. It lacks inner drama. We never think, for instance, of Washington or Jefferson caught in dark inner conflicts such as those Lincoln or Lee or Stonewall Jackson experienced. If Washington brooded in the night at Valley Forge, his trouble was not of that order.

But the Civil War—despite Southern nationalism and despite the Southern preference for the "War Between the States"—was, after all, a civil war. And a civil war is, we may say, the prototype of all war, for in the persons of fellow citizens who happen to be the enemy, we meet again, with the old ambivalence of love and hate and with all the old guilts, the blood brothers of our childhood. In a civil war—especially in one such as this when the nation shares deep and significant convictions and is not a mere handbasket of factions huddled arbitrarily together by historical happen-so—all the self-divisions of conflicts within individuals become a series of mirrors in which the plight of the country is reflected, and the self-division of the country a great mirror in which the individual may see imaged his own deep conflicts, not only the conflicts of political loyalties, but those more profoundly personal.

But to return to the contrast between the Revolution and the Civil War, it even seems that something had happened to the American character between 1776 and 1861. Perhaps the historians are right who say that if we look at the portraits of the Founding Fathers, we see the faces of men strong, practical, intelligent, and self-assured—and not burdened with excessive sensitivity. But we know that the strength of a Lincoln or a Grant was a different kind of strength, a strength somehow earned out of inner turmoil. Lee was, in a sense, more of an eighteenth-century character than any of them; but from the time of his great decision in 1861, when he said that he would "sacrifice anything but honor" for the Union, to the grim nights when, an old man, he walked the floor of the president's house at Washington College, he appears to us as a man living in the midst of moral scruples arbitrated by an iron will and endured by Christian faith.

The "inwardness" of the experience of the Civil War, in both personal and national terms, made for human sympathy that might, without blurring issues, overarch them, and might temper the bigotry of victory and the rancor of defeat. More than one historian has wondered how much the "nervous breakdown" of Lincoln, and the state of soul indicated by his ever-present but controlled melancholy, had to do with his great compassion—and the Gettysburg Address. We may remember how well Grant knew how narrow is the margin between being lost and being saved, and wonder how much the fact that only two years earlier he had had to be locked howling drunk in a steamboat cabin, contributed to the dignity and magnanimity of the morning at Appomattox.

We may remember General Simon Bolivar Buckner, CSA, calling on Grant in his last days of suffering—the same Buckner who had been a classmate at West Point, who had lent Grant money long ago when, destitute and out of the army, he had come to New York, and who later had surrendered to Grant at Fort Donelson—and remember how, when Buckner had come out from the dying man and the reporters demanded what had passed between them, he said, with tears in his eyes, that it was "too sacred." We may remember the Confederate generals, in their gray sashes, walking as pallbearers at the funeral of Grant.

Then, to round out the picture, we may remember the words of Charles Francis Adams, who had done his share of the fighting, but who said of Lee that had he been in his place he would have done exactly the same. "It may have been treason . . ." he said, "but he awaits sentence at the bar of history in a very respectable company . . ." including John Hampden, Oliver Cromwell, Sir Henry Vane, and George Washington, "a Virginian of note."

The whole context of Southern life made for some sort of self-division. The old romantic unionism survived in the South, and had, as we have said, a pervasive influence. Even in 1860, Virginia's vote for Bell for President, against Breckenridge, indicated the strength of Union sentiment. But more significant than unionism as a source of self-division was the universalist conception of freedom based on natural law, inherited from the Revolution. In addition to the notion of freedom, there were Jacksonian democracy and Christian doctrine, and more than one slaveholder is on record as sympathizing with the distress of a certain Gustavus Henry, who admitted to his wife that "I sometimes think my feelings unfit me for a slaveholder."

The eminent Southern editor Duff Green wrote, in the *United States Telegraph:* "It is only by alarming the consciences of the weak and feeble and diffusing among our people a morbid sensibility on the question of slavery, that the Abolitionists can accomplish their object." The editor, in other words, recognized in his fellow Southerners a dangerous proneness to bad conscience and morbid sensibility, ready to be tapped. The greatest danger to slavery was, in one perspective, the Southern heart. Long back, John Randolph of Roanoke, who was no starry-eyed reformer, when asked who was the greatest orator he had ever heard, replied: "A slave, sir. She was a mother and her rostrum was the auction block." And even Calhoun, who as early as 1837 had risen in the Senate to declare slavery not a necessary evil but a positive good, and who was the chief draftsman of the blueprint for Southern society, privately condemned the domestic slave trade.

The philosophy of slavery was shot through with what Louis Hartz calls "agonies and contradictions"—agonies and contradictions clearly exemplified in the fact that the very Constitution of the Confederacy, in forbidding the slave trade, implied that slavery itself was an evil. Behind the formidable façade of logic and learning, human beings

struggled with the actual process of life. When the Confederate shoul-
dered his musket and marched away, he carried something of this
burden. It would not make him falter, for, as General Beauregard said,
political and philosophical considerations dwindled when Federal
troops set foot on the soil of Virginia, just as such considerations
dwindled, for millions in the North, when the first gun was fired at the
flag over Sumter.

But for the Confederate the rub was, indeed, real. It was as real as
the inner rub we find in documents like this letter written home by a
Yankee corporal at Savannah, Georgia, in 1864: "The cruelties practiced on this campaign towards citizens have been enough to blast a
more sacred cause than ours. We hardly deserve success."

The inwardness of the story of those characters from the Civil War
gives the attraction of drama. In the struggle to define clear aims and
certain commitments in the complexity of life, in the struggle to
achieve identity and human charity, we find the echo of our own lives,
and that fact draws our imagination. We are smuggled into the scene
and endure the action.

Here, however, a paradox enters. The similarity to us of those men,
the named and nameless, attracts us. But their differences attract us, too.

For we must remember that those men, from conflict and division,
rose to strength. From complication they made the simple cutting edge
of action. They were, in the deepest sense, individuals; that is, by moral
awareness they had achieved, in varying degrees, identity. In our age
of conformity, of "other-directedness," of uniformity and the gray
flannel suit, of personality created by a charm school, Dale Carnegie,
or the public relations expert, when few exhibit "that manly candor
and masculine independence of opinion" the dwindling of which
de Tocqueville could already deplore before the Civil War—how nostalgically, how romantically, we look back on those powerful and suggestive images of integrity.

As a corollary to our secret yearning for the old-fashioned concept
of the person, we may glance, for a moment, at the notion of community. For one thing, the mere sense of place, of a locality clustered about
by shared sentiments, looms large in the Civil War. The regimental
designations were more than conveniences. Boys marched off from
home together and stayed together. Some sense of community went
with them. Today, we can scarcely imagine a commander saying what
Pickett said to his men as they dressed lines for the fatal charge: "Don't
forget today that you are from Old Virginia!" It is absurd—and romantic. But it carries the nostalgic appeal; for the notion of place has a

natural relation to the notion of identity in community, in the shared place.

Ultimately, it is the same appeal, even more romantic, which we feel when the old words *duty* and *honor* are spoken by those men. No doubt then many a rogue laid tongue to the words, and no doubt now many a man acts in duty and honor without using the words; but the words speak to us across time of a world of joyfully recognized obligations to the self and to society, and for some, even to God.

In our world of restless mobility, where every Main Street looks like the one before and the throughway is always the same, of communication without communion, of the ad-man's nauseating surrogate for family sense and community in the word *togetherness,* we look back nostalgically on the romantic image of some right and natural relation of man to place and man to man, fulfilled in worthy action. The corrosive of historical realism cannot quite disenthrall us of this, nor can our hope that somehow in our modern world we may achieve our own new version, humanly acceptable, of identity and community. In fact, the old image may feed our new hope.

Beyond nostalgia, and the criticism of ourselves which the nostalgia implies, the Civil War catches the imagination because it raises in an acute and dramatic form a fundamental question, the question of will and inevitability. Back in 1858, William H. Seward, one of the "extreme men" whom Lincoln, the "moderate," was to defeat for the nomination of 1860, had called the struggle between the North and South the "irrepressible conflict," and for generations, historian after historian has asked whether this conflict, arising, as Allan Nevins has said, in a situation of "political drift, cowardice, and fanaticism," and ending in blood, was really irrepressible. Could intelligence, tact, will, and good will have averted the arbitrament of force? Was there no solution short of the resolution by blood? Or if the ultimate collision had been averted at that time, would this have meant a mere postponement with more brutal consequences compounded for the future? Or if the conflict became inevitable at a certain date, what was that date—when did the ever-narrowing circle make men so desperate that they had to break out at any cost?

Here we are dealing, of course, with the question of historical inevitability, and the historians do not agree. We find, for example, James G. Randall calling the men of the 1850's the "Blundering Generation." And we find Arthur Schlesinger, Jr., retorting that a society like the

South "closed in the defense of evil institutions thus creates moral differences far too profound to be solved by compromise." Or we can turn to Charles A. Beard and find not the moral determinism of Schlesinger but the emphasis on economic factors. But Pieter Geyl, writing on the Civil War, says that the general question of inevitability "is one on which the historian can never form any but an ambivalent opinion. He will now stress other possibilities, then again speak in terms of a coherent sequence of cause and effect. But if he is wise, he will in both cases remain conscious that he has not been able to establish a definite equilibrium between the factors, dissimilar and recalcitrant to exact valuation as they are, by which every crisis situation is dominated." Or to go further, we find that David Donald, in a recent biography of Charles Sumner, can say, quoting André Gide, that "it is the part of wisdom to ask not why, but how events happen." And Kenneth Stampp agrees with Vann Woodward that the whole question "is one for the metaphysician and not the historian."

Strictly speaking, the question of evitability or inevitability is one for the metaphysician, but historians are human, and as human beings they turn, under the shock of event, to consider the "might have been," the road not taken. And as human beings, the historians do not arrive at their conclusions in a vacuum. The speculations of each period arise, of course, in the climate of that period. The history written in the last period of the nineteenth century, with its emphasis on reconciliation in the new nationalism, is very different from that written in the 1930's under the shadow of Karl Marx. Or more to our present concern, the history written in the 1920's, in a revulsion from war, with aspiration toward a rational internationalism, and with faith in progress, tended to see the Civil War as avoidable—the consequence of strong emotions and weak thinking. And in contrast with this view, we find the historians of our grim period of the Cold War rebuking the implicit optimism of the "revisionists" of the 1920's who held that the Civil War was avoidable.

More than the climate of a period may, however, condition the historian's speculations about inevitability. As human beings, the historians run the risk of letting their view of the objective question of inevitability serve as a mask for gratifying personal need. Southerners, for instance, tend to the view that the Civil War was evitable. And for Southerners this view may serve as a device to share the guilt—just as emphasis on racism in the North may make the Southerner feel a little less lonely in his guilt about slavery. If the War could have been avoided, it is an easy step, then, to show how both sides participated

in the responsibility, how the guilt can be spread around. The Southerner may feel that he is stuck with *some* guilt. But he would certainly
enjoy the inestimable privilege of being able to call the kettle black. So
the evitability theory, though philosophically contradicting the determinism implicit in the Great Alibi, works to the same happy end, the
diminishing of guilt.

Northerners, from different motives at different periods, tend to
favor the view that the Civil War was inevitable. In one perspective,
for some members of earlier generations, living under the bruising and
bloody shock of the event, one appeal of the inevitability theory may
have been that it relieved the Northerner of certain unpleasant speculations about his own hand in the proceedings. In another perspective,
with the inevitability theory there was full justification for the gesture
of reconciliation: the Southerner had merely enacted his inevitable role,
and might even be congratulated on having enacted it well, for we are
all shriven by History. In another perspective, and in another temper,
the inevitability theory could be used with equal ease to re-allocate all
guilt to the South. The guilt of the South might be taken primarily as
a failure to understand the national destiny, or the laws of economics,
or the logic of technology, and the virtue of the North would, then,
lie in identifying itself with whatever the Wave of the Future might be
taken to be. Or the guilt of the South might be put into moral terms:
the evil of the South made the Civil War *morally* inevitable, and the
North was merely the bright surgical instrument in the hand of God,
or History. There is one feature that most versions of the inevitability
theory share—any of them may be invoked to demonstrate the blame-
lessness of the instrument in the hand of the surgeon. So the inevitability theory may work to the same happy end as the Treasury of Virtue.

The Great Alibi and the Treasury of Virtue—they come back again
to us as soon as we begin to speculate about the inevitability of the Civil
War and undertake the sorting out of causes which that entails. This
does not mean that historians should give up the topic. It merely means
that historians, and readers of history too, should look twice at themselves when the topic is mentioned. It means that we should seek to end
the obscene gratifications of history, and try to learn what the contemplation of the past, conducted with psychological depth and humane
breadth, can do for us. What happens if, by the act of historical imagination—the historian's and our own—we are transported into the documented, re-created moment of the past and, in a double vision, see the
problems and values of that moment and those of our own, set against
each other in mutual criticism and clarification? What happens if, in

innocence, we can accept this process without trying to justify the present by the past or the past by the present? We might, then, ask the question about inevitability in the only way that is fruitful—in the recognition that there can never be a *yes-or-no* answer, but that the framing of perspectives of causality and context, as rigorously as possible even though provisionally, fulfills our urgent need to try to determine the limits of responsibility in experience.

The asking and the answering are bound to be ambiguous, for experience carries no labels. But there is a discipline of the mind and heart, a discipline both humbling and enlarging, in the imaginative consideration of possibilities in the face of the unique facts of the irrevocable past. The asking and the answering which history provokes may help us to understand, even to frame, the logic of experience to which we shall submit. History cannot give us a program for the future, but it can give us a fuller understanding of ourselves, and of our common humanity, so that we can better face the future.

In any case, the historians, as human beings, are bound to pick the scab of our fate. They are bound to turn to the question underlying the assessment of all experience: To what extent is man always—or sometimes—trapped in the great texture of causality, of nature and history? Most of us are not metaphysicians and do not often consider the questions abstractly, but as men, we know that our "felt" answer to it, the answer in our guts, gives the tone to our living and conditions the range and vigor of our actions.

The contemplation of the Civil War does not bring this question to us abstractly. It brings it to us not only in the very tissue of drama, in the passions of the actors in the drama, but also as echoed in the drama we now live and in our own passions. The Civil War is urgently our war, and, as we have said, reaches in a thousand ways into our blood-stream and our personal present. But more urgently, the present momentous crisis of our history, when our national existence may be at stake, makes us demand what we can learn—if, alas, anything—from that great crisis of our national past. Does a society like the USSR, "closed in the defense of evil institutions," create "moral differences far too profound to be solved by compromise"? If so, when do we start shooting? Or to drop the moral concern, does the naked geopolitical confrontation with Russia doom us to the struggle? Or the mounting economic rivalry? Can we, in fact, learn only that we are victims of nature and of history? Or can we learn that we can make, or at least have a hand in the making of, our future?

The basic question is anguishing and fascinating, and part of the anguish and fascination is that the question always leads back, past all other problems, to the problems of our personal histories and individual acts. We are living not only in a time of national crisis but in a time of crucial inspection of the nature and role of the individual. And so the Civil War draws us as an oracle, darkly unriddled and portentous, of personal, as well as national, fate.

In any case, the Civil War occurred. "Whether or not the war was inevitable," as Bernard de Voto says, "the crisis was." The conflicts had to be solved, but the fact that "they were not solved short of war is our greatest national tragedy." Or as Sidney Hook has put it: "If the war was inevitable, it was tragic. If it was not inevitable, it was even more tragic."

The word *tragedy* is often used loosely. Here we use it at its deepest significance: the image in action of the deepest questions of man's fate and man's attitude toward his fate. For the Civil War is, massively, that. It is the story of a crime of monstrous inhumanity, into which almost innocently men stumbled; of consequences which could not be trammeled up, and of men who entangled themselves more and more vindictively and desperately until the powers of reason were twisted and their very virtues perverted; of a climax drenched with blood but with nobility gleaming ironically, and redeemingly, through the murk; of a conclusion in which, for the participants at least, there is a reconciliation by human recognition. As Oliver Wendell Holmes, Jr., said, long before his great fame: "You could not stand up day after day in those indecisive contests where overwhelming victory was impossible because neither side would run as they ought when beaten without getting at least something of the same brotherhood for the enemy that the north pole of a magnet has for the south. . . ."

This is the Southern story, as we read it in the records, have heard it from the lips of old men, or see it in the powerful projections of Faulkner's imagination. But it is more than the Southern story. It is a communal story, as Lincoln said in the Second Inaugural: God gave "to both North and South this terrible war, as the woe due to those by whom the offense came. . . ."

The communal aspect of the story, as Lincoln puts it, means communal guilt as well as communal reconciliation. But in what sense? A writer in the *Journal* of Evansville, Indiana, back in 1861, had taken it that the guilt of the North was in having "winked at the wrongful business" of slavery. Therefore, he said, "the North must not expect to escape the penalty of her lack of principle. She must suffer like the South." Lincoln could scarcely have meant anything that simple; Lincoln had a very clear mind, and the writer of Evansville, Indiana, implies one or the other of two very dubious propositions. First, that if the North had ceased to "wink," there would have been no war; or second, that if there had been a war, it would, somehow, have been without suffering.

No, we may hazard that what Lincoln had in mind is a deeper and more complex communal involvement in the event, and in the history of the event, an involvement of all the unworthiness and blunderings of human nature, even of virtues perverted by being abstracted from the proper human context.

From the guilt we turn to the purgation of the Gettysburg Address: "The brave men, living and dead, who struggled here have consecrated it [the cemetery] far above our poor power to add or detract." The soil is hallowed, if Carl Sandburg is right in his reading, by the blood shed communally, the blood of men dying valorously in the common tragic entrapment, and by their valor rising to dignity beyond the entrapment.

Or we can turn to that profoundly revealing moment, shot through with deep ambiguities, when Lincoln, returning by water to Washington from his visit to the fallen Richmond and the headquarters of the victorious army, paused over a passage of the play of Shakespeare which he was reading to his companions. The words he paused to brood over and repeat are, at first glance, peculiar—not words about the ambitious and murderous Macbeth, but words about the good dead victim:

> Duncan is in his grave;
> After life's fitful fever he sleeps well;
> Treason has done his worst; nor steel, nor poison,
> Malice domestic, foreign levy, nothing,
> Can touch him further.

What comes over to us in this strange moment is no easy applicability, schematically perfect, to the occasion, but rather, the tragic aura of the event. The tone is that of the end of Herman Melville's Supplement to *Battle Pieces,* his poems of the Civil War, issued in 1866: "Let us pray that the terrible historic tragedy of our time may not have been enacted without instructing our whole beloved country through pity and terror. . . ."

Have we been "instructed" by that catharsis of pity and terror?

Sadly, we must answer no. We have not yet achieved justice. We have not yet created a union which is, in the deepest sense, a community. We have not yet resolved our deep dubieties or self-deceptions. In other words, we are sadly human, and in our contemplation of the Civil War we see a dramatization of our humanity; one appeal of the War is that it holds in suspension, beyond all schematic readings and claims to total interpretation, so many of the issues and tragic ironies —somehow essential yet incommensurable—which we yet live.

But there is a deeper appeal. Beyond the satisfaction it may give to rancor, self-righteousness, spite, pride, spiritual pride, vindictiveness, armchair blood lust, and complacency, we can yet see in the Civil War an image of the powerful, painful, grinding process by which an ideal emerges out of history. That should teach us humility beyond the Great Alibi and the Treasury of Virtue, but at the same time, it draws us to the glory of the human effort to win meaning from the complex and confused motives of men and the blind ruck of event.

Looking back on the years 1861–65 we see how the individual men, despite failings, blindness, and vice, may affirm for us the possibility of the dignity of life. It is a tragic dignity that their story affirms, but it may evoke strength. And in the contemplation of the story, some of that grandeur, even in the midst of the confused issues, shadowy chances, and brutal ambivalences of our life and historical moment, may rub off on us. And that may be what we yearn for, after all.

POETRY

*This symbol is used to indicate a space between sections of a poem wherever such spaces are lost in pagination.

THE RETURN: AN ELEGY

The east wind finds the gap bringing rain:
Rain in the pine wind shaking the stiff pine.
Beneath the wind the hollow gorges whine.
The pines decline.
Slow film of rain creeps own the loam again
Where the blind and nameless bones recline.

   all are conceded to the earth's absolute chemistry
   they burn like faggots in—of damp and dark—the monstrous
                                bulging flame.
   calcium phosphate lust speculation faith treachery
   it walked upright with habitation and a name

    tell me its name

The pines, black, like combers plunge with spray
Lick the wind's unceasing keel.
It is not long till day
The boughs like hairy swine in slaughter squeal.
They lurch beneath the thunder's livid heel.
The pines, black, snore *what does the wind say?*

    tell me its name

I have a name: I am not blind.
Eyes, not blind, press to the Pullman pane
Survey the driving dark and silver taunt of rain.
What will I find

What will I find beyond the snoring pine?
O eyes locked blind in death's immaculate design
Shall fix their last distrust in mine.

> give me the nickels off your eyes
> from your hands the violets
> let me bless your obsequies
> if you possessed conveniently enough three eyes
> then I could buy a pack of cigarettes

In gorges where the dead fox lies the fern
Will rankest loop the battened frond and fall
Above the bare tushed jaws that turn
Their insolence unto the gracious catafalque and pall.
It will be the season when milkweed blossoms burn.

> the old bitch is dead
> what have I said!
> I have only said what the wind said
> wind shakes a bell the hollow head

By dawn, the wind, the blown rain
Will cease their antique concitation.
It is the hour when old ladies cough and wake,
The chair, the table, take their form again
And earth begins the matinal exhalation.

> *does my mother wake*

Pines drip without motion.
The hairy boughs no longer shake.
Shaggy mist, crookbacked, ascends.
Round hairy boughs the mist with shaggy fingers bends.
No wind: no rain:
Why do the steady pines complain?
Complain

> *the old fox is dead*
> what have I said

*

Locked in the roaring cubicle
Over the mountains through darkness hurled
I race the daylight's westward cycle
Across the groaning rooftree of the world.
The mist is furled.

   a hundred years they took this road
   the lank hunters then men hard-eyed with hope:
   ox breath whitened the chill air: the goad
   fell: here on the western slope
   the hungry people the lost ones took their abode
   here they took their stand:
   alders bloomed on the road to the new land
   here is the house the broken door the shed
   the old fox is dead

The wheels hum hum
The wheels: I come I come.
Whirl out of space through time O wheels
Pursue down backward time the ghostly parallels
Pursue past culvert cut embankment semaphore
Pursue down gleaming hours that are no more.
The pines, black, snore

   turn backward turn backward O time in your flight
   and make me a child again just for tonight
   good lord he's wet the bed come bring a light

What grief has the mind distilled?
The heart is unfulfilled
The hoarse pine stilled.
I cannot pluck
Out of this land of pine and rock
Of red bud their season not yet gone
If I could pluck
(In drouth the lizard will blink on the hot limestone)

   the old fox is dead
   what is said is said
   heaven rest the hoary head

what have I said!
. . . I have only said what the wind said
honor thy father and mother in the days of thy youth
for time uncoils like the cottonmouth

If I could pluck
Out of the dark that whirled
Over the hoarse pine over the rock
Out of the mist that furled
Could I stretch forth like God the hand and gather
For you my mother
If I could pluck
Against the dry essential of tomorrow
To lay upon the breast that gave me suck
Out of the dark the dark and swollen orchid of this sorrow.

KENTUCKY MOUNTAIN FARM

I. REBUKE OF THE ROCKS

Now on you is the hungry equinox,
O little stubborn people of the hill,
The season of the obscene moon whose pull
Disturbs the sod, the rabbit, the lank fox,
Moving the waters, the boar's dull blood,
And the acrid sap of the ironwood.

But breed no tender thing among the rocks.
Rocks are too old under the mad moon,
Renouncing passion by the strength that locks
The eternal agony of fire in stone.

Then quit yourselves as stone and cease
To break the weary stubble-field for seed;
Let not the naked cattle bear increase,
Let barley wither and the bright milkweed.

Instruct the heart, lean men, of a rocky place
That even the little flesh and fevered bone
May keep the sweet sterility of stone.

II. AT THE HOUR OF THE
BREAKING OF THE ROCKS

Beyond the wrack and eucharist of snow
The tortured and reluctant rock again
Receives the sunlight and the tarnished rain.
Such is the hour of sundering we know,
Who on the hills have seen stand and pass
Stubbornly the taciturn
Lean men that of all things alone
Were, not as water or the febrile grass,
Figured in kinship to the savage stone.

The hills are weary, the lean men have passed;
The rocks are stricken, and the frost has torn
Away their ridged fundaments at last,
So that the fractured atoms now are borne
Down shifting waters to the tall, profound
Shadow of the absolute deeps,
Wherein the spirit moves and never sleeps
That held the foot among the rocks, that bound
The tired hand upon the stubborn plow,
Knotted the flesh unto the hungry bone,
The redbud to the charred and broken bough,
And strung the bitter tendons of the stone.

III. HISTORY AMONG THE ROCKS

There are many ways to die
Here among the rocks in any weather:
Wind, down the eastern gap, will lie
Level along the snow, beating the cedar,
And lull the drowsy head that it blows over
To startle a cold and crystalline dream forever.

The hound's black paw will print the grass in May,
And sycamores rise down a dark ravine,

Where a creek in flood, sucking the rock and clay,
Will tumble the laurel, the sycamore away.
Think how a body, naked and lean
And white as the splintered sycamore, would go
Tumbling and turning, hushed in the end,
With hair afloat in waters that gently bend
To ocean where the blind tides flow.

Under the shadow of ripe wheat,
By flat limestone, will coil the copperhead,
Fanged as the sunlight, hearing the reaper's feet.
But there are other ways, the lean men said:
In these autumn orchards once young men lay dead—
Gray coats, blue coats. Young men on the mountainside
Clambered, fought. Heels muddied the rocky spring.
Their reason is hard to guess, remembering
Blood on their black mustaches in moonlight.
Their reason is hard to guess and a long time past:
The apple falls, falling in the quiet night.

IV. WATERSHED

From this high place all things flow.
Land of divided streams, of water spilled
Eastward, westward, without memento . . .
Land where the morning mist is furled
Like smoke above the ridgepole of the world.

The sunset hawk now rides
The tall light up the climbing deep of air.
Beneath him swings the rooftree that divides
The east and west. His gold eyes scan
The crumpled shade on gorge and crest
And streams that creep and disappear, appear,
Past fingered ridges and their shrivelling span.
Under the broken eaves men take their rest.

Forever, should they stir, their thought would keep
This place. Not love, happiness past, constrains,
But certitude. Enough, and it remains,
Though they who thread the flood and neap

Of earth itself have felt the earth creep;
In pastures hung against the rustling gorge
Have felt the shuddering and sweat of stone,
Knowing thereby no constant moon
Sustains the hill's lost granite surge.

V. THE RETURN

Burly and clean, with bark in umber scrolled
About the sunlit bole's own living white,
The sycamore stood, drenched in the autumn light.
The same old tree. Again the timeless gold
Broad leaf released the tendoned bough, and slow,
Uncertain as a casual memory,
Wavered aslant the ripe unmoving air.
Up from the whiter bough, the bluer sky,
That glimmered in the water's depth below,
A richer leaf rose to the other there.
They touched; with the gentle clarity of dream,
Bosom to bosom, burned, one on, one in, the quiet stream.

But, backward heart, you have no voice to call
Your image back, the vagrant image again.
The tree, the leaf falling, the stream, and all
Familiar faithless things would yet remain
Voiceless. And he, who had loved as well as most,
Might have foretold it thus, for well he knew
How, glimmering, a buried world is lost
In the water's riffle or the wind's flaw;
How his own image, perfect and deep
And small within loved eyes, had been forgot,
Her face being turned, or when those eyes were shut
Past light in that fond accident of sleep.

PONDY WOODS

The buzzards over Pondy Woods
Achieve the blue tense altitudes,
Black figments that the woods release,
Obscenity in form and grace,
Drifting high through the pure sunshine
Till the sun in gold decline.

Big Jim Todd was a slick black buck
Laying low in the mud and muck
Of Pondy Woods when the sun went down
In gold, and the buzzards tilted down
A windless vortex to the black-gum trees
To sit along the quiet boughs,
Devout and swollen, at their ease.

By the buzzard roost Big Jim Todd
Listened for hoofs on the corduroy road
Or for the foul and sucking sound
A man's foot makes on the marshy ground.
Past midnight, when the moccasin
Slipped from the log and, trailing in
Its obscured waters, broke
The dark algae, one lean bird spoke.

"Nigger, you went this afternoon
For your Saturday spree at the Blue Goose saloon,
So you've got on your Sunday clothes,
On your big splay feet got patent-leather shoes.
But a buzzard can smell the thing you've done;
The posse will get you—run, nigger, run—
There's a fellow behind you with a big shot-gun.
Nigger, nigger, you'll sweat cold sweat
In your patent-leather shoes and Sunday clothes
When down your track the steeljacket goes
Mean and whimpering over the wheat.

*

"Nigger, your breed ain't metaphysical."
The buzzard coughed. His words fell
In the darkness, mystic and ambrosial.
"But we maintain our ancient rite,
Eat the gods by day and prophesy by night.
We swing against the sky and wait;
You seize the hour, more passionate
Than strong, and strive with time to die—
With Time, the beaked tribe's astute ally.

"The Jew-boy died. The Syrian vulture swung
Remotely above the cross whereon he hung
From dinner-time to supper-time, and all
The people gathered there watched him until
The lean brown chest no longer stirred,
Then idly watched the slow majestic bird
That in the last sun above the twilit hill
Gleamed for a moment at the height and slid
Down the hot wind and in the darkness hid.
Nigger, regard the circumstance of breath:
Non omnis moriar, the poet saith."

Pedantic, the bird clacked its gray beak,
With a Tennessee accent to the classic phrase;
Jim understood, and was about to speak,
But the buzzard drooped one wing and filmed the eyes.

At dawn unto the Sabbath wheat he came,
That gave to the dew its faithless yellow flame
From kindly loam in recollection of
The fires that in the brutal rock once strove.
To the ripe wheat fields he came at dawn.
Northward the printed smoke stood quiet above
The distant cabins of Squiggtown.
A train's far whistle blew and drifted away
Coldly; lucid and thin the morning lay
Along the farms, and here no sound
Touched the sweet earth miraculously stilled.
Then down the damp and sudden wood there belled
The musical white-throated hound.

*

In Pondy Woods in the summer's drouth
Lurk fever and the cottonmouth.
And buzzards over Pondy Woods
Achieve the blue tense altitudes,
Drifting high in the pure sunshine
Till the sun in gold decline;
Then golden and hieratic through
The night their eyes burn two by two.

HISTORY

Past crag and scarp,
At length way won:
And done
The chert's sharp
Incision,
The track-flint's bite.
Now done, the belly's lack,
Belt tight
—The shrunk sack,
Corn spent, meats foul,
The dry gut-growl.

Now we have known the last,
And can appraise
Pain past.
We came bad ways,
The watercourses
Dry,
No herb for horses.
(We slew them shamefastly,
Dodging their gaze.)
Sleet came some days,
At night no fuel.

*

And so, thin-wrapt,
We slept:
Forgot the frosty nostril,
Joints rotten and the ulcered knee,
The cold-kibed heel,
The cracked lip.
It was bad country of no tree,
Of abrupt landslip,
The glacier's snore.
Much man can bear.

How blind the passes were!

And now
We see, below,
The delicate landscape unfurled,
A world
Of ripeness blent, and green,
The fruited earth,
Fire on the good hearth,
The fireside scene.
(Those people have no name,
Who shall know dearth
And flame.)
It is a land of corn and kine,
Of milk
And wine,
And beds that are as silk:
The gentle thigh,
The unlit night-lamp nigh.
This much was prophesied:
We shall possess,
And abide
—Nothing less.
We may not be denied.
The inhabitant shall flee as the fox.
His foot shall be among the rocks.

In the new land
Our seed shall prosper, and
In those unsifted times

Our sons shall cultivate
Peculiar crimes,
Having not love, nor hate,
Nor memory.
Though some,
Of all most weary,
Most defective of desire,
Shall grope toward time's cold womb;
In dim pools peer
To see, of some grandsire,
The long and toothèd jawbone greening there.
(O Time, for them the aimless bitch
—Purblind, field-worn,
Slack dugs by the dry thorn torn—
Forever quartering the ground in which
The blank and fanged
Rough certainty lies hid.)

Now at our back
The night wind lifts,
Rain in the wind.
Downward the darkness shifts.
It is the hour for attack.
Wind fondles, far below, the leaves of the land,
Freshening the arbor.
Recall our honor,
And descend.
We seek what end?
The slow dynastic ease,
Travail's cease?
Not pleasure, sure:
Alloy of fact?
The act
Alone is pure.
What appetency knows the flood,
What thirst, the sword?
What name
Sustains the core of flame?
We are the blade,
But not the hand
By which the blade is swayed.

Time falls, but has no end.
Descend!

The gentle path suggests our feet;
The bride's surrender will be sweet.
We shall essay
The rugged ritual, but not of anger.
Let us go down before
Our thews are latched in the myth's languor,
Our hearts with fable gray.

LATE SUBTERFUGE

The year dulls toward its eaves-dripping end.
We have kept honor yet, or lost a friend;
Observed at length the inherited defect;
Known error's pang—but then, what man is perfect?
The grackles, yellow-beaked, beak-southward, fly
To the ruined ricelands south, leaving empty our sky.

This year was time for decision to be made.
No time to waste, we said, and so we said:
This year is time. Our grief can be endured,
For we, at least, are men, being inured
To wrath, to the unjust act, if need, to blood;
And we have faith that from evil may bloom good.

Our feet in the sopping woods will make no sound,
The winter's rot begun, the fox in ground,
The snake cold-coiled, secret in cane the weasel.
In pairs we walk, heads bowed to the long drizzle—
With women some, and take their rain-cold kiss;
We say to ourselves we learn some strength from this.

RANSOM

Old houses, and new-fangled violence;
Old bottles but new wine, and newly spilled.
Doom has, we know, no shape but the shape of air.
That much for us the red-armed augurs spelled,
Or flights of fowl lost early in the long air.

The mentioned act: barbarous, bloody, extreme,
And fraught with bane. The actors: nameless and
With faces turned (I cannot make them out).
Christ bled, indeed, but after fasting and
Bad diet of the poor; wherefore thin blood came out.

What wars and lecheries! and the old zeal
Yet unfulfilled, unrarefied, unlaced.
At night the old man coughs: thus history
Strikes sum, ere dawn in rosy buskins laced
Delivers cool with dew the recent news-story.

Defeat is possible, and the stars rise.
Our courage needs, perhaps, new definition.
By night, my love, and noon, infirm of will
And young, we may endeavor definition;
Though frail as the claspèd dream beneath the blanket's wool.

THE GARDEN

On prospect of a fine day in early autumn

How kind, how secret, now the sun
Will bless this garden frost has won,
And touch once more, as once it used,
The furled boughs by cold bemused.
Though summered brilliance had but room

In blossom, now the leaves will bloom
Their time, and take from milder sun
An unreviving benison.

No marbles whitely gaze among
These paths where gilt the late pear hung:
But branches interlace to frame
The avenue of stately flame
Where yonder, far more bold and pure
Than marble, gleams the sycamore,
Of argent torse and cunning shaft
Propped nobler than the sculptor's craft.

The hand that crooked upon the spade
Here plucked the peach, and thirst allayed;
Here lovers paused before the kiss,
Instructed of what ripeness is:
Where all who came might stand to prove
The grace of this imperial grove,
Now jay and cardinal debate,
Like twin usurpers, the ruined state.

But he who sought, not love, but peace
In such rank plot could take no ease:
Now poised between the two alarms
Of summer's lusts and winter's harms,
Only for him these precincts wait
In sacrament that can translate
All things that fed luxurious sense
From appetite to innocence.

TO A FACE IN A CROWD

Brother, my brother, whither do you pass?
Unto what hill at dawn, unto what glen,

Where among the rocks the faint lascivious grass
Fingers in lust the arrogant bones of men?

Beside what bitter waters will you go
Where the lean gulls of your heart along the shore
Rehearse to the cliffs the rhetoric of their woe?
In dream, perhaps, I have seen your face before.

A certain night has borne both you and me;
We are the children of an ancient band
Broken between the mountains and the sea.
A cromlech marks for you that utmost strand

And you must find the dolorous place they stood.
Of old I know that shore, that dim terrain,
And know how black and turbulent the blood
Will beat through iron chambers of the brain

When at your back the taciturn tall stone,
Which is your fathers' monument and mark,
Repeats the waves' implacable monotone,
Ascends the night and propagates the dark.

Men there have lived who wrestled with the ocean;
I was afraid—the polyp was their shroud.
I was afraid. That shore of your decision
Awaits beyond this street where in the crowd

Your face is blown, an apparition, past.
Renounce the night as I, and we must meet
As weary nomads in this desert at last,
Borne in the lost procession of these feet.

ELEVEN POEMS
ON THE SAME THEME
(1942)

MONOLOGUE AT MIDNIGHT

Among the pines we ran and called
In joy and innocence, and still
Our voices doubled in the high
Green groining our simplicity.

And we have heard the windward hound
Bell in the frosty vault of dark.
(Then what pursuit?) How soundlessly
The maple shed its pollen in the sun.

Season by season from the skein
Unwound, of earth and of our pleasure;
And always at the side, like guilt,
Our shadows over the grasses moved,

Or moved across the moonlit snow;
And move across the grass or snow.
Or was it guilt? Philosophers
Loll in their disputatious ease.

The match flame sudden in the gloom
Is lensed within each watching eye
Less intricate, less small, than in
One heart the other's image is.

The hound, the echo, flame, or shadow—
And which am I and which are you?

And are we Time who flee so fast,
Or stone who stand, and thus endure?

Our mathematic yet has use
For the integers of blessedness:
Listen! the poor deluded cock
Salutes the coldness of no dawn.

BEARDED OAKS

The oaks, how subtle and marine,
Bearded, and all the layered light
Above them swims; and thus the scene,
Recessed, awaits the positive night.

So, waiting, we in the grass now lie
Beneath the languorous tread of light:
The grasses, kelp-like, satisfy
The nameless motions of the air.

Upon the floor of light, and time,
Unmurmuring, of polyp made,
We rest; we are, as light withdraws,
Twin atolls on a shelf of shade.

Ages to our construction went,
Dim architecture, hour by hour:
And violence, forgot now, lent
The present stillness all its power.

The storm of noon above us rolled,
Of light the fury, furious gold,
The long drag troubling us, the depth:
Dark is unrocking, unrippling, still.

Passion and slaughter, ruth, decay
Descend, minutely whispering down,

Silted down swaying streams, to lay
Foundation for our voicelessness.

All our debate is voiceless here,
As all our rage, the rage of stone;
If hope is hopeless, then fearless is fear,
And history is thus undone.

Our feet once wrought the hollow street
With echo when the lamps were dead
At windows, once our headlight glare
Disturbed the doe that, leaping, fled.

I do not love you less that now
The caged heart makes iron stroke,
Or less that all that light once gave
The graduate dark should now revoke.

We live in time so little time
And we learn all so painfully,
That we may spare this hour's term
To practice for eternity.

PICNIC REMEMBERED

That day, so innocent appeared
The leaf, the hill, the sky, to us,
Their structures so harmonious
And pure, that all we had endured
Seemed the quaint disaster of a child,
Now cupboarded, and all the wild
Grief canceled; so with what we feared.

We stood among the painted trees:
The amber light laved them, and us;
Or light then so untremulous,

So steady, that our substances,
Twin flies, were as in amber tamed
With our perfections stilled and framed
To mock Time's marveling after-spies.

Joy, strongest medium, then buoyed
Us when we moved, as swimmers, who,
Relaxed, resign them to the flow
And pause of their unstained flood.
Thus wrapped, sustained, we did not know
How darkness darker staired below;
Or knowing, but half understood.

The bright deception of that day!
When we so readily could gloze
All pages opened to expose
The trust we never would betray;
But darkness on the landscape grew
As in our bosoms darkness, too;
And that was what we took away.

And it abides, and may abide:
Though ebbed from the region happier mapped,
Our hearts, like hollow stones, have trapped
A corner of that brackish tide.
The jaguar breath, the secret wrong,
The curse that curls the sudden tongue,
We know; for fears have fructified.

Or are we dead, that we, unmanned,
Are vacant, and our clearest souls
Are sped where each with each patrols,
In still society, hand in hand,
That scene where we, too, wandered once
Who now inherit a new province:
Love's limbo, this lost under-land?

The *then*, the *now:* each cenotaph
Of the other, and proclaims it dead.
Or is the soul a hawk that, fled
On glimmering wings past vision's path,

Reflects the last gleam to us here
Though sun is sunk and darkness near
—Uncharted Truth's high heliograph?

ORIGINAL SIN: A SHORT STORY

Nodding, its great head rattling like a gourd,
And locks like seaweed strung on the stinking stone,
The nightmare stumbles past, and you have heard
It fumble your door before it whimpers and is gone:
It acts like the old hound that used to snuffle your door and moan.

You thought you had lost it when you left Omaha,
For it seemed connected then with your grandpa, who
Had a wen on his forehead and sat on the veranda
To finger the precious protuberance, as was his habit to do,
Which glinted in sun like rough garnet or the rich old brain
$\qquad$ bulging through.

But you met it in Harvard Yard as the historic steeple
Was confirming the midnight with its hideous racket,
And you wondered how it had come, for it stood so imbecile,
With empty hands, humble, and surely nothing in pocket:
Riding the rods, perhaps—or Grandpa's will paid the ticket.

You were almost kindly then, in your first homesickness,
As it tortured its stiff face to speak, but scarcely mewed.
Since then you have outlived all your homesickness,
But have met it in many another distempered latitude:
Oh, nothing is lost, ever lost! at last you understood.

It never came in the quantum glare of sun
To shame you before your friends, and had nothing to do
With your public experience or private reformation:
But it thought no bed too narrow—it stood with lips askew
And shook its great head sadly like the abstract Jew.

*

Never met you in the lyric arsenical meadow
When children call and your heart goes stone in the bosom—
At the orchard anguish never, nor ovoid horror,
Which is furred like a peach or avid like the delicious plum.
It takes no part in your classic prudence or fondled axiom.

Not there when you exclaimed: "Hope is betrayed by
Disastrous glory of sea-capes, sun-torment of whitecaps
—There must be a new innocence for us to be stayed by."
But there it stood, after all the timetables, all the maps,
In the crepuscular clutter of *always, always,* or *perhaps.*

You have moved often and rarely left an address,
And hear of the deaths of friends with a sly pleasure,
A sense of cleansing and hope which blooms from distress;
But it has not died, it comes, its hand childish, unsure,
Clutching the bribe of chocolate or a toy you used to treasure.

It tries the lock. You hear, but simply drowse:
There is nothing remarkable in that sound at the door.
Later you may hear it wander the dark house
Like a mother who rises at night to seek a childhood picture;
Or it goes to the backyard and stands like an old horse cold in the
                                                                    pasture.

REVELATION

Because he had spoken harshly to his mother,
The day became astonishingly bright,
The enormity of distance crept to him like a dog now,
And earth's own luminescence seemed to repel the night.

Rent was the roof like loud paper to admit
Sun-sulphurous splendor where had been before
But a submarine glimmer by kindly countenances lit,
As slow, phosphorescent dignities light the ocean floor.

*

By walls, by walks, chrysanthemum and aster,
All hairy, fat-petaled species, lean, confer,
And his ears, and heart, should burn at that insidious whisper
Which concerns him so, he knows; but he cannot make out the
                                                            words.

The peacock screamed, and his feathered fury made
Legend shake, all day, while the sky ran pale as milk;
That night, all night, the buck rabbit stamped in the moonlit glade,
And the owl's brain glowed like a coal in the grove's combustible
                                                            dark.

When Sulla smote and Rome was racked, Augustine
Recalled how Nature, shuddering, tore her gown,
And kind changed kind, and the blunt herbivorous tooth dripped
                                                            blood;
At Inverness, at Duncan's death, chimneys blew down.

But, oh! his mother was kinder than ever Rome,
Dearer than Duncan—no wonder, then, Nature's frame
Thrilled in voluptuous hemispheres far off from his home;
But not in terror: only as the bride, as the bride.

In separateness only does love learn definition,
Though Brahma smiles beneath the dappled shade,
Though tears, that night, wet the pillow where the boy's head was
                                                            laid,
Dreamless of splendid antipodal agitation;

And though across what tide and tooth Time is,
He was to lean back toward that irredeemable face,
He would think, than Sulla more fortunate, how once he had
                                                            learned
Something important above love, and about love's grace.

SELECTED POEMS: 1923-1943

THE BALLAD OF BILLIE POTTS

(When I was a child I heard this story from an old lady who was a relative of mine. The scene, according to her version, was in the section of western Kentucky known as "Between the Rivers," the region between the Cumberland and the Tennessee. The name of Bardstown in the present account refers to Bardstown, Kentucky, where, it is said, the first race track west of the mountains was laid out late in the eighteenth century.)

Big Billie Potts was big and stout
In the land between the rivers
His shoulders were wide and his gut stuck out
Like a croker of nubbins and his holler and shout
Made the bob-cat shiver and the black-jack leaves shake
In the section between the rivers.
He would slap you on your back and laugh.

Big Billie had a wife, she was dark and little
In the land between the rivers,
And clever with her wheel and clever with her kettle,
But she never said a word and when she sat
By the fire her eyes worked slow and narrow like a cat.
Nobody knew what was in her head.

They had a big boy with fuzz on his chin
So tall he ducked the door when he came in,
A clabber-headed bastard with snot in his nose
And big red wrists hanging out of his clothes
And a whicker when he laughed where his father had a bellow
In the section between the rivers.

They called him Little Billie.
He was their darling.

(It is not hard to see the land, what it was.
Low hills and oak. The fetid bottoms where
The slough uncoils, and in the tangled cane,
Where no sun comes, the muskrat's astute face
Is lifted to the yammering jay; then dropped.
A cabin where the shagbark stood and the
Magnificent tulip-tree; both now are gone.
But the land is there, and as you top a rise,
Beyond you all the landscape steams and simmers
—The hills, now gutted, red, cane-brake and black-jack yet.

The oak leaf steams under the powerful sun.
"Mister, is this the right road to Paducah?"
The red face, seamed and gutted like the hill,
Slow under time, and with the innocent savagery
Of Time, the bleared eyes rolling, answers from
Your dream: "They names hit so, but I ain't bin.")

Big Billie was the kind who laughed but could spy
The place for a ferry where folks would come by.
He built an inn and folks bound West
Hitched their horses there to take their rest
And grease the gall and grease the belly
And jaw and spit under the trees
In the section between the rivers.
Big Billie said: "Git down, friend, and take yore ease!"
He would slap you on your back and set you at his table.

(Leaning and slow, you see them move
In massive passion colder than any love:
Their lips move but you do not hear the words,
Nor trodden twig nor fluted irony of birds,
Nor hear the rustle of the heart
That, heave and settle, gasp and start,
Heaves like a fish in the ribs' dark basket borne
West from the great water's depth whence it was torn.

Their names are like the leaves, but are forgot
—The slush and swill of the world's great pot

That foamed at the Appalachian lip, and spilled
Like quicksilver across green baize, the unfulfilled
Disparate glitter, gleam, wild symptom, seed
Flung in the long wind: silent, they proceed
Past meadow, salt-lick, and the lyric swale;
Enter the arbor, shadow of trees, fade, fail.)

Big Billie was sharp at swap and trade
And could smell the nest where the egg was laid.
He could read and cipher and they called him squire,
And he added up his money while he sat by the fire,
And sat in the shade while folks sweated and strove,
For he was the one who fatted and throve
In the section between the rivers.
"Thank you kindly, sir," Big Billie would say
When the man in the black coat paid him at streak of day
And swung to the saddle, was ready to go,
And rode away and didn't know
That he was already as good as dead,
For at midnight the message had been sent ahead:
"Man in black coat, riding bay mare with star."

(There was a beginning but you cannot see it.
There will be an end but you cannot see it.
They will not turn their faces to you though you call,
Who pace a logic merciless as light,
Whose law is their long shadow on the grass,
Sun at the back; who pace, pass,
And passing nod in that glacial delirium
While the tight sky shudders like a drum
And speculation rasps its idiot nails
Across the dry slate where you did the sum.

The answer is in the back of the book but the page is gone.
And Grandma told you to tell the truth, but she is dead.
And heedless, their hairy faces fixed
Beyond your call or question now, they move
Under the infatuate weight of their wisdom,
Precious but for the preciousness of their burden,
Sainted and sad and sage as the hairy ass, these who bear
History like bound faggots, with stiff knees;

And breathe the immaculate climate where
The lucent leaf is lifted, lank beard fingered, by no breeze,
Rapt in the fabulous complacency of fresco, vase, or frieze:

And the testicles of the fathers hang down like old lace.)

Little Billie was full of vinegar
And full of sap as a maple tree
And full of tricks as a lop-eared pup,
So one night when the runner didn't show up,
Big Billie called Little and said, "Saddle up,"
And nodded toward the man who was taking his sup
With his belt unlatched and his feet to the fire.
Big Billie said, "Give Amos a try.
Fer this feller takes the South Fork and Amos'll be nigher
Than Badly or Buster, and Amos is sly
And slick as a varmint, and I don't deny
I lak business with Amos, fer he's one you kin trust
In the section between the rivers,
And it looks lak they's mighty few.
Amos will split up fair and square."

Little Billie had something in his clabber-head
By way of brains, and he reckoned he knew
How to skin a cat or add two and two.
So long before the sky got red
Over the land between the rivers,
He hobbled his horse back in the swamp
And squatted on his hams in the morning dew and damp
And scratched his stomach and grinned to think
How Pap would be proud and Mammy glad
To know what a thriving boy they had.
He always was a good boy to his darling Mammy.

(Think of yourself riding away from the dawn,
Think of yourself and the unnamed ones who had gone
Before, riding, who rode away from *goodbye, goodbye,*
And toward *hello,* toward Time's unwinking eye;
And like the cicada had left, at cross-roads or square,
The old shell of self, thin, ghostly, translucent, light as air;
At dawn riding into the curtain of unwhispering green,

Away from the vigils and voices into the green
World, land of the innocent bough, land of the leaf.
Think of your own face green in the submarine light of the leaf.

Or think of yourself crouched at the swamp-edge:
Dawn-silence past last owl-hoot and not yet at day-verge
First bird-stir, titmouse or drowsy warbler not yet.
You touch the grass in the dark and your hand is wet.
Then light: and you wait for the stranger's hoofs on the soft trace,
And under the green leaf's translucence the light bathes your face.

Think of yourself at dawn: Which one are you? What?)

Little Billie heard hoofs on the soft grass,
But squatted and let the rider pass,
For he wouldn't waste good lead and powder
Just to make the slough-fish and swamp-buzzards prouder
In the land between the rivers.
But he saw the feller's face and thanked his luck
It's the one Pap said was fit to pluck.
So he got on his horse and cantered up the trace.
Called, "Hi thar!" and the stranger watched him coming,
And sat his mare with a smile on his face,
Just watching Little Billie and smiling and humming.
Little Billie rode up and the stranger said,
"Why, bless my heart, if it ain't Little Billie!"

"Good mornen," said Billie, and said, "My Pap
Found somethen you left and knowed you'd be missen,
And Pap don't want nuthen not proper his'n."
But the stranger didn't do a thing but smile and listen
Polite as could be to what Billie said.
But he must have had eyes in the side of his head
As they rode along beside the slough
In the land between the rivers,
Or guessed what Billie was out to do,
For when Billie said, "Mister, I've brung it to you,"
And reached his hand for it down in his britches,
The stranger just reached his own hand, too.

*

"Boom!" Billie's gun said, and the derringer, "Bang!"
"Oh, I'm shot!" Billie howled and grabbed his shoulder.
"Not bad," said the stranger, "for you're born to hang,
But I'll save some rope 'fore you're a minute older
If you don't high-tail to your honest Pap
In the section between the rivers."
Oh, Billie didn't tarry and Billie didn't linger,
For Billie didn't trust the stranger's finger
And didn't admire the stranger's face
And didn't like the climate of the place,
So he turned and high-tailed up the trace,
With blood on his shirt and snot in his nose
And pee in his pants, for he'd wet his clothes,
And the stranger just sits and admires how he goes,
And says, "Why, that boy would do right well back on the
                                            Bardstown track!"

"You fool!" said his Pap, but his Mammy cried
To see the place where the gore-blood dried
Round the little hole in her darling's hide.
She wiped his nose and patted his head,
But Pappy barred the door and Pappy said,
"Two hundred in gold's in my money belt,
And take the roan and the brand-new saddle
And stop yore blubberen and skeedaddle,
And next time you try and pull a trick
Fer God's sake don't talk but do it quick."

So Little Billie took his leave
And left his Mammy there to grieve
And left his Pappy in Old Kaintuck
And headed West to try his luck,
For it was Roll, Missouri,
It was Roll, roll, Missouri.
And he was gone nigh ten long year
And never sent word to give his Pappy cheer
Nor wet pen in ink for his Mammy dear.
For Little Billie never was much of a hand with a pen-staff.

(There is always another country and always another place.
There is always another name and another face.

And the name and the face are you, and you
The name and the face, and the stream you gaze into
Will show the adoring face, show the lips that lift to you
As you lean with the implacable thirst of self,
As you lean to the image which is yourself,
To set lip to lip, fix eye on bulging eye,
To drink not of the stream but of your deep identity,
But water is water and it flows,
Under the image on the water the water coils and goes
And its own beginning and its end only the water knows.

There are many countries and the rivers in them
—Cumberland, Tennessee, Ohio, Colorado, Pecos, Little Bighorn,
And Roll, Missouri, roll.
But there is only water in them.

And in the new country and in the new place
The eyes of the new friend will reflect the new face
And his mouth will speak to frame
The syllables of the new name
And the name is you and is the agitation of the air
And is the wind and the wind runs and the wind is everywhere.

The name and the face are you.
The name and the face are always new,
But they are you,
And new.

For they have been dipped in the healing flood.
For they have been dipped in the redeeming blood.
For they have been dipped in Time.
For Time is always the new place,
And no-place.
For Time is always the new name and the new face,
And no-name and no-face.

For Time is motion
For Time is innocence
For Time is West.)

*

Oh, who is coming along the trace,
Whistling along in the late sunshine,
With a big black hat above his big red face
And a long black coat that swings so fine?
Oh, who is riding along the trace
Back to the land between the rivers,
With a big black beard growing down to his guts
And silver mountings on his pistol-butts
And a belt as broad as a saddle-girth
And a look in his eyes like he owned the earth?
And meets a man riding up the trace
And squints right sharp and scans his face
And says, "Durn, if it ain't Joe Drew!"
"I reckin it's me," says Joe and gives a spit,
"But whupped if I figger how you knows it,
Fer if I'm Joe, then who air you?"
And the man with the black beard says: "Why, I'm Little Billie!"
And Joe Drew says: "Wal, I'll be whupped."

"Be whupped," Joe said, "and whar you goen?"
"Oh, just visiten back whar I done my growen
In the section between the rivers,
Fer I bin out West and taken my share
And I reckin my luck helt out fer fair,
So I done come home," Little Billie said,
"To see my folks if they ain't dead."
"Ain't dead," Joe answered, and shook his head,
"But that's the best a man kin say,
Fer it looked lak when you went away
You taken West yore Pappy's luck."
Little Billie jingled his pockets and said: "Ain't nuthen wrong with
                                                    my luck."

And said: "Wal, I'll be gitten on home,
But after yore supper why don't you come
And we'll open a jug and you tell me the news
In the section between the rivers.
But not too early, fer it's my aim
To git me some fun 'fore they know my name,
And tease 'em and fun 'em, fer you never guessed

I was Little Billie that went out West."
And Joe Drew said: "Durn if you always wasn't a hand to git yore
fun."

(Over the plain, over mountain and river, drawn,
Wanderer with slit-eyes adjusted to distance,
Drawn out of distance, drawn from the great plateau
Where the sky heeled in the unsagging wind and the cheek burned,
Who stood beneath the white peak that glimmered like a dream,
And spat, and it was morning and it was morning.
You lay among the wild plums and the kildees cried.
You lay in the thicket under the new leaves and the kildees cried,
For all your luck, for all the astuteness of your heart,
And would not stop and would not stop
And the clock ticked all night long in the furnished room
And would not stop
And the *El-*train passed on the quarters with a whish like a terrible
broom
And would not stop
And there is always the sound of breathing in the next room
And it will not stop
And the waitress says, "Will that be all, sir, will that be all?"
And will not stop,
For nothing is ever all and nothing is ever all,
For all your experience and your expertness of human vices and of
valor
At the hour when the ways are darkened.

Though your luck held and the market was always satisfactory,
Though the letter always came and your lovers were always true,
Though you always received the respect due to your position,
Though your hand never failed of its cunning and your glands
always thoroughly knew their business,
Though your conscience was easy and you were assured of your
innocence,
You became gradually aware that something was missing from the
picture,

And upon closer inspection exclaimed: "Why, I'm not in it at all!"
Which was perfectly true.
Therefore you tried to remember when you had last had

Whatever it was you had lost,
And you decided to retrace your steps from that point,
But it was a long way back.
It was, nevertheless, absolutely essential to make the effort,
And since you had never been a man to be deterred by difficult
                                            circumstances,

You came back.
For there is no place like home.)

He joked them and teased them and he had his fun
And they never guessed that he was the one
Had been Mammy's darling and Pappy's joy
When he was a great big whickering boy
In the land between the rivers.
He jingled his pockets and took his sop
And patted his belly which was full nigh to pop
And wiped the buttermilk out of his beard
And took his belch and up and reared
Back from the table and cocked his chair
And said: "Old man, ain't you got any fresh drinken water, this
                                here ain't fresher'n a hoss puddle?"
And the old woman said: "Pappy, take the young gentleman down
                                to the spring so he kin git it good and fresh?"
The old woman gave the old man a straight look.
She gave him the bucket but it was not empty but it was not water.

The stars are shining and the meadow is bright
But under the trees is dark and night
In the land between the rivers.
The leaves hang down in the dark of the trees,
And there is the spring in the dark of the trees,
And there is the spring as black as ink,
And one star in it caught through a chink
Of the leaves that hang down in the dark of the trees.
The star is there but it does not wink.
Little Billie gets down on his knees
And props his hands in the same old place
To sup the water at his ease;
And the star is gone but there is his face.

*

"Just help yoreself," Big Billie said;
Then set the hatchet in his head.
They went through his pockets and they buried him in the dark of
                                                          the trees.
"I figgered he was a ripe 'un," the old man said.
"Yeah, but you wouldn't done nuthen hadn't bin fer me," the old
                                                          woman said.

(The reflection is shadowy and the form not clear,
For the hour is late, and scarcely a glimmer comes here
Under the leaf, the bough, in innocence dark;
And under your straining face you can scarcely mark
The darkling gleam of your face little less than the water dark.

But perhaps what you lost was lost in the pool long ago
When childlike you lost it and then in your innocence rose to go
After kneeling, as now, with your thirst beneath the leaves:
And years it lies here and dreams in the depth and grieves,
More faithful than mother or father in the light or dark of the leaves.

So, weary of greetings now and the new friend's smile,
Weary in art of the stranger, worn with your wanderer's wile,
Weary of innocence and the husks of Time,
You come, back to the homeland of no-Time,
To ask forgiveness and the patrimony of your crime;

And kneel in the untutored night as to demand
What gift—oh, father, father—from that dissevering hand?)

"And whar's Little Billie?" Joe Drew said.
"Air you crazy," said Big, "and plum outa yore head,
Fer you knows he went West nigh ten long year?"
"Went West," Joe said, "but I seen him here
In the section between the rivers,
Riden up the trace as big as you please
With a long black coat comen down to his knees
And a big black beard comen down to his guts
And silver mountens on his pistol-butts,
And he said out West how he done struck
It rich and wuz bringen you back your luck."
"I shore-God could use some luck," Big Billie said,

But his woman wet her lips and craned her head,
And said: "Come riden with a big black beard, you say?"
And Joe: "Oh, it wuz Billie as big as day."

And the old man's eyes bugged out of a sudden and he croaked like a
    sick bull-frog and said: "Come riden with a long black coat?"

The night is still and the grease-lamp low
And the old man's breath comes wheeze and slow.
Oh, the blue flame sucks on the old rag wick
And the old woman's breath comes sharp and quick,
And there isn't a sound under the roof
But her breath's hiss and his breath's puff,
And there isn't a sound outside the door
As they hearken but cannot hear any more
The creak of saddle or the plop of hoof,
For a long time now Joe Drew's been gone
And left them sitting there alone
In the land between the rivers.
And so they sit and breathe and wait
And breathe while the night gets big and late,
And neither of them gives move or stir.
She won't look at him and he won't look at her.
He doesn't look at her but he says: "Git me the spade."

She grabbled with her hands and he dug with the spade
Where leaves let down the dark and shade
In the land between the rivers.
She grabbled like a dog in the hole they made,
But stopped of a sudden and then she said,
"My hand's on his face."
They light up a pine-knot and lean at the place
Where the man in the black coat slumbers and lies
With trash in his beard and dirt on his face;
And the torch-flame shines in his wide-open eyes.
Down the old man leans with the flickering flame
And moves his lips, says: "Tell me his name."

"Ain't Billie, ain't Billie," the old woman cries,
"Oh, it ain't my Billie, fer he wuz little
And helt to my skirt while I stirred the kittle

And called me Mammy and hugged me tight
And come in the house when it fell night."
But the old man leans down with the flickering flame
And croaks: "But tell me his name."

"Oh, he ain't got none, he jist come riden
From some fer place whar he'd bin biden.
Ain't got a name and never had none—
But Billie, my Billie, he had one,
And hit was Billie, it was his name."
But the old man croaked: "Tell me his name."

"Oh, he ain't got none and it's all the same,
But Billie had one, and he was little
And offen his chin I would wipe the spittle
And wiped the drool and kissed him thar
And counted his toes and kissed him whar
The little black mark was under his tit,
Shaped lak a clover under his left tit,
With a shape fer luck, and I'd kiss hit—"

The old man blinks in the pine-knot flare
And his mouth comes open like a fish for air,
Then he says right low, "I had nigh fergot."
"Oh, I kissed him on his little luck-spot
And I kissed and he'd laugh as lak as not—"
The old man said: "Git his shirt open."
The old woman opened the shirt and there was the birthmark
                                        under the left tit.
It was shaped for luck.

(The bee knows, and the eel's cold ganglia burn.
And the sad head lifting to the long return,
Through brumal deeps, in the great unsolsticed coil,
Carries its knowledge, navigator without star,
And under the stars, pure in its clamorous toil,
The goose hoots north where the starlit marshes are.
The salmon heaves at the fall, and, wanderer, you
Heave at the great fall of Time, and gorgeous, gleam
In the powerful arc, and anger and outrage like dew,
In your plunge, fling, and plunge to the thunderous stream:

Back to the silence, back to the pool, back
To the high pool, motionless, and the unmurmuring dream.
And you, wanderer, back,
Brother to pinion and the pious fin that cleave
The innocence of air and the disinfectant flood
And wing and welter and weave
The long compulsion and the circuit hope
Back,

And bear through that limitless and devouring fluidity
The itch and humble promise which is home.

And the father waits for the son.

The hour is late,
The scene familiar even in shadow,
The transaction brief,
And you, wanderer, back,
After the striving and the wind's word,
To kneel
Here in the evening empty of wind or bird,
To kneel in the sacramental silence of evening
At the feet of the old man
Who is evil and ignorant and old,
To kneel
With the little black mark under your heart,
Which is your name,
Which is shaped for luck,

Which is your luck.)

PROMISES: POEMS
1954–1956

TO A LITTLE GIRL, ONE YEAR OLD,
IN A RUINED FORTRESS

To Rosanna

I. SIROCCO

To a place of ruined stone we brought you, and sea-reaches.
Rocca: fortress, hawk-heel, lion-paw, clamped on a hill.
A hill, no. On a sea cliff, and crag-cocked, the embrasures
                             commanding the beaches,
Range easy, with most fastidious mathematic and skill.

Philipus me fecit: he of Spain, the black-browed, the anguished,
For whom nothing prospered, though he loved God.
His arms, a great scutcheon of stone, once over the drawbridge,
                             have languished
Now long in the moat, under garbage; at moat-brink, rosemary
                   with blue, thistle with gold bloom, nod.

Sun blaze and cloud tatter, now the sirocco, the dust swirl is
                             swirled
Over the bay face, mounts air like gold gauze whirled; it traverses
                     the blaze-blue of water.
We have brought you where geometry of a military rigor survives
                     its own ruined world,
And sun regilds your gilt hair, in the midst of your laughter.

Rosemary, thistle, clutch stone. Far hangs Giannutri in blue air. Far
                     to that blueness the heart aches,
And on the exposed approaches the last gold of gorse bloom, in the
                     sirocco, shakes.

II. THE CHILD NEXT DOOR

The child next door is defective because the mother,
Seven brats already in that purlieu of dirt,
Took a pill, or did something to herself she thought would not hurt,
But it did, and no good, for there came this monstrous other.

The sister is twelve. Is beautiful like a saint.
Sits with the monster all day, with pure love, calm eyes.
Has taught it a trick, to make *ciao*, Italian-wise.
It crooks hand in that greeting. She smiles her smile without taint.

I come, and her triptych beauty and joy stir hate
—Is it hate?—in my heart. Fool, doesn't she know that the process
Is not that joyous or simple, to bless, or unbless,
The malfeasance of nature or the filth of fate?

Can it bind or loose, that beauty in that kind,
Beauty of benediction? We must trust our hope to prevail
That heart-joy in beauty be wisdom, before beauty fail
And be gathered like air in the ruck of the world's wind!

I think of your goldness, of joy, but how empires grind, stars are
                                                         hurled.
I smile stiff, saying *ciao*, saying *ciao*, and think: *This is the world.*

INFANT BOY AT MIDCENTURY

I. WHEN THE CENTURY DRAGGED

When the century dragged, like a great wheel stuck at dead center;
When the wind that had hurled us our half-century sagged now,
And only velleity of air somewhat snidely nagged now,
With no certain commitment to compass, or quarter: then you
                                                      chose to enter.

*

You enter an age when the neurotic clock-tick
Of midnight competes with the heart's pulsed assurance of power.
You have entered our world at scarcely its finest hour,
And smile now life's gold Apollonian smile at a sick dialectic.

You enter at the hour when the dog returns to his vomit,
And fear's moonflower spreads, white as girl-thigh, in our dusk of
                                                    compromise;
When posing for pictures, arms linked, the same smile in their eyes,
Good and Evil, to iron out all differences, stage their meeting at
                                                    summit.

You come in the year when promises are broken,
And petal fears the late, as fruit the early frost-fall;
When the young expect little, and the old endure total recall,
But discover no logic to justify what they had taken, or forsaken.

But to take and forsake now you're here, and the heart will compress
Like stone when we see that rosy heel learn,
With its first step, the apocalyptic power to spurn
Us, and our works and days, and onward, prevailing, pass

To pause, in high pride of unillusioned manhood,
At the gap that gives on the new century, and land,
And with calm heart and level eye command
That dawning perspective and possibility of human good.

2. BRIGHTNESS OF DISTANCE

You will read the official histories—some true, no doubt.
Barring total disaster, the record will speak from the shelf.
And if there's disaster, disaster will speak for itself.
So all of our lies will be truth, and the truth vindictively out.

Remember our defects, we give them to you gratis.
But remember that ours is not the worst of times.
Our country's convicted of follies rather than crimes—
We throw out baby with bath, drop the meat in the fire where the
                                                    fat is.

*

And in even such stew and stink as Tacitus
Once wrote of, his generals, gourmets, pimps, poltroons,
He found persons of private virtue, the old-fashioned stout ones
Who would bow the head to no blast; and we know that such are
                                                    yet with us.

He was puzzled how virtue found perch past confusion and wrath;
How even Praetorian brutes, blank of love, as of hate,
Proud in their craftsman's pride only, held a last gate,
And died, each back unmarred as though at the barracks bath.

And remember that many among us wish you well;
And once, on a strange shore, an old man, toothless and through,
Groped a hand from the lattice of personal disaster to touch you.
He sat on the sand for an hour; said *ciao, bello,* as evening fell.

And think, as you move past our age that grudges and grieves,
How eyes, purged of envy, will follow your sunlit chance.
Eyes will brighten to follow your brightness and dwindle of distance.
From privacy of fate, eyes will follow, as though from the shadow
                                                     of leaves.

DRAGON COUNTRY: TO JACOB BOEHME

This is the dragon's country, and these his own streams.
The slime on the railroad rails is where he has crossed the track.
On a frosty morning, that field mist is where his great turd steams,
And there are those who have gone forth and not come back.

I was only a boy when Jack Simms reported the first depredation,
What something had done to his hog pen. They called him a
                                                 God-damn liar.
Then said it must be a bear, after some had viewed the location,
With fence rails, like matchwood, splintered, and earth a bloody mire.

But no bear had been seen in the county in fifty years, they knew.
It was something to say, merely that, for people compelled to explain

What, standing in natural daylight, they couldn't believe to be true;
And saying the words, one felt in the chest a constrictive pain.

At least, some admitted this later, when things had got to the
                                                            worst—
When, for instance, they found in the woods the wagon turned on
                                                            its side,
Mules torn from trace chains, and you saw how the harness had
                                                            burst.
Spectators averted the face from the spot where the teamster had
                                                            died.

But that was long back, in my youth, just the first of case after case.
The great hunts fizzled. You followed the track of disrepair,
Ruined fence, blood-smear, brush broken, but came in the end to a
                                                            place
With weed unbent and leaf calm—and nothing, nothing, was there.

So what, in God's name, could men think when they couldn't
                                                            bring to bay
That belly-dragging earth-evil, but found that it took to air?
Thirty-thirty or buckshot might fail, but then at least you could say
You had faced it—assuming, of course, that you had survived the
                                                            affair.

We were promised troops, the Guard, but the Governor's skin got
                                                            thin
When up in New York the papers called him Saint George of
                                                            Kentucky.
Yes, even the Louisville reporters who came to Todd County
                                                            would grin.
Reporters, though rarely, still come. No one talks. They think it
                                                            unlucky.

If a man disappears—well, the fact is something to hide.
The family says, gone to Akron, or up to Ford, in Detroit.
When we found Jebb Johnson's boot, with the leg, what was left,
                                                            inside,
His mother said, no, it's not his. So we took it out to destroy it.

*

Land values are falling, no longer do lovers in moonlight go.
The rabbit, thoughtless of air gun, in the nearest pasture cavorts.
Now certain fields go untended, the local birth rate goes low.
The coon dips his little black paw in the riffle where he nightly
                                                    resorts.

Yes, other sections have problems somewhat different from ours.
Their crops may fail, bank rates rise, loans at rumor of war be called,
But we feel removed from maneuvers of Russia, or other great
                                                    powers,
And from much ordinary hope we are now disenthralled.

The Catholics have sent in a mission, Baptists report new
                                                    attendance.
But all that's off the point! We are human, and the human heart
Demands language for reality that has not the slightest dependence
On desire, or need—and in church fools pray only that the Beast
                                                    depart.

But if the Beast were withdrawn now, life might dwindle again
To the ennui, the pleasure, and the night sweat, known in the time
                                                    before
Necessity of truth had trodden the land, and our hearts, to pain,
And left, in darkness, the fearful glimmer of joy, like a spoor.

LULLABY: SMILE IN SLEEP

Sleep, my son, and smile in sleep.
You will dream the world anew.
Watching you now sleep,
I feel the world's depleted force renew,
Feel the nerve expand and knit,
Feel a rustle in the blood,
Feel wink of warmth and stir of spirit,
As though spring woke in the heart's cold underwood.
The vernal work is now begun.

Sleep, my son.
Sleep, son.

You will see the nestling fall.
Blood flecks grass of the rabbit form.
You will, of course, see all
The world's brute ox-heel wrong, and shrewd hand-harm.
Throats are soft to invite the blade.
Truth invites the journalist's lie.
Love bestowed mourns trust betrayed,
But the heart most mourns its own infidelity.
The greater, then, your obligation.
Dream perfection.
Dream, son.

When the diver leaves the board
To hang at gleam-height against the sky,
Trajectory is toward
An image hung perfect as light in his mind's wide eye.
So your dream will later serve you.
So now, dreaming, you serve me,
And give our hope new patent to
Enfranchise human possibility.
Grace undreamed is grace forgone.
Dream grace, son.
Sleep on.

Dream that sleep is a sunlit meadow
Drowsy with a dream of bees
Threading sun, and a shadow
Where you may lie lulled by their sunlit industries.
Let the murmurous bees of sleep
Tread down honey in the honeycomb.
Heart-deep now, your dream will keep
Sweet in that deep comb for time to come.
Dream the sweetness coming on.
Dream, sweet son.
Sleep on.

What if angry vectors veer
Around your sleeping head, and form?

There's never need to fear
Violence of the poor world's abstract storm.
For now you dream Reality.
Matter groans to touch your hand.
Matter lifts now like the sea
Toward that strong moon that is your dream's command.
Dream the power coming on.
Dream, strong son.
Sleep on.

LULLABY: A MOTION LIKE SLEEP

Under the star and beech-shade braiding,
Past the willow's dim solicitudes,
Past hush of oak-dark and a stone's star-glinted upbraiding,
Water moves, in a motion like sleep,
Along the dark edge of the woods.
So, son, now sleep.

Sleep, and feel how now, at woods-edge,
The water, wan, moves under starlight,
Before it finds that dark of its own deepest knowledge,
And will murmur, in motion like sleep,
In that leaf-dark languor of night.
So, son, sleep deep.

Sleep, and dream how deep and dreamless
The covered courses of blood are:
And blood, in a motion like sleep, moves, gleamless,
By alleys darkened deep now
In the leafage of no star.
So, son, sleep now.

Sleep, for sleep and stream and blood-course
Are a motion with one name,
And all that flows finds end but in its own source,

And a circuit of motion like sleep,
And will go as once it came.
So, son, now sleep

Till the clang of cock-crow, and dawn's rays,
Summon your heart and hand to deploy
Their energies to know, in the excitement of day-blaze,
How like a wound, and deep,
Is Time's irremediable joy.
So, son, now sleep.

YOU, EMPERORS, AND OTHERS: POEMS 1957–1960

TIBERIUS ON CAPRI

I

All is nothing, nothing all:
To tired Tiberius soft sang the sea thus,
Under his cliff-palace wall.
The sea, in soft approach and repulse,
Sings thus, and Tiberius,
Sea-sad, stares past the dusking sea-pulse
Yonder, where come,
One now by one, the lights, far off, of Surrentum.
He stares in the blue dusk-fall,
For all is nothing, nothing all.

Let darkness up from Asia tower.
On that darkening island behind him *spintriae* now stir.
In grot and scented bower,
They titter, yawn, paint lip, grease thigh,
And debate what role each would prefer
When they project for the Emperor's eye
Their expertise
Of his Eastern lusts and complex Egyptian fantasies.
But darkward he stares in that hour,
Blank now in totality of power.

2

There once, on that goat island, I,
As dark fell, stood and stared where Europe stank.
Many were soon to die—

From acedia snatched, from depravity, virtue,
Or frolic, not knowing the reason, in rank
On rank hurled, or in bed, or in church, or
Dishing up supper,
Or in a dark doorway, loosening the girl's elastic to tup her,
While high in the night sky,
The murderous tear dropped from God's eye;

And faintly forefeeling, forefearing, all
That to fulfill our time, and heart, would come,
I stood on the crumbling wall
Of that foul place, and my lungs drew in
Scent of dry gorse on the night air of autumn,
And I seized, in dark, a small stone from that ruin,
And I made outcry
At the paradox of powers that would grind us like grain, small and
dry.

Dark down, the stone, in its fall,
Found the sea: I could do that much, after all.

MORTMAIN

AFTER NIGHT FLIGHT SON REACHES BEDSIDE OF
ALREADY UNCONSCIOUS FATHER, WHOSE RIGHT
HAND LIFTS IN A SPASMODIC GESTURE, AS
THOUGH TRYING TO MAKE CONTACT: 1955

In Time's concatenation and
Carnal conventicle, I,
Arriving, being flung through dark and
The abstract flight-grid of sky,
Saw rising from the sweated sheet and
Ruck of bedclothes ritualistically
Reordered by the paid hand
Of mercy—saw rising the hand—

*

Christ, start again! What was it I,
Standing there, travel-shaken, saw
Rising? What could it be that I,
Caught sudden in gut- or conscience-gnaw,
Saw rising out of the past, which I
Saw now as twisted bedclothes? Like law,
The hand rose cold from History
To claw at a star in the black sky,

But could not reach that far—oh, cannot!
And the star horribly burned, burns,
For in darkness the wax-white clutch could not
Reach it, and white hand on wrist-stem turns,
Lifts in last tension of tendon, but cannot
Make contact—*oh, oop-si-daisy*, churns
The sad heart, *oh, atta-boy, daddio's got*
One more shot in the locker, peas-porridge hot—

But no. Like an eyelid the hand sank, strove
Downward, and in that darkening roar,
All things—all joy and the hope that strove,
The failed exam, the admired endeavor,
Prizes and prinkings, and the truth that strove,
And back of the Capitol, boyhood's first whore—
Were snatched from me, and I could not move,
Naked in that black blast of his love.

DEBATE: QUESTION, QUARRY, DREAM

Asking what, asking what?—all a boy's afternoon,
Squatting in the canebrake where the muskrat will come.
Muskrat, muskrat, please now, please, come soon.
He comes, stares, goes, lets the question resume.
He has taken whatever answer may be down to his mud-burrow
         gloom.

*

Seeking what, seeking what?—foot soft in cedar-shade.
Was that a deer-flag white past windfall and fern?
No, but by bluffside lurk powers and in the fern glade
Tall presences, standing all night, like white fox-fire burn.
The small fox lays his head in your hand now and weeps that you
go, not to return.

Dreaming what, dreaming what?—lying on the hill at twilight,
The still air stirred only by moth wing, the last stain of sun
Fading to moth-sky, blood-red to moth-white and starlight,
And Time leans down to kiss the heart's ambition,
While far away, before moonrise, come the town lights, one by one.

Long since that time I have walked night streets, heel-iron
Clicking the stone, and in dark in windows have stared.
Question, quarry, dream—I have vented my ire on
My own heart that, ignorant and untoward,
Yearns for an absolute that Time would, I thought, have prepared.

But has not yet. Well, let us debate
The issue. But under a tight roof, clutching a toy,
My son now sleeps, and when the hour grows late,
I shall go forth where the cold constellations deploy
And lift up my eyes to consider more strictly the appalling logic of
joy.

TALE OF TIME: POEMS 1960-1966

(*IN* SELECTED POEMS: NEW AND OLD 1923-1966)

WHAT WERE YOU THINKING, DEAR MOTHER?

What were you thinking, a child, when you lay,
At the whippoorwill hour, lost in the long grass,
As sun, beyond the dark cedars, sank?
You went to the house. The lamps were now lit.

What did you think when the mourning dove mourned,
Far off in those sober recesses of cedar?
What relevance did your heart find in that sound?
In lamplight, your father's head bent at his book.

What did you think when the last saffron
Of sunset faded beyond the dark cedars,
And on noble blue now the evening star hung?
You found it necessary to go to the house,

And found it necessary to live on,
In your bravery and in your joyous secret,
Into our present maniacal century,
In which you gave me birth, and in

Which I, in the public and private mania,
Have lived, but remember that once I,
A child, in the grass of that same spot, lay,
And the whippoorwill called, beyond the dark cedars.

INSOMNIA

I

If to that place. Place of grass.
If to hour of whippoorwill, I.
If I now, not a child. To.
If now I, not a child, should come to
That place, lie in
That place, in that hour hear
That call, would
I rise,
Go?

Yes, enter the darkness. Of.
Darkness of cedars, thinking
You there, you having entered, sly,
My back being turned, face
Averted, or
Eyes shut, for
A man cannot keep his eyes steadily open
Sixty years.

I did not see you when you went away.

Darkness of cedars, yes, entering, but what
Face, what
Bubble on dark stream of Time, white
Glimmer un-mooned? Oh,
What age has the soul, what
Face does it wear, or would
I meet that face that last I saw on the pillow, pale?

I recall each item with remarkable precision.

Would the sweat now be dried on the temples?

2

What would we talk about? The dead,
Do they know all, or nothing, and
If nothing, does
Curiosity survive the long unravelment? Tell me

What they think about love, for I
Know now at long last that the living remember the dead only
Because we cannot bear the thought that they
Might forget us. Or is
That true? Look, look at these—
But no, no light here penetrates by which
You might see these photographs I keep in my wallet. Anyway,
I shall try to tell you all that has happened to me.

Though how can I tell when I do not even know?

And as for you, and all the interesting things
That must have happened to you and that
I am just dying to hear about—

But would you confide in a balding stranger
The intimate secret of death?

3

Or does the soul have many faces, and would I,
Pacing the cold hypothesis of Time, enter
Those recesses to see, white,
Whiter than moth-wing, the child's face
Glimmer in cedar gloom, and so
Reach out that I might offer
What protection I could, saying,
"I am older than you will ever be"—for you
Are the child who once
Lay lost in the long grass, sun setting.

Reach out, saying: "Your hand—
Give it here, for it's dark and, my dear,
You should never have come in the woods when it's dark,

But I'll take you back home, they're waiting."
And to woods-edge we come, there I stand.

I watch you move across the open space.
You move under the paleness of new stars.
You move toward the house, and one instant,

A door opening, I see
Your small form black against the light, and the door
Is closed, and I

Hear night crash down a million stairs.
In the ensuing silence
My breath is difficult.

Heat lightning ranges beyond the horizon.

That, also, is worth mentioning.

4

Come,
Crack crust, striker
From darkness, and let seize—let what
Hand seize, oh!—my heart, and compress
The heart till, after pain, joy from it
Spurts like a grape, and I will grind
Teeth on flint tongue till
The flint screams. Truth
Is all. But

I must learn to speak it
Slowly, in a whisper.

Truth, in the end, can never be spoken aloud,
For the future is always unpredictable.
But so is the past, therefore

At wood's edge I stand, and,
Over the black horizon, heat lightning
Ripples the black sky. After

The lightning, as the eye
Adjusts to the new dark,
The stars are, again, born.

They are born one by one.

ELIJAH ON MOUNT CARMEL

To Vann and Glenn Woodward

(Elijah, after the miraculous fall of fire on his altar,
the breaking of the drouth, and the slaughter of the
priests of Baal, girds up his loins and runs ahead of the
chariot of Ahab to the gates of Jezreel, where Jezebel
waits.)

Nothing is re-enacted. Nothing
Is true. Therefore nothing
Must be believed,
But
To have truth
Something must be believed,
And repetition and congruence,
To say the least, are necessary, and
His thorn-scarred heels and toes with filth horn-scaled
Spurned now the flint-edge and with blood spurts flailed
Stone, splashed mud of Jezreel. And he screamed.
He had seen glory more blood-laced than any he had dreamed.

Far, far ahead of the chariot tire,
Which the black mud sucked, he screamed,
Screaming in glory
Like
A bursting blood blister.
Ahead of the mud-faltered fetlock,
He screamed, and of Ahab huddled in
The frail vehicle under the purpling wrack
And spilled gold of storm—poor Ahab, who,
From metaphysical confusion and lightning, had nothing to run to

But the soft Phoenician belly and commercial acuity
Of Jezebel: that darkness wherein History creeps to die.

How could he ever tell her? Get nerve to?
Tell how around her high altar
The prinking and primped
Priests,
Limping, had mewed,

And only the gull-mew was answer,
No fire to heaped meats, only sun-flame,
And the hairy one laughed: "Has your god turned aside to make
                                                    pee-pee?"
How then on that sea-cliff he prayed, fire fell, sky darkened,
Rain fell, drouth broke now, for God had hearkened,
And priests gave their death-squeal. The king hid his eyes in his coat.
Oh, why to that hairy one should God have hearkened, who
                                                    smelled like a goat?

Yes, how could he tell her? When he himself
Now scarcely believed it? Soon,
In the scented chamber,
She,
Saying, "Baby, Baby,
Just hush, now hush, it's all right,"
Would lean, reach out, lay a finger
To his lips to allay his infatuate gabble. So,
Eyes shut, breath scant, he heard her breath rip the lamp-flame
To blackness, and by that sweet dog-bait, lay, and it came,
The soft hand-grope he knew he could not, nor wished to, resist
Much longer. So prayed: "Dear God, dear God—oh, please, don't
                                                    exist!"

LOVE: TWO VIGNETTES

1. MEDITERRANEAN BEACH, DAY AFTER STORM

How instant joy, how clang
And whang the sun, how
Whoop the sea, and oh,
Sun, sing, as whiter than
Rage of snow, let sea the spume
Fling.

Let sea the spume, white, fling,
White on blue wild
With wind, let sun
Sing, while the world
Scuds, clouds boom and belly,
Creak like sails, whiter than,
Brighter than,
Spume in sun-song, oho!
The wind is bright.

Wind the heart winds
In constant coil, turning
In the—forever—light.

Give me your hand.

2. DECIDUOUS SPRING

Now, now, the world
All gabbles joy like geese, for
An idiot glory the sky
Bangs. Look!
All leaves are new, are
Now, are
Bangles dangling and
Spangling, in sudden air
Wangling, then
Hanging quiet, bright.

*

The world comes back, and again
Is gabbling, and yes,
Remarkably worse, for
The world is a whirl of
Green mirrors gone wild with
Deceit, and the world
Whirls green on a string, then
The leaves go quiet, wink
From their own shade, secretly.

Keep still, just a moment, leaves.

There is something I am trying to remember.

WHERE THE SLOW FIG'S PURPLE SLOTH

Where the slow fig's purple sloth
Swells, I sit and meditate the
Nature of the soul, the fig exposes,
To the blaze of afternoon, one haunch
As purple-black as Africa, a single
Leaf the rest screens, but through it, light
Burns, and for the fig's bliss
The sun dies, the sun
Has died forever—far, oh far—
For the fig's bliss, thus.

     The air
Is motionless, and the fig,
Motionless in that imperial and blunt
Languor of glut, swells, and inward
The fibers relax like a sigh in that
Hot darkness, go soft, the air
Is gold.

   When you
Split the fig, you will see
Lifting from the coarse and purple seed, its
Flesh like flame, purer
Than blood.

    It fills
The darkening room with light.

MASTS AT DAWN

Past second cock-crow yacht masts in the harbor go slowly white.

No light in the east yet, but the stars show a certain fatigue.
They withdraw into a new distance, have discovered our
unworthiness. It is long since

The owl, in the dark eucalyptus, dire and melodious, last called, and

Long since the moon sank and the English
Finished fornicating in their ketches. In the evening there was a
strong swell.

Red died the sun, but at dark wind rose easterly, white sea nagged
the black harbor headland.

When there is a strong swell, you may, if you surrender to it,
experience
A sense, in the act, of mystic unity with that rhythm. Your peace is
the sea's will.

But now no motion, the bay-face is glossy in darkness, like

An old windowpane flat on black ground by the wall, near the ash
heap. It neither

Receives nor gives light. Now is the hour when the sea

Sinks into meditation. It doubts its own mission. The drowned cat
That on the evening swell had kept nudging the piles of the pier
and had seemed

To want to climb out and lick itself dry, now floats free. On that
surface a slight convexity only, it is like

An eyelid, in darkness, closed. You must learn to accept the kiss of
fate, for

*

The masts go white slow, as light, like dew, from darkness
Condensed on them, on oiled wood, on metal. Dew whitens in
darkness.

I lie in my bed and think how, in darkness, the masts go white.

The sound of the engine of the first fishing dory dies seaward. Soon
In the inland glen wakes the dawn-dove. We must try

To love so well the world that we may believe, in the end, in God.

THE LEAF

A

Here the fig lets down the leaf, the leaf
Of the fig five fingers has, the fingers
Are broad, spatulate, stupid,
Ill-formed, and innocent—but of a hand, and the hand,

To hide me from the blaze of the wide world, drops,
Shamefast, down. I am
What is to be concealed. I lurk
In the shadow of the fig. Stop.
Go no further. This is the place.

To this spot I bring my grief.
Human grief is the obscenity to be hidden by the leaf.

B

We have undergone ourselves, therefore
What more is to be done for Truth's sake? I

Have watched the deployment of ants, I
Have conferred with the flaming mullet in a deep place.

*

Near the nesting place of the hawk, among
Snag-rock, high on the cliff, I have seen
The clutter of annual bones, of hare, vole, bird, white
As chalk from sun and season, frail
As the dry grass stem. On that

High place of stone I have lain down, the sun
Beat, the small exacerbation
Of dry bones was what my back, shirtless and bare, knew. I saw

The hawk shudder in the high sky, he shudders
To hold position in the blazing wind, in relation to
The firmament, he shudders and the world is a metaphor, his eye
Sees, white, the flicker of hare-scut, the movement of vole.

Distance is nothing, there is no solution, I
Have opened my mouth to the wind of the world like wine, I
                                                        wanted
To taste what the world is, wind dried up

The live saliva of my tongue, my tongue
Was like a dry leaf in my mouth.

Destiny is what you experience, that
Is its name and definition, and is your name, for

The wide world lets down the hand in shame:
Here is the human shadow, there, of the wide world, the flame.

c

The world is fruitful, In this heat
The plum, black yet bough-bound, bursts, and the gold ooze is,
Of bees, joy, the gold ooze has striven
Outward, it wants again to be of
The goldness of air and—blessedly—innocent. The grape
Weakens at the juncture of the stem. The world

Is fruitful, and I, too,
In that I am the father
Of my father's father's father. I,

Of my father, have set the teeth on edge. But
By what grape? I have cried out in the night.

From a further garden, from the shade of another tree,
My father's voice, in the moment when the cicada ceases, has called
to me.

D

The voice blesses me for the only
Gift I have given: *teeth set on edge.*

In the momentary silence of the cicada,
I can hear the appalling speed,
In space beyond stars, of
Light. It is

A sound like wind.

AUDUBON: A VISION (1969)

Jean Jacques Audubon, whose name was anglicized when, in his youth, he was sent to America, was early instructed in the official version of his identity: that he was the son of the sea captain Jean Audubon and a first wife, who died shortly after his birth in Santo Domingo, and that the woman who brought him up in France was a second wife. Actually, he was the son of Jean Audubon and his mistress during the period when Jean Audubon was a merchant and slave-dealer in Santo Domingo, and the woman who raised him was the wife his father had left behind him in France while he was off making his fortune. By the age of ten Audubon knew the true story, but prompted, it would seem, by a variety of impulses, including some sound practical ones, he encouraged the other version, along with a number of flattering embellishments. He was, indeed, a fantasist of talent, but even without his help, legends accreted about him. The most famous one—that he was the lost Dauphin of France, the son of the feckless Louis XVI and Marie Antoinette—did not, in fact, enter the picture until after his death, in 1851.

I WAS NOT THE LOST DAUPHIN

[A]

Was not the lost dauphin, though handsome was only
Base-born and not even able
To make a decent living, was only
Himself, Jean Jacques, and his passion—what
Is man but his passion?

*

Saw,

Eastward and over the cypress swamp, the dawn,
Redder than meat, break;
And the large bird,
Long neck outthrust, wings crooked to scull air, moved
In a slow calligraphy, crank, flat, and black against
The color of God's blood split, as though
Pulled by a string.

Saw

It proceed across the inflamed distance.

Moccasins set in hoar frost, eyes fixed on the bird,
Thought: "On that sky it is black."
Thought: "In my mind it is white."
Thinking: "*Ardea occidentalis,* heron, the great one."

Dawn: his heart shook in the tension of the world.

Dawn: and what is your passion?

[B]

October: and the bear,
Daft in the honey-light, yawns.

The bear's tongue, pink as a baby's, out-crisps to the curled tip,
It bleeds the black blood of the blueberry.

The teeth are more importantly white
Than has ever been imagined.

The bear feels his own fat
Sweeten, like a drowse, deep to the bone.

Bemused, above the fume of ruined blueberries,
The last bee hums.

The wings, like mica, glint
In the sunlight.

*

He leans on his gun. Thinks
How thin is the membrane between himself and the world.

II THE DREAM HE NEVER KNEW THE END OF

[A]

Shank-end of day, spit of snow, the call,
A crow, sweet in distance, then sudden
The clearing: among stumps, ruined cornstalks yet standing, the spot
Like a wound rubbed raw in the vast pelt of the forest. There
Is the cabin, a huddle of logs with no calculation or craft:
The human filth, the human hope.

Smoke,
From the mud-and-stick chimney, in that air, greasily
Brims, cannot lift, bellies the ridgepole, ravels
White, thin, down the shakes, like sputum.

He stands,
Leans on his gun, stares at the smoke, thinks: "Punk-wood."
Thinks: "Dead-fall half-rotten." Too sloven,
That is, to even set axe to clean wood.

His foot,
On the trod mire by the door, crackles
The night-ice already there forming. His hand
Lifts, hangs. In imagination, his nostrils already
Know the stench of that lair beyond
The door-puncheons. The dog
Presses its head against his knee. The hand
Strikes wood. No answer. He halloos. Then the voice.

[B]

What should he recognize? The nameless face
In the dream of some pre-dawn cock-crow—about to say what,

Do what? The dregs
Of all nightmare are the same, and we call it
Life. He knows that much, being a man,
And knows that the dregs of all life are nightmare.

Unless.

Unless what?

  [c]

The face, in the air, hangs. Large,
Raw-hewn, strong-beaked, the haired mole
Near the nose, to the left, and the left side by firelight
Glazed red, the right in shadow, and under the tumble and tangle
Of dark hair on that head, and under the coarse eyebrows,
The eyes, dark, glint as from the unspecifiable
Darkness of a cave. It is a woman.

She is tall, taller than he.
Against the gray skirt, her hands hang.

"Ye wants to spend the night? Kin ye pay?
Well, mought as well stay then, done got one a-ready,
And leastwise, ye don't stink like no Injun."

  [d]

The Indian,
Hunched by the hearth, lifts his head, looks up, but
From one eye only, the other
An aperture below which blood and mucus hang, thickening slow.

"Yeah, a arrow jounced back off his bowstring.
Durn fool—and him a Injun." She laughs.

                              The Indian's head sinks.
So he turns, drops his pack in a corner on bearskin, props
The gun there. Comes back to the fire. Takes his watch out.
Draws it bright, on the thong-loop, from under his hunter's-frock.

It is gold, it lives in his hand in the firelight, and the woman's
Hand reaches out. She wants it. She hangs it about her neck.

And near it the great hands hover delicately
As though it might fall, they quiver like moth-wings, her eyes
Are fixed downward, as though in shyness, on that gleam, and her
                                                                face
Is sweet in an outrage of sweetness, so that
His gut twists cold. He cannot bear what he sees.

Her body sways like a willow in spring wind. Like a girl.

The time comes to take back the watch. He takes it.
And as she, sullen and sunken, fixes the food, he becomes aware
That the live eye of the Indian is secretly on him, and soundlessly
The lips move, and when her back is turned, the Indian
Draws a finger, in delicious retardation, across his own throat.

After food, and scraps for his dog, he lies down:
In the corner, on bearskins, which are not well cured,
And stink, the gun by his side, primed and cocked.

Under his hand he feels the breathing of the dog.

The woman hulks by the fire. He hears the jug slosh.

[E]

The sons come in from the night, two, and are
The sons she would have. Through slit lids
He watches. Thinks: "Now."

                    The sons
Hunker down by the fire, block the firelight, cram food
Into their large mouths, where teeth
Grind in hot darkness, their breathing
Is heavy like sleep, he wants to sleep, but
The head of the woman leans at them. The heads
Are together in firelight.

*

He hears the jug slosh.

                    Then hears,
Like the whisper and *whish* of silk, that other
Sound, like a sound of sleep, but he does not
Know what it is. Then knows, for,
Against firelight, he sees the face of the woman
Lean over, and the lips purse sweet as to bestow a kiss, but
This is not true, and the great glob of spit
Hangs there, glittering, before she lets it fall.

The spit is what softens like silk the passage of steel
On the fine-grained stone. It whispers.

When she rises, she will hold it in her hand.

  [F]

With no sound, she rises. She holds it in her hand.
Behind her the sons rise like shadow. The Indian
Snores. Or pretends to.

                    He thinks: "Now."

                              And knows
He has entered the tale, knows
He has entered the dark hovel
In the forest where trees have eyes, knows it is the tale
They told him when he was a child, knows it
Is the dream he had in childhood but never
Knew the end of, only
The scream.

  [G]

But no scream now, and under his hand
The dog lies taut, waiting. And he, too, knows
What he must do, do soon, and therefore
Does not understand why now a lassitude
Sweetens his limbs, or why, even in this moment

Of fear—or is it fear?—the saliva
In his mouth tastes sweet.

"Now, now!" the voice in his head cries out, but
Everything seems far away, and small.

He cannot think what guilt unmans him, or
Why he should find the punishment so precious.

It is too late. Oh, oh, the world!

Tell me the name of the world.

[H]

The door bursts open, and the travelers enter:
Three men, alert, strong, armed. And the Indian
Is on his feet, pointing.

He thinks
That now he will never know the dream's ending.

[I]

Trussed up with thongs, all night they lie on the floor there.
The woman is gagged, for she had reviled them.
All night he hears the woman's difficult breath.

Dawn comes. It is gray. When he eats,
The cold corn pone grinds in his throat, like sand. It sticks there.

Even whiskey fails to remove it. It sticks there.

The leg-thongs are cut off the tied-ones. They are made to stand up.
The woman refuses the whiskey. Says: "What fer?"
The first son drinks. The other
Takes it into his mouth, but it will not go down.

The liquid drains, slow, from the slack of the mouth.

[J]

They stand there under the long, low bough of the great oak.
Eastward, low over the forest, the sun is nothing
But a circular blur of no irradiation, somewhat paler
Than the general grayness. Their legs
Are again bound with thongs.

They are asked if they want to pray now. But the woman:
"If'n it's God made folks, then who's to pray to?"
And then: "Or fer?" And bursts into laughing.

For a time it seems that she can never stop laughing.

But as for the sons, one prays, or tries to. And one
Merely blubbers. If the woman
Gives either a look, it is not
Pity, nor even contempt, only distance. She waits,

And is what she is,

And in the gray light of morning, he sees her face. Under
The tumbled darkness of hair, the face
Is white. Out of that whiteness
The dark eyes stare at nothing, or at
The nothingness that the gray sky, like Time, is, for
There is no Time, and the face
Is, he suddenly sees, beautiful as stone, and

So becomes aware that he is in the manly state.

[K]

The affair was not tidy: bough low, no drop, with the clients
Simply hung up, feet not much clear of the ground, but not
Quite close enough to permit any dancing.
The affair was not quick: both sons long jerking and farting, but she,
From the first, without motion, frozen
In a rage of will, an ecstasy of iron, as though
This was the dream that, lifelong, she had dreamed toward.

*

The face,
Eyes a-glare, jaws clenched, now glowing black with congestion
Like a plum, had achieved,
It seemed to him, a new dimension of beauty.

[L]

There are tears in his eyes.
He tries to remember his childhood.
He tries to remember his wife.
He can remember nothing.

His throat is parched. His right hand,
Under the deerskin frock, has been clutching the gold watch.

The magic of that object had been,
In the secret order of the world, denied her who now hangs there.

He thinks: "What has been denied me?"
Thinks: "There is never an answer."

Thinks: "The question is the only answer."

He yearns to be able to frame a definition of joy.

[M]

And so stood alone, for the travelers
Had disappeared into the forest and into
Whatever selves they were, and the Indian,
Now bearing the gift of a gun that had belonged to the

hanged-ones,
Was long since gone, like smoke fading into the forest,
And below the blank and unforgiving eye-hole
The blood and mucus had long since dried.

He thought: "I must go."

But could not, staring
At the face, and stood for a time even after
The first snowflakes, in idiotic benignity,

Had fallen. Far off, in the forest and falling snow,
A crow was calling.

             So stirs, knowing now
He will not be here when snow
Drifts into the open door of the cabin, or,
Descending the chimney, mantles thinly
Dead ashes on the hearth, nor when snow thatches
These heads with white, like wisdom, nor ever will he
Hear the infinitesimal stridor of the frozen rope
As wind shifts its burden, or when

The weight of the crow first comes to rest on a rigid shoulder.

III WE ARE ONLY OURSELVES

We never know what we have lost, or what we have found.
We are only ourselves, and that promise.
Continue to walk in the world. Yes, love it!

He continued to walk in the world.

IV THE SIGN WHEREBY HE KNEW

[A]

His life, at the end, seemed—even the anguish—simple.
Simple, at least, in that it had to be
Simply, what it was, as he was,
In the end, himself and not what
He had known he ought to be. The blessedness!—

*

To wake in some dawn and see,
As though down a rifle barrel, lined up
Like sights, the self that was, the self that is, and there,
Far off but in range, completing that alignment, your fate.

Hold your breath, let the trigger-squeeze be slow and steady.

The quarry lifts, in the halo of gold leaves, its noble head.

This is not a dimension of Time.

[B]

In this season the waters shrink.

The spring is circular and surrounded by gold leaves
Which are fallen from the beech tree.

Not even a skitter-bug disturbs the gloss
Of the surface tension. The sky

Is reflected below in absolute clarity.
If you stare into the water you may know

That nothing disturbs the infinite blue of the sky.

[C]

Keep store, dandle babies, and at night nuzzle
The hazelnut-shaped sweet tits of Lucy, and
With the piratical mark-up of the frontier, get rich.

But you did not, being of weak character.

You saw, from the forest pond, already dark, the great trumpeter
swan
Rise, in clangor, and fight up the steep air where,
At the height of last light, it glimmered, like white flame.

The definition of love being, as we know, complex,
We may say that he, after all, loved his wife.

*

The letter, from campfire, keelboat, or slum room in New Orleans,
Always ended, "God bless you, dear Lucy." After sunset,

Alone, he played his flute in the forest.

[D]

Listen! Stand very still and,
Far off, where shadow
Is undappled, you may hear

The tusked boar grumble in his ivy-slick.

Afterward, there is silence until
The jay, sudden as conscience, calls.

The call, in the infinite sunlight, is like
The thrill of the taste of—on the tongue—brass.

[E]

The world declares itself. That voice
Is vaulted in—oh, arch on arch—redundancy of joy, its end
Is its beginning, necessity
Blooms like a rose. Why,

Therefore, is truth the only thing that cannot
Be spoken?
It can only be enacted, and that in dream,
Or in the dream become, as though unconsciously, action, and he
                                                                stood,

At dusk, in the street of the raw settlement, and saw
The first lamp lit behind a window, and did not know
What he was. Thought: "I do not know my own name."

He walked in the world. He was sometimes seen to stand
In perfect stillness, when no leaf stirred.

Tell us, dear God—tell us the sign
Whereby we may know the time has come.

V THE SOUND OF THAT WIND

[A]

He walked in the world. Knew the lust of the eye.

Wrote: "Ever since a Boy I have had an astonishing desire
        to see Much of the World and particularly
        to acquire a true knowledge of the Birds of North
                                  America."

He dreamed of hunting with Boone, from imagination painted his
                                  portrait.
He proved that the buzzard does not scent its repast, but sights it.
He looked in the eye of the wounded white-headed eagle.

Wrote: ". . . the Noble Fellow looked at his Ennemies
        with a Contemptible Eye."

At dusk he stood on a bluff, and the bellowing of buffalo
Was like distant ocean. He saw
Bones whiten the plain in the hot daylight.

He saw the Indian, and felt the splendor of God.

Wrote: ". . . for there I see the Man Naked from his
        hand and yet free from acquired Sorrow."

Below the salt, in rich houses, he sat, and knew insult.
In the lobbies and couloirs of greatness he dangled,
And was not unacquainted with contumely.

Wrote: "My Lovely Miss Pirrie of Oackley Passed by Me
        this Morning, but did not remember how beautifull
        I had rendered her face once by Painting it
        at her Request with Pastelles."

*

Wrote: ". . . but thanks to My humble talents I can run
       the gantlet throu this World without her help."

And ran it, and ran undistracted by promise of ease,
Nor even the kind condescension of Daniel Webster.

Wrote: ". . . would give me a fat place was I willing to
       have one; but I love indepenn and piece more
       than humbug and money."

And proved same, but in the end, entered
On honor. Far, over the ocean, in the silken salons,
With hair worn long like a hunter's, eyes shining,
He whistled the bird-calls of his distant forest.

Wrote: ". . . in my sleep I continually dream of birds."

And in the end, entered into his earned house,
And slept in a bed, and with Lucy.

                            But the fiddle
Soon lay on the shelf untouched, the mouthpiece
Of the flute was dry, and his brushes.

                        His mind
Was darkened, and his last joy
Was in the lullaby they sang him, in Spanish, at sunset.

He died, and was mourned, who had loved the world.

Who had written: ". . . a world which though wicked enough
          in all conscience is *perhaps* as good
          as worlds unknown."

[B]

So died in his bed, and
Night leaned, and now leans,
Off the Atlantic, and is on schedule.
Grass does not bend beneath that enormous weight
That with no sound sweeps westward. In the Mississippi,

390

On a mud bank, the wreck of a great tree, left
By flood, lies, the root-system and now-stubbed boughs
Lifting in darkness. It
Is white as bone. That whiteness
Is reflected in dark water, and a star
Thereby.

       Later,
In the shack of a sheep-herder, high above the Bitterroot,
The candle is blown out. No other
Light is visible.

The Northwest Orient plane, New York to Seattle, has passed,
                               winking westward.

  [c]

For everything there is a season.

But there is the dream
Of a season past all seasons.

In such a dream the wild-grape cluster,
High-hung, exposed in the gold light,
Unripening, ripens.

Stained, the lip with wetness gleams.

I see your lip, undrying, gleam in the bright wind.

I cannot hear the sound of that wind.

VI LOVE AND KNOWLEDGE

Their footless dance
Is of the beautiful liability of their nature.
Their eyes are round, boldly convex, bright as a jewel,

And merciless. They do not know
Compassion, and if they did,
We should not be worthy of it. They fly
In air that glitters like fluent crystal
And is hard as perfectly transparent iron, they cleave it
With no effort. They cry
In a tongue multitudinous, often like music.

He slew them, at surprising distances, with his gun.
Over a body held in his hand, his head was bowed low,
But not in grief.

He put them where they are, and there we see them:
In our imagination.

What is love?

One name for it is knowledge.

VII TELL ME A STORY

[A]

Long ago, in Kentucky, I, a boy, stood
By a dirt road, in first dark, and heard
The great geese hoot northward.

I could not see them, there being no moon
And the stars sparse. I heard them.

I did not know what was happening in my heart.

It was the season before the elderberry blooms,
Therefore they were going north.

The sound was passing northward.

[B]

Tell me a story.

In this century, and moment, of mania,
Tell me a story.

Make it a story of great distances, and starlight.

The name of the story will be Time,
But you must not pronounce its name.

Tell me a story of deep delight.

FROM
OR ELSE-POEM/POEMS
1968-1974

I AM DREAMING OF A WHITE CHRISTMAS:
THE NATURAL HISTORY OF A VISION

For Andrew Vincent Corry

[I]

No, not that door—never! But,
Entering, saw. Through
Air brown as an old daguerreotype fading. Through
Air that, though dust to the tongue, yet—
Like the inward, brown-glimmering twilight of water—
Swayed. Through brown air, dust-dry, saw. Saw
It.

    The bed.

        Where it had
Been. Now was. Of all
Covering stripped, the mattress
Bare but for old newspapers spread.
Curled edges. Yellow. On yellow paper dust,
The dust yellow. No! Do not.

           Do not lean to
Look at that date. Do not touch
That silken and yellow perfection of Time that
Dust is, for
There is no Time, I,
Entering, see.

*

I,
Standing here, breathe the dry air.

[2]

See
Yonder the old Morris chair bought soon
After marriage, for him to rest after work in, the leather,
Once black, now browning, brown at the dry cracks, streaked
With a fungoid green. Approaching,
See.

See it.

The big head. Propped,
Erect on the chair's leather pillow, bald skin
Tight on skull, not white now, brown
Like old leather lacquered, the big nose
Brown-lacquered, bold-jutting yet, but with
Nostril-flanges gone tattered. I have not
Yet looked at the eyes. Not
Yet.

The eyes
Are not there. But,
Not there, they stare at what
Is not there.

[3]

Not there, but
In each of the appropriate twin apertures, which are
Deep and dark as a thumb-gouge,
Something that might be taken for
A mulberry, large and black-ripe long back, but
Now, with years, dust-dried. The mulberries,
Desiccated, each out of
Its dark lurking-place, stare out at
Nothing.

*

        His eyes
Had been blue.

[4]

        Hers brown. But
Are not now. Now staring,
She sits in the accustomed rocker, but with
No motion. I cannot
Be sure what color the dress once was, but
Am sure that the fabric now falls decisively away
From the Time-sharpened angle of knees. The fabric
Over one knee, the left, has given way. And
I see what protrudes.

        See it.

        Above,
The dry fabric droops over breastlessness.

Over the shrouded femurs that now are the lap, the hands,
Palm-down, lie. The nail of one forefinger
Is missing.

        On the ring-finger of the left hand
There are two diamond rings. On that of the right,
One. On Sundays, and some evenings
When she sat with him, the diamonds would be on the fingers.

The rings. They shone.

Shine now.

In the brown air.

On the brown-lacquered face
There are now no
Lips to kiss with.

[5]

The eyes had been brown. But
Now are not where eyes had been. What things
Now are where eyes had been but
Now are not, stare. At the place where now
Is not what once they
Had stared at.

There is no fire, on the cold hearth now,
To stare at.

[6]

On
The ashes, gray, a piece of torn orange peel.
Foil wrappings of chocolates, silver and crimson and gold,
Yet gleaming from grayness. Torn Christmas paper,
Stamped green and red, holly and berries, not
Yet entirely consumed, but warped
And black-gnawed at edges. I feel

Nothing. A red
Ribbon, ripped long ago from some package of joy,
Winds over the gray hearth like
A fuse that failed. I feel
Nothing.

Not even
When I see the tree.

Why had I not seen the tree before?
Why, on entering, had I not seen it?
It must have been there, and for
A long time, for
The boughs are, of all green, long since denuded.
That much is clear. For the floor
Is there carpeted thick with the brown detritus of cedar.

Christmas trees in our section were always cedar.

[7]

Beneath the un-greened and brown-spiked tree,
On the dead-fall of brown frond-needles, are,
I see, three packages. Identical in size and shape.
In bright Christmas paper. Each with red bow, and under
The ribbon, a sprig of holly.

But look!

The holly
Is, clearly, fresh.

I say to myself:

The holly is fresh.

And
My breath comes short. For I am wondering
Which package is mine.

Oh, which?

I have stepped across the hearth and my hand stretches out.

But the voice:

No presents, son, till the little ones come.

[8]

What shadow of tongue, years back unfleshed, in what
Darkness locked in a rigid jaw, can lift and flex?

The man and the woman sit rigid. What had been
Eyes stare at the cold hearth, but I
Stare at the three chairs. Why—
Tell me why—had I not observed them before? For
They are here.

*

The little red chair
For the baby. The next biggest chair
For my little sister, the little red rocker. Then,
The biggest, my own, me the eldest.

The chairs are all empty.

But
I am thinking a thought that is louder than words.
Thinking:

They're empty, they're empty, but me—oh, I'm here!

And that thought is not words, but a roar like wind, or
The roar of the night-freight beating the rails of the trestle,
And you under the trestle, and the roar
Is nothing but darkness alive. Suddenly,
Silence.

And no
Breath comes.

[9]

Where I was,
Am not. Now am
Where the blunt crowd thrusts, nudges, jerks, jostles,
And the eye is inimical. Then,
Of a sudden, know:

Times Square, the season
Late summer and the hour sunset, with fumes
In throat and smog-glitter at sky-height, where
A jet, silver and ectoplasmic, spooks through
The sustaining light, which
Is yellow as acid. Sweat,
Cold in armpit, slides down flesh.

What year it is, I can't, for the life of me,
Guess, but know that,
Far off, south-eastward, in Bellevue,

In a bare room with windows barred, a woman,
Supine on an iron cot, legs spread, each ankle
Shackled to the cot-frame,
Screams.

She keeps on screaming because it is sunset.

Her hair has been hacked short.

  [10]

Clerks now go home, night watchmen wake up, and the heart
Of the taxi-driver, just coming on shift,
Leaps with hope.

All is not in vain.

Old men come out from the hard-core movies.
They wish they had waited till later.

They stand on the pavement and stare up at the sky.
Their drawers are drying stiff at the crotch, and

The sky dies wide. The sky
Is far above the first hysteria of neon.

Soon they will want to go and get something to eat.

Meanwhile, down the big sluice of Broadway,
The steel logs jerk and plunge
Until caught in the rip, snarl, and eddy here before my face.

A mounted policeman sits a bay gelding. The rump
Of the animal gleams expensively. The policeman
Is some sort of dago. His jowls are swart.
His eyes are bright with seeing.

He is as beautiful as a law of chemistry.

[11]

In any case,
I stand here and think of snow falling. But am
Not here. Am
Otherwere, for already,
This early and summer not over, in west Montana—
Or is it Idaho?—in
The Nez Perce Pass, tonight
It will be snowing.

The Nez Perce is more than 7,000 feet, and I
Have been there. The first flakes,
Large, soft, sparse, come straight down
And with enormous deliberation, white
Out of unbreathing blackness. Snow
Does not yet cling, but the tall stalk of bear-grass
Is pale in darkness. I have seen, long ago,
The paleness of bear-grass in darkness.

                                         But tell me, tell me,
Will I never know
What present there was in that package for me,
Under the Christmas tree?

[12]

All items listed above belong in the world
In which all things are continuous,
And are parts of the original dream which
I am now trying to discover the logic of. This
Is the process whereby pain of the past in its pastness
May be converted into the future tense

Of joy.

READING LATE AT NIGHT,
THERMOMETER FALLING

[1]

The radiator's last hiss and steam-clang done, he,
Under the bare hundred-watt bulb that glares
Like revelation, blanket
Over knees, woolly gray bathrobe over shoulders, handkerchief
On great bald skull spread, glasses
Low on big nose, sits. The book
Is propped on the blanket.

        Thus—
But only in my mind's eye now:

          and there, in the merciless
Glitter of starlight, the fields, mile
On mile over the county, stretch out and are
Crusted with ice which, whitely,
Answers the glitter of stars.

        The mercury
Falls, the night is windless, mindless, and long, and somewhere,
Deep in the blackness of woods, the tendons
Of a massive oak bough snap with the sound of a
Pistol-shot.

      A beam,
Somewhere in the colding house where he sits,
Groans. But his eyes do not lift. Who,
Long back, had said to me:

"When I was young I felt like I
Had to try to understand how things are, before I died."

[2]

But lived long.

       Lived
Into that purity of being that may
Be had past all ambition and the frivolous hope, but who now
Lives only in my mind's eye,
          though I

Cannot see what book is propped there under that forever
Marching gaze—Hume's *History of England,* Roosevelt's
Winning of the West, a Greek reader,
Now Greek to him and held in his hands like a prayer, or
Some college textbook, or Freud on dreams, abandoned
By one of the children. Or, even,
Coke or Blackstone, books forbidding and blackbound, and once I,
Perhaps twelve then, found an old photograph:

                      a young man,
In black coat, high collar, and string tie, black, one hand out
To lie with authority on a big book (Coke or Blackstone?), eyes
Lifted into space.

        And into the future.

            Which
Had not been the future. For the future
Was only his voice that, now sudden, said:

"Son, give me that!"

He took the photograph from my hand, said:

"Some kinds of foolishness a man is due to forget, son."

Tore it across. Tore
Time, and all that Time had been, across. Threw it
Into the fire. Who,
Years later, would say:

*

"I reckon I was lucky enough to learn early that a man can be
happy in his obligations."

Later, I found the poems. Not good.

  [3]

The date on the photograph: 1890.

He was very young then. And poor.

Man lives by images. They
Lean at us from the world's wall, and Time's.

  [4]

Night of the falling mercury, and ice-glitter.
Drouth-night of August and the horned insect booming
At the window-screen.

Ice-field, dusty road: distance flees.

And he sits there, and I think I hear
The faint click and grind of the brain as
It translates the perception of black marks on white paper into
Truth.

      Truth is all.

          We must love it.

And he loved it, who once said:

"It is terrible for a man to live and not know."

Every day he walked out to the cemetery to honor his dead.
That was truth, too.

[5]

Dear Father—Sir—the "Sir" being
The sometimes disturbed recollection
Of the time when you were big, and not dead, and I
Was little, and all boys, of that time and place, automatically
Said that to their fathers, and to any other grown man,
White of course, or damned well got their blocks
Knocked off.

       So, Sir, I,
Who certainly could never have addressed you on a matter
As important as this when you were not dead, now
Address you on it for the last time, even though
Not being, after all my previous and sometimes desperate efforts,
Sure what a son can ever say to a father, even
A dead one.

       Indecipherable passion and compulsion—well,
Wouldn't it be sad to see them, of whatever
Dark root, dwindle into mere
Self-indulgence, habit, tic of the mind, or
The picking of a scab. Reality
Is hard enough to come by, but even
In its absence we need not blaspheme
It.

  Not that
You ever could, God knows. Though I,
No doubt, have, and even now
Run the risk of doing so when I say
That I live in a profound, though
Painful, gratitude to you for what
You could not help but be: i.e., yourself.

Who, aged eighty, said:

"I've failed in a lot of things, but I don't think anybody can say
                        that I didn't have guts."

*

Correct.

> And I,
> In spite of my own ignorance and failures,
> Have forgiven you all your virtues.

> > > Even your valor.

[6]

Who, aged eighty-six, fell to the floor,
Unconscious. Two days later,
Dead. Thus they discovered your precious secret:
A prostate big as a horse-apple. Cancer, of course.

No wonder you, who had not spent a day in bed,
Or uttered a single complaint, in the fifty years of my life,
Cried out at last.

You were entitled to that. It was only normal.

[7]

So disappeared.

> Simply not there.

> > And the seasons,
Nerve-tingling heat or premonitory chill, swung
Through the year, the years swung,

> > > and the past, great
Eater of dreams, secrets, and random data, and
Refrigerator of truth, moved
Down what green valley at a glacier's
Massive pace,

> moving
At a pace not to be calculated by the trivial sun, but by
A clock more unforgiving that, at
Its distance of mathematical nightmare,

Glows forever. The ice-mass, scabbed
By earth, boulders, and some strange vegetation, moves
So imperceptibly that it seems
Only more landscape.

                        Until,
In late-leveling light, some lunkhead clodhopper,
The clodhopper me,
The day's work done, now trudging home,
Stops.

       Stares.

            And there it is.

                     It looms.

The bulk of the unnamable and de-timed beast is now visible,
Erect, in the thinly glimmering shadow of now sun-thinned ice.
                                   Somehow yet
Alive.

                           The lunkhead
Stares.

       The beast,
From his preternatural height, unaware of
The cringe and jaw-dropped awe crouching there below, suddenly,
As if that shimmer of ice-screen had not even been there, lifts,

Into distance,

           the magisterial gaze.

  [8]

The mercury falls. Tonight snow is predicted. This,
However, is another country. Found in a common atlas.

BIRTH OF LOVE

Season late, day late, sun just down, and the sky
Cold gunmetal but with a wash of live rose, and she,
From water the color of sky except where
Her motion has fractured it to shivering splinters of silver,
Rises. Stands on the raw grass. Against
The new-curdling night of spruces, nakedness
Glimmers and, at bosom and flank, drips
With fluent silver. The man,

Some ten strokes out, but now hanging
Motionless in the gunmetal water, feet
Cold with the coldness of depth, all
History dissolving from him, is
Nothing but an eye. Is an eye only. Sees

The body that is marked by his use, and Time's,
Rise, and in the abrupt and unsustaining element of air,
Sway, lean, grapple the pond-bank. Sees
How, with that posture of female awkwardness that is,
And is the stab of, suddenly perceived grace, breasts bulge down in
The pure curve of their weight and buttocks
Moon up and, in that swelling unity,
Are silver, and glimmer. Then

The body is erect, she is herself, whatever
Self she may be, and with an end of the towel grasped in each hand,
Slowly draws it back and forth across back and buttocks, but
With face lifted toward the high sky, where
The over-wash of rose color now fails. Fails, though no star
Yet throbs there. The towel, forgotten,
Does not move now. The gaze
Remains fixed on the sky. The body,

Profiled against the darkness of spruces, seems
To draw to itself, and condense in its whiteness, what light
In the sky yet lingers or, from

The metallic and abstract severity of water, lifts. The body,
With the towel now trailing loose from one hand, is
A white stalk from which the face flowers gravely toward the high
                                                              sky.

This moment is non-sequential and absolute, and admits
Of no definition, for it
Subsumes all other, and sequential, moments, by which
Definition might be possible. The woman,

Face yet raised, wraps,
With a motion as though standing in sleep,
The towel about her body, under the breasts, and,
Holding it there, hieratic as lost Egypt and erect,
Moves up the path that, stair-steep, winds
Into the clamber and tangle of growth. Beyond
The lattice of dusk-dripping leaves, whiteness
Dimly glimmers, goes. Glimmers and is gone, and the man,

Suspended in his darkling medium, stares
Upward where, though not visible, he knows
She moves, and in his heart he cries out that, if only
He had such strength, he would put his hand forth
And maintain it over her to guard, in all
Her out-goings and in-comings, from whatever
Inclemency of sky or slur of the world's weather
Might ever be. In his heart
He cries out. Above

Height of the spruce-night and heave of the far mountain, he sees
The first star pulse into being. It gleams there.

I do not know what promise it makes to him.

CAN I SEE ARCTURUS FROM WHERE I STAND? POEMS 1975

(*IN* SELECTED POEMS: 1923-1975)

A WAY TO LOVE GOD

Here is the shadow of truth, for only the shadow is true.
And the line where the incoming swell from the sunset Pacific
First leans and staggers to break will tell all you need to know
About submarine geography, and your father's death rattle
Provides all biographical data required for the *Who's Who* of the dead.

I cannot recall what I started to tell you, but at least
I can say how night-long I have lain under stars and
Heard mountains moan in their sleep. By daylight,
They remember nothing, and go about their lawful occasions
Of not going anywhere except in slow disintegration. At night
They remember, however, that there is something they cannot
                                    remember,
So moan. Theirs is the perfected pain of conscience, that
Of forgetting the crime, and I hope you have not suffered it. I have.

I do not recall what had burdened my tongue, but urge you
To think on the slug's white belly, how sick-slick and soft,
On the hairiness of stars, silver, silver, while the silence
Blows like wind by, and on the sea's virgin bosom unveiled
To give suck to the wavering serpent of the moon; and,
In the distance, in *plaza, piazza, place, platz*, and square,
Boot heels, like history being born, on cobbles bang.

Everything seems an echo of something else.

*

And when, by the hair, the headsman held up the head
Of Mary of Scots, the lips kept on moving,
But without sound. The lips,
They were trying to say something very important.

But I had forgotten to mention an upland
Of wind-tortured stone white in darkness, and tall, but when
No wind, mist gathers, and once on the Sarré at midnight,
I watched the sheep huddling. Their eyes
Stared into nothingness. In that mist-diffused light their eyes
Were stupid and round like the eyes of fat fish in muddy water,
Or of a scholar who has lost faith in his calling.

Their jaws did not move. Shreds
Of dry grass, gray in gray mist-light, hung
From the side of a jaw, unmoving.

You would think that nothing would ever again happen.

That may be a way to love God.

EVENING HAWK

From plane of light to plane, wings dipping through
Geometries and orchids that the sunset builds,
Out of the peak's black angularity of shadow, riding
The last tumultuous avalanche of
Light above pines and the guttural gorge,
The hawk comes.

                    His wing
Scythes down another day, his motion
Is that of the honed steel-edge, we hear
The crashless fall of stalks of Time.

*

The head of each stalk is heavy with the gold of our error.

Look! Look! he is climbing the last light
Who knows neither Time nor error, and under
Whose eye, unforgiving, the world, unforgiven, swings
Into shadow.

        Long now,
The last thrush is still, the last bat
Now cruises in his sharp hieroglyphics. His wisdom
Is ancient, too, and immense. The star
Is steady, like Plato, over the mountain.

If there were no wind we might, we think, hear
The earth grind on its axis, or history
Drip in darkness like a leaking pipe in the cellar.

OLD NIGGER ON ONE-MULE CART ENCOUNTERED LATE AT NIGHT WHEN DRIVING HOME FROM PARTY IN THE BACK COUNTRY

Flesh, of a sudden, gone nameless in music, flesh
Of the dancer, under your hand, flowing to music, girl-
Flesh sliding, flesh flowing, sweeter than
Honey, slicker than Essolube, over
The music-swayed, delicate trellis of bone
That is white in secret flesh-darkness. What
The music, it says: *no name, no name!*—only
That movement under your hand, what
It is, and no name, and you shut your eyes, but
The music, it stops. O.K. Silence
Rages, it ranges the world, it will
Devour us, for
That sound I do now hear is not external, is

Simply the crinkle and crepitation,
Like crickets gone nuts, of
Booze in the blood. *Goodnight! Goodnight!*

I can't now even remember the name of the dancer, but

I must try to tell you what, in July, in Louisiana,
Night is. No moon, but stars whitely outrageous in
Blackness of velvet, the long lane ahead
Whiter than snow, wheels soundless in deep dust, dust
Pluming whitely behind, and ahead all
The laneside hedges and weed-growth
Long since powdered whiter than star-dust, or frost, but air
Hot. The night pants hot like a dog, it breathes
Off the blossoming bayou like the expensive whiff
Of floral tributes at a gangster's funeral in N.O.,
It breathes the smell love makes in darkness, and far off,
In the great swamp, an owl cries,
And does not stop. At the sharp right turn,
Hedge-blind, which you take too fast,
There it is: death-trap.

Oh the fool-nigger—ass-hole wrong side of
The road, naturally: And the mule-head
Thrusts at us, and ablaze in our headlights,
Outstaring from primal bone-blankness and the arrogant
Stupidity of skull snatched there
From darkness and the saurian stew of pre-history.
For an instant—the eyes. The eyes,
They blaze from the incandescent magma
Of mule-brain. Thus mule-eyes. Then
Man-eyes, not blazing, white-bulging
In black face, in black night, and man-mouth
Wide open, the shape of an *O,* for the scream
That does not come. Even now,
That much in my imagination, I see. But also
The cargo of junk the black face blooms amidst—
Rusted bed-springs on end, auto axle at God-knows-what
Angle up-canted, barbed wire on a fence rail wound,
Lengths of stove pipe beat-up. God-yes,
A death-trap. But

I snatch the wheel left in a dust-skid,
Smack into the ditch, but the ditch
Shallow, and so, not missing a beat, I'm out
And go on, and he's left alone on his cart there
Unmoving, and dust of the car's passage settles
White on sweat-sticky skin, black, of the forehead, and on
The already gray head. This,
Of course, under the high stars.

Perhaps he had screamed, after all.

And go on: to the one last drink, sweat-grapple in darkness, then
Sleep. But only until
The hour when small, though disturbing, gastric shifts
Are experienced, the hour when the downy
Throat of the swamp owl vibrates to the last
Predawn cry, the hour
When joy-sweat, or night-sweat, has dried to a microscopic
Crust on the skin, and some
Recollection of childhood brings tears
To dark-wide eyes, and the super-ego
Again throws the switch for the old recorded harangue.
Until waking, that is—and I wake to see
Floating in darkness above the bed the
Black face, eyes white-bulging, mouth shaped like an *O*, and so
Get up, get paper and pencil, and whittle away at
The poem. Give up. Back to bed. And remember
Now only the couplet of what
Had aimed to be—Jesus Christ—a sonnet:
One of those who gather junk and wire to use
For purposes that we cannot peruse.

As I said, Jesus Christ. But

Moved on through the years. Am here. Another
Land, another love, and in such latitude, having risen
In darkness, feet bare to cold boards, stare,
Through ice-glitter of glass and air purer
Than absolute zero, into
The white night and star-crackling sky over
The snow-mountain. Have you ever,

At night, stared into the snow-filled forest and felt
The impulse to flee there? Enter there? Be
There and plunge naked
Through snow, through drifts floundering, white
Into whiteness, among
Spectral great beech-boles, birch-whiteness, black jag
Of shadow, black spruce-bulks snow-shouldered, floundering
Upward and toward the glacial assertion that
The mountain is? Have you ever
Had the impulse to stretch forth your hand over
The bulge of forest and seize trees like the hair
Of a head you would master? Well,
We are entitled to our fantasies, for life
Is only the fantasy that has happened to us, and

In God's name. But

In the lyrical logic and nightmare astuteness that
Is God's name, by what magnet, I demand,
Are the iron and out-flung filings of our lives, on
A sheet of paper, blind-blank as Time, snapped
Into a polarized pattern—and I see,
By a bare field that yearns pale in starlight, the askew
Shack. He arrives there. Unhitches the mule.
Stakes it out. Between cart and shack,
Pauses to make water, and while
The soft, plopping sound in deep dust continues, his face
Is lifted into starlight, calm as prayer. He enters
The dark shack, and I see
A match spurt, then burn down, die.

The last glow is reflected on the petal-pink
And dark horn-crust of the thumbnail.

And so I say:
Brother, Rebuker, my Philosopher past all
Casuistry, will you be with me when
I arrive and leave my own cart of junk
Unfended from the storm of starlight and
The howl, like wind, of the world's monstrous blessedness,
To enter, by a bare field, a shack unlit?

Entering into that darkness to fumble
My way to a place to lie down, but holding,
I trust, in my hand, a name—
Like a shell, a dry flower, a worn stone, a toy—merely
A hard-won something that may, while Time
Backward unblooms out of time toward peace, utter
Its small, sober, and inestimable
Glow, trophy of truth.

Can I see Arcturus from where I stand?

NOW AND THEN: POEMS 1976-1978

RED-TAIL HAWK AND PYRE OF YOUTH

To Harold Bloom

I

Breath clamber-short, face sun-peeled, stones
Loose like untruth underfoot, I
Had just made the ridge crest, and there,
Opening like joy, the unapprehensible purity
Of afternoon flooded, in silver,
The sky. It was
The hour of stainless silver just before
The gold begins.

Eyes, strangely heavy like lead,
Drew down to the .30-30 hung on my hand
As on a crooked stick, in growing wonder
At what it might really be. It was as though
I did not know its name. Nor mine. Nor yet had known
That all is only
All, and part of all. No wind
Moved the silver light. No movement,

Except for the center of
That convex perfection, not yet
A dot even, nameless, no color, merely
A shadowy vortex of silver. Then,
In widening circles—oh, nearer!
And suddenly I knew the name, and saw,
As though seeing, it come toward me,

Unforgiving, the hot blood of the air:
Gold eyes, unforgiving, for they, like God, see all.

2

There was no decision in the act,
There was no choice in the act—the act impossible but
Possible. I screamed, not knowing
From what emotion, as at that insane range
I pressed the cool, snubbed
Trigger. Saw
The circle
Break.

3

Heart leaping in joy past definition, in
Eyes tears past definition, by rocky hill and valley
Already dark-devoured, the bloody
Body already to my bare flesh embraced, cuddled
Like babe to heart, and my heart beating like love:
Thus homeward.

But nobody there.

So at last
I dared stare in the face—the lower beak drooping,
As though from thirst, eyes filmed.
Like a secret, I wrapped it in newspaper quickly
And hid it deep
In the ice chest.

Too late to start now.

4

Up early next morning, with
My father's old razor laid out, the scissors,
Pliers and needles, waxed thread,
The burlap and salt, the arsenic and clay,
Steel rods, thin, and glass eyes

Gleaming yellow. Oh, yes,
I knew my business. And at last a red-tail—

Oh, king of the air!

And at that miraculous range.

How my heart sang!

Till all was ready—skull now well scraped
And with arsenic dried, and all flesh joints, and the cape
Like a carapace feathered in bronze, and naturally anchored
At beak and at bone joints, and steel
Driven through to sustain wing and bone
And the clay-burlap body there within.
It was molded as though for that moment to take to the air—
though,

In God's truth, the chunk of poor wingless red meat,
The model from which all was molded, lay now
Forever earthbound, fit only
For dog tooth, not sky.

5

Year after year, in my room, on the tallest of bookshelves,
Regal, it perched on its bough-crotch to guard
Blake and *Lycidas,* Augustine, Hardy and *Hamlet,*
Baudelaire and Rimbaud, and I knew that the yellow eyes,
Unsleeping, stared as I slept.

Till I slept in that room no more.

6

Years pass like a dream, are a dream, and time came
When my mother was dead, father bankrupt, and whiskey
Hot in my throat while there for the last

Time I lay, and my heart
Throbbed slow in the
Meaningless motion of life, and with

Eyes closed I knew
That yellow eyes somewhere, unblinking, in vengeance stared.

Or *was* it vengeance? What could I know?

Could Nature forgive, like God?

7

That night in the lumber room, late,
I found him—the hawk, feathers shabby, one
Wing bandy-banged, one foot gone sadly
Askew, one eye long gone—and I reckoned
I knew how it felt with one gone.

And all relevant items I found there: my first book of Milton,
The *Hamlet*, the yellow, leaf-dropping Rimbaud, and a book
Of poems friends and I had printed in college, not to mention
The collection of sexual Japanese prints—strange sex
Of mechanical sexlessness. And so made a pyre for
The hawk that, though gasoline-doused and wing-dragging,
Awaited, with what looked like pride,
The match.

8

Flame flared. Feathers first, and I flinched, then stood
As the steel wire warped red to defend
The shape designed godly for air. But
It fell with the mass, and I
Did not wait.

What left
To do but walk in the dark, and no stars?

9

Some dreams come true, some no.
But I've waked in the night to see
High in the late and uncurdled silver of summer
The pale vortex appear once again—and you come

And always the rifle swings up, though with
The weightlessness now of dream,
The old .30-30 that knows
How to bind us in air-blood and earth-blood together
In our commensurate fate,
Whose name is a name beyond joy.

10

And I pray that in some last dream or delusion,
While hospital wheels creak beneath
And the nurse's soles make their *squeak-squeak* like mice,
I'll again see the first small silvery swirl
Spin outward and downward from sky-height
To bring me the truth in blood-marriage of earth and air—
And all will be as it was
In that paradox of unjoyful joyousness,
Till the dazzling moment when I, a last time, must flinch
From the regally feathered gasoline flare
Of youth's poor, angry, slapdash, and ignorant pyre.

YOUTH STARES AT MINOAN SUNSET

On the lap of the mountain meadow,
At the break of the Cretan cliff-quarry where
Venetians had once sawed their stone, soft
Nag of surf far below foot, he
Stares seaward the distance to sunset.

The sky is rose-hearted, immense, undisturbed.
In that light the youth's form is black, without motion,
And birds, gull nor other, have no transaction
In the inflamed emptiness of sky. Mountainward,
No bird cries. We had called once,
But we were too far, too far.

*

Molten and massy, of its own weight flattened,
The sun accelerates downward, the sea,
From general slate-blue, flaming upward.
Contact is made at the horizon line.

On that line, one instant, one only,
The great coin, flame-massy and with
The frail human figure thereon minted black,
Balances. Suddenly is gone. A gull
Defiles at last the emptiness of air.

We are closer now. The black
Silhouette, yet small, stares seaward. To our cry
It does not turn. Later,
It will, and turning, see us with a slow
And pitying happiness of recognition born of
A knowledge we do not yet have. Or have forgotten.

He spreads his arms to the sky as though he loves it—and us.

He is so young.

AH, ANIMA!

Watch the great bough lashed by wind and rain. Is it
A metaphor for your soul—or Man's—or even

Mine in the hurricane of Time? Now,
In the gray and splintered light, in the scything

Tail of the hurricane, miles of forest around us
Heave like the sea, and the gray underside of leaf is exposed

Of every tree, non-coniferous. The tall
Pines blackly stagger. Beyond,

*

The bulk and backdrop of mountain is
Obscured. Can you locate yourself

On the great chart of history?
In the distance a tree crashes.

Empires have fallen, and the stream
Gnashes its teeth with the *klang* of boulders.

Later, sleep. Tomorrow, help
Will come. The Governor promises. Roads will be rebuilt,

And houses. Food distributed. But, meanwhile, sleep
Is a disaster area, too. You have lain down

In the shards of Time and the un-roar of the wind of being,
And when, in the dark, you wake, with only

The *klang* of distant boulders in your ears,
You may wish that you, even in the wrack and dark pelt of storm,

Had run forth, screaming as wind snatched your breath away
Until you were nameless—oh, anima!—and only

Your mouth, rounded, is in the night there, the utterance gone.
                                                            Perhaps
That is the only purity—to leave

The husk behind, and leap
Into the blind and antiseptic anger of air.

THE MISSION

In the dark kitchen the electric icebox rustles.
It whispers like the interior dialogue of guilt and extenuation,

And I wake from a dream of horses. They do not know
I am dreaming of them. By this time they must be long dead.

Behind barbed wire, in fog off the sea, they stand.
Two clumps of horses, uncavorting, like gray stone, stand,
Heavy manes unrustling in even the gray sea wind.
The sea is gray. Night falls. Later, the manes will rustle,

But ever so little, in new wind lifting off the Bay of Biscay. But no—
They are dead. *La boucherie chevaline,* in the village,
Has a gold horse-head above the door. I wake
From my dream, and know that the shadow

Of the great spruce close by my house must be falling
Black on the white roof of winter. The spruce
Wants to hide the house from the moon, for
The moon's intentions have never been quite clear.

The spruce does not know that a secret square of moonlight lies
                                                     cunningly on
The floor by my bed, and I watch it and think how,
On the snow-locked mountain, deep in a fissure
Under the granite ledge, the bear

Huddles inside his fur like an invalid inside
A charity-ward blanket. Fat has thinned on bone, and the fur
Is too big for him now. He stirs in sleep, farts
Gently in the glacial blackness of the cave. The eyes

Do not open. Outside, in moonlight,
The ledges are bearded with ice, and the brook,
Black, crawls under ice. It has a mission, but,
In that blackness, has forgotten what. I, too,

Have forgotten the nature of my own mission. This
May be fortunate, for if I stare at the dark ceiling
And try to remember, I do not have to go back to sleep,
And not sleeping, will not again dream

Of clumps of horses, fog-colored in sea fog, rumps
To the sea wind, standing like stone primitively hewn,

While the fields, gray, stretch beyond them, and distance dies.
Perhaps that lost mission is to try to understand

The possibility of joy in the world's tangled and hieroglyphic beauty.

HEART OF AUTUMN

Wind finds the northwest gap, fall comes.
Today, under gray cloud-scud and over gray
Wind-flicker of forest, in perfect formation, wild geese
Head for a land of warm water, the *boom*, the lead pellet.

Some crumple in air, fall. Some stagger, recover control,
Then take the last glide for a far glint of water. None
Knows what has happened. Now, today, watching
How tirelessly *V* upon *V* arrows the season's logic,

Do I know my own story? At least, they know
When the hour comes for the great wing-beat. Sky-strider,
Star-strider—they rise, and the imperial utterance,
Which cries out for distance, quivers in the wheeling sky.

That much they know, and in their nature know
The path of pathlessness, with all the joy
Of destiny fulfilling its own name.
I have known time and distance, but not why I am here.

Path of logic, path of folly, all
The same—and I stand, my face lifted now skyward,
Hearing the high beat, my arms outstretched in the tingling
Process of transformation, and soon tough legs,

With folded feet, trail in the sounding vacuum of passage,
And my heart is impacted with a fierce impulse
To unwordable utterance—
Toward sunset, at a great height.

BEING HERE:
POETRY 1977–1980

WHY HAVE I WANDERED THE ASPHALT
OF MIDNIGHT?

Why have I wandered the asphalt of midnight and not known why?
Not guilt, or joy, or expectation, or even to know how,
When clouds are tattered, the distance beyond screams its rage,
Or when fog breaks
To clarity—not even to know how the strict
Rearrangement of stars communicates
Their mystic message to
The attent corpuscles hurrying heartward, and from.

Why did I stand with no motion under
The spilt-ink darkness of spruces and try to hear,
In the soundlessness of falling snow,
The heartbeat I know as the only self
I know that I know, while History
Trails its meaning like old cobwebs
Caught in a cellar broom?

Why should I clamber the cliff now gone bone-white in moonlight?
Just to feel blood dry like a crust on hands, or watch
The moon lean westering to the next range,
The next, and beyond,
To wash the whole continent, like spume?
Why should I sit till from the next valley I hear
The great bear's autumnal sex-hoot
Or the glutted owl make utterance?

*

Why should I wander dark dunes till rollers
Boom in from China, stagger, and break
On the beach in frothed mania, while high to the right
The North Star holds steady enough to be Truth?

Yes, why, all the years, and places, and nights, have I
Wandered and not known the question I carried?
And carry? Yes, sometimes, at dawn,
I have seen the first farmer

Set bright the steel share to the earth, or met,
Snowshoed, the trapper just set on his dawn-rounds.
Or even, long back, on a streetcar
Bound cityward, watched some old workman
Lean over his lunch box, and yawn.

ANTINOMY: TIME AND WHAT HAPPENED

I

Alone, alone, I lie. The canoe
On blackness floats. It must
Be so, for up to a certain point
All comes back clear. I saw,
At dock, the canoe, aluminum, rising ghost-white on blackness.
This much is true. Silent,
As entering air, the paddle, slow, dips. Silent,
I slide forth. Forth on,
Forth into,
What new dimension? Slow
As a dream, no ripple at keel, I move through
The stillness, on blackness, past hope or despair
Not relevant now to illusion I'd once
Thought I lived by. At last,
Shores absorbed in the blackness of forest, I lie down. High,
Stars stare down, and I

See them. I wonder
If they see me. If they do, do they know
What they see?

2

Do I hear stars speak in a whisper as gentle as breath
To the few reflections caught pale in the blackness beneath?
How still is the night! It must be their voices.
Then strangely a loon-cry glows ember-red,
And the ember in darkness dims
To a tangle of senses beyond windless fact or logical choices,
While out of Time, Timelessness brims
Like oil on black water, to coil out and spread
On the time that seems past and the time that may come,
And both the same under
The present's darkening dome.

3

A dog, in the silence, is barking a county away.
It is long yet till day.

4

As consciousness outward seeps, the dark seeps in.
As the self dissolves, realization surrenders its burden
And thus fulfills your fictionality.
Night wind is no more than unrippling drift.
The canoe, light as breath, moves in a dignity
As soundless as a star's mathematical shift
Reflected light-years away
In the lake's black parodic sky.

I wonder if this is I.

5

It is not long till day.

6

Dawn bursts like the birth pangs of your, and the world's, existence.
The future creeps into the blueness of distance.
Far back, scraps of memory hang, rag-rotten, on a rusting
                                                barbed-wire fence.

7

One crow, caw lost in the sky-peak's lucent trance,
Will gleam, sun-purpled, in its magnificence.

SAFE IN SHADE

Eyes, not bleared but blue,
Of the old man, horizonward gazed—
As on horizons and years, long lost, but now
Projected from storage in that capacious skull.

He sat in his big chair propped
Against reddish tatter of
Bole-bark of the great cedar. I,
The boy who on the ground sat, waited.

I waited for him to speak.

I waited for him to come back to me
From the distances he traveled in.
I waited for him to speak. I saw
The cob pipe in the liver-spotted hand
Now propped on a knee, on the washed blue-jeans.
Smoke, frail, slow, blue—as blue
As the jeans but not the eyes—
Rose to thread the cedar-dark.
Around us in our shade and hush
Roared summer's fierce fecundity,

And the sun struck down,
In blare and dazzle, on the myth of the world, but we,
Safe in the bourne of distance and shade,
Sat so silent that, from woods coming down
To the whitewashed fence but yards behind me,
I heard the secret murmur and hum
That in earth, on leaf, in air, seethed. Heard
One jay, outraged, scream.
The old blue eyes, they fixed on me.

I waited for him to speak. He spoke.

Now into the world hurled,
In later times and other places,
I lived but as man must
In all the garbled world's compulsions,
By fate perforce performed
Acts evil or good, or even
Both in the same act, in
That paradox the world exemplifies.

And Time, like wind-tattered smoke,
Blew by for one who, like all men, had flung,
In joy and man's maniacal
Rage, his blood
And the blind, egotistical, self-defining
Sperm into
That all-devouring, funnel-shaped, mad and high-spiraling,
Dark suction that
We have, as the Future, named.

Where is my cedar tree?

Where is the Truth—oh, unambiguous—
Thereof?

RUMOR VERIFIED:
POEMS 1979-1980

LOOKING NORTHWARD, AEGEANWARD:
NESTLINGS ON SEACLIFF

Chalky, steel-hard, or glass-slick, the cliff
That you crawl up, inch up, or clamber, till now,
Arms outspread, you cling to rotting scrub roots, and at last
See what you'd risked neck to see, the nub
Of rock-shelf outthrust from the shaded recess where,
From huddle of trash, dried droppings, and eggshell, lifts
The unfeathered pitiless weakness of necks that scarcely uphold
The pink corolla of beak-gape, the blind yearning lifeward.

In sun-blast, around and above, weave
The outraged screams that would net your head,
And wings slash the air with gleaming mercilessness,
While for toehold, or handhold, downward you grope,
Or for purchase to pause on and turn to the sun-crinkled sea,
To watch it fade northward into the
Horizon's blue ambiguity. You think
How long ago galleys—slim, black, bronze-flashing—bore
Northward too, and toward that quarter's blue dazzle of distance.
Or of a tale told.

And then think how, lost in the dimness of aeons, sea sloshed
Like suds in a washing machine, land heaved, and sky
At noon darkened, and darkness, not like any metaphor, fell,
And in that black fog gulls screamed as the feathers of gull-wing
From white flash to flame burst. That was the hour
When rooftree or keystone of palaces fell, and

*

Priest's grip drew backward the curls of the king's son until
Throat-softness was tightened, and the last cry
Was lost in the gargle of blood on bronze blade. The king,
In his mantle, had buried his face. But even
That last sacrifice availed naught. Ashes
Would bury all. Cities beneath sea sank.

In some stony, high field, somewhere, eyes,
Unbelieving, opened. They saw, first,
The sky. Stared long. How little
They understood. But, slowly, began,
In new ignorance, the nature of Time.

You think of necks, unfeathered and feeble, upholding
The pink corolla of beak-gape—that blind yearning lifeward.

RUMOR VERIFIED

Since the rumor has been verified, you can, at least,
Disappear. You will no longer be seen at the Opera,
With your head bowed studiously, to one side a little,
Nor at your unadvertised and very exclusive
Restaurant, discussing wine with the sommelier,
Nor at your club, setting modestly forth your subtle opinion.

Since the rumor has been verified, you can try, as in dream,
To have lived another life—not with the father
Of rigid self-discipline, and x-ray glance,
Not with the mother, overindulgent and pretty,
Who toyed with your golden locks, slipped money on the side,
And waved a witch's wand for success, and a rich marriage.

Since the rumor has been verified, you may secretly sneak
Into El Salvador, or some such anguished spot,
Of which you speak the language, dreaming, trying to believe

That, orphaned, you grew up in poverty and vision, struggling
For learning, for mankind's sake. Here you pray with the sick, kiss
lepers.

Since the rumor has been verified, you yearn to hold
A cup of cold water for the dying man to sip.
You yearn to look deep into his eyes and learn wisdom.
Or perhaps you have a practical streak and seek
Strange and derelict friends, and for justification lead
A ragtag squad to ambush the uniformed patrol.

Well, assuming the rumor verified—that may be
The only logical course: at any price,
Even bloodshed, however ruthless, to change any dominant order
And the secret corruption of power that makes us what we seem.
Yes, what is such verification against a strength of will?

But even in the face of the rumor, you sometimes shudder,
Seeing men as old as you who survive the terror
Of knowledge. You watch them slyly. What is their trick?
Do they wear a Halloween face? But what can you do?
Perhaps pray to God for strength to face the verification
That you are simply a man, with a man's dead reckoning, nothing
more.

MOUNTAIN MYSTERY

On the mountain trail, all afternoon,
Gravel, uncertain, grinds under hoof.
On left side, with scrub growth, the cliff hangs.
On right, hypnotic emptiness.

Far down, in distance, a stream uncoils,
Like nothing more than a glittering wire
Tangled in stone-slots, lost on the plain,
In distance dissolved, or down canyon, gone.

*

You stop. You turn and know what already
You know: snow commanding west ranges, sun
Yet high. Again, eastward turn, and the sun's
Hot hand, fingers spread, is pressed against your shoulders.

Soaring in sunlight, eastward, the eagle
Swings to a height invisible
Except when light catches a bright flash of wing.
You open your lips in infinite thirst for

The altitude's wine. All, all of the past
Is gone. Yet what is the past but delusion?
Or future? In timeless light the world swims.
Alone, alone, you move through the timeless

Light. Toward what? The ranch in the valley,
Some ten miles away—what but delusion?
Alone, but not alone, for if
You lift your eyes, you see, some forty

Feet off, her there—unless, of course,
The track now rounds an abutment, and she
Has ceased to exist, and you are alone
In the world's metaphysical beauty of light.

Only alone do you then think of love.
Eyes shut, you think how, in saddle, that narrow
Waist sways. You think how, when soon the trail straightens,
She will lean back to smile. Her eyes will be bright.

You pass the abutment. Beyond, the great mesa
Sinks blue. The world falls away, falls forever.
But she sways in the saddle, turns, smiles, and your heart
Leaps up. Then cries out: *Oh, what is enough?*

That night you will lie in your bed, not alone—
But alone. In dark paradox, you lie
And think of the screaming gleam of the world
In which you have passed alone, lost—

And in dark, lost, lain, hearing frailty of breath beside.

WHAT VOICE AT MOTH-HOUR

What voice at moth-hour did I hear calling
As I stood in the orchard while the white
Petals of apple blossoms were falling,
Whiter than moth-wing in that twilight?

What voice did I hear as I stood by the stream,
Bemused in the murmurous wisdom there uttered,
While ripples at stone, in their steely gleam,
Caught last light before it was shuttered?

What voice did I hear as I wandered alone
In a premature night of cedar, beech, oak,
Each foot set soft, then still as stone
Standing to wait while the first owl spoke?

The voice that I heard once at dew-fall, I now
Can hear by a simple trick. If I close
My eyes, in that dusk I again know
The feel of damp grass between bare toes,

Can see the last zigzag, sky-skittering, high,
Of a bullbat, and even hear, far off, from
Swamp-cover, the whip-o-will, and as I
Once heard, hear the voice: *It's late! Come home.*

HAVE YOU EVER EATEN STARS?

(A Note on Mycology)

Scene: A glade on a bench of the mountain,
      Where beech, birch, and spruce meet
      In peace, though in peace not intermingled,
      Around the slight hollow, upholstered

In woods-earth damp, and soft, centuries old—
Spruce needle, beech leaf, birch leaf, ground-pine
belly-crawling,
And fern frond, and deadfall of birch, grass blade
So biblically frail, and sparse in that precinct where
The sunray makes only its brief
And perfunctory noontide visitation.
All, all in that cycle's beneficence
Of being are slowly absorbed—oh, slowly—into
What once had fed them. And now,
In silence as absolute as death,
Or as vision in breathlessness,
Your foot may come. Or mine,
As when I, sweat-soaked in summer's savagery,
Might here come, and stand
In that damp cool, and peace of process,
And hear, somewhere, a summer-thinned brook descending,
Past stone, and stone, its musical stair.

But late, once in the season's lateness, I,
After drouth had broken, rain come and gone,
And sky been washed to a blue more delicate,
Came. Stood. Stared. For now,
Earth, black as a midnight sky,
Was, like sky-darkness, studded with
Gold stars, as though
In emulation, however brief.
There, by a deer trail, by deer dung nourished,
Burst the gleam, rain-summoned,
Of bright golden chanterelles.
However briefly, however small and restricted, here was
A glade-burst of glory.

Later, I gathered stars into a basket.

Question: What can you do with stars, or glory?
I'll tell you, I'll tell you—thereof
Eat. Swallow. Absorb. Let bone
Be sustained thereof, let gristle
Toughen, flesh be more preciously
Gratified, muscle yearn in

Its strength. Let brain glow
In its own midnight of darkness,
Under its own inverted, bowl-shaped
Sky, skull-sky, let the heart
Rejoice.
             What other need now
Is possible to you but that
Of seeing life as glory?

FEAR AND TREMBLING

The sun now angles downward, and southward.
The summer, that is, approaches its final fulfillment.
The forest is silent, no wind-stir, bird-note, or word.
It is time to meditate on what the season has meant.

But what is the meaningful language for such meditation?
What is a word but wind through the tube of the throat?
Who defines the relation between the word *sun* and the sun?
What word has glittered on whitecap? Or lured blossom out?

Walk deeper, foot soundless, into the forest.
Stop, breath bated. Look southward, and up, where high leaves
Against sun, in vernal translucence, yet glow with the freshest
Young tint of the lost spring. Here now nothing grieves.

Can one, in fact, meditate in the heart, rapt and wordless?
Or find his own voice in the towering gust now from northward?
When boughs toss—is it in joy or pain and madness?
The gold leaf—is it whirled in anguish or ecstasy skyward?

Can the heart's meditation wake us from life's long sleep,
And instruct us how foolish and fond was our labor spent—
Us who now know that only at death of ambition does the deep
Energy crack crust, spurt forth, and leap

From grottoes, dark—and from the caverned enchainment?

BROTHER TO DRAGONS: A NEW VERSION (1979)

*In the middle of December 1811, a terrible crime was com-
mitted. Two brothers, Lilburne and Isham Lewis, brutally
murdered a Negro slave for a reason so trivial as to seem
almost meaningless. Their act is a matter of record, but
would long since have taken its place with other forgotten
episodes of gratuitous cruelty and violence, of which history provides such numerous examples, were it not that
they were the sons of Thomas Jefferson's sister. Jefferson,
despite the fact that the crime was a matter of common
knowledge and reported in the press, apparently could not
bring himself to comment on or even acknowledge it.*

*The events leading up to the murder, and the even more
astonishing aftermath, provide the narrative framework
of* Brother to Dragons. *The form of the poem, as the
author states in a foreword, is that of a "dialogue spoken
by characters, but it is not a play. The main body of the
action is in the remote past—in the earthly past of the
characters long dead—and now they meet at an unspecified place and at an unspecified time to try to make
sense of that action. We may take them to appear, and
disappear, as their inner urgencies, and the urgencies of
argument, swell and subside. The place of this meeting is,
we may say, 'no place,' and the time is 'any time.' "*

*Thus the story itself is related by the principal actors in
it and partly in direct narrative and commentary by the
poet. The philosophical core of the poem is concerned with
the idealism of Thomas Jefferson, who appears as one of the
main speakers. In the course of the dialogue, Jefferson,
confronted by the bitter fact of this monstrousness in the
family blood, and other evidences of evil in American
history since his time, is forced to re-examine his belief in
the innate goodness and perfectibility of man and to fash-*

*ion, on a broader and more realistic base, a new definition
of human hope.*

In the course of writing Brother to Dragons, *Warren
obtained permission to make two explorations of the site
of Lilburne Lewis's house, on a bluff in Kentucky overlooking the Ohio River. His accounts of these visits, and
the reflections and memories they evoked, are included
here; one comes near the beginning of the poem, the other
is its conclusion.*

—A.E.

Well, after all, I had permission now. So down the road,
In the best shade there was, I parked the car
And left my father drowsing there,
For he was old, already pushing eighty.
No truth on mountains any more for him,
Nor marvel in the bush that burns and yet is not consumed.
Yes, he had climbed his mountain long ago,
And met what face—ah, who can tell?
He will not, who has filled the tract of Time
With rectitude and natural sympathy,
Past hope, ambition, and despair's delectable anodyne.
What face he had met I do not know, but know
That once, in a café in Paris, when an old friend said,
"Tell me about your father," my heart suddenly
Choked on my words, and in that throttlement
Of inwardness and coil, light fell
Like one great ray that gilds the deepest glade,
And thus I saw his life a story told,
Its glory and reproach domesticated.

The failures of our fathers are failures we shall make,
Their triumphs the triumphs we shall never have.
But remembering even their failures, we are compelled to praise,
And for their virtues hate them while we praise,
And praising, wonder, caught in the sudden and corrosive glare
Of speculation like the enemy rocket
Exploding above the torn and terror-bit terrain
Where darkness is the only comfort left—
We wonder, even as we consider their virtue:

What is wisdom and what the dimming of faculty?
What kindliness, and what the guttering of desire?
What philosophic wisdom, and what the fatigue of the relaxed nerve?

But still, despite all naturalistic considerations,
Or in the end because of naturalistic considerations,
We must believe in the notion of virtue. There is no
Inland path around that rock-ragged
And spume-nagged promontory. For past
All appetite and alibi, and past
Your various studies and reasonable ambitions,
Infidelities and chronic self-deception,
And the odor of fresh hay on the night wind
Like the perfume of a woman's parts,
You know that virtue, painful as a syllogism,
Waits, and will wait, as on
The leaf the lethal mantis at his prayer,
And under those great hands, spiked, Gothic, barbed,
Clasped high to arch the summer blue of heaven,
You pass, like ant or aphid in the season's joy, while he,
That green, crank nightmare of the dear green world,
All day, in sun and shade, maintains
His murderous devotion.
For you will come and under the barbed arch meet
The irremediable logic of all the anguish
Your cunning could invent or heart devise.
Or is any answer as complete as that?

Who has seen man in his naked absoluteness?

It was remembering my father that flushed these thoughts.
But now speculation settles like dust
When wind drops, and there is only the great quiet
Of a sunlit space,
For I recall one Sunday afternoon,
How, after the chicken dinner and ice cream,
Amid the comics, and headlines of the world's disaster,
I saw him sit and with grave patience teach
Some small last Latin to a little child,
My brother's child, aged five, and she would say
The crazy words, and laugh, they were so crazy.

*

There's worse, I guess, than in the end to offer
Your last bright keepsake, some fragment of the vase
That held your hopes, to offer it to a child.
And the child took the crazy toy, and laughed.

I wish you could tell me why I find this scene so sweet.

I left my father in the car to drowse
And went to climb the hill.
Like Boyle* had said, I was a fool,
A God-damned fool, and all that brush to fight.
Saw-vine and sassafras, passion-vine, wild rose,
But the roses gone, and bloom of the passion vine,
And blackberry, man-high, dry-snagging for your blood,
And up the bluff, where cedar clambered rock,
The tall, hot gloom of oak and ironwood,
Canted and crazed but tall, and from their boughs
The great grapevine, a century old, hung in its jungle horror,
Swayed in its shagged and visceral delight,
Convolved from bough to bough, halyard, reefline, and forebrace—
The rotten rigging of that foundered hill.

But I went on, and hit the carriage road
Old Lewis' Negroes had chopped from the live rock.
I hoped to God it wasn't in July
Black hands had grabbled and black sweat dropped.
But niggers don't mind heat. At least, not much.
And sure, somebody's got to build the road.
Did I say road? Well, that's an overstatement.
You see the fallen buttressing, that's all,
Poor nigger stonework, generations gone,
And sluicing winter and the oak-root's heave
Have done their duty. So
I damned the saw-briar, slapped the damned sweat-bee.
Went on, and all at once from the last green tangle, burst.

There was the quiet, high glade,
Blue grass set round with beeches, quietest tree.
The air was suddenly sweet, a hint of cool,

*Present owner of the Lewis property.

I stood in the new silence and heard my heart.
And there it was: the huddled stones of ruin,
Just the foundation and the tumbled chimneys,
To say the human hand, once here, had gone,
And never would come back, though the bright stars
Shall weary not in their appointed watch
And the broad Ohio devotedly seek the sea.
I went up close to view the ruin, and then
It happened. You know,
When you have clambered hard and fought the brush
And breath comes short and both lungs full of cotton,
And shirt is soaked and holds your hide like glue,
And heat runs prickling in your blood like ants—
Then if you stop, even in sun-blaze,
It's like malaria shook your bones like dice.

Well, standing there, I'd felt, I guess, the first
Faint tremor of that natural chill, but then,
In some deep aperture among the stones,
I saw the eyes, their glitter in that dark,
And suddenly the head thrust forth, and the fat, black
Body, molten, out-flowed, as though those stones
Bled forth earth's inner darkness to the day—
As though the bung had broke on that intolerable inwardness.
Thus, now divulged, focused, and compacted,
The thing that haunts beneath earth's soldered sill
Flowed forth, and the scaled belly of abomination
Rustled on stone, reared up
In regal indolence and swag.
I saw the soiled white of belly bulge,
And in that muscular distension, the black side scales
Show their faint yellow flange and tracery of white.

It climbed the paralyzed light.

On those heaped stones, taller than I,
Taller than any man,
The swollen head hung
Haloed and high in light; then in that splendid
Nimb the hog-snout parted, and with girlish
Fastidiousness the faint-tongue flicked to finick in the sun.

*

That fastidiousness was, I suppose, the ictus of horror,
And my natural tremor of fatigue
Was converted into the metaphysical chill, and my soul
Sat in my hand and could not move.

But, after all, the manifestation was only natural—
Not Apophis that Egypt feared and the great god
Ra, redemptive, at each dawn slew, but did not slay.
Nor that Nidhogg whose cumbrous coils and cold dung chill
The root of the world's tree, nor even
Eve's interlocutor by Eden's bough.
No, none of these, nor more modestly in Kentucky
The quintessential evil of that ruin,
Nor spirit of the nigger boy named John,
Whose anguish spangled midnight once like stars,
Nor symbol of that black lust all men fear and long for.

No, none of these, no spirit, symbol, god,
Or Freudian principle, but just a snake,
Black Snake, Black Pilot Snake, the Mountain Blacksnake,
Hog-snout or Chicken Snake, but in the books
Elaphe obsoleta obsoleta,
And not to be confused with the Black Racer,
Coluber constrictor—oh, I remember
That much from the old times when, like a boy,
I thought to name the world and hug it tight,
And snake and hawk and fox and ant and day and night
All moved in a stately pavane of great joy
And naked danced before the untouchable Ark of Covenant,
Like Israel's king, and never one fell down.
But when you're not a boy you learn one thing:
You settle for what you get. You find that out.
But if that's all you settle for, you're good as dead.

But to return: old *obsoleta*'s big,
Eight feet—though rarely. But this was big, and he reared
Up high, and scared me, for a fact. Then
The bloat head sagged an inch, the tongue withdrew,
And on the top of that strong stalk the head
Wagged slow, benevolent and sad and sage,

As though it understood our human limitation,
And forgave all, and asked forgiveness, too.

With no haste, it was gone.
This really happened, the big black son-of-a-bitch
Reared from the stones, and scared me, for a fact.
There's no harm in them, though. And they kill rats.

R.P.W.: The actual body of Lilburne, or what remains,
Lies sixty paces, more or less, beyond
The ruin of the Lewis house, about northwest.
At last I went again.
It was December then. We left for Smithland,
And under the paleness of the lemon light,
The heart of the earth drew inward, and was still,
And a voice speaking, or a dog's bark,
Carried with calm and frosted ceremony
In sad perfection past the field and farm,

Tonight the heel will ring on the earth, like iron.

Now under the lemon light we move,
My father and I,
Across the landscape of his early experience.
We pass the land where stood the house of his first light.
No remnant remains of stone gone fire-black. The plow-point
Has passed where the sill lay.

The old house, square, set on limestone, by cedars
That I, in my mind, see,
Is not a house I have seen. It is
A fiction of human possibility past.
We whirl past the spot it held, now woods.
The grave of my father's father is lost in the woods.
The oak-root has heaved down the headstone.

My father says: "About this time, December,
I recollect my father, how he'd take

Some yellow percoon, the root, and mash it
And bark of prickly ash, and do the same,
And cram it in a gallon jug, with whiskey."

"What for?" I asked. "A drink?"

"No, medicine, to wait three months on the shelf.
And spring came on, and then he'd call us boys—
All boys—we were a house of boys he had—
And line us up and give it, morn and night."

"What for?" I said.

"It's old-folks talk, but then they held it true,
My father said how winter thicked boys' blood
And made 'em fit for devilment, and mean.
But he'd sure fix that. Percoon would wry your tongue."

"But what's percoon?" And he: "Why, Son,
I just don't recollect. But it's percoon."

And so we passed that land and the weight of its mystery.
We passed the mystery of years and their logic,
And I have been a stranger in many nations.
I have been a stranger in my bed at night,
And with a stranger.
I have been a stranger when the waiter turned for my order.
I have been a stranger at the breaking of bread.
For isolation is the common lot
Which makes all mankind one.

And there was Smithland.
No, not Sam Clemens' town now, after all.
Sure, there's the jail, courthouse, and river,
And even now it's no metropolis,
In spite of a traffic signal, red and green,
And paint on houses, and new stores,
And money jingling in the local jeans.

Who would begrudge such solvency?
And who's to blame if there's a correlation

Between it and the dark audit of blood
In some Korean bunker, at the midnight concussion?
Yes, who's to blame? For in the great bookkeeping
Of History, what ledger has balanced yet?

In any case, Mr. Boyle's not home today—
Down in Paducah, I guess, for Christmas shopping.
But white, with new paint, the house shines in the sun.

I enter the barn lot. I see the new difference.
The barn's been propped, and in the bright
Cold sun the cattle stand. Some twenty head,
And whiteface, too. The jaws
Move slow. The bright drool drips in sun,
And under the glossy flanks the full flesh bulges
With the deep delight of being flesh, for flesh
Is its own blessing, and nobility.

Why am I here? But there's the bluff. I'd better climb.

Strange now, today it doesn't look so high,
Not like it did the first time here.
July it was—and I damned the heat and briar,
Then clambered through the tall, hot gloom
Of oak and ironwood, where grapevine, big as boas,
Had shagged and looped
In jungle convolvement and visceral delight.
For that's the way I had remembered it.

But, no, it's not quite that. At least, not now,
And never was, perhaps, but in my head.
There's grapevine, sure, and big,
But hanging like it's tired
From trees gone leafless now, and not so tall.
So I'm prepared for what I find up yonder:
The ruin now shrunken to a heap,
And those fine beech trees that I'd celebrated,
They just aren't there at all, or two or three,
Just piddling shag-barks, walnuts two or three,
And oaks to middling, not to brag on.

*

So winter makes things small, all things draw in.

I had plain misremembered,
Or dreamed a world appropriate for the tale.
One thing, however, true: old *obsoleta*
Had reared that day, and swayed against the sun.
But not today. He's keeping home this weather,
Down in the rocks, I reckon, looped and snug
And dark as dark: in dark the white belly glows,
And deep behind the hog-snout, in that blunt head,
The ganglia glow with what cold dream is congenial
To fat old *obsoleta*, winterlong.

All things draw inward with the winter's will.
The snow lies thin and pure, and I lift my eyes
Beyond the bluff and flatlands farther
Where the river gleams.
Its gleam is cold.

And I think of another bluff and another river.
I think of snow on brown leaves, and below
How cold and far was light on a northern river,
And think how her mouth and mine together
Were cold on the first kiss. We kissed in the cold
Logic of hope and need.

Who is to name delusion when the flesh shakes?

So in this other year by another river,
Far in Kentucky there, I raised my eyes
And thought of the track a man may make through Time,
And how the hither-coming never knows the hence-going.
Since then I have made new acquaintance
With snow on brown leaves.
Since then I have made new acquaintance
With the nature of joy.

I stood on the bluff and thought how men
Had moved on that broad flood—the good, the bad,
The strong, the weak, the drawn, the driven,
The fortunate, the feckless, all men, a flood

Upon the flood, and I,
In that cold light, was impelled to apostrophize:

River, who have on your broad bosom borne
Man and man's movement, and endured the oar,
Keel-pole and paddle, sweep and paddle-wheel.
And suffered the disturbance of the screw's bronze blade,
And tissued over that perpetual scarification
With instant sweetness and confident flow—
You who have suffered filth and the waste
Of the human establishment,
Ordure of Louisville and the slick of oil,
The drowned cow, swollen, from the mountain cove,
And junk jammed on the sand bar in the sun—
I take you as an image
Of that deep flood that is our history,
And the flood that makes each new day possible
And bears us westward to the new land.
I take you as image and confirmation
Of some faith past our consistent failure,
And the filth we strew.

And so I thought of the dead beneath my feet.
Of Lilburne on his mountain here,
Who brought no light into the dark, so died.
And of another mountain, far away,
In Albemarle, where Lilburne's kinsman sleeps,
And thought of all
Who had come down the great river and are
Nameless. What if
We know the names of the niggers hunkering by the wall,
Moaning? For yes, we know each name,
The age, the sex, the price, from the executor,
Who listed all to satisfy the court.

And know the names of all who went with Meriwether*
To lie on night-mats in rain, and hear the utterance of ocean.

*

*Meriwether Lewis, cousin and protégé of Jefferson, famed leader of the Lewis and Clark expedition (1804–06).

We know that much, but what is knowledge
Without the intrinsic mediation of the heart?

Returned to St. Louis. Were mustered out. Took pay,
And stepped into the encroachment of shadow.
So years go by, but on some village bench,
Or in some grog-shop where the candle stutters
On shadowy foulness of fat fumes,
The gaffer leans, befogged by drink or age,
And strikes his knee, or table top,

And says: "God-durn, I seen it, I was thar!"
And they: "Hell, Pap, shet up, you're drunk again."

Yes, Pap, you saw it. We believe you, Pap.
For we were there, too, and saw it, and heard
The mountain, like a bell,
Lonely, boom, though no geologist admits it possible.
We have seen the great bear die.
We have lifted the meat-axe in the elation of love and justice.
We have seen a small boy, wide-eyed, stand on the hearthstone
And accept from his father's hand
The bitter dose of percoon.

We have yearned in the heart for some identification
With the glory of the human effort. We have devised
Evil in the heart, and pondered the nature of virtue.
We have stumbled into the act of justice, and caught,
Only from the tail of the eye, the flicker
Of joy, like a wing-flash in thicket.

And so I stood on the headland and stared at the river
In the last light of December's, and the day's, declension.
I thought of the many dead and the places where they lay.
I looked at the shrunken ruin, and the trees leafless.
The winter makes things small. All things draw in.

It is strange how that shift of scale may excite the heart.

*

I leaned above the ruin and in my hand picked up
Some two or three pig-nuts, with the husks yet on.
I put them in my pocket. I went down.

Perhaps never to come back, for I did not know
What here remained, at least for me;
And to this day have not gone back, but hold,
In my heart, that landscape.

I crossed the evening barn lot, opened
The sagging gate, and was prepared
To go into the world of action and liability.
I had long lived in the world of action and liability.
But now I passed the gate into a world

Sweeter than hope in that confirmation of late light.

CHIEF JOSEPH
OF THE NEZ PERCE
(1983)

Joseph, Chief of the Nez Perce Indians, having been be-
trayed a third time by the United States government, tried
in 1877 to lead his people from Idaho through Montana to
freedom over the Canadian border. Pursued and attacked
all the way by various army units, Joseph eluded or de-
feated every one, until the last battle in northern Mon-
tana, where, believing he was already in Canada,
he relaxed security.
In this section, Joseph reflects on the nature of treaties and
of gold, and decides that rather than submit to an as-
signed reservation, his people will seek a new land.

—A.E.

"But what is a piece of white paper, ink on it?
What if the Father, though great, be fed
On lies only, and seeks not to know what
Truth is, or cannot tell Truth from Lie?
So tears up the paper of Truth, and the liars,
Behind their hands, grin, while he writes a big Lie?

"Yes, what is a piece of white paper with black
Marks? And what is a face, white,
With lips tight shut to hide forkèd tongue?
Too late, too late, we knew what was the white spot
In distance—white cover of cloth, leather-tough,
On wagons that gleamed, like white clouds adrift
Afar, far off, over ridges in sunlight:
But they knew where they went, and we knew.
This knowledge, like lead of a rifle, sagged heavy in flesh—
Healed over, but there. It ached in the night."

*

*But no recollection of former services could stand
before the white man's greed.*

MAJOR J. C. TRIMBLE

"My father held my hand, and he died.
Dying, said: 'Think always of your country.
Your father has never sold your country.
Has never touched white-man money that they
Should say they have bought the land you now stand on.
You must never sell the bones of your fathers—
For selling that, you sell your Heart-Being.' "

*I think it a great mistake to take from Joseph and his band
of Nez Perces Indians that valley [Wallowa].*

GENERAL O. O. HOWARD

"Into a dark place my father had gone.
You know how the hunter, at dawn, waits,
String notched, where the buck comes to drink. Waits,
While first light brightens highest spruce bough, eyes slitted
Like knife wounds, breath with no motion. My father
Waits thus in his dark place. Waiting, sees all.
Sees the green worm on green leaf stir. Sees
The aspen leaf turn though no wind, sees
The shadow of thought in my heart—the lie
The heel must crush. Before action, sees
The deed of my hand. My hope is his Wisdom.

"Oh, open, Great Spirit, my ears, my heart,
To his sky-cry as though from a snow-peak of distance!"

*It cannot be expected that Indians . . . will . . . submit
without any equivalent to be deprived of their homes and
possessions or to be driven off to some other locality where
they cannot find their usual means of subsistence . . . It
. . . is repugnant to the dictates of humanity and the
principals of natural justice.*

OREGON SUPERINTENDENT OF INDIAN AFFAIRS

"Does a grain of gold, in the dark ground, lie
Like a seed-sprout? What color of bloom
Will it bear? What cunning has it to make
Men rive raw rock where it hides like a murderous secret?
What cunning to lie in innocent brightness
Like wet sand in water? In water, what dives
The deepest—deep, deeper than the lead pellet?

"For all things live, and live in their nature.
But what is the nature of gold?

"In the deepest dark what vision may find it?
On its stone-bed of vision what secret name be divulged?
If it could dance in the name-dance, what
Name would gold dance? Would it be—
Death-that-in-darkness-comes-smiling?

"Or is it man's nature this thing not to know?"

> *. . . to attempt to restrain miners would be like attempting
> to restrain the whirl wind.*
>
> C. H. HALE, SUPERINTENDENT OF INDIAN AFFAIRS
> FOR WASHINGTON TERRITORY

"Years fled. But with heart grown small, as from fear,
What man can live forever? True,
We had long back made the promise of peace.
We had sworn no white blood to shed, our tongue was not forkèd.
But now we breathed the stink of the wind of Time,
As when wind comes bad from the death of the promise of peace—
As when on the big plain from upwind taint comes
From the age-dead old buffalo cow that rots in the sun.
You wake at night, not believing the dream's stink.
You try to think: 'I lie here as always,
In my own tepee, at peace with all men.'

"But think of your father's eyes in his darkness.

"The sun rises up. No end to the dream's stink."

I call him [the Indian] *a savage, and I call a savage something wholly desirable to be civilized off the face of the earth.*

CHARLES DICKENS

"You stand in the sun. You think: 'Am I Joseph?'
You find yourself watching the white man's horse-soldiers,
How they ride two-by-two, four-by-four, how they swing
Into line, charge or stop, dismount.
How the holders of horses fall back, while others
Are forming for skirmish. Or deploying for cover.

"The white horse-soldiers, they mount from the left.
We from right. Can that be a difference?

"Still as a stone, I stand watching, then suddenly know
How the young men watch me. Tears come to my eyes,
For I think how bodies, dead, in moonlight would shine.
I watch how the horse-soldiers wheel into line.
The young men watch me. One finger I touch
To my brow. Trace lines there. Then lay
A hand to my breast. It is hard to stand
And not know what self you have lived with, all years.
Oh, how can such two Truths kiss in your heart?

"For now you know what a treaty is—
Black marks on white paper, black smoke in the air.
For the greatest white war-chief—they call him Chief One-Arm—
Chief Howard—now in a loud voice he calls.
At a council of those who would take us away
From our land forever, at last I stood.

"In my weakness, tongue dry to the arch of my mouth,
I stood. My people waited. They waited
For words, for wisdom, to pass my lips—
Lips more dry than dust. Before me, I saw
All the blue coats, the buttons of gold, the black
Coats buttoned up tight
Over bellies that bulged—
White and sweaty, you knew, under that cloth—

And softer than dough. My words
Could not come. I saw
Their lips curl. I saw them,
Behind hands held up, in secret sneer.
'Oh, who will speak!' cried the heart in my bosom.
'Speak for the Nimipu, and speak Truth!'

"But then, my heart, it heard
My father's voice, like a great sky-cry
From snow-peaks in sunlight, and my voice
Was saying the Truth that no
White man can know, how the Great Spirit
Had made the earth but had drawn no lines
Of separation upon it, and all
Must remain as He made, for to each man
Earth is the Mother and Nurse, and to that spot
Where he was nursed, he must
In love cling."

> *The earth, my mother and nurse, is very sacred to me: too*
> *sacred to be valued, or sold for gold or for silver . . . and my*
> *bands have suffered wrong rather than done wrong.*

CHIEF JOSEPH TO THE COMMISSIONERS OF 1876

"Howard understood not. He showed us the rifle.
The rifle is not what is spoken in peace-talk.
He says we must leave the Winding Waters
Forever, forever—
Or come the horse-soldiers.
We must live afar with a shrunk-little heart,
And dig in the ground like a digger of roots—at Lapwai,
The Place of the Butterflies—how pretty
That name for a reservation to puke on!
Far from the fatherly eyes that stare in darkness.
Far from my father's words—and my promise!
So my chin to my chest dug deep. For I knew
One-Arm's numbers, and all those behind him.
I knew the strange gun that spits bullets like hail.
It sits on its wheels and spits bullets like hail.

*

"Worse—thirty days only to leave Wallowa,
With horses and herds, our old, young, and sick.
Horses and herds, they swam, though the Snake,
In thaw-flood, snatched off the weak colts, the weak calves,
And whites stole the rest left with poor guard.
But in round boats of buffalo hide, the people
Already were over, four strong horses and riders
To swim with each boat, and push for the shore.

"Even so, our young braves, they swallowed their rage,
Like bile that burns in the belly, and waits.
No, not ours it was who brought the great grief,
But young men of Chief White Bird.
They fled, burned houses, soaked earth with blood."

ALTITUDES AND EXTENSIONS: 1980-1984

(*IN* NEW AND SELECTED POEMS: 1923-1985)

MORTAL LIMIT

I saw the hawk ride updraft in the sunset over Wyoming.
It rose from coniferous darkness, past gray jags
Of mercilessness, past whiteness, into the gloaming
Of dream-spectral light above the last purity of snow-snags.

There—west—were the Tetons. Snow-peaks would soon be
In dark profile to break constellations. Beyond what height
Hangs now the black speck? Beyond what range will gold eyes see
New ranges rise to mark a last scrawl of light?

Or, having tasted that atmosphere's thinness, does it
Hang motionless in dying vision before
It knows it will accept the mortal limit,
And swing into the great circular downwardness that will restore

The breath of earth? Of rock? Of rot? Of other such
Items, and the darkness of whatever dream we clutch?

CARIBOU

Far, far southward, the forest is white, not merely
As snow of no blemish, but whiter than ice yet sharing
The mystic and blue-tinged, tangential moonlight,
Which in unshadowed vastness breathes northward.
Such great space must once
Have been a lake, now, long ages, ice-solid.

Shadows shift from the whiteness of forest, small
As they move on the verge of moon-shaven distance. They grow
                                                    clear,
As binoculars find the hairline adjustment.
They seem to drift from the purity of forest.
Single, snow-dusted above, each shadow appears, each
Slowly detached from the white anonymity
Of forest, each hulk
Lurching, each lifted leg leaving a blackness as though
Of a broken snowshoe partly withdrawn. We know
That the beast's foot spreads like a snowshoe to support
That weight, that bench-kneed awkwardness.

The heads heave and sway. It must be with spittle
That jaws are ice-bearded. The shoulders
Lumber on forward, as though only the bones could, inwardly,
Guess destination. The antlers,
Blunted and awkward, are carved by some primitive craftsman.

We do not know on what errand they are bent, to
What mission committed. It is a world that
They live in, and it is their life.
They move through the world and breathe destiny.
Their destiny is as bright as crystal, as pure
As a dream of zero. Their destiny
Must resemble happiness even though
They do not know that name.

I lay the binoculars on the lap of the biologist. He
Studies distance. The co-pilot studies a map. He glances at

A compass. At mysterious dials. I drink coffee. Courteously,
The binoculars come back to me.

I have lost the spot. I find only blankness.

                                       But
They must have been going somewhere.

FAR WEST ONCE

Aloud, I said, with a slight stir of heart,
"The last time"—and thought, years thence, to a time
When only in memory I might
Repeat this last tramp up the shadowy gorge
In the mountains, cabinward, the fall
Coming on, the aspen leaf gold, sun low
At the western end of the gun-barrel passage
Waiting, waiting the trigger-touch
And the blast of darkness—the target me.

I said, "I'll try to remember as much
As a man caught in Time cannot forget,"
For I carried a headful of summer, and knew
That I'd never again, in the gloaming, walk
Up that trail, now lulled by the stone-song of waters;
Nor again on path pebbles, noon-plain, see
The old rattler's fat belly twist and distend
As it coiled, and the rattles up from dust rise
To vibrate mica-bright, in the sun's beam;
Nor again, from below, on the cliff's over-thrust,
Catch a glimpse of the night-crouching cougar's eyes
That, in my flashlight's strong beam, had burned
Coal-bright as they swung,
Detached, contemptuous, and slow,
Into the pine woods' mounting mass
Of darkness that, eventually,

Ahead, would blot out, star by star,
The slot of the sky-slice that now I
Moved under, and on to dinner and bed.

And to sleep—and even in sleep to feel
The nag and pretensions of day dissolve
And flow away in that musical murmur
Of waters; then to wake in dark with some strange
Heart-hope, undefinable, verging to tears
Of happiness and the soul's calm.

How long ago! But in years since,
On other trails, in the shadow of
What other cliffs, in lands with names
Crank on the tongue, I have felt my boots
Crush gravel, or press the soundlessness
Of detritus of pine or fir, and heard
Movement of water, far, how far—

Or waking under nameless stars,
Have heard such redemptive music, from
Distance to distance threading starlight,
Able yet, as long ago,
Despite scum of wastage and scab of years,
To touch again the heart, as though at a dawn
Of dew-bright Edenic promise, with,
Far off, far off, in verdurous shade, first birdsong.

RUMOR AT TWILIGHT

Rumor at twilight of whisper, crepuscular
Agitation, from no quarter defined, or something
Like the enemy fleet below the horizon, in
Its radio blackout, unobserved. In a dark cave,
Dark fruit, bats hang. Droppings
Of generations, soft underfoot, would carpet the gravel—

That is, if you came there again. Have you ever felt,
Between thumb and forefinger, texture
Of the bat's wing? Their hour soon comes.

You stand in the dark, under the maples, digesting
Dinner. You have no particular
Financial worries, just nags. Your children
Seem to respect you. Your wife is kind. Fireflies
Punctuate the expensive blackness of shrubbery,
Their prickling glows—here, there—like the phosphorescent
Moments of memory when, in darkness, your head first
Dents the dark pillow, eyes wide, ceilingward.
Can you really reconstruct your mother's smile?

You stand in the dark, heart even now filling, and think of
A boy who, drunk with the perfume of elder blossoms
And the massiveness of moonrise, stood
In a lone lane, and cried out,
In a rage of joy, to seize, and squeeze, significance from,
What life is, whatever it is. Now
High above the maples the moon presides. The first bat
Mathematically zigzags the stars. You fling down
The cigarette butt. Set heel on it. It is time to go in.

OLD DOG DEAD

I

Cocker. English. Fifteen years old. Tumor
Of testes. Vet promising nothing. So did it.

Inevitable, but inevitable, too, the
Recollection of the first time, long back,
Seen—puppy-whirl
Of flopping forepaws, flopping ears oversize, stub
Tail awag, eyes bright. And brighter yet,

Dancing in joy-light, the eyes
Of a little girl with her new love. Holding
It up to show. That was what my eyes, open in darkness,
Had now just seen.

And what, no doubt, the eyes now closed beside me
Had, too, been seeing in darkness. With no confirmation needed
To pass between. And now
That breath beside me was at last
Even in sleep. I thought of the possible time
When evenness—in what ears?—
Might be of silence
Only.

Fingering familiar dark, I made
My way out.

2

Boots on, pullover over
Night shirt, on shoulders camp blanket,
Barberry-ripped—whatever
Came handy in anteroom. Then,
I was standing in starlight, moon
Long since behind the mountain, mountain blackness at my back.
On mossed stone sitting, I, streamward,
Stare, intent
On the stream's now messageless murmur of motion.

The stars are high-hung, clearly
Defined in night's cloudlessness,
But here, below, identity blurred
In the earth-bound waver of water.

Upward again I look. See Jupiter, contemptuous,
Noble, firmly defined,
The month being June, the place Vermont.

3

I shut eyes and see what
I had not in actuality seen—the

Raw earth, red clay streaked with
Black of humus under
The tall pine, anonymous in
The vet's woodlot.

Will I ever go back there? Absurdly,
I think I might go and put, stuck in the clay,
A stone—any stone large enough. No word, just something
To make a change, however minute,
In the structure of the universe.

4

I think of Pharaoh's
Unblinking gaze across
Sands endless.

If we can think of timelessness, does it exist?

5

Now Jupiter, southwest, beyond the sagging black spur
Of the mountain, in the implacable
Mathematics of a planet,
Has set. Tell me,
Is there a garden where
The petal, dew-kissed, withereth not?
And where, in darkness, beyond what bramble and flint,
Would iron gate, on iron hinge, move without sound?

Far off, a little girl, little no longer, would,
If yet she knew,
Lie in her bed and weep
For what life is.

6

Who will be the last to remember tonight?

Perhaps, far off, long later, an old woman,
Who once was the child,

Now alone, waking before dawn to fumble for
Something she painfully knows but cannot lay hand to, in
The unlabeled detritus and trash of Time.

AFTER THE DINNER PARTY

You two sit at the table late, each, now and then,
Twirling a near-empty wine glass to watch the last red
Liquid climb up the crystalline spin to the last moment when
Centrifugality fails: with nothing now said.

What is left to say when the last logs sag and wink?
The dark outside is streaked with the casual snowflake
Of winter's demise, all guests long gone home, and you think
Of others who never again can come to partake

Of food, wine, laughter, and philosophy—
Though tonight one guest has quoted a killing phrase we owe
To a lost one whose grin, in eternal atrophy,
Now in dark celebrates some last unworded jest none can know.

Now a chair scrapes, sudden, on tiles, and one of you
Moves soundless, as in hypnotic certainty,
The length of table. Stands there a moment or two,
Then sits, reaches out a hand, open and empty.

How long it seems till a hand finds that hand there laid,
While ash, still glowing, crumbles, and silence is such
That the crumbling of ash is audible. Now naught's left unsaid
Of the old heart-concerns, the last, tonight, which

Had been of the absent children, whose bright gaze
Over-arches the future's horizon, in the mist of your prayers.
The last log is black, while ash beneath displays
No last glow. You snuff candles. Soon the old stairs

*

Will creak with your grave and synchronized tread as each mounts
To a briefness of light, then true weight of darkness, and then
That heart-dimness in which neither joy nor sorrow counts.
Even so, one hand gropes out for another, again.

OLD-TIME CHILDHOOD IN KENTUCKY

When I was a boy I saw the world I was in.
I saw it for what it was. Canebrakes with
Track beaten down by bear paw. Tobacco,
In endless rows, the pink inner flesh of black fingers
Crushing to green juice tobacco worms plucked
From a leaf. The great trout,
Motionless, poised in the shadow of his
Enormous creek-boulder.
But the past and the future broke on me, as I got older.

Strange, into the past I first grew. I handled the old bullet-mold.
I drew out a saber, touched an old bayonet, I dreamed
Of the death-scream. Old spurs I tried on.
The first great General Jackson had ridden just north to our state
To make a duel legal—or avoid the law.
It was all for honor. He said: "I would have killed him
Even with his hot lead in my heart." This for honor. I longed
To understand. I said the magic word.
I longed to say it aloud, to be heard.

I saw the strategy of Bryce's Crossroads, saw
The disposition of troops at Austerlitz, but knew
It was far away, long ago. I saw
The marks of the old man's stick in the dust, heard
The old voice explaining. His eyes weren't too good,
So I read him books he wanted. Read him
Breasted's *History of Egypt.* Saw years uncoil like a snake.
I built a pyramid with great care. There interred

Pharaoh's splendor and might.
Excavation next summer exposed that glory to man's sight.

At a cave mouth my uncle showed me crinoid stems,
And in limestone skeletons of the fishy form of some creature.
"All once under water," he said, "no saying the millions
Of years." He walked off, the old man still with me. "Grandpa,"
I said, "what do you do, things being like this?" "All you can,"
He said, looking off through treetops, skyward. "Love
Your wife, love your get, keep your word, and
If need arises, die for what men die for. There aren't
Many choices.
And remember that truth doesn't always live in the number of
voices."

He hobbled away. The woods seemed darker. I stood
In the encroachment of shadow. I shut
My eyes, head thrown back, eyelids black.
I stretched out the arm on each side, and, waterlike,
Wavered from knees and hips, feet yet firm-fixed, it seemed,
On shells, in mud, in sand, in stone, as though
In eons back I grew there in that submarine
Depth and lightlessness, waiting to discover
What I would be, might be, after ages—how many?—had rolled
over.

COVERED BRIDGE

Another land, another age, another self
Before all had happened that has happened since
And is now arranged on the shelf
Of memory in a sequence that I call Myself.

How can you think back and know
Who was the boy, sleepless, who lay

In a moonless night of summer, but with star-glow
Gemming the dewy miles, and acres, you used to go?

You think of starlight on the river, star
By star declaring its motionless, holy self,
Except at the riffle by the sandbar.
You wondered if reflection was seen by the sky's star.

Long, long ago, some miles away,
There was an old covered bridge across that stream,
And if impact of hoof or wheel made the loose boards sway,
That echo wandered the landscape, night or day.

But if by day, the human bumble and grind
Absorbed the sound, or even birdsong
Interfered in its fashion, and only at night might you find
That echo filling the vastness of your mind,

Till you wondered what night, long off, you would set hoof
On those loose boards and then proceed
To trot through the caverning dark beneath that roof.
Going where? Just going. That would be enough.

Then silence would wrap that starlit land,
And you would sleep—who now do not sleep
As you wonder why you cannot understand
What pike, highway, or path has led you from land to land,

From year to year, to lie in what strange room,
Where to prove identity you now lift up
Your own hand—scarcely visible in that gloom.

RE-INTERMENT: RECOLLECTION OF A GRANDFATHER

What a strange feeling all the years to carry
It in your head! Once—say almost

A hundred and sixty-odd years ago, and
Miles away—a young woman carried it
In her belly, and smiled. It was
Not lonely there. It did not see
Her smile, but knew itself part of the world
It lived in. Do you remember a place like that?

How strange now to feel it—that presence, lonely
But not alone, locked in my head.
Are those strange noises
All night in my skull
But fingers fumbling to get out?
He knows few others there or what they talk about.
More lonely than ever he must feel with the new, strange voices.

I hear in dream the insane colloquy and wrangling.
Is that his croak demanding explanation
Of the totally illegal seizure? Then tussle and tangling.
But whence the choked weeping, manic laughter, lips moving in
                                                    prayer?
It's a mob scene of some sort, and then
Zip and whish, like bat wings in dark air,
That sometimes fill the great dome my shoulders bear.
But sometimes silence; and I seem to see
How out of the jail of my head he comes free.
And in twilight,
His lips move without sound, his hands stretch out to me there.
But his face fades from my sight.

Then sometimes I wake, and I know what will wake me.
It's again the fingernails clawing to get out,
To get out and tell me a thousand things to make me
Aware of what life's obligation is. Nails dig at a skull-seam.
They are stronger and sharper each year. Or is that a dream?
Each year more clawlike—as I watch hair go thin and pate gleam.
I strain to hear him speak, but words come too low
From that distance inside my skull,
And there's nothing to do but feel my heart full
Of what was true more than three-score years ago.

*

Some night, not far off, I'll sleep with no such recollection—
Not even his old-fashioned lingo and at dinner the ritual grace,
Or the scratched-in-dust map of Shiloh, and Bloody Pond,
Or the notion a man's word should equal his bond,
And the use of a word like *honor* as no comic disgrace.
And in our last communal trance, when the past has left no trace,
He'll not feel the world's contempt, or condescending smile,
For there'll be nobody left, in that after-while,
To love him—or recognize his kind. Certainly not his face.

MUTED MUSIC

As sultry as the cruising hum
Of a single fly lost in the barn's huge, black
Interior, on a Sunday afternoon, with all the sky
Ablaze outside—so sultry and humming
Is memory when in barn-shade, eyes shut,
You lie in hay, and wonder if that empty, lonely,
And muted music was all the past was, after all.
Does the past now cruise your empty skull like
That blundering buzz at barn-height—which is dark
Except for the window at one gable, where
Daylight is netted gray with cobwebs, and the web
Dotted and sagged with blunderers that once could cruise and hum.

What do you really know
Of that world of decision and
Action you once strove in? What
Of that world where now
Light roars, while you, here, lulled, lie
In a cunningly wrought and mathematical

Box of shade, and try, of all the past, to remember
Which was *what, what, which.* Perhaps
That sultry hum from the lone bumbler, cruising high
In shadow, is the only sound that truth can make,

And into that muted music you soon sink
To hear at last, at last, what you have strained for
All the long years, and sometimes at dream-verge thought

You heard—the song the moth sings, the babble
Of falling snowflakes (in a language
No school has taught you), the scream
Of the reddening bud of the oak tree

As the bud bursts into the world's brightness.

PLATONIC LASSITUDE

Not one leaf stirs, though a high few,
As they hang without motion, shine translucently green
Against the depth of the sky's depthless blue.
The brook is shrunk. It meditates in serene

Silence. You see the warbler's throat palpitate
With heat. That is the only motion you see.
The mountain seems to float, to have no weight.
It may even sway, drift away into infinity,

Like a child's balloon at a circus. No fly, no gnat,
Stirs through the bright unreality of air.
Your lungs seem to have no function, and you have forgot
The substance breathed, and the *near* and the *far* where-

by you locate yourself, and the world
You're in, seem to lose distinction. No utterance
May come again, and the smoke that is curled
From a chimney may never uncurl in greater or lesser distance.

By brookside, by woodsedge, no bird sings or woodpecker taps,
And like the collage of a child to blue paper glued, the sun

Hangs, and you lie in the world's ontological collapse,
And ask if all is accomplished, all now done,

And even the past dissolves like a dream of mist,
Which is a new joy, that unlike the old, cannot end.
So, lulled, you loll in the lap of Time's wave, and the great crest,
With its tattered glory and gleam of foam-fringe, will never descend.

Or will it? To remind you
That nothing defines itself in joy or sorrow,
The crow calls from the black cliff forgotten but beckoning behind
                                                                you.
Had you forgotten that history is only the fruit of tomorrow?

THE PLACE

From shelving cliff-darkness, green arch and nave
Skyward aspire, translucently, to heights
Where tattered gold tags of sunlight twirl, swing,
Or downward sift to the upturned eye. Upward,
The eye probes infinite distance, infinite
Light, while foot, booted, tangled in fern,
Grips stone. Fern
Bleeds on stone.

                        This
Is the hour of the unbounded loneliness. This
Is the hour of the self's uncertainty
Of self. This is the hour when
Prayer might be a possibility, if
It were. This
Is the hour when what is remembered is
Forgotten. When
What is forgotten is remembered, and
You are not certain which is which.
But tell me:

*

How had you ever forgotten that spot
Where once wild azalea bloomed? And what there passed? And
                                                            forgotten

That truth may lurk in irony? How,
Alone in a dark piazza, as the cathedral clock
Announced 3 A.M. to old tiles of the starless city, could you bear
To remember the impossible lie, told long before, elsewhere?
But a lie you had found all too possible.

Self is the cancellation of self, and now is the hour.
Self is the mutilation of official meanings, and this is the place.
You hear water of minor musical utterance
On stone, but from what direction?
You hear, distantly, a bird-call you cannot identify.
Is the shadow of the cliff creeping upon you?
You are afraid to look at your watch.

You think of the possibility of lying on stone,
Among fern fronds, and waiting
For the shadow to find you.
The stars would not be astonished
To catch a glimpse of the form through interstices
Of leaves now black as enameled tin. Nothing astounds the stars.
They have long lived. And you are not the first
To come to such a place seeking the most difficult knowledge.

LITTLE GIRL WAKES EARLY

Remember when you were the first one awake, the first
To stir in the dawn-curdled house, with little bare feet
Cold on boards, every door shut and accurst,
And behind shut doors no breath perhaps drew, no heart beat.

You held your breath and thought how all over town
Houses had doors shut, and no whisper of breath sleeping,

And that meant no swinging, nobody to pump up and down,
No hide-and-go-seek, no serious play at housekeeping.

So you ran outdoors, bare feet from the dew wet,
And climbed the fence to the house of your dearest friend,
And opened your lips and twisted your tongue, all set
To call her name—but the sound wouldn't come in the end,

For you thought how awful, if there was no breath there
For answer. Tears start, you run home, where now mother,
Over the stove, is humming some favorite air.
You seize her around the legs, but tears aren't over,

And won't get over, not even when she shakes you—
And shakes you hard—and more when you can't explain.
Your mother's long dead. And you've learned that when loneliness
                                                          takes you
There's nobody ever to explain to—though you try again and again.

YOUTHFUL PICNIC LONG AGO:
SAD BALLAD ON BOX

In Tennessee once the campfire glowed
With steady joy in its semi-globe
Defined by the high-arched nave of oaks against
Light-years of stars and the
Last scream space makes beyond space. Faces,

In grave bemusement, leaned, eyes fixed
On the fingers white in their delicate dance
On the strings of the box. And delicate
Was the melancholy that swelled each heart, and timed
The pulse in wrist, and wrist, and wrist—all while
The face leaned over the box
In shadow of hair that in fire-light down-gleamed,
Smoother than varnish, and black. And like
A silver vine that upward to darkness twines,

The voice confirmed the sweet sadness
Young hearts gave us no right to.

No right to, yet. Though some day would,
As Time unveiled,
In its own dancing parody of grace,
The bony essence of each joke on joke.

But even back then perhaps we knew
That the dancing fingers enacted
A truth far past the pain declared
By that voice that somehow made pain sweet.

Would it be better or worse, if now
I could name the names I've lost, and see,
Virile or beautiful, those who, entranced, leaned?
I wish I knew what wisdom they had there learned.

The singer—her name, it flees the fastest!
If only she'd toss back that varnished black screen
Of beautiful hair, and let
Flame reveal the grave cheek-curve, eye-shine,
Then I'd know that much.
If not her name.

Even now.

HISTORY DURING NOCTURNAL SNOWFALL

Dark in the cubicle boxed from snow-darkness of night,
Where that soundless paradox summarizes the world,
We lie, each alone, and I reach a finger laid light
To a wrist that does not move, as I think of a body curled—

Is it an inch, or a world, away—a watch-tick
Or a century off? In darkness I compress my eyes

And wonder if I might devise the clever trick
Of making heartbeat with heartbeat synchronize.

Each has come a long way to this wordless and windless burrow,
Each, like a mole, clawing blindly, year after year,
Each clawing and clawing through blindness of joy and sorrow,
And neither knowing how the world outside might appear.

Could one guess the other's buried narrative?
How the other, in weal or woe, might have found
White darkness where, a finger on wrist, one might live
In the synchronized rhythm of heart, and heart, with no sound?

Was it a matter of chance? Or miracle?
Or which is which—for logic laughs at both?
Could it matter less as whiteness and darkness blending fall
And my finger touches a pulse to intuit its truth.

WHATEVER YOU NOW ARE

In the depth and rustle of midnight, how do you know
What is the dream and who the dreamer? Oh yes,
You fell asleep to the star-bit and murmurous flow
Of the stream beneath your window, but frontierless
Are the stream and the Self conjunct all night long.
How is the difference defined between singer and song?

Is it you that flows from distance, to distance,
With the tune of time and blood intertwined forever?
Or does the dark stream of log-ripple and stone-chance
Define the pattern of your whole life's endeavor?
What elements, shadowy, in that dream interlace
In a region past categories of Time and Space?

Yes, think of the pale transparencies that lave
Stone, riffle, algae, and the moon-bright sandbar,

While music drifts to your shadowy cave
Of consciousness, whoever you now are—
But dawn breaks soon, and that self will have fled away.
Will a more strange one yet inhabit the precinct of day?

IT IS NOT DEAD

It is not dead. It is simply weighty with wisdom.
A long way and painful, it has come to become
What it is. In nameless heat under
Nameless pressure, liquefied,
It has tried
To find its true nature, seething in depth and darkness when earth
Was not yet ready to be torn asunder,
But heaved in silence, like throttled thunder.

What eons remained still
To await what cataclysmic birth
That exploded, roared, glowed
To change its liquid mind to hardness like glass, to iron will?
What name had the plowshare that plowed
It wide to the fury of light on a high place?
What determination interminable,
What years, did the crowbar of ice take
To pry from the crag-face
That mass to make
A scythe to reduce some undefined forest to splinters? Then the
                                                            might
Of the first unmerciful grasp of the glacier, the grind,
The trundling descent in darkness, white
But absolute. What timeless thoughts ground in its downward
                                                            mind?
Then fingers of water, weak but uncontrollable,
Worked in their tangle of multitudinous will,
Age after age, until
Half in, half out, of my brook it lies,

Honed to perfection, perfect in structure, moss-idle, sunlit.
And, naked, I lie on it,
Brooding on our common destinies.
Against the declaration of sunlight I close my eyes.

All night, it will lie there under the stars,
Attent to the riffle, and I lie, in brotherhood, where I lie,
Hearing the riffle too, though a curtain bars
Me in darkness except in one twisted spot where I spy
A fleeting fracture of the immensity of the night sky.

MYTH OF MOUNTAIN SUNRISE

Prodigious, prodigal, crags steel-ringing
To dream-hoofs nightlong, proverbial
Words stone-incised in language unknowable, but somehow singing
Their wisdom-song against disaster of granite and all
Moonless non-redemption on the left hand of dawn:
The mountain dimly wakes, stretches itself on windlessness. Feels
                        its deepest chasm, waking, yawn.

The curdling agony of interred dark strives dayward, in stone
                                 strives though
No light here enters, has ever entered but
In ageless age of primal flame. But look! All mountains want slow-
ly to bulge outward extremely. The leaf, whetted on light, will cut
Air like butter. Leaf cries: "I feel my deepest filament in dark
                                     rejoice.
I know that the density of basalt has a voice."

How soon will the spiderweb, dew-dappled, gleam
In Pompeian glory! Think of a girl-shape, birch-white sapling,
                                rising now
From ankle-deep brook-stones, head back-flung, eyes closed in first
                                    beam,

While hair—long, water-roped, past curve, coign, sway that no
                                        geometries know—
Spreads end-thin, to define fruit-swell of haunches, tingle of
                                        hand-hold.
The sun blazes over the peak. That will be the old tale told.

ABOUT THE AUTHOR

ROBERT PENN WARREN was born in Guthrie, Kentucky, in 1905. After graduating summa cum laude from Vanderbilt University (1925), he received a master's degree from the University of California (1927), and did graduate work at Yale University (1927–28) and at Oxford as a Rhodes Scholar (B. Litt., 1930).

Mr. Warren has published many books, including ten novels, sixteen volumes of poetry, and a volume of short stories; also a play, a collection of critical essays, a biography, three historical essays, a critical book on Dreiser and a study of Melville, and two studies of race relations in America. This body of work was published in a period of fifty-six years—a period during which Mr. Warren also had an active career as a professor of English.

All the King's Men (1946) was awarded the Pulitzer Prize for Fiction. The Shelley Memorial Award recognized Mr. Warren's early poems. *Promises* (1957) won the Pulitzer Prize for Poetry, the Edna St. Vincent Millay Prize for the Poetry Society of America, and the National Book Award. In 1944–45 Mr. Warren was the second occupant of the Chair of Poetry at the Library of Congress. In 1952 he was elected to the American Philosophical Society; in 1959 to the American Academy of Arts and Letters; and in 1975 to the American Academy of Arts and Sciences. In 1967 he received the Bollingen Prize in Poetry for *Selected Poems: New and Old 1923–1966*, and in 1970 the National Medal for Literature, and the Van Wyck Brooks Award for the book-length poem *Audubon: A Vision*. In 1974 he was chosen by the National Endowment for the Humanities to deliver the third Annual Jefferson Lecture in the Humanities. In 1975 he received the Emerson-Thoreau Award of the American Academy of Arts and Sciences. In 1976 he received the Copernicus Award from the Academy of American Poets, in recognition of his career but with special notice of *Or Else—Poem/Poems 1968–1974*. In 1977 he received the Harriet Monroe Prize for Poetry and the Wilma and Roswell Messing, Jr. Award. In 1979, for *Now and Then*, a book of new poems, he received his third Pulitzer Prize. In 1980 he received the Award of the Connecticut Arts Council, the Presidential Medal of Freedom, the Common Wealth Award for Literature, and the Hubbell Memorial Award (The Modern Language Association). In 1981 he was a recipient of a Prize Fellowship of the John D. and Catherine T. MacArthur Foundation. In 1986 he was designated as this country's first official Poet Laureate.

Mr. Warren lives in Connecticut with his wife, Eleanor Clark (author of *The Bitter Box, Rome and a Villa, The Oysters of Locmariaquer, Baldur's Gate, Eyes, Etc.: A Memoir,* and *Gloria Mundi*). They have two children, Rosanna and Gabriel.